MONEY, MARKETS, AND THE STATE

Social Democratic Economic Policies since 1918

Social democrats generally hold mass unemployment to be the main scourge of the market economy. Yet, social democratic policies for full employment have met with strikingly different levels of success. *Money, Markets, and the State* provides in-depth explanations for the various successes and failures of the economic policies of social democratic governments in five Western European countries: Germany, Great Britain, Sweden, Norway, and the Netherlands. Dr. Notermans examines these economies from the inflation following the conclusion of World War I, through the Great Depression, and up to the present-day conditions of mass unemployment. Drawing on a wide range of historical and statistical sources, Dr. Notermans argues that the fate of social democratic economic policy hinges on the political and institutional success of maintaining price stability, and not on structural economic factors such as changing supply-side conditions or the increasing globalization of economic relations. Although social democracy has repeatedly been declared obsolete, this study concludes that successful social democratic policies for growth and full employment remain possible even under the present conditions of an increasingly globalized economy.

Ton Notermans is Senior Researcher for the Advanced Research on the Europeanization of the Nation-State (ARENA) Program in the Political Science Department at the University of Tromsø in Norway. Dr. Notermans is coeditor with Douglas J. Forsyth of *Regime Changes: Macroeconomic Policy and Financial Regulation in Europe from the 1930s to the 1990s* (1997) and has published articles in *Politics and Society, Stato E Mercato,* and the *European Journal of Political Research.*

CAMBRIDGE STUDIES IN COMPARATIVE POLITICS

General Editor

PETER LANGE   Duke University

Associate Editors

ROBERT H. BATES   Harvard University
ELLEN COMISSO   University of California, San Diego
PETER HALL   Harvard University
JOEL MIGDAL   University of Washington
HELEN MILNER   Columbia University
RONALD ROGOWSKI   University of California, Los Angeles
SIDNEY TARROW   Cornell University

OTHER BOOKS IN THE SERIES

(Continued on page following the index)

MONEY, MARKETS, AND THE STATE

Social Democratic Economic Policies since 1918

TON NOTERMANS

University of Tromsø

CAMBRIDGE
UNIVERSITY PRESS

PUBLISHED BY THE PRESS SYNDICATE OF THE UNIVERSITY OF CAMBRIDGE
The Pitt Building, Trumpington Street, Cambridge, United Kingdom

CAMBRIDGE UNIVERSITY PRESS
The Edinburgh Building, Cambridge CB2 2RU, UK   http://www.cup.cam.ac.uk
40 West 20th Street, New York, NY 10011-4211, USA   http://www.cup.org
10 Stamford Road, Oakleigh, Melbourne 3166, Australia
Ruiz de Alarcón 13, 28014 Madrid, Spain

First published 2000

Printed in the United States of America

Typeface Garamond #3 10.5/12 pt.   *System* DeskTopPro$_{/UX}$ [BV]

A catalog record for this book is available from the British Library.

Library of Congress Cataloging in Publication data

Notermans, Ton.
  Money, markets, and the state : social democratic economic
  policies since 1918 / Ton Notermans.
      p.   cm. – (Cambridge studies in comparative politics)
    Includes bibliographical references and index.
    ISBN 0-521-63339-7
      1. Europe, Western – Economic policy Case studies.   2. Socialism –
  Europe, Western Case studies.   I. Title.   II. Series.
  HC240.N68   2000
  338.94 – dc21   99-24406
                                                                              CIP

ISBN 0 521 63339 7 hardback

To my father

CONTENTS

TABLES AND FIGURES

TABLES

FIGURES

ABBREVIATIONS

ADGB	Allgemeiner Deutscher Gewerkschaftsbund
AES	Alternative Economic Strategy
AfA	Allgemeiner freier Angestelltenbund
ARP	Anti-Revolutionaire Partij
BdL	Bank deutscher Länder
BF	Bondeförbundet
BoE	Bank of England
BP	Bondepartiet
CDU	Christlich Demokratische Union
CDU(NL)	Christen-Democratische Unie
CHU	Christelijk Historische Unie
CSU	Christlich Soziale Union
DGB	Deutscher Gewerkschaftsbund
DNA	Det Norske Arbeiderparti
DNB	De Nederlandsche Bank
DNVP	Deutsch-Nationale Volkspartei
DP	Deutsche Partei
DVP	Deutsche Volkspartei
ECB	European Central Bank
EEA	Exchange Equalization Account
ECU	European Currency Unit
EMS	European Monetary System
EMU	Economic and Monetary Union
FIEF	Fackföreningsrörelsens Institut för Ekonomisk Forskning
KVP	Katholieke Volkspartij
LO(N)	Landsorganisasjon i Norge
LO(S)	Landsorganisasjon i Sverige

LSP	Liberale Staatspartij
NAF	Norges Arbeidsgiver Fordbundet
NOU	Norges Offentlige Utredninger
NSDAP	National Sozialistische Deutsche Arbeiterpartei
NUPE	National Union of Public Employees
NVV	Nederlands Verbond van Vakverenigingen
OECD	Organization for Economic Cooperation and Development
ÖTV	Gewerkschaft Öffentliche Dienste, Transport und Verkehr
PBO	Publiekrechtelijke Bedrijfsorganisatie
PPR	Politieke Partij Radicalen
PvdA	Partij van de Arbeid
RKSP	Rooms-Katholieke Staatspartij
SAF	Svenska Arbetsgivareföreningen
SAK	Statens Arbetslöshetskommission
SAL	Sveriges Allmänna Lantbrukssällskap
SAP	Sveriges Socialdemokratiska Arbetareparti
SDAP	Sociaal-Democratische Arbeiderspartij
SER	Sociaal Economische Raad
SOU	Statens Offentliga Utredningar
SPD	Sozialdemokratische Partei Deutschlands
SV	Sosialistisk Valgforbund / Sosialistisk Venstreparti
TUC	Trade Union Congress
USPD	Unabhängige Sozialdemokratische Partei Deutschlands
VDB	Vrijzinnig Democratische Bond
ZAG	Zentralarbeitsgemeinschaft der industriellen und gewerblichen Arbeitgeber und Arbeitnehmer Deutschlands

ACKNOWLEDGMENTS

This manuscript has traveled a long road to completion. I first became interested in questions of economic policy in advanced industrial nations while attending Manfred Schmidt's seminars at the Freie Universität Berlin during the mid-eighties. At the time, I felt that Schmidt's emphasis on domestic politics and institutions was becoming less appropriate in an increasingly globalized economy. More than a decade later I realize that Schmidt was right from the beginning: domestic political processes, rather than international economic pressures, were and are the decisive driving forces of economic policy making. That I eventually came to realize this was in no small amount the result of my regular discussions with Lars Mjøset of the University of Oslo. One of my early attempts to make sense of economic policy making drew his comment that it did not seem to apply particularly well to the Scandinavian countries. Lars was right. I hope the present argument will be more acceptable to him.

During my time at the Freie Universität I also regularly visited Hajo Riese's seminars in macroeconomics. Riese convinced me that any account of economic policy making would have to be centered on money and monetary policy. The years that have passed since then have only made my conviction stronger.

Having finished my master's thesis at the Freie Universität, I applied to the doctoral programs of several U.S. universities, though with little hopes of being accepted or being able to finance such an undertaking. To my great surprise, the Department of Political Science at the Massachusetts Institute of Technology not only accepted my application but also provided me with a fellowship, hence allowing me to spend some years in what is probably one of the most stimulating intellectual environments in the world.

During my first semester at MIT, I had the great luck of meeting Andrew Martin of the Center for European Studies at Harvard University. Without

Andy's intellectual and moral support this manuscript probably never would have been written. The argument advanced here has been shaped in more ways by Andy's comments than he probably realizes himself. Douglas Forsyth of MIT's Department of History was one of the few who shared my interest in money and finance. During my last years at MIT, we talked almost on a daily basis. His incisive comments have greatly helped clarify my own thoughts on the subject. Another person who provided crucial support in times of need was Helen Ray of the MIT political science department. Without her uplifting presence I probably would not have lasted as long at MIT as I did.

It was also at MIT where I met my wife, Simona Piattoni. I am still surprised that she never got tired of carefully reading numerous versions of the same argument. Without Simona the manuscript might have been finished earlier, but it would certainly have been much less fun writing it.

The list of people who at some point or another provided helpful comments would probably fill several pages. In order not to make an already long manuscript even longer I just mention five people who have been particularly helpful: Jos de Beus, Lars Hörngren, Lars Jonung, Charles Sabel, and Richard Samuels. Interviews with policy makers have been of crucial importance, but, as is common in this type of study, I will not mention them by name.

Affiliations with three institutions, in particular, have been most helpful. In Oslo the hospitality of the Institute for Social Research has made my stays both more fruitful and more pleasant. I would like to thank in particular its director, Frederik Engelstad, Trond Nordby, Geir Høegsnes, and the staff of the library for their kind assistance. The Swedish Trade Union Institute for Economic Research (FIEF) most probably is the ideal research environment for someone interested in economic policy and social democracy. Without the invaluable assistance of the people at FIEF the Swedish part of this study could not have been written. In particular I would like to express my gratitude to FIEF's director, Villy Bergström, and to Anders Vredin and Cesar Fuentes-Godoy. In Germany I greatly benefited from my stay at David Soskice's Labor Market and Employment Research Group at the Wissenschaftszentrum Berlin.

While working on the historical parts of this study, access to various archives has been of crucial importance. I would like to thank the board of directors of Norges Bank, the general secretary of the SAP, and the boards of the Norwegian and Swedish LO for granting me access to their respective archives. Dr. Turid Wammer, head of the Archives of Norges Bank, has most kindly sacrificed a considerable amount of her time to help me locate relevant material. Equally kind and helpful assistance was received from Anneli Alrikson at the LO (S) Archives in Stockholm. In addition, I wish to thank the staff at the Archives of the Labor Movement in Oslo and Stockholm.

Financial assistance for this study has been received from the Department of Political Science at MIT, the MacArthur doctoral scholarship program of the Center for International Studies at MIT, the Program for the Study of Germany and Europe of the Center for European Studies at Harvard University, and the

Social Science Research Council in New York. Finally I would like to thank Johan Olsen of the ARENA Program of the Norwegian Research Council for giving me a chance to broaden my horizon.

This book is dedicated to my father, who finished school during the Great Depression just to join the army of the unemployed, and who died at a time when Western European governments again were doing their best to keep millions of people out of work.

A NOTE ON TERMINOLOGY

The terms *inflation* and *deflation* will be used in their technical meaning of a continuous rise or fall in the price level. This is in contrast to the interwar use of the term *inflation* when it frequently meant an expansion of the money supply, and a common present use of the word *deflation* as denoting restrictive demand management policies. *Reflation* denotes the recovery of the price level from a preceding deflation. Inflationary and deflationary policies accordingly are policies that lead to a continuous rise or fall of the price level, while reflationary policies are aimed at a once-and-for-all increase in the price level. Disinflationary policies, in contrast to deflationary policies, are aimed at reducing the rate of inflation rather than depressing the overall price level. The terms *restrictive* and *expansionary* will be used for policies aiming to reduce or increase overall demand, irrespective of their effect on the price level. A currency will be called convertible if it can be freely exchanged against other currencies. Also this is in contrast to the usage of the interwar period, when convertibility frequently meant that the currency in question maintained a fixed parity with respect to gold. In accordance with standard usage in economics, policies are said to have nominal effects if they lead to a change in the absolute price level and real effects if they alter relative prices, growth employment, overall demand, and so on. This is not to suggest that real effects are what matters whereas nominal effects are merely epiphenomenal. In effect, the argument presented here rests on something akin to the contrary. In the case of the two Scandinavian countries, non–social democratic governments are referred to as bourgeois governments. This is in accordance with the common usage in Norway and Sweden, and it is not meant to suggest that these governments somehow are the political wing of the "bourgeoisie." The word *liberal* is used in the European sense of a political movement, which advocates minimal interference with free markets. Finally, one billion equals one thousand millions.

1

SOCIAL DEMOCRACY IN THE MACROECONOMY

The social democratic vision of society envisaged a world in which human beings control their circumstances rather than being controlled by them. One essential characteristic of such a society would be that it guaranteed its members a decent livelihood. Rather than large sections of the population being condemned to inactivity by recurring economic crisis, all those able to take up employment should have the possibility of doing so. Those who temporarily or permanently lack the ability to provide for themselves should be able to count on the solidarity of society to provide them with the means for a decent livelihood. The inability to work should not be a condemnation to live a marginalized existence. Sickness should not be an economic catastrophe and the health care received should be determined by need rather than by ability to pay. Likewise, education should be provided according to ability rather than according to social status or wealth. In addition, such a society should be democratic. A society that achieved freedom from economic want by subjecting its members to the whims of an overpowering state would defeat its own purpose. In short, the social democratic program aimed to reform the market economy so as to combine political and economic liberty.

During the first couple of decades after its birth in the second half of the nineteenth century, the social democratic struggle focused primarily on achieving political liberties. Not only was political democracy a goal in itself, it also seemed a necessary and sufficient condition for realizing the economic goals of the labor movement. In a society in which a narrow elite reserved for itself the right to appoint the political leadership, the state would inevitably consider it its task to defend the economic privileges of the few rather than to promote the well-being of the many. After the struggle for democracy was crowned with success shortly after the end of World War I, social democrats had little doubt that their economic program would soon be realized too. Looking back at more than eighty years of social democratic policies in democratic societies, however, one must conclude that, rather than creating the conditions under which humans can control their own economic fate the social democratic program itself has been subjected to the whims of economic conditions.

At times, it appeared that the social democratic program was the only viable program for the management of the economy in a democratic polity. The economic malaise of the interwar period also convinced center-right political parties that interventionist policies were required to achieve acceptable economic outcomes and that cutting wages, taxes, and welfare benefits was not a promising avenue to economic prosperity. In the decades following the Great Depression, social democrats thus saw much of their policy program realized, even in those countries where they did not manage to obtain a dominant position in government. Yet, this "golden age" of social democracy was bracketed by two periods in which even social democrats found it hard to deny the liberal critique that generous welfare arrangements, a strong union movement, and extensive political management of the economy undermined the wellsprings of economic prosperity. During the 1920s and again since the mid-seventies, Western European social democrats proved unable to provide an economic policy program that could effectively address stagnation, unemployment, and inequality. Rather than providing an effective remedy against mass unemployment, social democratic policies seemed to make matters worse. Improving the income of labor and extending welfare state arrangements appeared to threaten the prosperity of the business sector on which the well-being of labor ultimately depended.

This study provides an explanation of the historical vagaries of the social democratic program. It focuses on the economic policies of social democratic governments in five countries. Sweden and Norway boast the strongest social democratic parties in the Western world. Ever since they came to power in the midst of the Great Depression, they have been the dominant political forces in their countries. The Swedish social democratic party (SAP, Sveriges Socialdemokratiska Arbetareparti) governed uninterruptedly from 1932 to 1976, and with a three-year interruption in the early nineties, has been in power again since 1982. Interrupted only by the German occupation, the Norwegian social democrats (DNA, Det Norske Arbeiderparti) governed from 1935 until 1963. In the thirty-five years since, they have been in office for roughly twenty-three years. German and Dutch social democrats, in contrast, have found themselves in a rather weak position. While the German Social Democratic Party (SPD, Sozialdemokratische Partei Deutschlands) became the strongest political force after the collapse of the German Empire, its fortunes turned with the onset of recession in the early twenties. Except for a two-year period in the late twenties, it was out of office from 1924 to 1966. It suffered a similar fate in the recession of the early eighties, when it was forced to leave office after its liberal coalition partner deserted in 1982. It has only been able to return to office in 1998. The Dutch social democrats traditionally required the consent of the Christian democrats to enter government and had to remain on the opposition benches until 1939. They became a regular coalition partner after the war, but their ability to pursue their preferred policies always remained sharply constrained by the pivotal position of the Christian democrats. As economic pressures mounted in the mid-seventies, they had to leave office and were unable to return until 1989. However, as before, since 1989 it, too, has governed on the basis of a coalition in which it confronted parties of equal or greater strength. The British Labour Party occupies a middle position. Due to the absence of coalition governments, it can wield considerable power when in office, yet it managed to govern on a regular basis only during the decades of prosperity after 1945. Apart from two short-lived governments, it was out of office in the interwar period. Mainly due to its inability to handle the economic crisis, it was voted out of office in 1979 and did not manage to return until 1997.

The main argument of this study is that rather than being determined by the political strength of social democratic parties, the success or failure of the social democratic program depends crucially on the institutional and political ability to combine growth with a fair degree of price stability. The economic growth required to achieve the goals of full employment and a well-developed welfare state can only be brought about by an expansionary macroeconomic regime. Macroeconomic policies, however, can concentrate on growth only if labor market institutions can assume a major part of the responsibility for keeping inflation down.

THREE REGIME CHANGES

Three fundamental turning points in the fate of the social democratic policy program in Western Europe can be distinguished since 1918. In the tense political and economic situation following the end of the war, full employment and growth enjoyed top priority. While many wartime regulations were quickly abolished, frequently at the behest of labor, monetary policies remained expansionary so as to promote growth. Within five years after the armistice, however, all governments had come to see the attempt to foster growth and employment by means of discretionary macroeconomic management as a mistake. Full employment was accompanied by rampant inflation, which was perceived to be the result of ill-guided attempts to mitigate domestic distributional conflicts by means of fiscal expansion and the printing press. Accordingly, the resurrection of the fixed exchange rate regime of the gold standard was to provide a "knave-proof" protection against politically caused economic instability, limiting as much as possible the access of domestic political actors to monetary policy decisions. The deflationary policies required to return to the gold standard at the prewar parity initiated a long period of mass unemployment. But, since the experience of high inflation had allegedly shown that macroeconomic policies could not durably alter output, responsibility for growth and employment apparently could not be placed with the state but instead had to rest with civil society. Especially with respect to demands for employment policies, governments stressed that the unobstructed operation of the labor market was the most promising road to full employment. In this zero-sum situation the accommodation between capital and labor that had started during the war could not proceed.

Although, with the exception of Sweden, non–social democratic governments initiated the return to the gold standard, social democrats saw no alternative. As a result, they found themselves confronting the dilemma of having to agree that the major impulse to growth and employment had to come from domestic cost reduction, while at the same time being unable to politically accept the consequences in terms of social security and wages. Unable to identify a viable policy alternative, many social democrats relapsed into a sort of Marxist fatalism, which postponed all practical policies for the improvement of the lot of the working class to that mythical time when the socialist revolution would arrive.

The liberal policy regime ended abruptly in the Great Depression of the 1930s. The liberal belief in the self-regulating market now came to be widely considered erroneous, and not only by social democrats. The price governments apparently had to pay for their abstention from discretionary policies was the worst economic recession in recorded history and a threat to the legitimacy of liberal democracy. Governments now resorted to widespread regulation of prices and quantities in order to halt what was diagnosed as a process of ruinous competition in unregulated markets. In a full U-turn, independent central banks, which in the preceding decade were heralded as the strong institutions that would restore monetary discipline, came to be seen during the depression as one of the major villains in the piece, who had sacrificed the interests of society in favor of the interests of *haute finance*. Moreover, Keynes's contention that contracyclical fiscal policies rather than unobstructed wage adjustment were required in order to maintain full employment became a generally accepted dogma for most governments after World War II.

Politically the Great Depression ushered in the golden age of social democracy. The social democratic critique that the liberal management of the economy at best benefited a narrow elite while subjecting the economy to instability and crises now seemed incontrovertible. Social democracy's political opponents on the center and right of the political spectrum also had to recognize the bankruptcy of laissez-faire and accordingly found themselves on the ideological defensive. Moreover, at the moment when market regulation was deemed necessary to prevent ruinous competition, and growth and employment were to be achieved by macroeconomic stimulation, welfare arrangements and organized economic interests no longer appeared as impediments to prosperity but rather could be interpreted as valuable stabilizing elements in an inherently unstable market economy. Accordingly, the polarization between capital and labor gradually gave way to accommodation.

It was not until the early seventies that this policy consensus was fundamentally challenged. Confronted with escalating inflation, the reemergence of mass unemployment, unstable exchange rates, burdensome social welfare systems, and rising budget deficits, governments throughout Western Europe found it necessary to reconsider the policy convictions inherited from the Great Depression. Government intervention now came to be seen as the main source of, rather than the cure for, economic instability. British Labour prime minister James Callaghan's (1987: 426) famous recantation of macroeconomic interventionism at the 1976 Labour Party annual congress would gradually come to be shared by most parties on the Continent: "We used to think that you could spend your way out of a recession, and increase employment by cutting taxes and boosting government expenditure. I tell you in all candour that that option no longer exists, and that in so far as it ever did exist, it only worked on each occasion since the war by injecting a bigger dose of inflation into the economy, followed by a higher level of unemployment as a next step." Not unlike the twenties, maintaining price stability now again came to be considered the only legitimate task for macroeconomic policies. Growth and employment again thus began to be considered microeconomic matters, which inevitably cast extensive welfare arrangements and high wages in the role of main culprits for stagnation and crisis.

Politically the advent of a disinflationary regime in the seventies and eighties marked the decline of social democratic ideological hegemony. In the period following the first oil price shock, Western European social democratic governments either changed from the government bench to that of the opposition or, when remaining in office, abandoned their commitment to full employment and pursued economic policies that implicitly admitted the correctness of much of the liberal critique. As social democrats could not identify an alternative to the new macroeconomic policy interpretation in what was diagnosed as an increasingly global economy, they came to agree that competitiveness held the key to economic prosperity. And since any reference to socialism had become utterly unattractive after the Soviet experience, they were left to present themselves as the party that could implement the neoliberal program in a more efficient or more humane way.

Like the interwar gold standard regime, the disinflationary regime of the eighties and nineties was very effective in combating inflation but did nothing to solve the problems of stagnation and mass unemployment. As the memory of inflation waned, so did the popularity of neoliberal policies. With unemployment the dominant problem, it seemed to many voters that social democrats again had a more promising recipe for managing the economy, especially since most parties had decisively broken with the policies that had caused the economic dislocations of the seventies. Starting around the midnineties, European social democrats scored a string of impressive election victories. Whether the new political dominance of social democracy will bring about a regime change in macroeconomic policy making remains to be seen, however.

PRECONDITIONS FOR THE SOCIAL DEMOCRATIC PROGRAM

In sociological terms, social democracy traditionally has considered itself the political representation of the working class. Its historical roots lie in the firm-level struggle between workers and owners in an industrial economy. In the labor movements' own understanding of its internal division of labor, trade unions are to represent workers' interests in the bargaining process, while social democratic parties represent their political interests on the level of the state. A potential tension exists, however, between the firm-level conflict of interests between workers and employers and the macrolevel desirability of a market economy. The electoral logic of a political movement, which derives much of its strength from a close association with trade unions, requires that social democrats cannot be seen as wholeheartedly embracing the interests of the employers, while its advocation of a market economy requires that it must promote conditions under which privately owned business can prosper.

This tension implies that social democracy finds it difficult to thrive in a world where the microlevel pursuit of workers' interests is considered antithetical to the prosperity of the market economy. Instead, the success of the social democratic program rests on an economic policy regime in which macroeconomic management is considered to hold the key to growth and employment. In technical terms, social democratic policies only come to be seen as constituting a superior mode of managing the economy when macroeconomic policy management is informed by the conviction that money is not neutral, that is, the belief that monetary expansion can have real and not only nominal effects.

The conviction that money is neutral implies that the state, on the macroeconomic level, cannot mitigate the microlevel zero-sum game between business and labor. Expansionary monetary policies per definition only result in higher inflation. The same argument, however, also implies that fiscal management cannot durably alleviate unemployment and stagnation. Without monetary expansion, fiscal expansion requires that increased budget deficits be financed either by increasing taxes or by loans. In either case, no aggregate positive effect can be expected as the funds that the private sector could have employed for expansion are used by the state, and the additional purchasing power is neutralized by heavier taxation. Financing a deficit by creating money does not help because it is the equivalent of expansionary monetary policies. Moreover, to the extent that the desire to prevent inflationary monetary policies has been institutionalized by means of a fixed exchange rate arrangement and the acceptance of unobstructed international financial flows, the possible consequences for the currency will generally be sufficient to prevent attempts at expansionary fiscal management.

In regimes like the interwar gold standard or the present neoliberal one in which macroeconomic policies are primarily assigned the goal of price stability, the low growth and mass unemployment that tend to be characteristic of such periods hence are inevitably attributed to microeconomic causes. Extensive social welfare systems, the trade unions' resistance to more labor market flexibility, cartel agreements, and insufficient innovation come to be seen as the main impediments to renewed prosperity. In such a constellation, social democracy faces the unpleasant dilemma of either supporting trade unions' efforts, thereby risking the loss of electoral support for appearing to lack a policy that can benefit society as a whole, or concentrating on what are considered sound economic policies, thereby sacrificing their conviction that the market economy is not incompatible with the legitimate demands of labor. In practice, such a situation generally entails that social democrats lose the political initiative as they move uneasily between the two sides of this dilemma.

To be sure, during periods when the inevitability of a restrictive macroeconomic regime is generally accepted, the political left tries to regain the initiative by presenting its own version of supply-side theory, which denies that the microlevel interests of the labor force are antithetical to overall prosperity. The leftist version, not surprisingly, inverts the neoclassical contention that a weak labor movement is beneficial for economic performance. Improving productivity and the attractiveness of the product mix, rather than cost cutting, is presented as the key to prosperity. Strong trade unions and high real wages, in this view, promote overall prosperity because they prevent the employers from choosing the low-cost road to competitiveness, forcing them instead to continuously innovate and compete on the basis of quality rather than price.[1] But while this may seem ideologically attractive, social democracy has historically been unable to build an attractive alternative program based on microeconomic strategies, simply because such strategies are economically and organizationally inappropriate.

Just as their liberal (neoclassical) counterpart, social democratic supply-side policies for improved competitiveness have been unable to provide an effective answer to the core problem of mass unemployment because they rest on a fallacy of composition. Competitiveness is a relative term: not every firm or country can improve its competitiveness simultaneously. Even if a firm manages to improve competitiveness, either by cost reduction, improved productivity, or a more attractive product mix, there is no reason to assume that this will lead to an increase of aggregate employment. Aggregate employment increases only if production is increased by more than productivity gains. By itself, increased competitiveness for one firm means loss of market shares for another firm, whereas increased productivity of the economy means that the same level of production will require less labor. Instead of solving the problem of unemployment and stagnation, a policy that relies on microeconomic strategies for employment under a restrictive macroeconomic regime is likely to contribute to increased inequality between a highly paid, highly educated sector of the economy and an increasingly marginalized, underemployed, and undereducated sector.

To avoid confusion, the point is not that supply-side policies are unnecessary or ineffective, but that it is inadmissible to treat microeconomic policies as a functional equivalent of macroeconomic policies.[2] It is indeed hard to see how a healthy economy can be based on high wages and low productivity. Especially in an international system in which other countries pursue such policies, neglect of the supply side will have high costs. The level of productivity traditionally had to be an important concern for social democracy because it determines firm-level competitiveness and the feasible real wage.[3] But there is no reason why a high-productivity, high-wage economy cannot be at the same time a low-growth, high-unemployment economy, and vice versa.

Social democratic supply-side policies are organizationally inappropriate because, in the longer run, they tend to undermine the cohesion of organized labor and hence are unable to prevent the cost-cutting policies to which they were meant to provide an alternative. Because they historically have failed to remedy mass unemployment, they cannot provide an effective response to the tendency of the workforce in individual firms, or even individual workers to break away from collective bargaining in order to save their own employment. As will be shown in Chapter 3, beginning in the late twenties the unions started to exert massive pressure on social democratic parties to seek macroeconomic solutions to high unemployment precisely because the existing economic constellation had become an acute threat to their internal cohesion. At present, even the huge German metalworking union IG Metall, which has long been considered the star witness for the argument that high wages can benefit competitiveness by serving as a productivity whip, finds itself increasingly unable to enforce its collective agreements in the face of massive unemployment.

In contrast, the general acceptance of the postulate that discretionary monetary (macroeconomic) management can durably affect growth and employment, from roughly the midthirties to the midseventies, removed the contradiction between the pursuit of firm-level interest and overall prosperity. Cuts in wages and social security were no longer necessary preconditions for economic prosperity. Rather, stable wages and extensive welfare arrangements could now be argued to play a fundamental role in maintaining effective demand. Hence social democrats could abandon the defensive view that high wages and social security benefits perhaps had some negative economic consequences but were desirable from a social and moral viewpoint and embrace the politically rather more effective argument that such arrangements were beneficial to growth and economic stability. Moreover, the view that markets are crisis prone and that only interventionist policies can safeguard prosperity allowed social democrats to reconcile such policies with their traditional ideological conception that a capitalist system needs to be subjected to social control, while avoiding politically and economically dangerous experiments with socialization of the means of production. Hence, it became possible for social democrats to successfully extend their appeal beyond the narrow base of manual workers. Understandably, social democrats generally consider the period from the end of the Great Depression to the seventies as the golden age.

THE POLITICAL CONSEQUENCES OF PRICE FLEXIBILITY

Explaining the historical pattern of success and failure of the social democratic program hence essentially comes down to explaining the dynamics of economic policy regimes. Why have the political consequences of major economic crises of this century differed so radically? Why did the crises of the early twenties and the seventies and eighties give rise to a (neo) liberal policy regime while the depression of the thirties established the ideological hegemony of social democratic concepts? Why was the solution to persistent mass unemployment during the twenties and the seventies and eighties sought in removing obstacles to the operation of the free market, while mass unemployment during the Great Depression came to be interpreted as a failure of free markets?

As most political parties operating under democratic conditions, social democrats have tended to assume that the success of their program depends on the amount of power resources – in particular, votes – they can muster relative to their opponents. Given their roots in the capital-labor conflict, this assumption generally amounts to explaining the success of social democracy in terms of the relative strength of the working class versus business. Indeed, a substantial social science literature attempts to understand the development of Western European social democracy exactly in these terms.[4]

There is good cross-national evidence that strong social democratic parties leave a specific imprint on the political management of the economy. In Norway and Sweden, where social democrats have enjoyed a hegemonic position since World War II, welfare state arrangements came to be more extensive and more interventionist than in countries with a weaker social democracy. Likewise, defending full employment enjoyed higher priority than in the rest of Western Europe. Yet the conclusion that social democracy was simply politically too weak to prevent a change to an unfavorable regime in the early twenties and during the last two decades is obviously inaccurate. Regime changes in most cases do not coincide with a change in governing party. More important, both during the twenties and at present social democrats themselves came to accept the prevailing mode of macroeconomic management as, if not desirable, at least inevitable. The crisis of social democratic policies in both historical instances was not confined to electorally defeated parties but affected all.

Despite its strong position at the end of World War I, the labor movement was not able to prevent the change from the expansionary policies pursued immediately after the war to the restrictive policy regime of the gold standard. Whereas the regime shift of the early twenties was completed throughout Western Europe within a span of five years, it took almost eighteen years, from the Copernican turn of the German Bundesbank to monetarist policies in 1973 to the advent of mass unemployment in Sweden in 1991, for the interventionist Keynesian welfare state policies of the post–Great Depression era to be replaced with a rather more liberal regime. At some point during the eighties, it hence might have seemed that indeed the crisis of social democracy was confined to those countries where it was weak.[5] Yet, by the early nineties the conclusion could only be that the social democratic policy program was in disarray everywhere. Despite the undeniable, and undeniably important, cross-national differences in economic management, social democratic policies at several instances in history seem to have encountered rather definite limits.

As the crisis of social democratic policies proved to be of a rather general nature, political explanations gave way to structural ones.[6] Social democrats themselves discovered the argument, familiar from the interwar period, that the internationalization of the economy, and in particular the openness of financial markets, frustrated their policies as international investors would rather seek refuge in countries less friendly to labor. Conservatives and liberals in turn came to argue again that the program of an extensively regulated economy simply is economically inappropriate as it gradually destroys those conditions under which a market economic can function well. Yet, the more often these structuralist arguments make a historical appearance, the less convincing they become.

International capital mobility, contrary to what is often argued, is not a phenomenon unique to the present period. The interwar period was equally characterized by highly open, and at times highly erratic, financial flows. Yet, financial openness in most cases did not provide an obstacle to a rather fundamental reorientation of macroeconomic policies once the fixed exchange rate constraint of the gold standard was abandoned. Likewise, in the present period, flexible management of the exchange rate has allowed countries that so desired to pursue more expansionary policies despite open financial markets.

The main liberal explanation for the failures of the social democratic program – namely, that macroeconomic policies only have nominal and not real effects in the long run and hence should be oriented toward the goal of price stability instead of full employment in order to avoid inflationary mayhem – is even less convincing. If money is indeed neutral (i.e., if inflation is stimulating in the short run but has no real effects in the long run), price stability should be a rather irrelevant policy goal. Moreover, the prediction that disinflationary policies would not affect the real economy in the longer run was generally disappointed, as both the policies of the early twenties and the midseventies ushered in a long period of mass unemployment. The longer-run result of the disinflationary regime initiated in the early twenties was not a return to full employment but the Great Depression and a shift to more expansionary policies. Similarly in the present period the long-run result of the disinflationary policies of the seventies and eighties does not seem to be a return to prosperity but an increasing doubt concerning their appropriateness.

This study argues that the historical successes and failures of the social democratic policy program have to be explained in terms of the compatibility or incompatibility of governments' macroeconomic policy orientations and the institutional preconditions required for the successful implementation of those policies. A policy regime that successfully promotes growth and full employment by macroeconomic means has to rely on the ability of labor market institutions to contain inflation by not employing their market power to the full. Tight labor markets inevitably imply upward pressure on nominal wages, and if the central bank is prevented from pursuing consistently tight policies for fear of creating unemployment, inflation can only be contained if unions and employers can be brought to exercise moderation in wage and price setting. Conversely, a liberal regime characterized by mass unemployment and restrictive macroeconomic policies requires labor market institutions that can maintain some degree of nominal wage stability despite an excess supply of labor in order to prevent the price level from falling.

Contrary to what is implied by most standard economic theories, a failure of labor market institutions to show moderation in tight labor markets does not leave the government the choice of either tolerating inflation or increasing unemployment. Nor is it feasible for governments to ignore deflation in the longer run in order to pursue restrictive macroeconomic policies. In the neoclassical model world, in which money has no real function, rapid and prolonged changes in nominal prices may be irrelevant. In the monetary economies of the real world, prolonged inflation or deflation undermines the conditions under which a market can function properly.

Major disturbances of price level stability are such a crucial problem because they tend to become cumulative. Expectations of a falling price level increase the attractiveness of hoarding money relative to investing in industry. Consequently, investment and growth decline while unemployment increases. Debt defaults due to the emerging recession further reduce the willingness to finance investment. Prolonged periods of unemployment tend, moreover, to fragment the trade unions' power in wage setting. The resulting drop in the price level prompts further hoarding and a further increase in unemployment, which in turn lead to an additional decrease in nominal wages in a downward spiral. The result is a total cessation of investment and a total collapse of the economy. Inflation is very much a mirror image of this. Expectations of inflation make it unattractive to hold money and more attractive to invest and speculate. Higher investment activity reduces unemployment. As prolonged scarcity of labor fragments the trade unions because employers start bidding up wages in order to attract workers, the labor market amplifies the inflationary impulse. Yet as inflation accelerates, short-term speculation rather than longer-term engagements in productive ventures come to appear as a more appropriate means to safeguard or increase the value of monetary assets. The final stage of such a cycle is a so-called flight out of money – heavy speculation in real estate and other real assets and a collapse of real investment.

If the interaction of policy choices and financial and labor markets comes to cumulatively reinforce price level trends, then the state will eventually be left with no other option than to terminate the old regime. At that point, the question is no longer whether but *when* policies will change. Rather than operating in a neoclassical or Keynesian economy in which intervention can be aimed at realizing politically determined goals, governments will first of all have to ensure the conditions under which a market economy can function properly.[7] The progressing loss of control over the economy and the ineffectiveness of traditional instruments may lead governments to stop inflationary or deflationary cycles at an early stage. Alternatively, a regime change may have to await the collapse of the economy. Strong social democratic governments may exhibit a higher degree of tolerance for inflation than their conservative or liberal counterparts for fear of creating unemployment. Yet, if it lacks the institutional means to contain inflation, a parliamentary majority will be of little help for social democrats intent on pursuing their traditional program.

It is the politico-economic dynamic of monetary economies that ultimately determined the political fate of Western European social democracy during the twentieth century. Analyses of the development of social democracy generally centered on the concepts of liberal democracy and a capitalist economy, which automatically directs the attention to issues of political mobilization and the systemic power of the owners of the means of production. Yet, the major problems that have confronted social democracy, and which have driven its political and ideological fate, are rooted in the coordination of a monetary economy.

The failures of social democracy to realize its program cannot be attributed to the systemic power of "capitalists," nor are social democracy's successes the outcome of a mobilization of power resources, which enabled it to overcome the opposition of "capital." The arrangement reached after the Great Depression in which extensive welfare benefits and full employment were combined with private ownership of the means of production was not a temporary compromise that was to be discarded as soon as social democracy had accumulated enough power resources to expropriate the bourgeoisie.[8] Nor can the "failure" of social democracy to establish a socialist economy be attributed to the electoral logic that requires social democrats to water down their program in a situation where the working class comprises less than half of the electorate, or to the electoral unfeasibility of a program that would lead to superior economic outcomes in the long run but cause economic dislocations in the short run.[9]

Being unable both to provide an alternative solution to inflationary pressures and to politically tolerate the unemployment and wage cuts following from the gold standard regime, social democrats during the twenties were structurally unable to govern or advance their goals. And again during the last two decades of the century, the disintegration of institutional devices designed to contain inflation and the subsequent shift to a disinflationary policy regime have marked the loss of ideological and political initiative on the part of social democracy and the acceptance of a substantial part of the conservative or neoliberal policy recommendations. Conversely, as the strategy of tight macroeconomic policies coupled with microeconomic flexibility drove Western European economies into the deflation of the Great Depression, economic liberalism's ideological shipwreck became inevitable. While social democrats generally did not initiate the new policies, they eventually were to reap the electoral and ideological benefits of liberalism's failure. After the cataclysm of the Great Depression, liberals now had to pay the price for labeling the interventionist policies of the gold standard a free-market regime, while social democrats could claim that history had shown their postulate of the need for political regulation of a capitalist economy to be correct.

OUTLINE OF THIS VOLUME

The structure of this book is as follows: Chapter 2 reviews the main economic views commonly underlying political analysis and sketches an alternative view in which the general orientation of economic policies (i.e., the regime) is seen to be informed by the need to combat or prevent cumulative movements in nominal prices. The following three chapters provide a historical overview of the three policy regime changes of this century. Chapter 3 argues that the pursuit of expansionary monetary policies in the absence of appropriate institutional and political instruments for the microeconomic control of inflation aborted a nascent social democratic policy regime around the early twenties. Chapter 4 interprets the regime change during the Great Depression as a response to the destructive effects of price deflation. In contrast to a still widespread view, it is argued that the decisive character of the new regime did not consist in a shift to Keynesian contracyclical policies but rather in the elimination of the need for further deflation by abandoning the gold standard, a policy of cheap money, and a proliferation of institutional devices designed to promote downward nominal rigidity. Chapter 5 argues that the advent of disinflationary policy regimes during the seventies and eighties is ultimately a story about the slow disintegration of the ability to contain inflationary pressures without having recourse to macroeconomic restriction and unemployment. Chapter 6 analyzes the prospects for the social democratic policy program at the end of the twentieth century.

2

POLITICS, ECONOMICS, AND POLITICAL ECONOMY

POLITICS, POLICY PREFERENCES, AND ECONOMIC THEORY

Commonly, politics can be understood as a process in which competing groups try to affect the distribution of (political) goods in their favor, within a stable framework of rules and institutions. The analysis of policy making in such stable periods can generally be conducted fairly satisfactorily in terms of the relative political power resources of the competing groups. However, while institutions and policies usually tightly interlock, the cohesion of the institutional network seems to be radically weakened during certain periods. At those critical junctures in history, politics is mainly concerned with the reshaping of the framework of rules and institutions within which political competition is to take place.

In the field of economic policy making, regime changes are marked primarily by a reinterpretation of the relation between policy instruments and outcomes and a redefinition of the responsibilities of political actors. On a general level, two such different regimes can be distinguished. In liberal regimes, such as those of the 1920s and today, maintaining price stability is considered the foremost responsibility of the macroeconomic authorities whereas the causes of unemployment are primarily located in the functioning of the labor market, which implies that the social partners carry the main responsibility for it. In the social democratic regime, which historically separated the two liberal regimes, the assignment of instruments to outcomes is inverted: unemployment is interpreted primarily as a macroeconomic problem. Inflation instead is seen as a phenomenon that originates in the labor market, which implies that employers and unions carry the major responsibility for it.[1]

The justification for such regime changes is commonly couched in terms of

14

economic theories, with neoclassical doctrines justifying the policy assignments of liberal regimes and Keynesian views underpinning the assignments of the social democratic regime. New economic ideas, in other words, would seem to play a crucial role in bringing about new policies. Yet, such a conclusion would be valid only if regime changes could not be interpreted in terms of interest, and if at any time there were several viable alternatives to the new policies actually implemented.

Political scientists in particular have learned to be skeptical of the official justifications provided by policy makers and instead are inclined to interpret different theoretical views on the management of the economy as rationalizations of particular interests. Competing economic theories, in this approach, are employed to enhance the political acceptability of arguments based on political preferences by presenting them as the outcome of neutral scientific reasoning.[2] Regime changes accordingly would appear as politics by other means, in the sense that they share the same driving forces but have a different object, namely, the rules, theoretical interpretations, and institutions rather than the distribution of political goods.

Given that the political left historically has displayed a closer affinity with Keynesian views whereas the political right generally seems more attracted to neoclassical reasoning, such an argument might seem to have some validity. Yet, the attempt to reduce economic theories to political preferences is unconvincing. There is no reason to deny that in the daily policy process economic theory is sometimes used as a cloak for political preferences. Yet, it is ultimately impossible to reduce economic theories to political interests. Even if it is assumed that the structure of industrialized societies necessarily creates groups with a priori preferences concerning goals – high profits and high demand for employers and high real wages and full employment for employees – it is the economic theory employed that will determine how these preferences are to be translated into demands for policy. But, if economic theories are prior to *policy* preference formation, explanations of regime changes in terms of the changing balance of power in civil society must necessarily be inadequate. On the contrary, because economic theories specify which goals economic policies can affect, and what the links between policies and outcomes are, they structure the boundaries between state and civil society and mold the policy preferences of the actors.

If it is not possible to reduce competing economic models to political interests, political analyses of economic policy making also will have to address the arguments of economic theory. It is not possible to analyze economic policy making without reference to at least a rudimentary model of the economy. Yet the choice of an economic theory has a crucial influence on the focus of analysis as well as the conclusions drawn, if only because, as Charles Maier and Leon Lindberg (1985: 570) note, "each of today's major economic doctrines also presupposes a model of society and politics." Is one to embrace a neoclassical view and direct the attention in periods of inflation to the weakness of the state and the conflicts between social groups, or a Keynesian view and focus on the organization of the labor market? Is one to understand the political accommodation between capital and labor in the wake of the Great Depression in a neoclassical fashion as the result of an exogenous process of growth, or as the outcome of a reorientation of policy? Does the persistence of mass unemployment require us to analyze the sociological process of microlevel interaction between employers and employees, or is the political process of macropolicy formation the more appropriate focus for analysis? Is one to understand the changes in economic policies since the seventies in terms of adjustment to structural and external forces like international capital mobility or technological change, or in terms of the destabilizing effects of previous policies?

In a positivist understanding of science, it should be possible to decide the debates between competing economic doctrines in an empirical manner. Yet, we know since the work of Pierre Duhem and W. V. O Quine that it is well-nigh impossible to refute theories by means of empirical evidence.[3] Historically, the shift in economic orthodoxies speaks strongly against the possibility of deciding the debate between Keynesians and neoclassics in favor of either one of them. Charles Kindleberger (1987: 6) pointed out that the debate between neoclassics – or monetarists as he labels them – and Keynesians "did not have its origin in the 1920s or 1930s, as many students of the subject think, but can be traced back to the seventeenth century and beyond." Instead of observing a process whereby the interplay between theoretical reflection and historical reality leads to the crystallization of a commonly accepted economic theory, the historical shifts in politically dominant economic theories seems to describe some sort of sinus curve in which some core positions – always in different historical forms – replace each other as the dominant interpretation.[4]

In the absence of a generally accepted criterion for selecting from among the several available candidates, political scientists and historians ultimately cannot refrain from justifying their economic views. The remainder of this chapter does just that. The next section provides a critique of Keynesian and neoclassical views. The third section briefly sketches an alternative, and the concluding section draws the implications for economic policy making.

KEYNESIANS AND NEOCLASSICS

The essence of the Keynesian perspective is that macroeconomic policies can exert a decisive influence on the level of income and employment. Whereas the neoclassical analysis of the determinants of employment is microeconomic in nature (i.e., is located on the level of the interaction of market participants), the Keynesian tradition is macroeconomic in nature. Total employment is a function of total output, which in turn is determined by demand. Equations 2.1 to 2.4 present a rudimentary Keynesian model. Equilibrium requires that total output (Y) equal aggregate demand, which consists of consumption (C), investment (I), and government spending (G) (Equation 2.1). Because households do not spend their total income, but save and pay taxes, equilibrium implies that the sum of saving (S) and taxes (T) must equal the sum of government spending and investment (Equation 2.2). Keynesian equilibrium does not imply full employment. As long as Equation 2.2 holds, total output remains unchanged, but that level of output may or may not be sufficient to provide employment to all those wishing to work. In other words, there is no reason to expect market economies to gravitate toward full-employment.

$$Y = C + I + G \tag{2.1}$$
$$S + T = G + I \tag{2.2}$$

In addition to deriving the possibility of an unemployment equilibrium, Keynesians argue that total output tends to fluctuate over time, mainly because of the inherent instability of private investment. Investment is a commitment for the future, but what the future will bring is inherently uncertain. Accordingly, private investment can be strongly affected by changes in confidence. A more pessimistic outlook will reduce investment and hence aggregate demand. The resulting drop in output implies a reduction in income and hence lower savings. The process continues until savings and investment become equal again at a lower level of total output.

However, since the state also affects aggregate demand by means of its spending, it has the ability to cure the instability and unemployment endemic to market economies by means of discretionary demand management. Since consumption is assumed to be a function of disposable income, and since disposable income equals total income minus taxes (tY),[5] C can be rewritten as follows:

$$C = c(Y - tY) \tag{2.3}$$

Substituting Equation 2.3 in 2.1 and rearranging the terms yields the famous Keynesian income multiplier (Equation 2.4), which shows how a change in spending will affect total output. Maintaining full employment accordingly appears as a technical problem of correctly estimating and timing changes in public spending.

$$Y = 1/1 - c(1 - t) \cdot (I + G) \tag{2.4}$$

Although it is recognized that it cannot continue indefinitely without monetary accommodation by the central bank, inflation is primarily interpreted as a phenomenon that originates in the labor market under conditions of full employment. Confronted with high demand and no possibility to expand production, employers will increase prices (profit inflation) and employees will successfully bargain for higher nominal wages (wage inflation). This relation can be graphically represented in the form of a downward-sloping Phillips curve (P_1, Figure 2.1). The Phillips curve, which became rather popular during the sixties, is commonly interpreted as presenting a menu of combinations of unemployment and inflation from which the government can choose. If, for example, the inflation rate at point A is deemed too high, restrictive policies that will move the economy to, say, point B are called for. To reduce inflation without increasing unemployment (i.e., a downward shift of the curve) will require changing the wage- and price-setting behavior of unions and employers. Historically Keynesian-inspired governments have therefore sought recourse in income policies rather than restrictive monetary policies to contain inflationary pressures.

Generally, Keynesians place great trust in public intervention, quite in contrast to their neoclassical colleagues. But because governments can maintain full employment, Keynesians required an explanation of why they, at times, did not do so. In practice, this means that Keynesians have displayed an affinity for interpretations that argue that governments were either misled by wrong economic ideas or prevented from pursuing correct policies due to external constraints on demand management in open economies.

In the seventies, Keynesianism came under heavy attack from neoclassical/ monetarist scholars. The main criticism was that the Phillips curve in the somewhat longer run in fact was vertical (P_2, Figure 2.1), the implication being that rather than reducing unemployment, expansionary demand management policies only resulted in a higher price level.

In the neoclassical perspective, the level of unemployment (UN, Figures 2.1 and 2.2) is determined at the microeconomic, not the macroeconomic, level. Figure 2.2 represents the core of the neoclassical labor market analysis. The level of employment is simultaneously determined by the demand and supply for labor. The supply curve (S) is upward sloping as workers will have to be compensated with higher real wages in order to forgo an additional unit of leisure time. Given the capital stock, an additional unit of labor employed will have a lower marginal productivity. Since for profitable production to be possible the real wage cannot exceed the marginal productivity, the demand curve (D) is downward sloping.

In contrast to the Keynesian perspective, the implication is that market economies in principle do exhibit a tendency toward full employment. If labor markets, like any well-behaved market, react to an excess supply with a reduction in price (i.e., the real wage), unemployment will disappear. If nevertheless historically extended periods of high unemployment have occurred, this must accordingly reflect either wage earners' preferences for leisure versus work or obstructions to wage adjustment. Existing unemployment is voluntary, to the extent that wage earners refuse to forgo additional units of leisure time at the real wage that would clear the labor market, or to the extent that institutional factors like trade unions or minimum wage legislation prevent wages from reaching the market-clearing level.

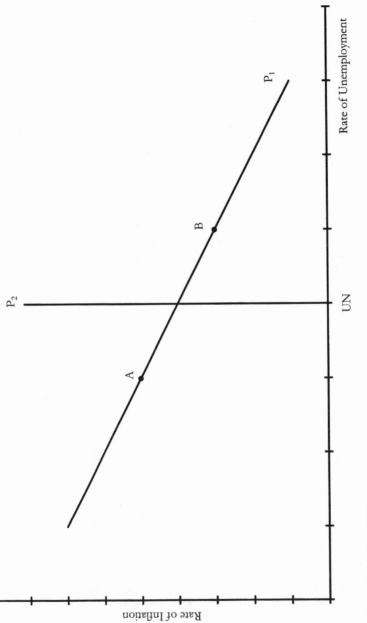

Figure 2.1. The Phillips curve

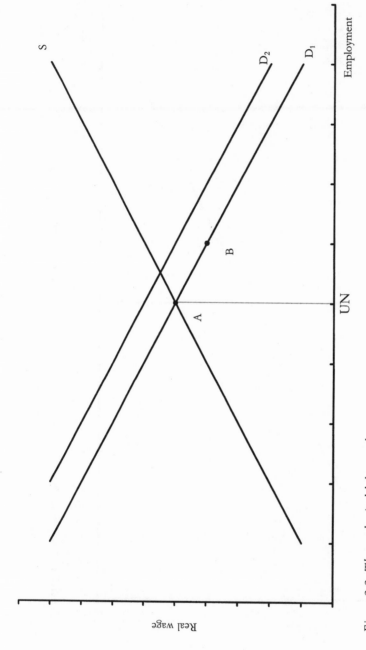

Figure 2.2. The neoclassical labor market

Yet, even assuming the presence of obstructions to wage adjustment it does not necessarily follow that the state cannot bring about full employment. The demand curve in Figure 2.2. assumes a fixed capital stock. An increase in the capital stock shifts the D_1 curve to the right (D_2). At the new equilibrium point B, both the volume of employment and the real wage have increased. If it were possible to increase the capital stock by means of expansionary monetary policies, the conclusion that a reduction in unemployment mainly depends on the behavior of the labor market parties would not hold anymore.

Yet, the neutrality-of-money doctrine argues that the state cannot do so.[6] In the simple version the argument goes as follows: the demand and supply for credit (loanable funds) are determined in standard fashion by a downward-sloping demand curve and an upward-sloping supply curve. As the marginal productivity of capital is a decreasing function of the amount of capital employed relative to labor, industrialists can only be induced to borrow in order to expand their capital stock by means of a lower interest rate. The supply curve is upward sloping because in order to be induced to save (i.e., supply loanable funds) instead of consuming an increasing portion of their income, households require a higher interest rate. In addition to holding savings, households hold a certain amount of money for transaction purposes (real cash balances). The amount of cash balances is assumed to be a fraction of the households' real income so that nominal balances will increase if nominal income increases.

If the state should want to bring about an increase in the capital stock, it would have to lower the market interest rate and it can attempt to do so by means of injecting more money into the economy. Lower interest rates will induce firms to demand more loanable funds, but the supply will not be forthcoming because households will consume more and save less. Consequently, firms cannot expand their capital stock and production cannot expand either. As a result of the expansionary monetary policies households find themselves with excessive cash balances. These higher balances will not be channeled into saving but consumed. Higher demand for goods at an unchanged level of production, however, can only mean higher prices. The rise in nominal incomes will induce households to hold higher nominal balances to maintain the same real balances. Equilibrium will be reached again at the same real interest rate, the same capital stock, and the same amount of real savings but at a higher nominal income and higher nominal cash balances. Given that monetary policies cannot affect private investment, and assuming the propensity to save to be fixed, the level of unemployment is uniquely determined in the labor market. Therefore the Phillips curve is vertical (P_2, Figure 2.1), and expansionary demand management accordingly only creates higher inflation.

According to the neoclassical critique, Keynesian policies could only be successful under so-called money illusion. Money illusion denotes a situation in which wage earners do not perceive the reduction in real wages resulting from a rise in the price level. Because a reduction in unemployment requires a reduction in the real wage, the government can reduce unemployment by engineering a higher price level while the nominal wage remains fixed.

In "The General Theory of Unemployment," Keynes (1973: 15) suggested that the labor market was characterized by downward rigidity of money wages. Because individual groups of wage earners were primarily concerned about their relative position versus other wage earners, they would resist lower money wages but not an across-the-board real wage cut. Accordingly, a macroeconomic policy that increased the price level would succeed in lowering real wages. "Every trade union will put up some resistance to a cut in money-wages, however small. But since no trade union would dream of striking on every occasion of a rise in the cost of living, they do not raise the obstacle to any increase in aggregate employment which is attributed to them by the classical school." However, as the rapid spread of wage indexation mechanisms during the sixties seemed to indicate, wage earners were not willing to accept government-engineered cuts in real wages. In terms of Figure 2.2, demand management policies forced wage earners off their supply curve to, for example, point B. In the next bargaining round, workers would increase their nominal wages so as to return to their supply curve. The economy thus returns to the original unemployment rate at A, albeit at a higher price level.

A further implication is that inflation originates not in the labor market but from the macroeconomic authorities, that is, the central bank. The neoclassical analysis of inflation is best summarized in terms of the quantity theory of money. In the standard notation of Equation 2.5, the quantity theory can be characterized as the triple proposition that the level of total real output (T) is determined in the market by the standard supply and demand mechanisms; the volume of money (M) is determined by the political authorities (the central bank); and the velocity of money (V) is stable.[7] In that case, the price level (P) is a function of the money supply.

$$M \cdot V = P \cdot T \tag{2.5}$$

Because the price level is determined by the volume of money and because the volume of money is exogenously set by the political authorities, it follows that inflation is a political phenomenon. Historical inflations accordingly are explained with reference to misguided political interventionism. Inflations are the outcome either of a weak state, which by printing money attempts to satisfy the incompatible distributional demands of social groups, or of a calculating government that tries to maximize its own electoral popularity by engineering a short-term boom at election time at the cost of long-term inflation. Put differently, whereas Keynesians required the state to stabilize an inherently unstable economy, the state now comes to be seen as a destabilizing element in an otherwise stable market economy. As a consequence, the quantity view generally gives rise to the demand to isolate the conduct of monetary policy from the demands of civil society and governments by awarding central banks political independence and/or removing the possibility for policy discretion by tying the currency to an external anchor.

THE MYTH OF THE INVISIBLE HAND

The idea that in a market economy the pure pursuit of self-interest results in the optimal employment of society's economic resources is one of the ideological pillars of modernity. Although it dates back to the eighteenth century, it continues to underpin many modern views on the economy and economic policy making. Yet, paradoxically, modern economics has failed to confirm Adam Smith's notion of an invisible hand. The concept of an uncoordinated, decentralized system tending toward a predetermined equilibrium may be appropriate for the physical sciences, where an environment that is independent of the actions of the individual elements can be assumed. In the social sciences, where the environment the individual actor faces is basically the sum of the actions of the other individuals, the notion of an uncoordinated system tending toward a predetermined position is simply inappropriate because an exogenously given point on which convergence can take place is lacking.

Neoclassical theory has to confront this problem at the point where it makes the step from partial equilibrium theory (i.e., the analysis of individual markets) to general equilibrium theory (i.e., the analysis of the interaction of all markets). General equilibrium theory, which constitutes the theoretical core of modern economics, recognizes that this reflexive process whereby individuals adjust to market conditions and thereby change the market conditions that face all other actors will establish a general equilibrium only by pure coincidence.[8] Contrary to a widespread misunderstanding, neoclassical theory does not show that even in a perfect world, market-driven adjustment processes will establish equilibrium. In order to arrive at a general equilibrium in a neoclassical market economy it is necessary to eliminate the element of reflexivity. This can be done by assuming perfect foresight – by assuming that each individual is perfectly informed about the actions other individuals will undertake. However, apart from being obviously unrealistic, this device is logically questionable to the extent that in order for each individual to decide upon a course of action the decision of all other individuals most already be known.[9] Alternatively economic theorists have introduced a so-called auctioneer as a (fictitious) coordinating agent who operates outside the market, and who is assigned the task of determining the vector of prices that will establish equilibrium and make it known to market actors before trade takes place.[10] In sum, modern neoclassical research has established that, in order for general equilibrium to obtain, one cannot trust the "invisible hand." As a result, theorists involved in developing general equilibrium theory, like Frank Hahn, have come to regard it as an analytical device, useful for establishing what the notion of an invisible hand would actually have to imply, but rather useless as a description of anything that is going on in the real world.[11]

The reflexivity of economic interaction implies that actors necessarily make decisions under uncertainty. In the words of Jan Kregel:

> The "non-ergodicity" of the system then ultimately results from the fact that individual actions are constrained by the actions of other individuals which cannot be predicted with certainty and thus when taken together form an aggregate or global or macroeconomic constraint which is not the simple, linear, and, therefore, predictable summation of individual behavior. Thus it is not macroeconomics that has to be brought into closer touch with microeconomics, but rather one must try to formulate a macrofoundation for uncertain individual decisions. (Kregel 1987: 528)

Given that economic actors necessarily operate under uncertainty, expectations come to play a crucial role in determining economic behavior. It therefore cannot be assumed any longer that an unambiguous relationship exists between market or policy signals and economic behavior. Instead, market actors will have to place these signals in a broader context or, to use a sociological term, attribute meaning to them. Is a given recession just a short-term phenomenon and hence no reason to adjust longer-term production or investment plans, or is it the prelude to a long period of stagnation? Is a lowering of the discount rate to be interpreted as the initial step in a durable policy of cheap money, or is it more likely to be a short-term measure with no significant longer-term consequences? Is a lower price for a certain good a reason for purchasing more because it is a one-shot event, or should purchases be postponed because it is the prelude to further price cuts?

Because expectations necessarily influence behavior, the state has much less control over the economy than is assumed in both the Keynesian and the neoclassical perspective. If the concept of a market as a dynamic and decentralized system of decision making is to be taken seriously, then the role of the state in the economy can adequately be captured neither by the liberal concept of a disturbing factor in an otherwise stable real economy nor by the social democratic concept of a political determination of macroeconomic policy goals and the precise manipulability of the real economy.

Because neoclassical theory cannot show that even a pure market will tend toward (Pareto optimal) equilibrium, the habit of the quantity theory to introduce a stable real sector on which a destabilizing monetary sphere is superimposed (see Equation 2.5) is simply a normative assumption that stands in contradiction to its own theoretical analysis.[12] Moreover, the radical separation of the monetary from the real sphere, which is necessary to conclude that macroeconomic policies cannot affect employment, is implausible and ultimately based on the assumption that there is no uncertainty. In a world characterized by uncertainty, it is implausible to assume that savings (i.e., the supply of funds for investment) are purely determined by the interest rate or nominal cash balances by nominal income. Credit contracts are by definition not spot transactions but contracts over time, and their conditions are thus very sensitive to expectations. Banks, for example, cannot afford to lend indiscriminately to those willing to pay the highest interest rate, but they must form an opinion about whether the potential borrower will be able to fulfill the credit contract. Given more pessimistic expectations about the future, the supply of credit to industry might be lower and cash balances (money holdings) higher despite higher interest rates. Similarly, the idea that the central bank is able to precisely control the volume of money and the price level does not conform to reality. While the central bank may be able to control the volume of so-called high-powered money,[13] it has no direct control over the activities of commercial banks and individual wealth holders nor, therefore, over the velocity of circulation.

Keynesians at times have emphasized the role of expectations and uncertainty, yet their approach is open to a similar critique. The textbook version, as it became popular after World War II, simply interpreted Keynesianism as the short-run version of a long-run neoclassical model in which money was neutral. Due mainly to the presence of trade unions, nominal prices did display some downward rigidity, but in the long run, when price adjustments had taken place, the neoclassical results would hold. Historically this meant that much of the discussion between the advocates of the respective views was based on different judgments on the extent of price rigidities in real-world economies. But if it remains unclear what outcomes flexible markets would produce, it must also remain unclear how relevant such an analysis is.

The more "fundamentalist" interpretation of Keynes instead stresses the instability of market economies due to the erratic fluctuations of private investment demand in response to changes in expectations about the future.[14] Yet, the concept of uncertainty here is used very selectively. As Alan Coddington (1982) has pointed out, it is rather inconsistent to introduce uncertainty as an explanation of instability while maintaining at the same time that macroeconomic management has precise control over the economy. Deficit spending, for example, is an uncertain remedy against recession. If deficit spending fails to improve confidence sufficiently to reignite private investment, it will eventually have to be abandoned owing to burgeoning budget deficits and, quite possibly, current account deficits.

THE CONCEPT OF A MONETARY ECONOMY

This section sketches the outline of a model of a monetary economy, that is, an economy in which the monetary sector exerts a decisive influence on the real economy. Such views have a long lineage. Elements are to be found in mercantilist thought[15] and in modern times in the writings of, for example, Knut Wicksell and Irving Fisher. In the interwar period the most important proponent of such views was, of course, Keynes himself.[16] The version presented in this section rests primarily on the interpretations of Hajo Riese (1986, 1987 A, B), Heinz-Peter Spahn (1986), and James Tobin (1980).

The analysis of a monetary economy starts with a wealth owner who is endowed with a certain sum of money, the volume of money being determined by the central bank. Each wealth owner has several options with respect to the form in which this financial portfolio is to be held. In the simple case, the wealth owner has two options: either to hold money or to lend to industrialists in order for them to undertake production. Lending implies that the wealth owner will be able to enjoy interest income whereas holding money yields no interest. Yet, due to the need for daily transactions, holding certain amounts of money will be convenient.[17] Lending involves the risk of debt default, that is, the loss of wealth. Because each individual faces uncertainty, each lender will have to form a subjective opinion of the creditworthiness of potential borrowers. Accordingly, the level of lending activity is not purely a function of the interest rate but also of the state of expectations about future economic developments.[18]

For each given state of expectations the willingness to depart with liquidity – the so-called liquidity preference schedule (j, Figure 2.3)[19] – can be graphically represented as a downward-sloping function. In order to forgo an additional amount of liquidity, wealth owners need to be offered a higher interest rate so as to compensate for the higher proportion of their portfolio exposed to risk. Given the liquidity preference schedule and the rate of interest (i), which is exogenous from the point of view of each individual wealth holder, the amount of liquidity held in portfolios and the amount of credit wealth owners are willing to supply can be determined. In terms of Figure 2.3, suppose a wealth holder can dispose of an amount of money (M) of 0-B. The amount to the left of the intersection of the i and j curves (0-A) will be held as liquidity. The remainder (A-B) will be supplied to the credit market. A more pessimistic view of the future will cause the j curve to shift to the right, leading to higher money balances and a smaller supply of credit for each given rate of interest.

On the credit market the supply by wealth owners (Gs, Figure 2.4) meets the demand (Gd) from entrepreneurs who need to finance production. The interaction of demand and supply determines the interest rate. Entrepreneurs at any given time have a stock of physical capital, and they will have an incentive to change their productive capacity if the interest rate does not equal their expected profit rate. If an entrepreneur believes that the demand prospects for his products are so good that an extension of capacity will yield a profit rate greater than the expected real interest rate which will have to be paid to finance that investment,[20] net investment will take place. In the opposite case, capacity will contract. For any given state of expectations about the future, the demand for credit is inversely related to the interest rate because an expansion of production under these conditions is expected to lead to lower profits. The interaction between wealth owners and entrepreneurs, at a given volume of money, hence determines the interest rate and the capital stock.

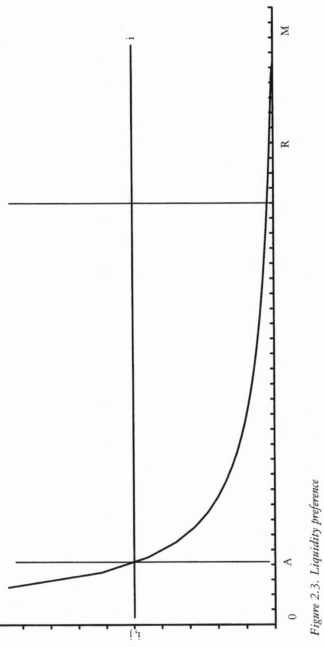

Figure 2.3. Liquidity preference

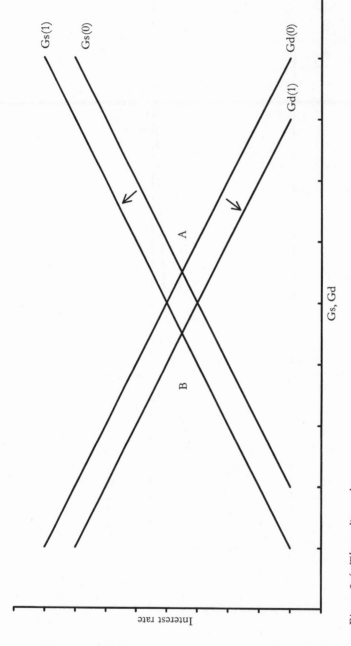

Figure 2.4. The credit market

It is important to note that the equilibrium reached in the credit market is not a unique equilibrium. More pessimistic expectations about the future will lead to less demand and supply of credit; that is, both curves will shift to the left. Figure 2.4 shows an equidistant shift to the left of the Gs (0) and Gd (0) curves. The new equilibrium, at the intersection of the Gs (1) and Gd (1) curves, is characterized by both a lower demand for and supply of credit and unchanged interest rates.

How much will be produced with a given stock of capital depends on the entrepreneurs' expectations concerning the short-term level of aggregate demand. For a given state of expectations concerning demand hence, the level of production is given, but with a given capital stock, also the level of employment is determined.

This stands in stark contrast to the neoclassical analysis in which at a given level of demand and capital stock, changes in the money wage at a fixed price level determine the level of employment. Yet, as Keynes already had pointed out,[21] because the nominal wage level affects the price level it is no longer obvious that changes in money wages affect the real wage. Wage earners can only signal their willingness to accept lower real wages by accepting lower nominal wages. For each *individual* firm a reduction in the nominal wage of its workforce will lead to a proportional reduction in its real wage costs because the overall price level can be assumed fixed. Accordingly, the demand for that firm's products, and with it employment, may be expected to rise. Yet, if wage earners throughout the economy attempt to lower real wages by lowering nominal wages, the assumption of a fixed price level is not justified anymore. Rather, the price level may be expected to fall proportionately. Keynes concluded therefore, that the level of employment was completely inelastic with respect to the money wage.

Since nominal wage changes affect the price level, the real wage can no longer be understood as the result of (unionized) wage bargaining. Instead, the real wage is a residual category, which at a given capital stock and interest rate results from the demand-determined level of employment. On the labor market then, not the real wage and the level of employment but the nominal wage is set and with it the price level.[22] Keynes retained the inverse relation between real wages and employment as depicted in the neoclassical labor demand curve, but inverted the interpretation. The level of employment determined the real wage, and not vice versa.

It is doubtful, however, whether the neoclassical labor-supply curve is of any great practical relevance simply because firms do not normally operate at their technical capacity limit. If firms, however, do not produce at full capacity the marginal cost calculus cannot provide a basis for price setting. Instead, it seems more realistic to interpret price setting as a markup of cost over prices, with the implication that also in the short run, that is, at a given level of the capital stock, changes in employment do not require inverse changes in the real wage.

Whereas in the short term generalized wage cutting fails to boost employ-ment because of the interaction of nominal wages and the price level,[23] in the somewhat longer term, falling nominal wages and prices are apt to actually *reduce* the volume of employment. To see this the effects of price changes on income determination need to be considered.

Deflation implies that money holdings, although earning no interest, will in fact earn a yield. As the price level falls, money holdings will increase in value, and this in itself will lead to a desire to increase money holdings. Decisive, however, is that the liquidity preference increases and the expected profit rate decreases because of (expected) deflation. Deflation for industrialists implies that their real indebtedness increases and their expected profit rate decreases.[24] The latter effect is strengthened by the time that necessarily elapses between the purchase of material for production and the sale of finished goods. Increased indebtedness and reduced profit expectations will reduce not only the demand for credit but also its supply as it becomes less likely that debtors will be able to fulfill their commitments.[25] Banks, for example – a crucial category of wealth holders – will become more conservative in lending to firms that experience increased indebtedness and reduced prospects of profitability. The curtailment of credit to industry implies a contraction in income and hence a reduction in demand. This effect may be exacerbated if consumers hold off on purchases in expectation of a future fall in prices. As Irving Fisher pointed out with reference to the Great Depression, firms having difficulties meeting their financial commitments may resort to liquidation of stocks of products and assets in order to obtain liquidity. This process in itself, however, aggravates defla-tion.[26] If sufficiently severe, the widespread debt default of industry will threaten the solidity of the banking system and cause a run of depositors on the banks.[27] A well-behaved – in the neoclassical sense – labor market will be a major propagator of deflation. If wage earners in general react to an increase in unemployment by lowering wages, deflationary problems and hence the eco-nomic collapse are intensified. Politically this implies that in a deflationary crisis, weak trade unions sooner or later must become a problem for the economy and the state. Or, to be a bit sarcastic, full price and wage flexibility in practice can only be held out as the remedy to all economic evils only as long as they do not actually occur.

There is a possible countervailing force, namely, that deflation increases the value of money holdings and hence might stimulate spending.[28] However, under strong deflationary dynamics this price level effect is likely to be swamped by reduced income due to reduced investment, destruction of financial wealth due to debt default, and reduced consumption in expectation of further deflation. To quote Tobin (1980: 18): "Now expected deflation increases the demand for money, making it more attractive relative to other goods and equities in goods. This effect counters the price level effect and may be stronger. If so, deflation does not correct the initial deficiency in aggregate demand that triggered it. Then deflation has no stopping point. The symmetrical case is hyper-inflation, in which the velocity of money rises astronomically."

As Tobin suggests, inflationary processes can be understood very much as the mirror image of deflationary processes. Inflation undermines the value of money holdings and hence makes them less attractive. Decreasing real indebtedness and the time lag between the beginning of production and sales increases expected profit rates. High activity and rising prices will make industry more willing to borrow, especially because it can expect a decline in real indebtedness. Inflation will hence have a stimulating effect on production as both demand and supply of credit increase. Banks will pursue a more liberal lending policy as the likelihood of borrowers being able to fulfill their commitments increases; increased demand, in turn, further improves profit prospects and this effect is stronger if households decide to increase consumption in expectation of future price increases. Again, well-behaved trade unions will aggravate inflationary problems if they react to lower unemployment with higher nominal wage demands. Moreover, as the labor market becomes increasingly tight, even centralized trade unions will be less and less able to deliver wage moderation. Even centralized trade unions will have difficulties preventing their members at the local level from accepting higher wages. In times of tight labor markets and increasing profits and prices, the leadership of centralized unions will thus find it increasingly difficult to contain wage increases.

In a deflation, lenders will profit at the expense of borrowers if the latter are able to fulfill their debt contracts. As deflation continues, however, debt default becomes increasingly likely with the result of a "flight into money," that is, the only assets protected against debt default as well as bank failures. Rising inflation rates, however, imply that the value of debt contracts is eroded. Yet, holding liquidity obviously provides no protection against the erosion of wealth. While in its initial stages inflation may stimulate industrial activity, holding real assets sooner or later becomes more attractive than lending to industry. For it is only real assets, like real estate and durable consumption goods, which provide protection against the erosion of the value of money and debt contracts. Increased demand for such assets in turn increases inflationary pressures. The result is that continued inflation leads to a so-called flight out of money, in which all wealth holders try to liquidate financial assets and money for real assets and where speculation becomes a more promising way of increasing and safeguarding wealth than financing the production of goods.

ECONOMIC POLICY MAKING IN MONETARY ECONOMIES

THE PRIORITY OF PRICE STABILITY

The political hue of the government does, as political scientists have frequently argued,[29] exert a significant influence on economic policies. Yet power politics operates within definite limits, given by the extent to which the institutions of the market and civil society can maintain the compatibility between a given economic policy program and the requirement of price stability.

Growth and full employment are the most crucial goals for social democratic governments, not only because full employment in itself is crucial for the welfare of wage earners, but also because in the longer run mass unemployment makes it impossible to finance social democracy's welfare state programs. Growth and full employment, however, can only be maintained on the basis of an expansionary macroeconomic regime in which the labor market parties are able to contain inflationary pressures. Because in the somewhat longer run the government's readiness to tolerate inflation is likely to spark a cumulative spiral at the end of which stands the collapse of the financial system and the economy, a parliamentary majority for social democratic parties provides insufficient protection against policies that will introduce unemployment as the main instrument in the fight against inflation. The increasing destabilization of the economy may prompt conservative or liberal governments to initiate a restrictive macroeconomic regime at a relatively early stage. But, when the financial system explodes in a speculative flight out of money, even social democrats are left with no policy options. At this point they either change policies, or they are elected out of office because obviously incompetent.

Conversely, conservative or liberal governments cannot indefinitely pursue a restrictive macroregime that seeks economic recovery mainly by means of domestic cost cutting if they lack the appropriate institutions that can contain deflationary pressures. The unemployment consequences of such a constellation may prompt strong social democratic governments to change policies at an early stage. Yet when a massive flight into money ruins the banking system and brings the real economy to a standstill, business and farmers also will start to have grave doubts about the wisdom of deflation. Again this leaves liberal and conservative governments the option of changing their policies or being elected out of office.

In sum, because of the possibility of cumulative processes in decentralized monetary economies, price stability is a policy priority that no government can avoid pursuing in the long run.[30] Accordingly, the concept of a monetary economy suggests that a historical analysis of economic policy making will eventually have to distance itself from the assumption that regime changes can be interpreted in terms of a process of political competition among interest groups for policy outcomes, as well as from the assumption that policy making is informed primarily by the goal of facilitating the optimal development of the real sector. Historically, the view that economic policies will always attempt to avoid crises and to promote growth and employment sits uneasily with those instances in which policy, primarily in the form of monetary restriction, attempts to reduce growth and full employment as during the return to gold in the twenties, the initial phases of the Great Depression, and the disinflation of the eighties and nineties. The three regime changes of this century instead must be interpreted as ultimately driven by the need to break cumulative processes – an inflationary process during the early twenties and the past two decades, and a deflationary process during the thirties.

POLICY REGIMES AND EXPECTATIONS

Once it is realized that expectations play a crucial role in the economic process, it becomes analytically necessary to distinguish between the government's day-to-day policies and its long-term policy orientation – namely, the policy regime. Policy authorities may find that market dynamics at times counteract their short-term policy measures. Yet, the state does exert a powerful influence over economic developments through the way in which the policy regime shapes the long-term expectations of the actors.

Realizing that the propensity to invest, and with it the prospect for growth and prosperity, ultimately depends on the confidence in future prosperity, Keynes (1973: 161) stressed the importance of spontaneous shifts from optimism to pessimism; the famous "animal spirits": "Most, probably, of our decisions to do something positive, the full consequences of which will be drawn out over many days to come, can only be taken as a result of animal spirits – of a spontaneous urge to action rather than inaction, and not as the outcome of a weighted average of quantitative benefits multiplied by quantitative probabilities." Yet as witnessed by, for example, the thirty-year boom after World War II or the durable recession of the past two decades, long-term expectations have frequently been more resilient than would have to be expected if they were driven by spontaneous animal spirits.

The emphasis on animal spirits underestimates the role of the state as a common point of orientation for market actors, and hence as an agent that can shape and stabilize expectations. By explicitly embracing a specific policy "philosophy" (i.e., by prioritizing some goals over others and by assigning specific instruments to specific tasks, the state embeds its short-term policy activity within a longer-term framework of meaning and hence provides an important focal point for the expectations of market actors. Or, as Peter Temin (1989: 91) defines policy regimes:

> The regime is an abstraction from any single policy decision; it represents the systematic and predictable part of all decisions. It is the thread that runs through the individual choices that governments and central banks have to make. It is visible even though there inevitably will be some loose ends, that is, some decisions that do not fit the general pattern. These isolated actions have little impact because they represent exceptions to the policy rule, not new policy regimes.

The alternations of long periods of growth and recession that Western Europe has witnessed since 1918 accordingly are not the result of the fickleness of animal spirits. Rather, stagnation and prosperity can be understood as the outcome of the set of expectations created by the long-term policy orientation of governments. A policy regime that gives priority to combating inflation by means of restrictive macropolicies will have a powerful negative impact on expectations about future growth prospects and hence depress private invest-ment. The unemployment of the interwar period and the seventies and eighties was primarily the result of a restrictive policy regime which, in terms of Figure 2.4, shifted both curves to the left, reducing the (growth rate of the) level of productive capacity and thereby the demand for labor. To attempt Keynesian deficit spending in combination with a restrictive regime is to ensure the former's failure. As restrictive regimes discourage investment, fiscal deficit spending may mitigate a drop in overall demand but is quite unlikely to provide the initial spark for recovery of private investment and will thereby perpetuate budget deficits. Historically, this has meant that the decision to employ restric-tive monetary policies in order to combat inflation or maintain the fixed exchange rate as in the early and late twenties, the early thirties, and the seventies and eighties necessarily also implied the failure of deficit spending strategies.

Conversely, a regime that can successfully contain inflationary pressures without recourse to restrictive policies will have the opposite effect. The higher gross domestic product (GDP) growth is expected to be, the more attractive it would seem to invest in additional productive capacity to satisfy growing demand; and the more vigorous private investment, the higher growth. A credible commitment to a growth regime, which dissipates the fear that pros-perity may provoke central banks to seek a return to unemployment for fear of rising inflation, can set in motion and maintain such a virtuous circle. This was the main driving force behind the long post-1945 boom. And because of the buoyancy of private investment, Keynesian deficit spending was unnecessary.

LAISSEZ-FAIRE VERSUS INTERVENTIONISM?

In the common understanding of the history of economic policy making, re-gimes are interpreted as different methods to pursue the same goal of growth and full employment. In contrast to many ethical questions, for example, the issue of abortion, the discourse about economic policy making is generally characterized by agreement on the ultimate goals but disagreement on the appropriate methods. Whatever their differences, virtually all political parties generally agree that growth, full employment, and price stability are the most important economic goals the state should strive for. Indeed, in a democratic polity any other policy priorities would seem hardly viable electorally. The disagreement rather seems to concern the policies to be employed. Is economic prosperity best served by giving as much free rein as possible to market forces, or does it require substantial intervention and regulation?

Accordingly, the three regime changes of this century are frequently inter-preted as a movement from laissez-faire to Keynesian interventionism and back to a more liberal reliance on market forces. The 1920s have entered the history books as a period of liberal economic policies. In the view of Keynes, the laissez-faire of the 1920s was at the root of the economic evils of that time.[31] Conversely, the thirties appeared as a transition from the liberal laissez-faire to a politically regulated economy. According to Karl Polanyi, for example, the thirties marked the end of the self-regulating market.[32] Also in the eyes of most social democrats the transformation starting with the Great Depression marked the end of laissez-faire and the beginning of the dominance of the political over the economic system.[33] And although the seventies and eighties have seen neither the return to a gold standard type of deflationary policies nor the full-scale dismantling of welfare states, the period to most observers is characterized by a decisive turn toward neoliberalism.

Yet, such an interpretation does not conform to the needs of a monetary economy, which requires discretionary policy management with the goal of long-term price stability. Accordingly, regimes cannot be usefully distinguished in terms of interventionism versus laissez-faire because they are all necessarily interventionist. At the same time, the Keynesian notion of a discretionary regime aimed at growth and full employment is equally inappropriate because, in case of a conflict, the goal of price stability will prevail over the goal of employment.

Instead, it is more accurate to characterize regimes in terms of the specific assignment of instruments to goals. Historically, one can distinguish, on the one hand, interventionist regimes that maintain high unemployment and a fixed exchange rate in order to combat inflation while relegating the concern for growth and employment to microeconomic policies and, on the other hand, interventionist regimes in which growth and full employment are assigned to macroeconomic policies, while the concern for price stability is delegated primarily to the microeconomic level of wage bargaining.

If there ever was a policy regime after 1918 that deserved to be called liberal, it must apply to the period 1918–21. Letting currencies float meant that exchange rate levels were to be determined by market forces. The rapid deregulation of wartime controls also entrusted wage and price formation to the market. Finally, accommodating monetary policies implied that the supply of money was determined by market demand. With the decision to deflate and return to gold, the "liberal" regime ended, and it has not returned since.

To consider the interwar gold standard as well as the present regime variations of liberalism is inaccurate for three reasons. First, because monetary instability is a fundamental threat to a market economy, liberals have in practice come to accept price stability – and in many cases fixed exchange rates – as a goal of macroeconomic policies. However, by accepting the goal of price stability, direct intervention in the market becomes unavoidable. The decision to impose a specific target for what should have been the outcome of market processes necessarily compromises the core principle of liberalism as it makes the principle of nonintervention subordinate to a teleology. As Polanyi (1957: 233) noted with respect to the interwar period: "Though opposed in theory to interventionism and inflation alike, economic liberals had chosen between the two and set the sound currency ideal above that of non-intervention." A truly liberal regime instead should be indifferent with respect to market outcomes, including monetary ones. Accordingly, the only consistent liberal regime would be one that awarded all commercial banks the privilege of note issue rather than relying on the government-sanctioned monopoly of a central bank and allowing the market to find its own price level and exchange rate.[34] Why should the market be left to determine the quantity and price of all goods except in the monetary field?

The response to such criticism has generally been to call attention to the automatic, or nondiscretionary, character of the macroeconomic policies employed in order to reach the goal of price stability. According to most advocates of the interwar gold standard, the system removed all room for political discretion as it made the conduct of monetary policies totally subordinate to the fixed exchange rate target. In our day, the practice of monetary targeting is said to remove discretion in the conduct of monetary policies. But calling for a nondiscretionary or automatic monetary policy cannot conceal that the acceptance of the need for a political determination of the quantity and price of money is a fundamental breach with the liberal principle of noninterference. There is really no good reason that a policy that fixes the money supply at an arbitrary rate or varies the supply of money only in response to the requirements of the exchange rate should be called more market based or liberal and less interventionist than a policy that automatically varies the money supply and/or the budget deficit in response to a deviation of the unemployment rate from a politically determined target value. Yet, the latter type of policy would be unacceptable to those who profess to be economic liberals.

Second, if only because, as argued earlier, the velocity of money cannot be a priori assumed to be stable, automatic, or nondiscretionary, monetary policies are inappropriate tools for achieving a given target level of the price level and/ or exchange rate. Given that in both "liberal" regimes preventing inflation enjoyed the utmost priority, the implication was that macroeconomic, and in particular monetary, policies were conducted in a highly discretionary manner just as in what is generally considered the interventionist regime.[35]

Restoring and maintaining the interwar gold standard required highly discretionary monetary policies, as did membership in the European monetary system (EMS). Nor has the rise of monetarist targeting in some countries since the seventies reduced the discretionary character of monetary policies. No single country ever accepted Milton Friedman's prescriptions of constitutionally determined money supply rates in order to stabilize inflation. Rather than a fixed rate of money growth giving rise to stable prices, changes in inflation came to function as an indicator for discretionary changes in monetary policy. As Victor Argy, Anthony Brennan, and Glenn Stevens (1990: 58) argued after surveying the practice of monetary targeting in nine countries: "Targets were never interpreted as monetary rules (that probably would be a revolution). Over-runs were not usually reversed; neither were under-runs, but they were far less frequent. The aggregates concerned were switched when considered necessary, and the targets themselves were ignored at times when other considerations intruded. Some countries eventually abandoned targeting altogether."

Third, the inability to adhere to the liberal principle of noninterference with market outcomes went far beyond the monetary sphere. Because both so-called (neo) liberal regimes were based on the assumptions that automatic or rule-based monetary policies are a sufficient condition for monetary stability, and that restrictive monetary policies did not affect growth and employment, the inevitable disparity between theory and reality gave rise to far-reaching interventions. The durable mass unemployment, which invariably, characterized both "liberal" regimes, drew policy makers into supply-side policies, rather than causing them to change macroeconomic course. But a perceived need for supply-side policies by definition signals distrust in the automatic healing forces of the market. During the interwar gold standard, governments were generally convinced that rationalization of industry held the key to improved industrial performance. In the twenties the Bank of England (BoE), for example, became actively involved in industrial restructuring in an effort to deflate political opposition against the role of banks in industrial finance and to increase exports, thereby strengthening the pound and improving overall economic performance.[36] Similarly, at present most governments accept the need for interference in the labor market to promote flexibility, product innovation, and adoption of new technologies as important means of improving the performance of the economy.

THE POLITICS OF ECONOMIC IDEAS

Since regime changes can hardly be explained within the framework of normal political competition, economic ideas have received increasing attention as a potential explanatory variable.[37] To focus on ideas would seem a theoretically and empirically plausible route as regime changes are generally accompanied by dramatic shifts in policy orthodoxy. The policy changes since the seventies have frequently been characterized as a transition from Keynesianism to monetarism. The regime change in the aftermath of the Great Depression is commonly understood as a shift from neoclassical to Keynesian views. Less well known perhaps, the dramatic changes in macroeconomic policies that accompanied the resurrection of the gold standard during the early 1920s also saw a change in policy orthodoxy from "Keynesian"-inspired views to neoclassical ones.

Yet, such an interpretation is unsatisfactory. As will be argued in the next three chapters, the actual policies pursued frequently did not conform to the theoretical interpretation governments claim to have embraced. More important perhaps, the Duhem-Quine thesis that it is well-nigh impossible to refute theories by means of empirical evidence also implies that virtually any policy measure can be justified in terms of a given theory by varying the auxiliary assumptions. And indeed, historically, the degree of policy convergence during regime changes has been considerably greater than the convergence of theoretical justifications; that is, the same policies can be and have been justified on the basis of different theoretical frameworks.

In fact, the hypothesis that new economic ideas determine the character of the new policies during regime changes reverses cause and effect. Instead, the periodic changes in the ideas informing economic policies can be understood as the mechanism by which conflicts between the inherent policy priorities of a monetary economy and the requirements of democratic party competition are solved. The cumulative nature of the inflationary and deflationary constellations that gave rise to regime changes implied that the basic character of the new economic policies was predetermined. The adoption of new ideas only served the function of providing an explanation for these changes that was satisfactory in terms of the basic ideological convictions of the main political groups. Instead, ideas do play a role in explaining policy continuity. The trauma of the deflationary or inflationary cycles that give birth to a new regime generally comes to dominate policy even after the original constellation that informed these policies has long gone. The new understanding of policy making prompted by a de- or inflationary crisis is institutionalized in a new form of economic policy assignment and hence acquires a high degree of inertia. As shall be argued later, during the midst of the deflationary depression many politicians feared a reemergence of runaway inflation. In our times, Western European macroeconomic authorities seem to be guided primarily by the fear of a new inflationary cycle despite mass unemployment and oftentimes falling unit labor costs. And because the core economic views informing a policy regime are basically impossible to refute empirically, they tend to structure opposition to its economic effect so as to produce demands that do not question its perpetuation.

The requirement that macroeconomic policies be conducted in a discretionary fashion, while giving priority to price stability, does not necessarily conform well to the needs of political parties in a democratic polity. The democratic constitution of the polity requires, as a rule, that political parties, which wish to enlist a political majority, must present an economic policy program that is said to promote growth and employment. In a deflationary constellation, generally no conflict exists as the policies required to halt the fall in prices are also those that will stimulate growth and employment. In an inflationary crisis, instead, macroeconomic policies sooner or later become necessary that will actually increase unemployment and reduce growth. Accordingly, regime changes require a change of interpretative framework.

Moreover, successful political competition requires that political parties distinguish themselves from their political opponents in order to maintain ideological credibility, which means that they must be able to justify economic policy strategies in terms of the general philosophy on which they are said to be founded. In general terms this means that the liberal tradition must find an explanation for both types of regimes that somehow makes reference to the superiority of market forces. For social democrats in turn the task is to find justifications that do not violate the conviction that markets need to be tamed and that political intervention and interest organizations potentially promote prosperity.

To avoid misunderstanding, it is not argued that politicians consciously advocate new ideas that they know to be false in order to defend their political interests. Politicians, like most others, will conduct the search for the new policies, which become necessary as de- or inflationary spirals increasingly demonstrate the inappropriateness of the old policies, quite naturally on the basis of their prior theoretical and ideological convictions. Only if satisfactory explanations cannot be found will the necessity of a fundamental adjustment of core beliefs be contemplated. Yet, the Duhem-Quine thesis implies that it will almost always be possible to find satisfactory explanations.

The liberal and conservative sides of the political spectrum generally adjust ideologically to inflationary constellations by resurrecting the neoclassical neutrality-of-money doctrine as a way of integrating the need for macroeconomic disinflation with their core ideological convictions. By postulating that there simply is no trade-off between growth, employment, and inflation, and that, therefore, a political debate about the relative priorities to be attached to these goals is simply pointless, the required priority of anti-inflation policies can be achieved without openly violating the political requirement that economic policies may not be seen to reduce growth and employment. Moreover, as follows from the quantity theory, the inflationary problems present must be attributed to political mismanagement.

At first sight, such an ideological adjustment may seem somewhat counterproductive because the neutrality-of-money doctrine does not provide a good ground at all for justifying a policy of disinflation or for more independent central banks. Because it argues that inflation has positive effects in the short run and no effects in the long run, inflation should be at worst irrelevant. Nor is it clear why governments should be able to profit electorally from expansionary policies in this model. If the effect of expansionary policies is indeed to reduce the real wage against the wage earners' wishes, it would be surprising if such a policy would motivate them, in their capacity as voters, to reward the government. However, if the government in this model cannot have an incentive to create inflation, there also is no reason why monetary policy would have to be isolated from political influences.

Yet, the argument that disinflation has no costs is quite useful once it is already recognized that inflation is highly disruptive and needs to be fought. The argument of the absence of a trade-off between inflation and unemployment does provide a formidable defense against diluting the priority of low inflation with any concerns for the real economy. The emergence of durable unemployment and recession in response to disinflationary policies does not cast doubt upon the neutrality-of-money postulate. Instead, following the overall liberal convictions, stagnation and unemployment are attributed to microeconomic obstructions to the free play of market forces (in particular, trade unions and excessive regulations), hence calling for an extension of liberal policies also to the supply side.

The expansionary macroeconomic policies that eventually become necessary to break a deflationary cycle, in the liberal perspective, are interpreted in a theoretical framework that derives the possibility of effective macroeconomic policies from the presence of, mainly union-inspired, nominal wage rigidities. As already briefly mentioned, the dominant liberal interpretation of the apparent success of Keynesian policies was that, if nominal wages are rigid, then expansionary macropolicies can bring about a reduction in real wages that the trade unions will not allow to take place by the usual market mechanisms. Whereas the neutrality-of-money argument stresses the long-run effects, it is now the short run that becomes the focus of attention. Ideologically, such an interpretation has the obvious advantage that it can justify discretionary macromanagement without having to reject the conclusion that a free market in principle would produce optimal outcomes.

For social democracy, the neoclassical justification of restrictive macroeconomic regimes is generally unattractive as it implies that policy mismanagement, welfare state arrangements, and the trade unions are to blame for inflation and unemployment. Somewhat paradoxically, perhaps, the neoclassical justification was much more amenable to Marxist thinking. The postulates that economic policies have no real effect in the longer run and that stagnation and unemployment are due to excessive wage demands could be seen to support their contention that the legitimate demands of labor could not be satisfied within the framework of capitalism. And indeed, as shall be argued in the next chapter, the gold standard policies did lead to a relapse into Marxist fatalism in some social democratic parties. Social democrats instead prefer to argue that restrictive macroeconomic policies were imposed on national governments by internationally mobile capital. Although the internationalization of financial markets and the restrictive consequences for domestic macromanagement allegedly following it are generally considered to be rather recent phenomena, they are in fact not without precedent. The 1920s were characterized by rather extensive international capital flows, and accordingly the view that abandoning the gold standard and the restrictive policies required by it would destroy the credibility of the currency with dire consequences for the whole economy could be frequently heard from social democratic politicians.

Historically, such a view was indeed not implausible as, in countries with open financial markets, the flight out of money accompanying ingrained expectations of further inflation might manifest itself as a flight out of the national currency. Accordingly, there seemed to be good empirical evidence for attributing domestic problems to external constraints, although such an argument in fact reversed cause and effect. Ideologically, the advantage of the external constraints hypothesis is that it allows social democrats to maintain their conviction that expansionary demand management policies in principle are feasible and necessary, and yet to adopt the same policy conclusions as their liberal opponents, namely, that restrictive macroeconomic policies are inevitable.[38] Hence, it is no coincidence at all that (various versions of) the quantity theory and the external constraints view tend to become popular simultaneously.

Obviously, social democrats could not hope to build an attractive platform on the argument that expansionary policies are unfortunately impossible at the moment. Social democrats needed a program for reducing unemployment, and, with the macro side blocked, this only left supply-side policies. Since it would be hard for social democrats to place the need for real wage cuts at the core of their policy program, cost cutting by means of improved productivity seemed the plausible alternative. By postulating that, in the long run, the resistance of unions against wage cuts benefits prosperity as it forces firms to "rationalize," the liberal supply-side views could be given a genuinely social democratic answer.

3

WHY WAS THERE NO SOCIAL DEMOCRATIC BREAKTHROUGH IN THE TWENTIES?

THE IRRELEVANCE OF SOCIALISM

For socialists the most puzzling feature of the post–World War I period has always been why the labor movement could not capitalize on its greatly strengthened position by making decisive headway toward a socialized economy. Yet, in retrospect one must recognize that this "failure" was not too surprising at all. While the goal of a socialist economy may at times have served an important rhetorical role for some social democratic parties, it remained largely irrelevant for the conduct of practical economic policies. During prosperous times, there seemed to be no reason to risk a socialist experiment, and, during periods of crises, it seemed unwise to further upset the complex machinery of the developed Western European economies. The political logic of a movement that wanted to improve the economic and social plight of its followers, yet could only see massive economic dislocations in the transition to a socialist economy, instead suggested a program of reformism within the framework of a market economy.

At the end of the war, social democracy was unable to give any concrete content to Marx's contention that the liberation of labor was the precondition for the liberation of society – specifically that public ownership of the means of production would benefit everyone. Germany was the only country in Western Europe in which a socialist revolution might have been politically feasible immediately after the collapse of the Wilhelmine Empire. Yet the SPD felt it was unwise to subject an already severely malnourished and underemployed population to the far-reaching economic dislocations of socialism, and instead decided to set up a commission to study the problem. The Dutch, Swedish, and Norwegian social democrats, none of whom were even remotely close to a revolutionary situation, created similar commissions, but they all failed to produce an answer.

The SPD came to embrace Rudolf Hilferding's theory of "organized capitalism," which argued that the goal of socialism did not call for any concrete measures because the organic development of capitalism itself would create the necessary preconditions. The Norwegian labor party's report, published in 1920, went into some detail concerning the order in which different sectors were to be nationalized, but it did not treat the question of how nationalized firms were to be managed and in what way nationalization would solve the firms' and the economy's problems.[1] The Dutch report, also published in 1920, focused mainly on the administrative structure of a socialized economy, but it, too, lacked any concrete analysis of how the economic problems of the period could be solved by means of socialization. The Swedish commission, however, did have the intention of providing concrete guidelines, and its fate is symptomatic of the inherent problems of a strategy of socialization. The commission was established in 1920. In the end, it would devote fifteen years to the task without being able to come up with substantive answers.[2]

Socialization appeared also to be a threat to the coherence of the labor movement itself. Socializing firms implied that decisions concerning wages and employment became internal political problems for the labor movement. The active participation of social democratic parties in the regulation of the wartime economy had shown that the administration of scarcity increased tensions both in and between the party and the unions. To a political movement dependent on an appeal to workers in general, political viability and unity required that such divisive issues remained external. Hence, it is not surprising that trade unions generally were skeptical. During the turbulent years of 1918–19 the German trade unions, for example, opposed far-reaching socialization because they feared it would destabilize the economy and undermine their own position.[3] The Swedish LO (Landsorganisasjon i Sverige) had similar views.

STRONG LABOR AND MACROECONOMIC POLICIES FOR GROWTH

What does seem surprising is that within three years of the end of hostilities virtually all countries embarked on severely restrictive macroeconomic policies at great cost to growth and employment. After the social and economic ravages wrought by the war, a policy of deflation held no appeal. The hardship in the trenches and at home had radicalized many; as a result, trade unions and social democratic parties generally recorded a rapid growth in membership. In addition, the introduction of general (male) suffrage further strengthened the position of the left. Norwegian, Dutch, and British social democrats all recorded significant gains in the first postwar elections, although they were too weak to enter government.[4] In Sweden and Germany, on the other hand, the growing strength of labor was translated into government participation. The Swedish social democrats entered government in 1917 as junior partners of the liberals. In the spring of 1920, they formed a minority government on their own, the first social democratic government in Swedish history. In Germany, the (M)SPD came to occupy a crucial position in the early years of the Weimar Republic. On February 13, 1919, Philipp Scheidemann became the first chancellor of the new republic and the first social democratic chancellor in German history.

But even in those countries where social democrats remained on the opposition benches, labor's growing strength and radicalism strongly impressed the need upon liberal and conservative parties to accommodate labor.[5] In Britain, the election manifesto of the liberal/conservative coalition of Lloyd George and Bonar Law, published in November 1918, emphasized the need to stimulate domestic production. In a famous election speech in late 1918, Liberal Prime Minister David Lloyd George promised "to make Britain a fit country for heroes to live in."[6] In order to do so, production had to be increased, a massive housing construction program started, and health care, child welfare, and education improved. On the basis of this program, the coalition scored an overwhelming victory in the elections of December 1918.

In Norway, the October elections also reconfirmed liberal (Venstre) Prime Minister Gunnar Knudsen, although here the liberals now had to govern on the basis of a parliamentary minority. Pursuing a policy of the "outstretched hand" toward labor was foremost on Knudsen's mind. In his inaugural speech, he announced increased spending on housing construction, social security reforms, and the eight-hour working day. Moreover, Knudsen sought to include DNA in his coalition. Since March 1918, however, DNA had come to define itself as a revolutionary Marxist party, and the conditions under which it would join a coalition proved to be unacceptable. But in order not to further alienate labor, the liberals continued to exclude the possibility of a coalition with the conservatives.

Even apart from any fear of working-class unrest, however, a host of other reasons compelled governments to pursue a strategy of economic growth. Also most non–social democratic parties felt sincerely that the soldiers should not be greeted by recession and unemployment when coming home. Given the high debt at the end of the war, a policy of cheap money aimed at stimulating private investment would seem the most promising strategy to improve the budgetary situation. Low interest rates also served to facilitate the debt service. Higher growth, moreover, would increase tax receipts and thereby facilitate deficit reduction. Finally, four long years of wartime destruction and insufficient investment in capital stock and infrastructure made the need for stimulating investment even more urgent after the war.

Moreover, a growth-oriented policy would seem the most politically promising strategy for liberal and conservative parties, in the face of the rapidly growing popularity of social democracy. Despite the rhetoric, for the majority

Table 3.1. *British governments during the interwar period*

Prime minister	Period	Labour	Conservatives	Liberals	National Liberals	National Labour	Percentage of parliament seats
Lloyd George	1/10/1919		R	X			72.0
Bonar Law	10/24/1922		X				55.9[a]
Baldwin	5/27/1923		X				55.9
MacDonald	1/23/1924	X					31.1
Baldwin	11/6/1924		X				67.5
MacDonald	6/8/1929	X		R			46.7
MacDonald	8/25/1931		R				51.9[b]
MacDonald	11/5/1931		R		R	X	84.7
Baldwin	6/7/1935		X		R	R	69.8[c]
Chamberlain	5/28/1937		X		R	R	69.8

Note: X: Party of prime minister. R: Party represented in coalition.

[a] Prior to November election 54.0%.

[b] Supported only by parts of Labour.

[c] Prior to November election 84.7%.

Source: Flora et al. 1983: 189.

Table 3.2. *Norwegian governments during the interwar period*

Prime minister	Period	Labor (DNA)	Conservatives (Høyre)	Left Liberals (Frisinnede Venstre)	Liberals (Venstre)	Farmers (BP)	Percentage of parliament seats
Knudsen	12/20/1919				X		40.5
Halvorsen I	6/21/1920		X	R			39.7
Blehr	6/22/1921				X		40.5
Halvorsen II	3/6/1923		X	R			38.0
Berge	5/30/1923		R	X			38.0
Mowinckel I	7/25/1924				X		24.7
Lykke	3/5/1925		X	R			36.0
Hornsrud	1/28/1928	X					39.3
Mowinckel II	2/15/1928				X		20.0
Kolstad	5/12/1931					X	16.7
Hundseid	3/14/1932					X	16.7
Mowinckel III	3/2/1933				X		22.0
Nygaardsvold I	3/20/1935	X					46.0
Nygaardsvold II	4/22/1940	X	R		R	R	98.0

Note: See Table 3.1.
Source: Flora et al. 1983.

of social democrats, socialization of the means of production was not an end in itself but a means to improve living conditions.[7] To abstain from a policy of reforms that might improve the lot of the working class was not, therefore, a viable policy option for social democrats. By proving that significant improvements of working-class conditions were possible under private ownership, liberals and conservatives could effectively undermine the case for nationalizing industry. In such a scenario, social democrats would have the choice of either concentrating on reforms within a market economy or remaining in opposition and clinging to their slogans of nationalization while losing the initiative to their political opponents.

Because of the expansionary policies unemployment remained low almost everywhere (see Table 3.3). Unemployment was virtually nonexistent in Norway and Britain until 1921 and in Germany until 1923. Dutch unemployment remained fairly high, although a significant decrease was recorded in 1920. Sweden seems the only country where the boom was not reflected in lower unemployment. Yet as the boom took place mainly during the last half of 1919 and the first half of 1920, annual data overestimate the amount of labor market slack. Most industrial sectors in Sweden showed a strong drop in unemployment starting with the third quarter of 1919. In the first six months of 1919, only 10 percent of industrial firms reported labor scarcity; by the first half of 1920, the figure had risen to 25.4 percent. In the second half of 1920 the figure dropped to 8.7 percent.[8]

The new decade, however, brought a radical change in policies. The decision to return to the fixed exchange rate system of the gold standard, taken, with the exception of Germany, around 1920–21, initiated a period of strongly deflationary policies. As a result unemployment skyrocketed. Although the situation subsequently improved somewhat, unemployment remained high throughout the decade.

According to a still widespread interpretation, the regime shift of the 1930s was the result of the mounting opposition from, in particular, the labor movement to unemployment and recession. And, as macroeconomic policies were reoriented toward stimulating growth, it proved possible to reduce unemployment without real wages cuts, thereby resolving the deadlock between the socialist demand for expropriation of the bourgeoisie and the employers' insistence on cost reduction. But, if the reorientation of macroeconomic policies during the thirties did indeed lay the foundation for the "golden age of social democracy," it must be asked why such changes did not take place in the twenties. If the political right and the employers felt compelled by the threat of social unrest to grant some of labor's long-standing demands, such as the eight-hour day and universal suffrage, and to renege on some of capital's prerogatives by initiating corporatist structures,[9] why could this cooperation not be durably extended to macroeconomic policies? If, as Keynes would argue a decade later, macroeconomic management could defuse the case for socialism, the early twenties rather than the thirties would seem the ideal political constellation for the

Table 3.3. *Unemployment rates, 1916–26*

	Germany	Netherlands	Norway	Sweden	Britain
1916	2.2	5.1	0.8	4.0	0.4
1917	1.0	6.5	0.9	4.0	0.6
1918	1.2	7.5	1.4	4.6	0.8
1919	3.7	7.7	1.6	5.5	3.4
1920	3.8	5.8	2.3	5.4	2.0
1921	2.8	9.0	17.6	26.6	11.3
1922	1.5	11.0	17.1	22.9	9.8
1923	10.2	11.2	10.6	12.5	8.1
1924	13.1	8.8	8.5	10.1	7.2
1925	6.8	8.1	13.2	11.0	7.9
1926	18.0	7.3	24.3	12.2	8.8

Note: Germany, up to 1929 unemployed trade union members, thereafter registered unemployed; Netherlands, proportion of possible days' work lost due to unemployment; Norway and Sweden, percentage of unemployed trade union members; Britain, registered unemployed.
Sources: Sweden, Silenstam 1970: 108. Remaining countries, Mitchell 1992.

birth of such a policy. Why then did the breakthrough to a social democratic type of economic policy making, which occurred in the wake of the depression, not take place in the aftermath of World War I?

WAITING FOR KEYNES?

One possible answer might be that Keynesian policies were a necessary precondition for a successful social democratic model, but such policies were not yet known during the early twenties. This view, however, is incorrect.[10] No sophisticated economic reasoning is required to arrive at the conclusion that public spending will alleviate the plight of at least some firms and workers during a crisis. Especially those industries that could hope to benefit directly from state procurement would hardly need to wait for the formulation of Keynesian theory to advocate increased state spending without tax increases. Even for the state itself, loan-financed contracyclical spending would seem attractive as recessions are generally characterized by lower interest rates, lower wages, and lower prices. Nor did social democrats have to wait for Keynes in order to advocate expansionary macromanagement. In times of crisis, when employers demanded wage reductions, high unemployment weakened the trade unions, and demands for higher real wages so as improve the purchasing power of the working class had at best rhetorical value, stimulation of demand by the state would almost automatically present itself as a convenient remedy. Klein (1975: 139) was right to point out that "the concept of public works as a remedy for unemployment is so obvious that some researchers have attempted to trace its origins to Ancient Egypt."[11]

In Britain, the Minority Report of the Royal Poor Law Commission, written largely by Beatrice Webb, has long been recognized as a forerunner of contracyclical government spending. In the same year in which the Minority Report was published (1909), the principle of contracyclical investment spending was endorsed by the British government in the Development and Road Fund Act.[12] Demands for contracyclical public works were already included in the Labour Party's 1918 program *Labour and the New Social Order*. Labour's pamphlet *Unemployment: A Labour Policy* (1921) likewise envisaged the use of contracyclical government spending along the lines of the minority report.[13]

Similarly in Norway, the idea of contracyclical policies had been part of the baggage of political parties long before Keynes. The Conservative Party, which especially after 1923 was the driving force behind the policy of budget retrenchment, had long stressed the need for the state to run a surplus and reduce debt in good years so as to be able to stimulate economic activity by means of tax reduction in times of recession.[14] A rather similar view was expressed in parliament by the financial spokesman of the labor party in 1922. In a passage that might have come from a Keynesian textbook, Christian Hornsrud argued:

> Under growth periods we should implement high and strongly progressive taxes, pay back debt and collect the biggest possible reserves until the recession comes. At that point the state and the communes must use their reserves for increased construction of railways, roads, etc. and thereby supplement the irregular, the inharmonic, speculative private activity. Our highest income we had from 1918 onward, but at that point it was not possible to get my point of view implemented.[15]

The DNA's eight-point program against unemployment of 1922 likewise called for increased spending on infrastructural works, to be financed partly by loans.[16] According to Gunnar Ousland (1949, vol. 2: 192), the Norwegian trade unions campaigned for contracyclical spending as early as 1902. Liberal prime minister and finance minister Gunnar Knudsen and the parliament's finance committee expressed their agreement with these views.[17] During 1918–20, Knudsen himself had frequently argued that public works should be reduced in a boom to be able to increase them during a recession.

In Sweden, contracyclical fiscal policies had found the support of parliament and the government before World War I.[18] The high unemployment of 1908–9 led the liberal government to spend an additional 36 million kronor on railroad and canal construction. According to Gustafsson (1974: 121), these policies were as expansionary as those presented by the SAP government in

1933–34. Furthermore the liberal government in 1908–9 apparently did not believe that downward adjustment of wages was the most suitable way to combat unemployment as the works programs it created paid market wages.[19]

The social democrats repeatedly presented proposals to parliament for increased spending on public works so as to alleviate unemployment. In contrast to the relief works of the 1920s, which paid below market wages so as not to obstruct the allegedly necessary wage adjustment, the SAP's proposals of 1908–12 explicitly stated that the wages paid in public works programs should match market wages. In 1912, they obtained a parliamentary majority for such proposals.[20] The ideas of 1908–12 were reiterated in 1919 in two motions to the Riksdag by SAP member of parliament C. I. Asplund.[21] It was only after 1921, when the decision to prepare for the return to gold had been taken, that the SAP shelved its demands for contracyclical policies, not to rediscover them until 1930.

Before World War I, many influential Swedish economists also believed in the usefulness of contracyclical policies. Eli Heckscher, who after the war would become one of the most vocal opponents of deficit spending, argued in 1906 that unemployment might be prevented by means of contracyclical government spending. Gustav Cassel, another advocate of restrictive policies in the twenties, held "Keynesian" views prior to the war.[22] Accordingly, the well-known Swedish economist M. Hamilton could, on good grounds, argue in 1914 that the view that the state should initiate public works instead of reducing spending in times of depression was generally accepted by economists as well as the state.

The SAP's proposals of the early 1900s in part drew inspiration from similar German policies. The SAP motion to the second chamber 1910:195 cited Chancellor Otto von Bismarck as a proponent of activist fiscal policies.[23] In late 1918, the SPD-led ministry of economic affairs formulated a contracyclical spending program to the amount of 5 billion reichsmarks in order to counteract the collapse of demand.[24] Although the program was expected to lead to a reduction of the reichsbank's gold reserves, this was considered acceptable in times of crisis when the role of the state should be to stimulate the economy. Similar "Keynesian" viewpoints were expressed in the short-term program of the economy ministry of December 1918.[25] In response to the rapid increase in unemployment during 1925–6, the SPD and the main trade union ADGB (Allgemeiner Deutscher Gewerkschaftsbund) again strongly advocated contracyclical works creation programs.[26] What is perhaps more surprising, the government at that time did actually pursue a policy of contracyclical deficit spending.

As for monetary policy, it is quite clear that the view that monetary expansion could produce favorable real effects did not have to await Keynes. According to Keynes himself, the belief that cheap money might stimulate growth underlay much of the thinking of mercantilist scholars.[27] In eighteenth-century Sweden, a political faction called "the Hats" held that expansion of the volume of money would benefit the growth of the economy and pursued economic policies accordingly.[28] In the so-called British Bullionist Controversy of the early nineteenth century, the banking school of thought argued that expansion of the money supply was a safe policy as long as the additional means were used to finance productive undertakings.[29] The Norwegian central bank accepted such views before 1914 as it was common to pursue an expansionary policy in times of crisis.[30] In Sweden, this view was not unknown either. In 1908, the well-known economist Knut Wicksell had advocated plentiful credit as a measure for combating crises.[31] Even the British Treasury, which consistently refused to heed Keynes's and Lloyd George's calls for fiscal expansion during the twenties, recognized that expansionary monetary policies could have a stimulating effect. In the words of Donald Moggridge (1990: vii), the Treasury Views entailed that "loan-financed public works, unaccompanied by monetary expansion, would invariably crowd out an equivalent amount of private investment and that monetary expansion could achieve the same end without this additional piece of machinery."[32]

STAGNATION AS FATE?

Given that political and ideational explanations are unconvincing, the most widespread interpretation of the twenties has come to rest on a structural argument in the form of the quantity theory. There was no social democratic breakthrough in the early twenties because that was simply economically impossible. Due to their inability to reconcile the demands of different political groups within the (exogenously) given level of national income, governments resorted to expansionary monetary and fiscal policies. Yet, following the basic tenet of the quantity theory, such a policy was doomed from the outset, as it could only result in more inflation rather than more growth and more room for distribution.[33] In the analysis of, for example, Charles S. Maier (1987) interwar inflation comes to be interpreted as the result of the necessarily futile attempt of the political system to expand the boundaries of an exogenously given real income.

Yet historically the position that views inflation as the result of a futile attempt to solve a distributional political crisis by excessive money creation suffers from the serious weakness that, on the one hand, it has to maintain that restrictive policies to combat inflation will have no long-term effects on economic activity, while, on the other hand, it has to invoke an exogenous structural crisis in order to account for the long-term reduction in growth and employment that accompanies restrictive regimes.[34] Unfortunately, the deflationary policies of the early twenties seem to have been followed by a long period of structural crisis, thereby making durable accommodation virtually impossible. Again during the seventies and eighties, something similar must

have occurred. The expansionary policies followed since the thirties must, fortunately, have coincided with an exogenous increase in growth rates, thereby
preventing a repetition of the inflation of the early twenties.

Instead, it will be argued here that what determined the failure to reach a
social democratic accommodation in the twenties was neither the lack of an
adequate economic theory, nor the political weakness of social democracy, nor
the insurmountable limits of an exogenously given growth level, but rather the
political and institutional inability to counteract an inflationary constellation by
other means than a restrictive macroeconomic regime.

CHEAP MONEY

Given the priority of stimulating private investment, governments embarked
on a policy of low interest rates immediately after the war.[35] In Britain, Lloyd
George and conservative Chancellor of the Exchequer Bonar Law were united in
their desire for low interest rates. Cheap money was considered essential not
only to prevent unemployment and industrial unrest, but also to reduce the cost
of servicing the debt and facilitate the issuing of bonds for the government's
program of housing construction.[36] Accordingly, the bank rate remained at 5
percent until November 1919 and was only raised again on November 6, 1920.
The rate for Treasury bills remained at 3.5 percent from February 1918 to
October/November, when it was raised to 5 percent.[37]

Such policies met with the opposition of Montague Norman, the governor
of the Bank of England. For Norman, the resurrection of the gold standard was
the first priority because he considered it a precondition for the revival of
international trade and for Britain to regain its dominant position in international finance. Moreover, the gold standard would impose the discipline on
domestic policies necessary to prevent inflationary excesses. In principle, the
government was also committed to a return to gold. In January 1918, Lloyd
George appointed the Cunliffe Commission, which was to report on how sterling was to return to gold.[38] The interim report, published in August 1918,
recommended a quick return to gold and was met with virtually unanimous
consent.[39] Yet, as Norman pointed out to the government, a policy of returning
to gold would require higher instead of lower interest rates. However, he found
few sympathetic ears within the government. For Lloyd George apparently the
reconstruction of the gold standard was a long-term policy aim that should not
be allowed to override the immediate concern for economic growth.

Whereas the BoE consistently advocated restrictive policies, central banks
in other countries were more worried about the prospects for the real economy.
After the war, Norges Bank believed that the discount rate should be kept low
so as not to obstruct economic activity.[40] It initially kept the discount rate at 6
percent, but decided to lower it to 5.5 percent in May 1919 and kept it there
until December 1919. Norges Bank director A. Sandberg argued that to pursue

a restrictive policy in order to stop inflation and stabilize the currency would be to put the cart before the horse. First the productive resources of the economy should be allowed to recover and only then would it be possible to achieve a stable currency and price level.[41] Norges Bank had, with the consent of the government, increased the volume of money more than it legally was allowed to during the war. Rather than contract the money supply after the war, Knudsen, on initiative from Norges Bank[42] in 1919 proposed "legalizing" the new situation by changing the rules for the bank.[43]

In Sweden, the Riksbank lowered its discount rate in April and June 1919. As the wholesale price level started to increase again in late 1919, after having fallen for most of the year, many Swedish economists suggested an increase of the discount rate. The board of the Riksbank refused because industry had to be kept going at all costs and a crisis had to be avoided.[44] Commercial banker Oscar Rydbeck, who during the policy debates of 1920–21 frequently functioned as spokesman for Riksbank,[45] pointed out that a high discount rate would cause more harm to industry than the stabilization of the price level would do good.[46] The same refusal to increase discount rates was reconfirmed by a joint declaration of the three Scandinavian central banks in late February 1920.

Like Sweden and Norway, the Netherlands had remained neutral during World War I. With a virtually unscathed productive apparatus, Dutch businessmen were strongly optimistic at the end of the war as they expected to have a competitive advantage in satisfying the anticipated reconstruction demand of other nations.[47] The Catholic-Protestant coalition government did not want to pursue a policy that might hinder the increase in production, nor did the central bank, DNB (De Nederlandsche Bank). Despite some critical voices from economists who preferred a high interest rate policy, the DNB accommodated the increasing demand from the economy.[48] In response to its critics, the DNB argued that the increased money supply was due to the fiscal policy of the government and that, therefore, a reduction in spending instead of an increase in discount rates was called for. The discount rate remained at 4.5 percent from July 1, 1915, to July 18, 1922. There was consensus that the guilder should return to gold, but also for the DNB this was a long-term goal, which should not interfere with its accommodating policy.

The disorganization of the economy and the unstable political situation in the young Weimar Republic meant that restrictive monetary policies were out of the question for German policy makers. The recovery of production had to enjoy absolute priority, and while the Reichsbank strongly argued in favor of a reduction in budget deficits, it largely shared the view that economic recovery should not be hindered by a policy of monetary contraction.[49] As Gerald Feldman (1993: 214) has argued, "There was a basic consensus in Germany on the need to subordinate financial to economic policy for the purpose of promoting reconstruction through the systematic effort to encourage agricultural and industrial production and maintain high employment, on the one hand, and a no less concentrated effort to maintain social peace and relieve hardships, on the other." Despite rapid inflation, the discount rate was kept at 5 percent from late 1914 to mid-1922, and the Reichsbank continued to pursue an accommodating policy until the stabilization of the reichsmark in 1923.[50]

FLOATING EXCHANGE RATES

The commitment to cheap money was incompatible, however, with a fixed exchange rate. As the release of pent-up import demand and the emerging boom led to a rapid deterioration of the current account in all five countries, the exchange rate with the dollar (the only currency on gold at that point) came under pressure. Instead of changing the course of monetary policies, central banks allowed currencies to float, and prohibitions on the export of gold were maintained or imposed.[51]

Britain left the gold standard on March 31, 1919, and let sterling float. As Susan Howson (1975: 11) notes, this decision marked the defeat of the advocates of restrictive monetary policies. With the outbreak of the war, Sweden also had suspended the gold standard. Partly because of Sweden's high current account surpluses under the war, the krona actually appreciated with respect to most currencies in November 1918. As the current account moved strongly into deficit after the war, the krona started to depreciate relative to the dollar, although it largely maintained its value relative to sterling. Whereas the krona's prewar parity with respect to the dollar[52] had been SEK 3.73/$, in December 1919 it had depreciated to SEK 4.68/$, and in November 1920 the lowest level was reached at SEK 5.27/$.[53] The government did not attempt to counteract the depreciation. When the krona reached its dollar parity in March 1919, the ban on the export of gold was maintained, which allowed the krona to depreciate further. One month later the discount rate was lowered.

Norway also had experienced large current account surpluses during the war and the krone had appreciated relative to most currencies at the end of the war. Also in Norway authorities were not willing to compromise their accommodating monetary policies by defending the exchange rate. The krone was floated at the end of the war. While the exchange rate had stood at 15.590 Norwegian Kroner (NOK) to the pound in 1918, it reached 18.120 in 1919 and 22.490 in 1920.[54]

The Dutch guilder had initially appreciated with respect to the dollar. During 1919, however, the exchange rate fell below its parity. Despite a public controversy in which a group of fourteen well-known economists published an appeal for the DNB to increase interest rates and defend the exchange rate,[55] the bank refused to comply. Finally, the reichsmark also depreciated significantly with respect to the dollar. By December 1919, the reichsmark/dollar index (1913 = 1) had risen to 11.14. In 1920, the depreciation of the mark slowed down a bit as the index stood at 17.38.[56] By the end of the hyperinflation in late 1923, the reichsmark had lost value almost altogether.

DEREGULATION AND BALANCED BUDGETS

Unlike the post–World War II period, which was preceded by increased state regulation of markets during the Great Depression, governments in 1918 believed that deregulation would promote economic recovery. Moreover, the experience of the war years had created massive opposition against continued regulations. After four years of war, regulations had become highly unpopular with business, labor, and agriculture.[57] Business and labor objected to the wartime regulations because they perceived them as obstacles to seizing the opportunities that the economic situation provided. As business in all countries expected a major upsurge in demand, rationing of imports and raw materials plus price controls seemed to stand in the way of expansion. Given the already high inflation during the war, trade unions generally favored maintaining price controls. At the same time, however, they wanted to abolish constraints on wages as quickly as possible and return to normal bargaining.

In Britain, the Labour Party's immediate postwar demands called for a mixture of increased and decreased state intervention in the economy. In its 1918 program, *Labour and the New Social Order*, it proposed nationalization of land and the key industries.[58] But at the same time, the lifting of many of the restrictions imposed during the war featured rather prominently on its list of priorities. The Labour Party adamantly objected to restrictions on the choice of place of employment and residence.[59] Also in Germany the labor movement advocated deregulation. One of the reasons for the increased cooperation between German employers and labor, which started in the last weeks of the war, was that both parties sought the lifting of wartime regulations, which they considered to unduly restrict their room to maneuver.[60]

As in the case of general suffrage or a shorter working day, labor's demands for deregulation were generally heeded. In Britain, controls on raw materials were abolished in the spring of 1919 and price controls were lifted in 1920. In March 1919, the ban on domestic capital issues was terminated, which was followed by a rapid increase in the flotation of shares. In 1919, food rationing was ended. In the Netherlands the apparatus of wartime regulations had been completely dismantled within eighteen months of the armistice.[61] Within six months of the armistice, all restrictions on imports had been lifted in Norway. During the first half of 1919, the system of maximum prices was abolished for most goods.[62]

Stimulating growth, however, did not imply a policy of deficit spending. Even in the nonbelligerent countries, the years 1914–18 had seen a drastic increase in state debt. In November 1918, therefore, governments generally realized that, in order to avoid escalation of debts, fiscal policy would have to be restrictive.

As Howson (1975: 23) has noted, in Britain, "budgetary measures were operating against the boom throughout its duration." Government revenues increased radically after the war from £889 million in the fiscal year 1918–19 to £1,339.6 million in the fiscal year 1919–20. During the same period, spending was drastically reduced from £2,579.8 million to 1,665.8 million. As a result, the budget deficit of £326.2 million for the fiscal year 1919–20 was about one-fifth of what it had been during the last year of the war. In the fiscal year, 1920–21 revenues increased further, although less radically, and spending fell. Consequently, the budget showed a surplus of £230.6 million.[63]

The Catholic-Protestant coalition that governed the Netherlands radically improved that nation's budget. Whereas the deficit[64] had amounted to 421 million Dutch guilders (NLG) in 1918, the budget showed a surplus of NLG 76 million in 1920.[65] Unlike in Britain, the budget improved despite an increase in spending. Also for the Dutch government, improvements in housing, education, and social welfare enjoyed a high priority after the war. Consequently, spending increased from NLG 333 million in 1918 to NLG 444 million in 1919 and NLG 613 million in 1921. Due to a booming economy, revenues largely kept pace without the need for drastic tax increases. In 1919, revenues increased to NLG 466 million compared to NLG 329 million in the previous year. In 1920, revenue amounted to NLG 614 million.

The Swedish liberal/labor government was as successful in turning around the budget. Whereas the budget for 1918 had shown a deficit of SEK 139 million, the following year's budget was in surplus to the amount of SEK 227 million. In 1920, when the SAP governed from March to October, the surplus was SEK 170 million.[66] The ministry of finance during these three years was headed by a social democrat, first Rickard Sandler and as of July 1, 1920, by F. V. Thorsson.

In contrast, the liberal government of Gunnar Knudsen in Norway was not as successful. Budgets had been in surplus from 1915 to 1917, but the fiscal years 1918–19 showed a deficit of NOK 62 million, which was reduced to NOK 30 Million in the next year. The fiscal year 1919–20 showed a significant improvement, but there was still a deficit to the amount of NOK 30 million.[67] The inability of the minority liberal government of Knudsen to eliminate the deficit was largely due to opposition from the conservatives and social democrats. According to Knudsen the state should save now so as to be able to pursue more expansionary fiscal policies when necessary. The majority of parliament, however, did not share Knudsen's views, and he repeatedly had to accept increases in spending against his wishes. Knudsen finally stepped down in June 1920 when a majority consisting of DNA and the conservatives voted in favor of increased spending on road construction.

In Germany, the situation was much bleaker. As Table 3.5 shows, the budget was in deficit from the end of the war until the end of hyperinflation in

Table 3.4. *Dutch governments during the interwar period*

Prime minister	Period	Labor (SDAP)	Protestants (ARP)	Protestants (CHU)	Liberals (LSP)	Liberals (VDB)	Catholics (RKSP)	Percentage of parliament seats
de Beerenbrouck	9/9/1918		R	R			X	50.0
de Beerenbrouck	9/18/1922		R	R			X	59.0
Colijn	8/4/1925		X	R			R	54.0
de Geer	3/8/1926		R	X			R	54.0
de Beerenbrouck	8/10/1929		R	R			X	53.0
Colijn	5/25/1933		X	R	R	R	R	65.0
Colijn	7/31/1935		X	R	R	R	R	65.0
Colijn	6/23/1937		X	R	R		R	56.0
Colijn	8/24/1939		X	R				29.0
de Geer	8/9/1939	R		R		R	R	68.0

Note: See Table 3.1.
Source: Flora et al. 1983: 182.

Table 3.5. *German budget deficits, 1919–23*

	Expenditures	Revenues	Deficit
1919	8,643	2,496	6,147
1920	7,098	3,171	3,927
1921	10,395	6,237	4,158
1922	6,240	4,029	2,211
1923	6,543	2,589	3,954

Note: In billions of gold marks; 1919 figures for last three quarters only.
Source: Eichengreen 1992: 138.

late 1923. While the deficit was significantly reduced in 1920, it increased again in 1921, but was virtually halved in the next year. By 1923, the level of 1922 had been reached again. The reparations payments imposed after the war constituted a major economic and political obstacle to deficit reduction. As German society generally considered reparation demands to be absurdly high and unjust, the willingness to bear tax increases and spending cuts was not very pronounced. Despite these political obstacles, the policy of the social democratic/ Catholic coalitions of the first years of Weimar did not rest on fiscal profligacy. In late 1919 and early 1920, SPD minister of finance Mathias Erzberger passed a reform package that provided for drastic tax increases, while at the same time trying to promote income equality in Germany. As Erzberger wrote in 1919: "Every individual German will be burdened with taxes up to the limit of his capacity, up to levels previously considered fantastic. Such a burden will only be borne if complete equality and absolute conformity is guaranteed."[68] Erzberger's reform was centered on a progressive tax on personal and corporate income. In addition, an emergency levy on property was assessed in late 1919. That Germany's public finances did not improve strongly despite these drastic measures was mainly the result not of reparations but of inflation. As Steven B. Webb (1989: 42) argued: "With extended price stability, the budget would have had small deficits, perhaps even surpluses. Inflation, on the other hand, quickly forced the government to borrow to cover most of its expenses."

In sum, the economic policy regime at the end of the war greatly facilitated a political accommodation between capital and labor. Instead of trying to depress their economies and return to the prewar gold parity, the three smaller countries oriented their exchange rate policies toward Britain. Since British monetary policy was relaxed at the end of the war, this did not imply the need for restrictive policies at home. Accommodating monetary policies allowed for a strong growth in private activity and a reduction in unemployment. At the same time economic growth meant that improvements in housing, welfare, and education could be undertaken without incurring unsustainable budget deficits. And as a growing economy defused the more radical tendencies within labor and mitigated distributional conflicts, it laid the groundwork for a cooperation between capital and labor that could endure beyond the bourgeoisie's fears of massive unrest in the first postwar months.

There thus seemed to be a distinct possibility that the logic of domestic political accommodation would lead governments to embark on a growth regime and thereby de facto relegate the return to gold to an ever more distant future. Instead, the nascent political accommodation between labor and capital was suddenly aborted in the early twenties. Confronted with accelerating inflationary pressures, which increasingly seemed to escape their control, governments resorted to sharply restrictive macroeconomic policies and decided to institutionalize the new macroregime by means of the resurrection of the gold standard. Consequently, mass unemployment came to characterize the rest of the decade.

THE DYNAMICS OF INFLATION

After a few months of hesitation, which primarily reflected private-sector insecurity with respect to the nature of the new regime, economic activity improved dramatically. The optimistic state of expectations concerning reconstruction and restocking demand ensured that banks would be more than willing to lend to industry so that sufficient liquidity would be available for a rapid increase in private investment. As R. H. Brand of Lloyds Bank noted: "My impression of Board meetings at that time was that we ladled out money; we did it because everybody said they were making and were going to make large profits, and while you had an uneasy feeling yet you thought that while they were making large profits there could be nothing said about ladling out money."[69] Within two years of the war, most economies found themselves in a constellation of virtual full employment.

Given the existing bottlenecks, strong demand was bound to lead to price increases. As unions tried to defend their real wage, such a profit inflation, combined with tight labor markets, might have been sufficient to set off a price-wage-price spiral. But when normal bargaining procedures were reinstated after the war, unions aimed for much more than to defend the real wage they had in 1918. In most cases, real wages had fallen significantly during the war, and after 1918 trade unions sought to undo this. The increase in union strength and the good liquidity position of business after the war hence made high wage agreements almost inevitable.

The decision to allow currencies to depreciate in order to protect domestic growth further contributed to inflationary pressures. Once inflation got under way and a policy reversal seemed unlikely in the near future, the increased monetary velocity added to the inflationary fuel central banks provided by means of their cheap money policy. Eventually widespread speculation in securities, commodities, and real estate started to occur.[70]

As the experience of the post-1945 years would show, the only possible strategy for preventing a policy that had to resort to unemployment in order to break inflation would have consisted of the simultaneous application of far-reaching price and income controls. After 1945, most countries kept tight controls on imports, investments, and wages. At the same time, a host of administrative measures was employed in order to bind the liquidity of the large monetary overhang. The rapid deregulation after 1918, however, left governments without such measures. Deregulation seemed a political necessity. Just like business, unions also had experienced the restrictions on wage bargaining as a restriction of their market power, and they favored a return to free bargaining after the war. Not even social democratic governments seemed to have an advantage in enlisting the cooperation of the unions. At a meeting of the LO(S) leadership April 28–29, 1919, SAP minister of finance Thorsson argued that unions should show some moderation in their wage demands, but his suggestion was not greeted enthusiastically.[71]

However, even if unions had taken a more moderate stance, the decision to abandon price and quantity controls would have doomed any attempt to contain wages. At the latest, when financial speculation spread in the wake of inflation, any income policy would have been interpreted as an attempt to contain workers' wages while some people were allowed to get rich quickly and effortlessly.[72] The liberal government in Norway, for example, did attempt to pursue wage policies. With the votes of the conservatives it decided in 1919 to prolong the wartime practice of compulsory mediation in wage bargaining; the DNA objected strongly. Given rapid inflation and the radicalism of labor, the state mediators awarded nominal hourly wage increases of nearly 25 percent. As DNA member of parliament Buen argued, the ongoing wage spiral was a result of the rise in prices, partly due to the depreciation of the krone. In order to stop inflation, prices rather than wages, therefore, had to be halted first.[73]

Given the inability to contain inflation by means of microeconomic regulations, there eventually was no alternative to a recession. The only politically relevant question left at this point was whether the political courage for such a policy could be mustered before or after the economy collapsed in hyperinflation. Most governments hesitated for about one year before changing the course of monetary and exchange rate policies.

Initially inflation was interpreted as a temporary phenomenon related mainly to the abnormal scarcity of supply. As the wartime distortions disappeared, inflation was expected to disappear with it. Deregulation and a policy of stimulating investment, hence, could even be understood as a policy that reduced inflationary pressures by promoting a recovery of supply.[74] Furthermore, as imports became more readily available, supply problems could also be expected to become less pressing. More important, the prospect of recession and unemployment militated strongly against a drastic tightening of monetary policies. Until mid-1920, governments were not convinced that there was no way to avert this choice.

Based on the British case, where the BoE called for more restrictive monetary policies right at the end of the war, the belated reaction to rising inflation is often attributed to the fact that governments, instead of central banks, were ultimately in charge of monetary policies. If, so the argument goes, central banks had had full control over monetary policies, the boom would not have had the chance to develop as far as it did and the subsequent bust would have been more moderate or even absent.

But the experience of Britain is not representative for the smaller countries. In those countries central banks, just as governments, perceived a dilemma between, on the one hand, stimulating growth and investment and, on the other hand, the need to contain inflationary pressures and speculative finance. Central banks, even the BoE, did not interpret inflation in a neoclassical manner as a mechanistic response to the increase in the volume of money. The boom clearly thrived on a radical change in expectations after the war, which had led banks to rapidly increase their lending activities. Accordingly, central banks would not have the option of fine-tuning the rate of inflation without hurting the real side of the economy. Modest increases in discount rates would not deter further borrowing, and a change in monetary policy strong enough to affect expectations would imply a recession.[75] Moreover, high interest rates were likely to have their immediate impact on the productive sector while leaving speculation and the public sector relatively unscathed. Accordingly, the best way to combat inflation was to try to change price-setting behavior of market agents rather than to administer a dose of restrictive monetary policy.

In order not to compromise their policy of cheap money, central banks resorted to appealing to commercial banks, the public, and the government to show moderation. The aim was to induce commercial banks to apply a voluntary form of credit rationing, by only lending to productive and not speculative undertakings. In May 1920, the Swedish Riksbank, for example, addressed a letter to commercial banks urging them to restrict lending:

> However good profit expectations may be, given the present situation in the money market, this is not a sufficient reason for approving loans to a new business transaction or a new industrial company. Nor should the fear for losing a customer that one would have liked to keep or gain be decisive with respect to the question of approving loans. If a reduction of the pressure on the Riksbank cannot be brought about by voluntary moderation of the banks lending . . . the Riksbank will have to use compulsory measures.[76]

Already at the end of 1918, the Norwegian Finance Council (Finansråd), headed by central bank governor Bomhoff, argued that an increase in discount rate would not be able to stem speculation. Other means had to be found, and the council proposed a concerted action of the commercial banks so as to reduce lending on the collateral of stocks.[77] In February 1920, Bomhoff repeated his appeal to commercial banks to exert moderation in their lending practices, but now also the need for moderation by the state and society in general was strongly stressed.[78] On July 8, 1920, shortly before the boom broke, Norges Bank again issued a widely noted appeal in which it called for moderation from the public, commercial banks, and the government.[79] However, because appeals to the public to reduce consumption did not have the desired effect and both the commercial banks and Norges Bank remained skeptical with respect to an increase in interest rates, the reintroduction of import restrictions was proposed. In a letter from Norges Bank as well as sixty-four private banks, dated September 7, 1920, it was pointed out that "several sides have appealed to the public in the strongest possible words without the desired results. Now the state authorities must take action." The banks, therefore, proposed that the government "impose without delay restrictions of imports and rationing of some of the big import activities. . . . It is unfortunate that restrictions have to be imposed on the citizens of the country and their freedom has to be constrained, but we think it is necessary if the good reputation of Norway is not to be lost."[80]

At the same time, central banks tried to shift the blame for inflation to fiscal policies. Because they were reluctant to pursue a tight money policy, which was likely to harm private investment, calling for a reduction in government spending seemed a logical way to reduce demand pressures. For example, G. Vissering, president of the DNB, initially rejected higher interest rates in order to combat inflation and speculation because budget deficits were seen as the root cause of inflationary pressures, and restrictive monetary policies would harm private business while having only negligible effects on government spending.[81] Yet, it was quite unlikely that a reduction in public spending would calm down the economy. The boom was not based on expectations of increased government spending. As was shown earlier, budgets were actually in surplus in Britain, the Netherlands, and Sweden. What was required to end the boom was to break the optimistic expectations about future demand and a continuing rise in prices. This was what governments resolved to do in 1920.

Figures 3.1 and 3.2 show the development of wholesale and consumer prices for four countries from 1916 to 1927. Except in the Netherlands, wholesale prices rose from the end of the war and started to fall around mid-1920. Britain showed the strongest increase in these two years with 37 percent. Wholesale price increases were more moderate in Sweden and Norway, with 12 percent and 6 percent, respectively. In the Netherlands, the decline in wholesale prices started in 1920. Consumer prices in all countries rose to a peak in 1920 and came down thereafter. In the Netherlands and Sweden, they rose by 17 percent and 20 percent, respectively. For Britain and Norway, the figures were 22 percent and 24 percent.

Nominal wages showed a similar pattern. The Swedish index of nominal

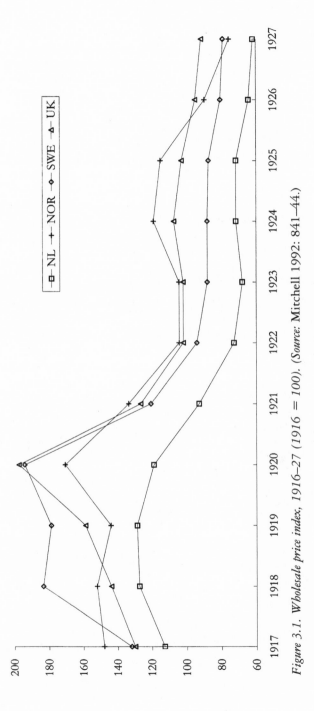

Figure 3.1. Wholesale price index, 1916–27 (1916 = 100). (Source: Mitchell 1992: 841–44.)

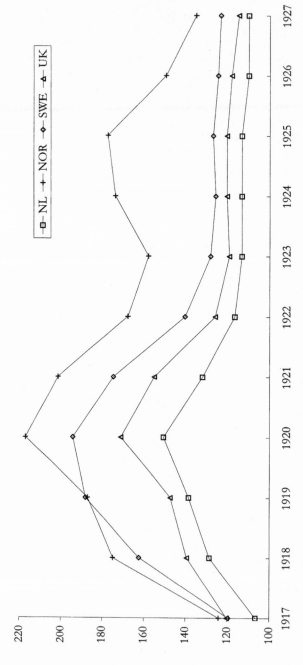

Figure 3.2. Consumer price index, 1916–27 (1916 = 100). (Source: Mitchell 1992: 848–50.)

wages in industry, construction, and trade rose from 200 in 1918 (1913 = 100) to 294 in 1920. By 1923, however, the index had fallen to 202 again.[82] In the Netherlands, the index of nominal wages (1913 = 110), which had stood at 167 in 1918, rapidly increased in the next three years to reach its peak of 274 in 1921.[83] In the United Kingdom, the money wage index rose from 72.0 in 1917 (1930 = 100) to 162 in 1920. Especially in the period 1918–20 nominal wages increased rapidly. In 1918, they grew by roughly 19 percent, in 1919 by 30 percent, and in 1920, the last year of inflation, by 34 percent.[84] Reliable figures for German nominal wage rises during 1918 and 1919 are not available. By February 1920, however, the index stood at 6.0 (1913 = 1). By February 1921 it had risen to 10 and in February 1922 it stood at 20.3.[85] In Norway, average hourly wages for men in manufacturing rose by roughly 60 percent from 1918 to 1920 and fell afterward. They reached their 1918 level again around 1928.[86]

DEAR MONEY AND THE RETURN TO GOLD

Compared to the rates of the seventies, the inflation of 1918–20 may seem no cause for alarm. But, for governments who had experienced price stability or even a moderate deflation in the decades before 1914, the rise in prices, which set in around mid-1919, was a clear sign that something had to be done.[87] More important than the actual extent of price increases was that the onset of inflation for governments who had just divested themselves of the wartime control apparatus meant a threatening loss of control over the economy. Germany and Austria, where hyperinflations were about to develop, became frightening examples of what might happen if the financial and monetary system was not brought under control. To governments that lacked the ability to directly interfere with wage and price setting, the onset of inflation had to appear as a more serious problem than, for example, the rise in prices during the first years after 1945. Given widespread speculation, an explosion in bank lending, highly optimistic entrepreneurs, and strong and radical trade unions, high inflation rates had to appear as a prelude to even higher rates. The economy seemed to be moving into a self-reinforcing inflationary cycle with ever-stronger speculative overtones. The widespread optimism about future growth kept investment demand up, and as investment increased, expectations were confirmed. Tight labor markets drove rapid nominal wage increases, and given the ample availability of money and tight demand conditions, employers had no problem in passing higher wages on into prices. R. H. Tawney (1943: 15) graphically described the mood in Britain at that time:

> That the future will necessarily resemble the immediate past; that trees, if let alone, will grow into the sky; and that upward movements, once started, will continue for ever, seems to be, if not the first article of the practical

man's faith, at least a superstition on which, given the opportunity, he is not averse from acting. To these believers in perpetual motion it appeared to be sound sense to buy with borrowed money, provided that the interest did not exceed the rate at which prices were thought certain to continue to rise for the cogent reason that they were already rising. So they bought, borrowed, and drove them still further up, with shrill cries of excitement, as of children on a merry-go-round.

Apparently, the postwar developments had proved right those who argued that cheap and plentiful money was bound to lead to inflationary chaos. Among economists and central bankers, the postwar developments rapidly came to be interpreted as evidence of the destabilizing effects of political intervention in the monetary sphere. Governments, however, generally did not interpret the developments of the postwar years in terms of an inherently stable economy that had been destabilized by misguided policies. Instead, economic actors were seen to have behaved perversely. Rather than to use the monetary leeway for reconstruction and expansion of productive resources, luxury imports and financial speculation had become rampant. In some sense governments felt betrayed: they had tried to provide favorable conditions for reconstruction by deregulating and by accommodating the monetary demand necessary for investment, but while doing so they had also unwillingly accommodated frivolous and speculative activities. The moralistic overtones accompanying the installation of the new regime were difficult to overhear. Especially in Protestant countries, the reaction of governments to inflation and speculation was frequently to diagnose civil society and market agents as suffering from a consumerist or speculative moral deficiency. In a way, market agents had "sinned" as they had preferred quick money to honest hard work. And as even appeals for moderation had sorted no effects, the state would have to impose discipline by imposing strict and inviolable monetary constraints. Certainly, such measures would hurt in the short run, but they seemed the only way to restore discipline to the economy.

Because politicians had primarily experienced the boom in terms of an economy that indulged in speculative excesses if monetary discipline was not tight, merely administering a dose of dear money was not enough. Because the root cause of inflation was a weakness of will, the institutionalization of inviolable constraints on macroeconomic policy making seemed indispensable in order to prevent a repetition. The gold standard was to serve this function. Under the gold standard, monetary policies would not be a matter for day-to-day politics, but would be conducted by independent central banks whose sole responsibility was the fixed exchange rate.

Given that at the end of the war the general presumption among politicians and central bankers was that currencies would eventually return to gold, the policy changes of 1920 might seem predetermined. In this view, the return of the European currencies to the gold standard in the twenties was rooted in the inability of policy makers to perceive any alternatives to such arrangements. The first postwar years would then appear as a mere delay caused by the special economic and political problems of those years, but not by any doubts about the system as such.

The experience of the postwar years suggests differently. In November 1918, the elites of Europe had realized that the old order had disappeared for good in the trenches of the war. It was not clear at all that the gold standard would not also fall victim to this need for change. Although committed to returning to gold *in the long run,* no government was initially willing to pursue the (short-run) policies required to do so. As with the goal of full employment since the seventies, relegating the gold standard to the long run might simply have been the most convenient way of abandoning it. That this did not happen was due to the postwar inflation and not to the inability to conceive of any other system. Given the economic disorganization, the prewar gold standard in fact now came to be seen in a more rosy light than contemporaries had.[88]

It also follows that the neoclassical interpretation, and the interpretation of many central bankers at that time, of the gold standard as a device that served to free monetary policy from political intervention does not capture the essence of the policy change. In theory it is quite impossible to isolate monetary policies from the political process, both because the decision to reconstruct the gold standard had to be a political one, and because governments at any point were free to abandon their exchange rate commitment again. Even in countries where the central banks legally enjoyed political independence, matters of exchange rate regime were the prerogative of the government.[89] In addition, the central bank law itself of course could be changed by political decision. The resurrection of the gold standard, then, was not primarily an attempt to isolate the central bank from politics, but a voluntary abdication of control by governments who feared to set free uncontrollable economic dynamics without such a constraint. Although the high interest rates and deflation required to restore and maintain the gold standard by no means enjoyed unanimous political support, such opposition was generally impotent, since virtually no political party during the twenties and up to the Great Depression dared to live without gold. The fear of having to face an uncontrollable economy without the gold standard constraint also explained why governments were so desperately trying to maintain it even in the midst of the depression. If governments had held, in line with the neoclassical interpretation, that the boom and inflation of 1919–20 were merely responses to an undue increase in the money supply, such a rigid constraint would not seem necessary. Surely, for example, British or Swedish politicians had enough confidence in themselves to believe that they would be able to refrain from setting the printing press in motion even without the discipline of the gold standard.

And because the resurrection of the gold standard was an attempt to institutionalize restrictive monetary policies, rather than restrictive monetary policies being brought about by a desire to return to gold, it follows that whether currencies were on gold or not was not necessarily crucial for the policy regime. As Table 3.6 shows, most countries only actually returned to the gold standard in the midtwenties. Yet, the decisions in favor of restrictive money of the early twenties and not the actual linking to gold marked the decisive change in policy regime.

In Norway, the beginning of the new regime can be dated to June 25, 1920. On that date Norges Bank raised the discount rate from 6 percent to 7 percent – the highest level in forty years – and again admonished banks to reduce lending. At the same time the bank, which at that time still had commercial banking operations, instructed its offices to reduce their lending. Norges Bank's vice governor Nicolai Rygg, who was to be promoted to governor on November 1, 1920, was the driving force behind the policy reorientation. In 1919, Rygg had strongly opposed Governor Bomhoff's proposal to relax the rules governing the gold and reserves backing of the money in circulation.[90] Instead he presented an alternative proposal for more restrictive policies.[91] Initially, Prime Minister Knudsen supported Bomhoff. In June 1920, he changed his mind as he argued that money was out of control and that more restrictive policies were needed.[92] A formal decision to return to gold at the prewar parity was never taken. Yet, because Rygg's views on the subject were well known, his appointment as governor, which was approved by parliament, was the equivalent of such a decision.

Also in Britain the inflation and widespread speculation, which set in around April 1919 and lasted for slightly more than a year, eventually made Lloyd George give in to the pressures from the Treasury and the BoE for higher interest rates and a return to gold. As in other countries, a rapid increase in bank lending financed much of the boom. Banks could easily obtain additional liquidity by reducing their holdings of state debt. Much of the war debt was in short-term (three months) Treasury bills. If the public in the aggregate decided to reduce its holdings of state debt, the government would be forced to refinance itself at the BoE in order to acquire the necessary liquidity. In order to stop fueling inflation, the government needed to induce the public to hold state debt, which required higher interest rates. By the end of 1919, the developing boom had convinced the government of the need for a change in policy. While de facto having ignored the Cunliffe Commission's recommendation, in December 1919, the Chancellor of the Exchequer announced that it accepted the need to stop borrowing from the BoE and to return to gold. Interest rates had been raised already in November 1919; another increase became necessary as the government experienced difficulties in selling treasury bills.[93] The boom broke shortly afterwards.[94]

Swedish social democrats, from early 1920 onward, were among the most vocal advocates of restrictive monetary policies and a return to gold. In response to a newspaper article by well-known economist Eli Heckscher of March 11, 1920, which encouraged the public to withdraw gold from the Riksbank, the bank immediately asked to be freed from its obligation to sell gold. The social democratic government of Karl Hjalmar Branting agreed. Yet social democratic

Table 3.6. *Restoration and decline of the gold standard*

| Country | Return to Gold | | End of Gold Standard | |
	Date	Government	Date	Government
Germany	1923		7/15/1931 (beg. of pervasive exchange controls)	Brüning, Catholic (presidential cabinet)
Netherlands	4/28/1925	Colijn, Christian Democrat	9/26/1936	Colijn, Christian Democrat
Norway	5/1/1928	Mowinckel, Liberal	9/27/1931	Kolstad, Farmers Party
Sweden	1924	Trygger, Conservative	9/27/1931	Ekman, Liberal
U.K.	4/28/1925	Baldwin, Conservative	9/21/1931	MacDonald, National Government (Conservative)

members of parliament like Ernst Wigforss, Rickard Sandler, and Anders Örne, joined the by now united front of Swedish economists and strongly protested. Both chambers of parliament would probably have accepted Branting's proposal if, as Wigforss (1951: 150–2) recounts, he and Örne had not proposed a postponement. Two days later (March 15, 1920), a public protest was organized at which, among others, Wigforss and Heckscher spoke. At the meeting, Wigforss likened the Riksbank's policy to that of a counterfeiter. In the Riksdag debate, Wigforss argued that inflation had to be stopped and the krona linked to gold again. Örne claimed that the most important effect of a raise in the discount rate would be to reduce the possibility of making profits off the poor.[95] Despite the opposition, the Riksdag did free the Riksbank from the obligation to sell gold, but only until September 30, 1920. Immediately afterward the Riksbank increased the discount rate by a full percentage point.

On April 30, 1920, the Branting government appointed a committee of experts to study Swedish monetary policy. Its report was published in August 1920, when Swedish prices were still rising. The committee proposed that energetic measures be taken to stop inflation, followed by measures to depress the price level, and that the krona be linked to gold again. By now the resistance within the SAP government against more restrictive monetary policies had disappeared. When the government in September 1920, in agreement with the commission's proposals, suspended the Riksbank's obligation to buy and sell gold for another three months, it declared that it concurred fully with the committee's recommendations. At the same time the discount rate was raised again. This then marked the decisive change in monetary policy orientation.[96] Wholesale prices started falling in the same month, and as of October unemployment increased rapidly.

The recession gave rise to a renewed discussion about monetary policy. Should the krona return to gold at is prewar parity or at a devalued parity? On April 19, 1921, the Riksdag's banking committee argued that deflation was very costly for the economy and that it really did not matter at what parity the krona was linked to gold as long as the domestic price level was stabilized. The social democratic newspaper *Social Demokraten* thus summarized the committee's views on deflation:

> The economic and social consequences of the deflation can mainly be summarized as follows: Production has decreased; business profitability has fallen; the value of all capital assets has been reduced; the purchase of capital goods for productive firms has been made more difficult; business initiative has been overcome by despondency; the credit restriction has reduced purchasing power and exacerbated the fall in prices; stoppages have increased in number and size; bankruptcies and defaults are rising; unemployment has grown; the reduction of wages that has followed deflation has caused extensive industrial disputes and consumption and investment goods have decreased.[97]

Nevertheless, the only committee member to advocate a return to the prewar parity was social democrat Ernst Wigforss.[98] If the gold standard was to function as a constraint, then the parity chosen should seem "natural" rather than arbitrary, and the obvious choice thus was the prewar parity. Hence Wigforss (1951: 152) argued that it was difficult to find some other value for the krona "that would not seem even more arbitrary."[99] The government and the overwhelming majority of the Riksdag shared his views. In addition, during the parliamentary debates the social democratic speakers unanimously expressed their desire to return to the old parity.

Nor did the trade unions exert any pressure on the SAP for more expansionary monetary policies. In April 1921 LO's chairman Arvid Thorberg stated that it was unavoidable to return from a price level that had been bloated by the abnormal circumstances of the war to a more normal price level. And since it was unavoidable that the price level be reduced, LO could not necessarily be expected to support all strikes that were staged for the purpose of preventing a reduction in wages.[100] At a LO board meeting later the same year some members voiced the opinion that the creation of additional money would lead to more jobs. Yet, the majority of the board, among them J. O. Johansson of the powerful metalworkers union, argued that expansionary monetary policy would only lead to inflation. Therefore, one should not mislead the people with talk about increasing the money stock.[101]

SOCIAL DEMOCRATS AND GOLD

Perhaps because it carried government responsibility, the SAP may have advocated dear money and the gold standard more outspokenly than its sister parties in Western Europe. But this was a difference in form and not in substance. For once European social democrats held a common view. Governments encountered little or no social democratic opposition against the monetary policy decisions of 1920–21.[102]

The most important reason for social democrats to advocate restrictive policies was that inflation undermined real wages. Already since the last years of the war, unions and social democrats had complained vocally about the rising price level. In Stockholm and Oslo large demonstrations were held. On a more moderate scale, the socialist NVV (Nederlands Verbond van Vakverenigingen) trade union organized a protest meeting against inflation in 1919.

DNA held that the depreciation of the krone since the end of the war had led to higher prices and hence to lower wages. In the budget debates in April 1920, Hornsrud argued strongly that the depreciation of the krone was a sign, that called for a change in policy.[103] Earlier that year also DNA member of parliament Buen had called for energetic policies against inflation.[104] The change in policy in mid-1920 and the onset of deflation were thus initially greeted by DNA as a development that would benefit the income position of workers. As Egil Nysæter (1973: 21) has shown, during 1920–21 the labor MPs were in full agreement with Norges Bank's policy of a slow contraction of the volume of money.[105]

Also in the Netherlands the argument that inflation undermined real wages was decisive in leading the majority of the social democrats to support restrictive policies. During the debate of the parliamentary group of the social democratic party SDAP (Sociaal-Democratische Arbeiderspartij) on the policies of Christian democratic finance minister H. Colijn in September 1922, chairman Vliegen argued that inflation ran counter to the interests of the working class as it led to real wage cuts. As a result, the reduction of public employment and the cuts in public service wages, which Colijn held necessary in order to defend the gold parity, were, tacitly, supported by the SDAP. Prominent SDAP members Albarda and Sannes had similar views while only Troelstra was skeptical.[106] The SDAP apparently also held that monetary policy was best left in the hands of an independent central bank as it declined to include the demand for socialization of the central bank in its program because this would merely lead to more printing of money.[107]

If inflation lowered real wages, then deflation would obviously increase them. SAP board member Nils Karleby, for example, argued that the business community preferred inflation as it allowed them to reduce wages through price increases. In a deflation, on the other hand, labor gained at the expense of capital. The widespread notion that deflation had a negative effect on the economy was, according to Karleby (1921: 303), therefore, false and simply an expression of the fact that "the ideas of the ruling class are always the leading ideas in society."

Moreover, many social democrats believed that deflation would reduce unemployment because it improved the competitiveness of domestic industry.[108] On the face of it, the argument seemed plausible: as the price level was falling in most European countries, those that did not join the trend would suffer a loss of export markets. Yet, such an argument could hardly be considered decisive. A lower rate of domestic deflation would only result in reduced competitiveness if the country in question were linked to its competitors by means of a fixed exchange rate. Germany, which suffered from massive inflation from 1918 to late 1923, actually experienced an improvement in export competitiveness because the exchange rate of the reichsmark would frequently depreciate faster than the domestic price level rose. Deflation hence could only seem an argument in favor of promoting employment once the decision to return to gold had been accepted by the labor movement. This did not mean, however, that social democrats were completely taken by surprise by the emerging unemployment. In line with what virtually all economists and politicians thought, they rather expected the rise in unemployment to be short lived.

In addition, the widespread financial speculation of the boom was a strong reason for organized labor to call for more restrictive policies. During the war, labor had urged governments to take firmer action against war profiteering, primarily by imposing a drastic duty on war profits. The financial speculation after the war was equally objectionable, especially in a time of low real wages that were being further undermined by inflation. It seemed that the economy had been taken over by speculators who were making quick money while workers suffered from low living standards.[109] Many social democrats in 1919–20 came to argue that monetary policy had stimulated speculation and hence should become more restrictive.

For some social democrats, finally, the resistance of some parts of business against deflationary policies may have been helpful in determining their own position on these issues. If, as some argued, capitalists opposed restrictive policies, that had to mean that such policies were in the interest of labor. And indeed, the little opposition that was voiced against the policy of deflation mainly came from business circles, although businessmen also generally hesitated to advocate abandoning the gold standard outright. In Norway, commercial banker Jebsen of Bergens Privatbank warned as early as November 1918 that any attempt by Norges Bank to reduce lending activity by means of higher interest rates might have dangerous consequences for the economy.[110] As of the midtwenties, the majority of Norwegian businesses felt that the krone should indeed go back to its old parity but at a very slow pace. Some businessmen, mainly in shipping and forestry, actually advocated devaluation, but they were a very small minority.[111]

Dutch commercial bankers were among the most vocal opponents of restrictive policies. When fourteen Dutch economists issued an appeal for dear money, seventeen so-called practical men, mainly bankers and businessmen, responded, arguing that this would have dire consequences for the economy. One of the signatories to this counterappeal was the president of the Rotterdamsche Bank, who, in the bank's annual report for 1919, had in fact argued that expansionary monetary policies were not inflationary as long as the additional liquidity was employed to finance productive undertakings.[112]

In Sweden, financier and industrialist Ivar Kreuger, who would become world famous when his financial empire crashed in 1932, was opposed to deflationary policies in the early twenties. Swedish industry also spoke out against high interest rates and deflation.[113] During the Riksdagsdebate in April 1921, Liberal member and chairman of the Swedish Export Association Nylander was one of the very few who felt that linking the krona to the gold standard was not necessary to prevent a resurgence of inflation. He in fact argued that, given high unemployment, a recovery of business would not lead to labor scarcity and hence also not to the wage-price spiral characteristic of inflations.[114] In Britain, industrialists' opposition to restrictive policies would become a constant feature as recession continued throughout the twenties. Also in the early twenties, industry voiced its skepticism with respect to the course of economic policies. In June 1920, the Federation of British Industries, for example, suggested to Lloyd George that he appoint a new committee on monetary policy matters, but unlike the Cunliffe Commission, industry should now also be represented.[115]

Just like the policy of tight money, the gold standard was never questioned by social democrats, not even during the Great Depression. Obviously, the rise of mass unemployment could not lead social democrats to call for a change in monetary policies. Social democrats had known all along that capitalism was fundamentally flawed, and the occurrence of periodic crisis hence was no surprise. The only effective cure was a socialist economy. They had also known all along that prosperity was created by labor and not by tinkering with the money supply. In the short run, as long as the conditions were not ripe for socialism, adherence to the gold standard could hence be interpreted as the only correct social democratic strategy for macroeconomic policies.

The Norwegian labor party was, to some extent, an exception to the uncritical acceptance of the gold standard. The prewar parity of the Norwegian krone was not established before 1928. The reason for this long delay was that the initial deflation produced a banking crisis, which forced the central bank to temporarily abandon its deflationary line in 1923–24. Unlike in other countries, exchange rate policies remained at the forefront of the Norwegian economic policy discussion up to 1928.

Once the consequences of deflation became manifest, DNA started to argue that Norway should exploit the freedom a floating currency gave it to pursue more expansionary monetary policies. During the budget debates of 1922, economic spokesman Hornsrud exclaimed: "For God's sake, don't stop the printing press now that the crisis has come. Everything possible has to be done to keep the economy going."[116] In the same debate DNA member Krogh argued that under a system of flexible exchange rates it is "the monetary policy the bank pursues that for a significant part determines to what extent business, production, and employment shall be kept going or whether it shall stagnate."[117] Yet, at the same time DNA did not question the gold standard as such but favored a parity that would not require further deflation.

Hence, it is unlikely that a DNA government would have established a new policy regime. It might have stabilized the krone at a value corresponding to the domestic price level, thereby sparing Norway a lot of economic hardship. But because Horsnrud, in particular, who had a decisive influence over the party's economic policy positions, feared that a floating currency would lead to inflation, speculation, and lower real wages, it had to accept the orientation of monetary policy toward external balance rather than toward employment. Indeed, as will be shown in the next chapter, DNA's first reaction to the devaluation of 1931 was to warn against inflation.

Moreover, once the prewar parity was established, DNA lacked the courage to call for a change. In fact, DNA's attachment to the fixed exchange rate was indirectly responsible for the fall of Norway's first labor government in 1928 after only eighteen days in office. In the election campaign, DNA had strongly emphasized its disagreement with the monetary policies of Norges Bank. The election was a great success. DNA and the Farmers' party BP (Bondepartiet) had polled 36.8 percent and 14.9 percent, respectively, and Hornsrud was called upon to form a government. Accordingly, devaluation might reasonably be expected. Capital outflows had already started before the government was formed and could not be stemmed by the new government's declarations that the currency was not to be devalued. The massive withdrawals acutely threatened the solidity of a banking system already weakened by Norges Bank's deflationary policies.

Yet, Hornsrud was very reluctant to support banks in difficulties, interpreting it as a subsidy to the wealthiest and most powerful capitalists. Using an argument quite reminiscent of present-day liberal views on subsidies to industry, the government held that, while a bank insurance fund may be helpful, it was in principle not correct that the state should give a guarantee for deposits, and that the state should not keep banks alive whose soundness, due to their own policies, had become doubtful.[118] DNA interpreted the deflationary policies as being mainly inspired by the interest of creditors, and the latter were taken to be represented by the banks. Similarly, the postwar inflation was attributed to financial speculation. In the view of the labor movement, canceling the debts that many had incurred during inflation and that had become a heavy burden under deflation would merely mean presenting the bill to those responsible: the banks. Yet, the government rejected Rygg's proposal for a bank insurance fund.[119] When Hornsrud refused to give his consent to a support scheme proposed by Norges Bank, Governor Rygg asked the leader of the liberal party to table a motion of no confidence against the government.

Hornsrud's foreign minister Edvard Bull expressed the general feeling of the DNA when he said that the government's fall had been dictated by financial capital. But, the lesson to be learned here was not that capital could dictate its wishes when markets were open, but quite simply that one should not talk of depreciation if one lacked the courage to implement it.

THE GERMAN HYPERINFLATION

In Germany, a policy that created a recession in order to break inflation was politically impossible. Monetary policies remained accommodating, and in sharp contrast to the other countries, the German economy recovered rapidly from the recession of 1920–21.[120] Indeed, recession and mass unemployment were absent until late 1923. Yet, because Germany could not dispose of any microeconomic mechanisms for containing prices and nominal wages, the expansionary monetary policy orientation simply implied tolerating whatever inflation rate would develop. The result was a spectacular hyperinflation that, in the end, disrupted the whole economy and created the mass unemployment policies had sought to avoid. From 1919 to 1920, wholesale prices rose by more than 250 percent whereas consumer prices "only" rose by somewhat more than 140 percent. In mid-1922, prices were already rising at more than 50 percent each month. One year later, the monthly inflation rate exceeded 1,000 percent. The exchange rate depreciated at a similar pace. In November 1923, when the currency was stabilized, one dollar bought 4.2 billion reichsmarks, one billion times more than before the war.

The interpretation of what caused the German hyperinflation would have profound consequences for the policies leading up to the Great Depression, and not only in Germany. In the view of those in charge of German economic policies after 1923, and especially in the view of German central bankers, fiscal profligacy was at the root of the inflation. For some, the inflation was the outcome of a sinister plan to convince the Allies that Germany could not pay the reparations burden. Rather than tax society, German governments had chosen to set the printing press in motion so as to create economic chaos that could be exploited to convince the Allies of the unreasonableness of their demands. For others, the recourse to the printing press was the result of the weakness of the German state vis-à-vis civil society. Confronted with a virulent conflict between capital and labor and with widespread rejection of the institutions of the Weimar Republic, the state had seen no other option than to try and accommodate competing and irreconcilable claims of the German national product by means of fiscal spending. The government could not raise taxes for fear of alienating the working class. Extensive spending on welfare programs and food subsidies was also unavoidable to pacify labor. Maintaining interest payments on the war debt was essential in order not to provoke the middle class. However, since this additional spending financed by printing money could not increase the size of the national product and hence could not mitigate distributional conflicts, hyperinflation was the inevitable result.

But irrespective of whether the German government had been unable or unwilling to balance its budget, the way to prevent a repetition was the same: the state should be denied access to the central bank. In response to Allied demands presented at the reparations meeting on January 13, 1922, in Cannes, the Reichstag on May 26, 1922, passed a law that made the Reichsbank independent of the government by revoking the right of the latter to issue directives to the bank.[121] Yet, as this did not lead to a change in monetary policies because the Reichsbank shared the views of the government,[122] the Allies decided to interfere with not only the form but also the substance of German monetary policy. The Dawes Plan of August 30, 1924, envisaged a radical reduction of Germany's ability to pursue an autonomous monetary policy by placing the reichsmark on the gold standard and introducing a strong element of foreign control over the reichsbank. Under the provision of the Dawes Plan, the parity of the reichsmark (RM) was fixed at 4.20 to the dollar. Forty percent of the note issue was to be covered by gold and foreign exchange reserves and the rest by qualified commercial bills. Like the arrangements in other countries, temporary violations of the 40 percent coverage requirement were not entirely ruled out. In such a case, however, the Reichsbank would have to pay a penalty to the government.

The new Reichsbank law of August 30, 1924, replaced the executive body of the Reichsbank with a general council consisting of seven German and seven foreign members. Henceforth the executive body of the bank was to be appointed by the general council. The government was not to have any influence on the composition of the general council: its German members were instead to be elected by the private shareholders of the Reichsbank. Section 25 placed a strict upper limit of RM 100 million to the Reichsbank's lending to the government. In addition, Section 19 provided for the appointment of a foreign commissioner for the note issue who was to ensure that the Reichsbank would abide by the rules of note issue as laid down in the Dawes Plan.[123]

The initial change in central bank law had failed to bring about a policy change. The second change was not decisive either, as German politicians themselves, by the time hyperinflation had run its course, also had become convinced that tying the currency to the gold standard and balancing the budget should enjoy absolute priority.

Yet, the quantity theory view does not fit well with the experience of the German hyperinflation. First of all, as many central banks would discover again in the seventies and eighties, there is no clear-cut relation between money growth and inflation. After the currency reform of 1923, the supply of money in Germany increased more than tenfold from November 16, 1923, to July 31, 1924, while the price level stabilized.[124] As Barry Eichengreen has argued (1992: 146), "Inflation depends not just on the supply of money but on the public's willingness to hold it." But if the increase in the volume of money is not a sufficient condition for inflation, then monetary financing of budget deficits cannot be held directly accountable for the observed inflation.

Eichengreen nevertheless concludes that the budget deficit was the main cause of the German hyperinflation as budget deficits created expectations of inflation by creating expectations of future increases in the money supply, whereas the political agreement on balancing the budget that was reached late in 1923 eliminated such expectations and consequently also inflation, even though the volume of money kept growing. Such a view seems unsatisfactory, however, because if it is assumed that budget deficits create expectations of inflation to the extent that they are considered to lead to an increase in the volume of money, a continued rapid growth in the money supply should maintain inflationary expectations even if the budget is brought under control. In other words, in a model in which the volume of money ultimately is considered the determining factor of inflation, changes in expectations should be related to monetary policies and not to fiscal policies.

Second, as countries like Britain and Sweden showed, budget deficits were not a necessary precondition for a reduced willingness to hold money and for the emergence of inflationary pressures. In Sweden, as we have seen, the budget had turned strongly positive in 1919 and remained so in 1920. Yet, inflation escalated in this and the following year. The successful fiscal retrenchment led the commercial banks to turn to the Riksbank to a larger extent, since late 1918.[125] In the UK, the monetary expansion of the late teens and early twenties seems to have been primarily demand determined as banks increased their lending activity by reducing their reserves and by drawing on the BoE.[126] Similarly in Norway, commercial banks rapidly increased their lending and reduced their liquid reserves after 1918. In 1918, private banks had net assets at Norges Bank of NOK 51.9 million, but in the next year their net borrowing from Norges Bank amounted to NOK 6.5 million. Put differently, expectations concerning money holding could change irrespective of budgetary policies, and as long as the central bank was willing to remain accommodating, the boom could continue without budget deficits.

Third, the view of a weak state forced into deficit spending to accommodate civil society does not fit well with the Erzberg tax reform package of 1919–20. As noted in the previous section, this reform package meant a rather drastic increase in tax rates that would have balanced budgets if prices had been stable. To quote Steven Webb (1989: 38) again: "Government spending was not extravagant. Net of expenses mandated by the Versailles Treaty and expenses taken over from the states, the central government spent about the same as before the war. Social spending after the war replaced the military spending of the pre-war arms race."

Finally, the contention that monetary expansion merely created inflation and did not enhance the distributional space by stimulating the real economy, as well as the conclusion that stabilization of prices would, therefore, also have no significant real costs for the economy, does not seem to be borne out by the facts. Initially the German government's refusal to initiate a stabilization crisis meant that the German economy performed better in terms of growth and employment during the early twenties than its neighbors.[127] Even Costantino Bresciani-Turroni, who provided the standard neoclassical interpretation of the German hyperinflation, had to admit that inflation had had a stimulating effect on production.[128] Initially the net domestic product in Germany fell sharply from RM 42.1 billion for 1914–17 to RM 34.2 billion in 1919. During the next three years production rose sharply to reach RM 42 billion again by 1922. At the same time unemployment remained relatively low. While the difficulties of the postwar year increased the unemployment rate, it recovered soon thereafter. Especially during the years 1920–22, the German unemployment rate was significantly below the level in other countries. During the last months of hyperinflation and during stabilization, production collapsed. GDP dropped to RM 37.9 billion in 1923.[129] Durable mass unemployment now also appeared in Germany as the low figures of the 1920s would not be reached again until the midthirties. Karsten Laursen and Jørgen Pedersen (1964: 85–88) compared output developments during the hyperinflation with those in countries that pursued a restrictive policy in order to break inflation.[130] They concluded: "In

Germany production was also low. However, it did not fall but rose or was maintained during the inflation years."

The German government did not, willingly or reluctantly, provoke an inflation, but rather decided to accommodate inflationary pressures for fear of the economic and political consequences of a disinflation strategy.[131] After the war, inflationary impulses mainly came from two sources. First, the reichsmark depreciated rapidly, thereby causing a rapid increase in prices of imported goods. For German policy makers at the time, for example, Karl Hellferich, the depreciation of the exchange rate was the favorite culprit because it shifted the blame from the government to the Allies.[132] The unreasonably high reparations payments, so the argument went, had caused the depreciation and forced the government to accommodate price rises in order not to create a recession. Yet, reparations were certainly not the only source of depreciation. The sorry state of the German productive apparatus at the end of the war and the acute food crisis left Germany with a huge demand for imports and little capacity for exports, even without reparations. Moreover, exchange rate depreciation did not necessarily have to lead to inflation. If the increase in import prices had not given rise to adjustments in domestic wages and hence prices – that is, if the depreciation had been not only nominal but also real – no inflationary spiral would have emerged but rather a once-and-for-all price increase. Yet, wages did not lag behind prices. Given both the acute food shortage[133] and the radicalization of labor during the war, it was not willing to greet the armistice with an additional cut in wages. Moreover, increasing nominal wages constituted an autonomous source of inflation as wages rose slightly faster than the consumer price index from November 1918 to July 1919.[134] Accommodating monetary policies allowed for passing nominal wage rises onto prices, and in this way a spiral was set in motion by which wages and prices would drive each other up during the next few years.

The stimulating effect of inflation implied that as time progressed, labor scarcity would come to add powerful pressures for the acceleration of nominal wages. During 1922, the unemployment rate fell below 2 percent. And as inflation eroded the willingness to hold money, the result was an increase in the supply of money even irrespective of the Reichsbank's policies. Budget deficits undoubtedly added to already high demand pressures. But, as we have seen, the Erzberger reforms failed to balance the budget mainly because of inflation. From 1920–21 onward, budget deficits mainly became a consequence rather than a cause of inflation. Rapid inflation reduced the real value of tax receipts. Moreover, as inflation continued, the public became less willing to hold government debt (i.e., nominal assets subject to rapid depreciation).[135] The result had to be a greater recourse to the Reichsbank.

The crucial difference between the German strategy and the one followed by other countries was, therefore, not primarily that Germany did not try to balance its budget, but that the German authorities were not willing to reorient monetary policies so as to break the inflationary tendencies in the economy. For

Table 3.7. *German governments during the interwar period*

Chancellor	Period	(Labor) SPD	Catholics (Zentrum)	DDP	DVP	BVP	DNVP	Middle-Class Party	Fascists (NSDAP)	Percentage of parliament seats
Scheidemann	2/13/1919	X	R	R							78.1
Bauer	6/21/1919	X	R	R							60.3[a]
Müller	3/27/1920	X	R	R							60.3
Fehrenbach	6/25/1920		X	R	R						36.6[b]
Wirth	5/10/1921	R	X	R							44.7[c]
Wirth	10/26/1921	R	X	R							44.7[d]
Cuno	11/22/1922		R	R	R	R					41.2
Stresemann	8/13/1923	R	R	R	X						58.8
Stresemann	10/6/1923	R	R	R	X						58.8
Marx	11/30/1923		X	R	R	R					41.2[e]
Marx	6/3/1924		X	R	R						29.2[f]
Luther	1/15/1925		R	R	R	R	R				55.6
Luther	1/20/1926		R	R	R	R					34.7[g]
Marx	5/16/1926		X	R	R	R					34.7
Marx	1/29/1927		X		R	R	R				49.1
Müller	6/28/1928	X	R	R	R	R					61.3
Brüning	3/20/1930		X	R	R	R		R			34.8[b]
Brüning	10/9/1931		X	Tolerated presidential cabinet							
von Papen	6/1/1932		X	Presidential cabinet							
von Schleicher	12/3/1932			Presidential cabinet							
Hitler	30/1/1933			Presidential cabinet						X	

Note: DDP, Deutsche Demokratische Partei; DVP, Deutsche Volkspartei; BVP, Bayrische Volkspartei; DNVP, Deutsch Nationale Volkspartei. See also Table 3.1.

[a] After DDP rejoined in October 78.1%.

[b] Tolerated by SPD and DNVP.

[c] Tolerated by USPD.

[d] Tolerated by USPD, including Bavarian Farmers League.

[e] Tolerated by SPD.

[f] Tolerated by SPD.

[g] Tolerated by SPD.

[h] Supported by DNVP, after 1930 elections 31.3%, including DNVP and excluding DDP, middle-class party.

Source: Flora et al. 1983: 173.

other countries, the spectacle of German hyperinflation strengthened their re-
solve to pursue restrictive monetary policies. Yet, when German policy makers
looked across the border to assess the likely effects of such a strategy, they
became determined not to follow a similar course. As argued earlier, it is a
weakness of the view that restrictive monetary regimes have no effects on real
variables that it has to invoke the occurrence of structural crisis in the wake of
such strategies in order to explain rising unemployment and recession. All
countries that pursued such a strategy in the early twenties suffered from serious
recessions. As Laursen and Pedersen (1964: 86–88) computed, the United States,
Great Britain, and Sweden all suffered a drop in real per capita income to below
prewar levels during the stabilization crisis. Given the radical impoverishment
Germany had suffered as a result of the war, German policy makers were simply
not willing to risk the consequences of such a strategy.[136]

In short, the political situation in Germany during the hyperinflation was
fairly unique in that it prevented governments from creating a recession in order
to stabilize the price level. Yet, at the same time the German experience also
showed that a political willingness to tolerate inflation ultimately does not allow
a country to escape recession and unemployment. At the point where the
confidence in the reichsmark had been eroded so much that it would not serve
anymore as a medium of credit contracts and finally did not even purchase
goods, inflation lost its stimulating effects.[137] Without an acceptable monetary
medium for credit contracts and the purchase of goods, the economy collapsed.
The collapse hence started not as a result of a policy to combat inflation, but as
the final result of inflation itself. During the final months of hyperinflation
unemployment rose from 3.5 percent in July 1923 to 19.1 percent in October
of the same year.[138] But with that, the rationale of the inflation regime had been
exhausted. In November 1923, the now largely functionless reichsmark was
replaced with a new currency and the price level could be stabilized. As the
German polity had not been able to overcome political resistance against a
policy of creating recession to break inflation, inflation brought about the
recession and thereby made a new policy regime politically possible. Because
inflation, rather than a feared counterinflationary policy, now had become the
cause of recession, business and agriculture in the summer of 1923 gave up
their resistance to such a strategy.

As in the other countries, the regime was based on strict adherence to gold,
balanced budgets, and high unemployment. German economic policies finally
converged with those of its neighbors.

THE END OF ACCOMMODATION

With the change in macroeconomic regime, the possibility of reaching an
accommodation between capital and labor based on the increasing distributional
space in a growing economy fell by the wayside. As the new regime turned the

Table 3.8. *Average annual man-days lost in labor disputes, 1910–69*[a]

	1910–19	1920–29	1930–39[c]	1940–49[d]	1950–59	1960–69
Germany	624.54	1154.25	95.06	N.A.	63.41	16.02
Netherlands[b]	366.44	660.26	170.85	135.03	26.73	21.30
Norway	1038.14	2400.07	1817.47	93.61	162.64	75.34
Sweden	624.62	2276.89	876.85	622.34	66.59	20.01
Britain	991.60	2359.23	185.47	107.14	160.75	168.18

[a]Per 1,000 nonagricultural wage earners. Both strikes and lockouts included.
[b]Up to 1929 man-days lost not available for all labor disputes.
[c]Germany, 1930–33.
[d]Netherlands, 1946–49, Norway 1945–49.
Source: Computed from Flora et al. 1987: 715–17, 730–33, 736–39, 740–43, 750–53.

relations between capital and labor into a zero-sum game, a high level of labor market conflict was unavoidable, at least as long as the effects of mass unemployment had not yet robbed the trade unions of their ability to pursue effective industrial action. While during 1919 strike activity was mainly informed by the problem of inflation and the general feeling of dissatisfaction that characterized labor at the end of the war, by the end of 1920 strikes in most countries except Germany took on a defensive character. The advent of crisis and mass unemployment inevitably signaled the beginning of a business offensive to reduce wages and social security benefits and to undo some of labor's recent gains like the eight-hour day. The social gains labor had made during and after the war now came to be seen by employers as (politically supported) obstruction to their profitability.[139] Lacking a sympathetic government and given high unemployment, labor increasingly had to concede to employers' demands.

The failure to reach a durable political accommodation is most clearly reflected by the high level of industrial conflicts during the decade (see Table 3.8). Compared to the teens, industrial disputes more than doubled in most cases. In Sweden, man-days lost increased by more than 260 percent. During 1920 alone, more working days were lost to industrial disputes than during the whole preceding decade. British labor market conflict reached its peak when the Trades Union Congress (TUC) called a general strike in May 1926 in support of the miners who were striking against a reduction in wages, the lengthening of working hours, and the abolition of national agreements in the industry[140] Due in part to a low degree of unionization and institutional fragmentation,[141] strike activity was traditionally low in the Netherlands. Yet, here also the twenties witnessed a strong increase in conflicts. Especially the metalworking strike of 1921–22 and the textile strike of 1923–24 – both erupted over employers' demand for wage cuts – were unusually large and long lasting. In Norway, the biggest strike in its history took place in 1921 when the blue-collar union LO (Landsorganisasjon i Norge) called a general strike over ship-owners' demands for wage cuts. In Germany, the year 1924 broke all previous records as 36 million working days were lost. Yet, in the absence of deflation labor market pressures still were less than in many other countries. As the crisis intensified toward the late twenties, so did labor conflicts. Signaling the advent of the Great Depression, official unemployment statistics showed more than 1 million unemployed since September 1928. Two months later the so-called *Ruhreisenstreit,* a labor conflict in the heavy industry of the Ruhr, marked the beginning of the employers' general attack on wages, working hours, and social security benefits.

Inevitably, the new regime implied the end of macrocorporatist arrangements between capital and labor, which had developed during or immediately after the war. Under mass unemployment, employers tended to favor a return to local bargaining. While from the employers' view, national bargaining in times of tight labor markets might help prevent local wage escalation, decentralization in times of high unemployment held the promise of facilitating wage cuts. Yet the new regime did not lead to an across-the-board intensification of capital-labor conflicts. The cooperation that had emerged during the previous years now frequently shifted to the microlevel as improving competitiveness through rationalization came to appear to be a promising way to reduce unemployment. Because it eliminated the need for direct wage cuts and thereby eliminated a major source of conflict, increasing firm-level competitiveness through increased productivity was a strategy inherently attractive to business and labor. Yet, cooperation on this level in practice had to remain confined to pockets of modern export-oriented firms.

In Germany the first victims of the stabilization were the eight-hour day and the cooperation between employers and labor in the so-called Zentralarbeits-gemeinschaft (ZAG). The ZAG was a bipartite national-level body of employers and unions that had been founded in late November 1918 during the revolution following Germany's military defeat. The agreement establishing the ZAG instituted the eight-hour day, granted trade unions full bargaining rights, and established management-labor councils in firms with more than fifty employees. The most important task of these management-labor councils was to ensure that the terms of collective agreements were respected. Moreover, business agreed to no longer support company unions. Since unions were rather skeptical about plans for socialization, the ZAG was an arrangement that realized some long-standing demands while at the same time promoting economic recovery. The rapid increase in unemployment during the last stages of the hyperinflation, however, unleashed a general business offensive against the eight-hour day and wage costs. At the same time the position of the unions weakened dramatically because the inflation wiped out virtually all their assets and the onset of mass unemployment provoked a dramatic loss of members. As business was no longer willing to adhere to the terms set out in the ZAG, the unions decided to withdraw in January 1924.

Somewhat similar to the ZAG, the Dutch Catholic employers and trade unions attempted to institutionalize corporatist cooperation after the war. The joint Easter Manifesto of 1919 envisaged the creation of management-labor councils and a national-level council of firms. The bipartite councils were to have responsibility for, among other things, wages, prices, and employment. After a good start, employers' interest in this form of cooperation waned quickly in the face of recession and unemployment. By 1921–22, the short-lived corporatist experiment had come to an end.[142] The end of the war also brought the establishment of a tripartite national body, the so-called High Council of Labor (Hoge Raad van Arbeid), whose purpose was both to advise the government on matters of social legislation and to provide a meeting ground for business and labor. In the same year (1919) the minister of social affairs P. J. M. Aalberse, who had played an important role in creating the council, introduced the eight-hour workday and the forty-five hour workweek. The deterioration of labor market relations since 1920, however, condemned the council to remain largely irrelevant. Only in the wake of the Great Depression, when the Dutch government recognized a need for public intervention so as to stabilize wages, would this body gain more importance.[143]

Building on a trend set in motion during the war, tripartite cooperation in Britain took the form of the National Industrial Conference (NIC). The first one was held in February 1919 and was fairly successful. The first conference also resolved to institutionalize this meeting on a permanent basis, but the NIC would not survive the strains of economic crisis. Within two years of its inception it was abandoned.[144] The same year saw the start of a massive employers' initiative aimed at a return to local instead of national bargaining.

Norwegian employers had steered a conciliatory course after World War I, but labor relations deteriorated markedly after 1920. When the krone finally reached its old parity in 1928, and the need for deflation had temporarily disappeared, labor relations improved. The Norwegian employers' association (NAF, Norges Arbeidsgiver Fordbundet) again assumed a more conciliatory stance and abandoned its absolute insistence on wage cuts. With the onset of depression and renewed deflation, labor relations in the early thirties again deteriorated rapidly.[145]

THE SOCIAL DEMOCRATIC DILEMMA

As the Great Depression showed, crisis and unemployment did not necessarily have to coincide with declining fortunes of social democracy. Nor did a high level of unemployment necessarily have to lead to more hostile relations between business and labor. However, social democracy could not thrive in a policy regime that excluded macroeconomic stimulation and instead pursued macroeconomic restriction for fear of rekindling inflation and jeopardizing exchange rate targets. Restrictive monetary policies, budget cuts, and a fall in prices and nominal, as well as real, wages now became the economic policy priorities. The acceptance of restrictive monetary policies and the return to the gold standard therefore implied the institutionalization of a political dilemma, which would haunt social democracy until the thirties.

Politically, the implication of the new regime was that labor had lost its allies. The coalition between labor and liberals, based on a common interest in electoral and social reform, could no longer be maintained. As the new economic policy interpretation implied that a strong labor movement was a hindrance to economic recovery, the liberals would evidently place the interest of the economy ahead of the interest of labor. At the end of March 1921, for example, Lloyd George ended state control of coal mines because the subsidy that had allowed owners and miners to reach a modus vivendi became too heavy a burden on the budget. The immediate result was a massive labor dispute. In Sweden, liberals now felt that the state should use its works creation programs to facilitate downward wage adjustment and promote strikebreaking. In Norway, relations between DNA and the bourgeois parties reached an absolute low in 1927 when a new law concerning labor disputes was passed. The law made exerting pressure against strikebreakers an offense punishable by imprisonment. In addition, the law held unions financially responsible for illegal strikes unless they had done their utmost to prevent such strikes.

In the Netherlands and Germany, the new regime implied that a political rapprochement between Christian democracy and labor became impossible. Partly owing to their own working-class constituency and papal teachings on social policy,[146] Catholic parties in principle could agree with labor on the need for more extensive social welfare and better labor legislation. Indeed, their shared views on social reform had provided much of the cement for the SPD-Zentrum coalition in the early Weimar Republic. Under the new policy regime, however, social reform for Christian democratic parties necessarily had to take a backseat. By the time the Catholic politician Heinrich Brüning formed his cabinet of 1930–32, deflation had become the first policy priority, and this required radical expenditure cuts instead of social reform. In the Netherlands, the Catholic party remained opposed to forming a coalition with the social democrats until shortly before World War II. But because the Christian democrats (i.e., Catholics and Protestants) came to dominate the political system after the electoral reform of 1917,[147] labor might have expected a more positive approach toward social reform. After 1945, these parties would indeed become the main forces behind the massive extension of the Dutch welfare state.[148] Yet, the exigencies of the interwar economic policy regime meant that the political dominance of confessional parties did not imply significant welfare state expansion.[149]

However, the social democratic political paralysis was not primarily due to its inability to muster political allies. As social democrats also came to consider the gold standard regime inevitable, they were hard pressed to find effective answers to the policies of the parties to their right. Given the fundamental economic policy choice the gold standard regime implied, social democrats were almost inevitably torn between what were now considered to be the exigencies of the economy and the demands of its own constituency. Basically, this left them only two options: they either criticized the government and proclaimed the superiority of socialism from the safety of the opposition benches, or they assumed office and risked alienating their constituency whenever the defense of the exchange rate required more wage and budget cuts.

Between the regime change in the early twenties and the regime change in the wake of the Great Depression, social democrats took office, either alone or as part of a coalition government, nine times in the five countries examined here. Seven out of nine governments fell over issues of economic policy.[150] The Dutch and Norwegian parties spent the decade rather unfruitfully on the opposition benches. In the Netherlands, the attitude of the confessional parties spared the SDAP from having to make a choice of its own. After a spell of eighteen days in office in 1928, the DNA was voted out of office when Prime Minister Hornsrud refused to support commercial banks in difficulties. The DNA remained on the opposition benches for the rest of the decade. Førsund's (1978: 30) remark about the parliamentary debates in 1930 also fairly accurately characterizes DNA's policies from 1922 onward: "DNA's answers to the bourgeois policy were criticism, motions of no-confidence, but no proposals for an alternative policy." The SPD confronted an even more unpleasant dilemma because the need to defend the feeble democracy of Weimar made outright opposition frequently impossible. Between the Kapp-Lüttwitz Putsch of 1920 and the second Müller government, the SPD lost much of its influence, frequently feeling forced to tolerate conservative governments for fear of jeopardizing the republic. Moreover, the Müller government disintegrated within two years over the issue of reducing unemployment benefits in the face of a rapid rise in unemployment. The British Labour Party, after its withdrawal from the War Coalition in mid-November 1918, only occupied government benches from late January to early October 1924. Labour would not return to government until June 1929, when the second MacDonald government was formed. Yet, MacDonald was as hapless as Müller, for in slightly more than two years the government and the Labour Party would split over cuts in unemployment benefits deemed necessary to defend sterling. Only the Swedish social democratic party SAP (Sveriges Socialdemokratiska Arbetareparti) fared better as it managed to govern – with interruptions and in a minority position – for roughly forty-eight months during the 1920s. But the SAP vacillated for much of the decade between, on the one hand, letting other parties take the blame for policies it thought inevitable, and, on the other, trying to limit the damage to the labor movement by assuming office itself.

WAGE CUTTING UNDER SOCIAL DEMOCRATIC GOVERNMENTS

The need for continued downward flexibility of domestic costs implied that collective organization of economic interest quite inevitably came to be considered a potential obstruction to the state's macroeconomic policy goals. Industrial or agricultural cartels, but particularly strong trade unions, increasingly became the target of government intervention in the twenties. Acceptance of returning to the prewar parity implied that social democrats had to agree to nominal wage cuts in order to depress the price level. Soon after the regime change, however, real – as opposed to nominal – cost reduction seemed unavoidable. In a regime in which the insight had been lost that macroeconomic policies actually do have a crucial impact on employment, the microlevel strategy of improving the competitiveness of domestic industry would also for social democrats appear to be the only feasible way to reduce unemployment.[151] Increasing competitiveness, however, might imply not only lower taxes on business, and higher productivity (rationalization), but also lower real wages. Accordingly, the new regime suggested that it would become difficult for social democrats to justify their resistance against any type of wage cuts. The SDAP, for example, admitted openly that wages were too high.[152] In October 1923, the SPD members temporarily left the coalition because they found it hard to agree with employers and the coalition's partners that the eight-hour day was too costly.

In Sweden, the three social democratic governments of the twenties actually fell over wage-related issues. While having been the only social democratic party to have initiated the new regime, the SAP was also its first victim. The same Branting government, which had accepted the need for deflation in the spring, realized in October that such policies were best observed from the opposition benches rather than pursued. The decision to step back was taken at the SAP board meeting (*partistyrelsen*) on October 13, 1920.[153] The leadership generally agreed that the present economic situation called for austerity and wage cuts.[154] At the same time, it was deemed politically impossible for a social democratic government to advocate such a policy. Accordingly, the best policy for the SAP at the moment would be not to pursue a policy at all but go into opposition. Finance minister Thorsson argued:

> It is going to be difficult for any government to govern under the coming period, but it is going to be most difficult of all for a social democratic government. We would be forced to violate too many points of our policy program if we continued to govern. That would only lead to an unprecedented gloating in the country. . . . It has to be said that there now has to be an end to talk about higher wages. However, the question is, do we have the courage for that? A different economic policy than we are able to pursue is simply necessary. We therefore serve the country best if we step back. The economic situation of the country is really precarious. Only by means of austerity and rationing can the situation be improved. But the social

democrats cannot do that. Isn't it better if we get a government that can solve the economic problems?[155]

Ernst Wigforss was no less outspoken: "We are unfit to govern. We do not agree on the economic questions; we very simply do not have a policy for the present situation. The government must go. The economic problems have to be solved according to the bourgeois recipe."[156]

Although it had declared itself unfit to govern in 1920, it was politically difficult for the SAP to remain voluntarily in opposition at a time when some of the most vital interests of its core constituency were threatened, especially given that the SAP had consistently polled the most votes since 1917. The gold standard dilemma, which at the same time made it unavoidable and impossible for the SAP to assume government responsibility, was the main reason for the rapid succession of governments in Sweden during the 1920s. Tage Erlander (1972: 172), who was to become SAP prime minister after World War II, summarized this conflict between the SAP's economic analysis and its general ideological outlook succinctly when he remarked that "social democracy experienced . . . an arduous conflict between the scientist's theoretical analysis of reality and feelings of justice which revolted against this reality."[157]

The remaining two SAP governments of the twenties fell over the question of how the labor market measures used to relieve unemployment should relate to the unions' efforts to prevent wage cuts. Labor market policies were the responsibility of a public commission – Statens Arbetslöshetskommission (SAK) – created in 1914. From its inception, the SAK had operated on the principle that public works were to be preferred to unemployment benefits. The wages paid at public works programs were the same as those paid for comparable work in the regular labor market. However, as unemployment increased rapidly beginning in the fall of 1920, the SAK changed its wage principles, and the wages in the public works programs now were kept below market wages. Moreover, to prevent crowding out regular employment, SAK was only to finance projects that were not likely to be undertaken in the near future. SAP and LO(S) in principle advocated market wages in labor market programs. In 1912, for example, the SAP had proposed public works at market wages, and from 1930 onward this again became one of the core points in its policy program.[158] Yet, given that the SAP had embraced the need for deflation it also had to accept the new SAK policy. Put differently, the need for deflation implied that the state, in those areas where its policies directly affected wage setting, had to try and promote a fall in (nominal) wages, and paying market wages for public works programs was incompatible with this goal.[159] Moreover such a policy would also help contain public spending, which seemed rather urgent given the rapidly rising budget deficit since 1920. But at the same time, it would be politically difficult for the SAP, especially in view of fierce protest from LO, to pursue a policy that undermined the already weakened bargaining power of the trade unions.

Table 3.9. *Swedish governments during the interwar period*

Prime minister	Period	Labor (SAP)	Liberals	Conservatives	Prohibitionist Liberals	Farmers Party	Swedish Liberals	Percentage of parliament seats
Edén	10/19/1917	R	X					64.3
Branting	3/10/1920	X						37.4
de Geer	10/27/1920	Caretaker	Cabinet					
von Sydow	2/23/1921	Caretaker	Cabinet					
Branting	10/13/1921	X						40.4
Trygger	4/19/1923			X				27.0
Branting^a	10/18/1924	X						45.2
Sandler	2/24/1925	X						45.2
Ekman	6/7/1926				X		R	14.3
Lindman	10/1/1928			X		R		43.5
Ekman	6/7/1930				X			12.2
Hamrin	8/6/1932	Caretaker	Cabinet					
Hansson	9/24/1932	X				R		60.9
Pehrsson-Bramstorp	6/19/1936				R	X		26.1
Hansson	9/28/1936	X				R		64.3
Hansson	3/13/1939	X	R	R		R		95.2

Note: See Table 3.1.

^a Tolerated by liberal parties.

Source: Flora et al. 1983.

Despite the fact that such policies were unpopular, the SAP agreed with the SAK's new pay principles.[160] Yet, the party could not go along with the SAK's policy on industrial disputes. The generally accepted principle was that the SAK should be neutral in industrial disputes, but business and labor had quite different views on what neutrality entailed. The issue revolved around two questions: (1) whether the SAK should suspend assistance, both in the form of unemployment benefits and public works, to sectors in which an industrial dispute was going on and (2) whether the SAK should be allowed to instruct unemployed workers to take employment at firms where the regular workforce was on strike. The logic of the new regime suggested that the answer to both questions had to be affirmative, because both types of measures were likely to promote downward wage adjustment. Yet the SAP could not agree with such labor market measures because, unlike the policy of paying below-market wages for public works, the interference of the SAK in industrial disputes directly threatened the ability of the trade union to operate effectively.

Initially the second Branting government had even agreed with the SAK's proposal to cut off assistance to all unemployed workers in an industry where a labor dispute took place because this would make it impossible for the SAK to use unemployed workers as strikebreakers. It soon turned out, however, that such a policy put excessive pressure on the finances of the unions concerned. On initiative from the LO, in February 1923 the second Branting government proposed a change in policy to the extent that those who had been unemployed uninterruptedly for at least six months should continue to receive support. The bourgeois parties in the Riksdag, including the liberals, voted down the proposal and Branting left office. Sandler's government fell in June 1926 over a similar conflict. In early March 1926, the SAK had granted a request from the Stripa mine in the town of Linde to be allocated workers on unemployment assistance in order to replace the striking workforce. Again mainly in response to pressure from LO the government decided to annul the decision of the SAK, but this decision in turn was voted down by the bourgeois Riksdag majority on initiative from the liberals. According to Tage Erlander (1972: 169), the Stripa conflict "was for me and surely many others the end of hopes about a cooperation between liberalism and social democracy."

FISCAL AUSTERITY AND SOCIAL DEMOCRATS

The decision in favor of a restrictive policy regime also implied that fiscal policies would be unavailable as an instrument to reduce unemployment and foster social accommodation. The stabilization crisis of the early twenties by itself aggravated debt problems due to the normal mechanism of reduced tax receipts and increased spending, in particular on unemployment benefits. And, with exchange rate policies unavailable, fiscal policy, along with domestic cost cutting, was one of the main instruments for restoring current account balance. High interest rates and a falling price level, moreover, implied a higher real indebtedness and accordingly a higher share of government receipts to be spent on debt service. And as under the gold standard regime balancing the budget came to be interpreted as the most important indicator of a government's willingness to pursue "sound" policies, fiscal austerity in general was unavoidable in order to maintain the credibility of the exchange rate commitment. Especially in Germany, which became quite dependent on U.S. capital imports after the stabilization of the reichsmark, politicians feared that budget deficits would be interpreted as a return to inflationary policies and hence would destroy the creditworthiness of the country. British policy makers had similar fears, as they continuously needed to revolve a large short-term debt stemming from World War I. However, because of its resistance to cuts in unemployment benefits and its pressure for more effective measures to combat unemployment, a strong labor movement also appeared as a threat to balanced budgets.

For the SAP, the advent of the new regime meant that its early demands for fiscal expansion as a way to relieve unemployment without relying on wage cuts had to be shelved. As Tage Erlander (1972: 176) pointed out, one of the reasons why the SAP did not pursue its earlier ideas on combating unemployment during the twenties was that the early part of the decade was completely dominated by the debate about problems of inflation. The DNA still proposed deficit spending partly to be financed by loans in its 1922 crisis program but the issue was forgotten afterward and would not be revived until 1933. The SDAP also could offer no alternatives to budget cuts. During 1923, the SDAP had vigorously campaigned against increasing the budget for the navy at a time of general reduction in spending. But as chairman Willem Hubert Vliegen remarked at a meeting of the party leadership in October 1923, even without additional spending for the navy the budget could not be balanced and austerity would hence also have been a necessity for a government with SDAP participation.[161]

The emergence of restrictive fiscal policies did not mean that all fiscal programs of particular interest to labor were to be reduced. The rapid rise in unemployment during the early twenties prompted most governments to allocate additional means to works creation programs or unemployment insurance. Despite cuts in social services, to which Labour was bitterly opposed, Lloyd George's government found room within a reduced overall budget to extend both the period for which unemployed workers could collect benefits and the amount of borrowing from the Treasury the Unemployment Insurance Fund was permitted. In addition, spending on relief programs like road construction was stepped up.[162] But while British budgets were balanced in the 1920s with the exception of 1926 (see Table 4.4), the Norwegian state recorded sizable deficits financed by borrowing.[163] In Norway, as well, part of the deficit was due to discretionary spending increases on unemployment relief. The number of workers in emergency work-creation programs (Nødsarbeid), for example, increased from 13,856 in 1920–21 to 58,434 in 1921–22.[164] The Swedish reaction to the rapid rise in unemployment showed a similar pattern. Public spending on work-creation programs rose from SEK 26.8 million in 1921 to SEK 43.8 million in 1922.[165] Both the caretaker cabinets of Louis de Geer and Oscar von Sydow plus the second Branting government allocated additional means for improving the communication infrastructure with the specific aim of reducing unemployment.

In Germany, the high unemployment of 1925–26 even led the bourgeois coalition to pursue what was in fact a Keynesian contracyclical policy. Politically the need for such a policy was perhaps greater in Weimar than in other countries given the additional strains an economic recession would exert on the polity. Economically such a policy was possible because the state budget was actually in surplus. The contracyclical program of 1926 initially was centered on substantial tax cuts for business but soon was complemented by export subsidies. Later in the year a work-creation program was added, which consisted not only of increased spending on unproductive emergency work programs but also of the rather traditional Keynesian measure of spending increases for productive purposes like infrastructure and housing construction.[166]

However, these initial reactions to rising unemployment could not be sustained. As argued in Chapter 2 fiscal expansion pursued in combination with a strong commitment to a restrictive regime is unlikely to spark off increased private investment. While the relief programs of the early twenties, and the midtwenties for the case of Germany, certainly helped mitigate unemployment, the failure of the economy to recover meant that such programs put increasing strains on the budget and thereby also came to be considered as a potential threat to the exchange rate parity. As mass unemployment failed to disappear, the commitment to gold hence implied that considerations of containing the growth in budget deficits had to become paramount. Despite continued high unemployment, governments therefore saw no option but to reduce spending on unemployment relief. In Norway, the number of workers in emergency relief programs, for example, was reduced from 58,343 in 1921–22 to 5,270 in 1925–26 and 4,037 in 1926–27. Yet in 1921–22, about 17 percent of trade union members were unemployed, whereas the figures in 1926 and 1927 were 24.3 and 25.4, respectively. In Sweden, spending on emergency work-creation dropped from SEK 26.8 million in 1921 to SEK 3.1. million in 1924. By 1924, unemployment had come down significantly from its level of 26.6 percent in 1921, but with an unemployment rate over 10 percent, the reduction in relief spending was more than proportional.

In Germany, the spending programs of 1926 indirectly caused the fall of SPD chancellor Hermann Müller in 1930 – the last democratic government of the Weimar Republic. The rapid increase in unemployment since 1925 caused doubts whether increased productivity (rationalization) could indeed be a strategy to improve the labor market situation. Fritz Tarnow, for example, chairman of the woodworkers union and one of the authors of the famous expansionist WTB plan of 1932, revised his earlier enthusiasm about rationalization during these years.[167] At the same time, the ADGB argued that spending on productive works was to be preferred to the unproductive emergency work-creation programs.

The failure of the economy to recover sufficiently in response to the German programs of 1926, however, had the implication for the Müller government that it inherited a budget deficit from its predecessor. In addition, the onset of the crisis had led to a rapid increase in unemployment in the winter of 1928–29, and, as a result, the government needed to finance a sizable deficit in the unemployment benefits program. Given that the flow of foreign capital had largely dried up, the deficit had to be financed domestically. Under the pressures of the economic crisis, however, the compromise between the SPD and the industry-friendly DVP (Deutsche Volkspartei) disintegrated. The ADGB proposed an increase in both employer and employee contributions. Yet the SPD's coalition partner, the DVP, insisted that the burden to industry should be eased and demanded a reduction in the level of benefits. As the ADGB was not willing to accept that, the SPD withdrew from the government and a presidential cabinet under Heinrich Brüning of the Catholic Center Party was formed.

The second social democratic government to fall over fiscal spending was the second Labour government of Ramsay MacDonald. While Labour still had advocated extensive contracyclical programs in 1921, enthusiasm for such measures became much less pronounced after its experience in government during 1924. Given the depressed state of the economy, local authorities, who should have carried out most of the programs, could not afford to do so. And at the national level, the rapidly increasing demand on the national unemployment insurance fund and the decided aim of returning to gold eliminated any available room for more aggressive fiscal spending. Indeed, the inability to find an effective cure for unemployment, despite the high hopes it had created when assuming office, marked the most conspicuous failure of MacDonald's first term as prime minister.

MacDonald's second government fell in August 1931 as he, similar to Müller, failed to obtain approval from the party for radical cuts in unemployment benefits so as to balance the budget and thereby relieve pressure on sterling. In late July, the May Commission predicted in its report that, if no change in policy was brought about, Britain would have a budget deficit to the amount of £120 million by the next spring. The pound had been under pressure more or less continuously since 1928, and the European banking crisis of the summer of 1931 intensified outflows. The publication of the May Commission's report further undermined confidence in sterling, which successive increases in the discount rate were apparently not able to restore. For MacDonald and Philip Snowden, his Chancellor of the Exchequer, and indeed for most of the country, radical budget cuts in order to avert a deficit seemed the only way to prop up the pound. The Labour Party had been able to reach internal agreement on spending cuts of £56 million by mid-August, a significant part of which was to come from savings on the unemployment insurance fund. The conservatives and the liberals, notwithstanding Lloyd George's plans for deficit spending, held these cuts to be insufficient. In response, MacDonald and Snowden proposed additional cuts on unemployment benefits, yet the cabinet, and especially those ministers close to the trade unions, felt unable to accept the new proposals as they seemed to place an unfair share of the burden on labor. Unable to secure cabinet approval, MacDonald resigned and with support from conservatives and liberals formed a so-called national government. In response to what was considered a betrayal, both MacDonald and Snowden, who was to remain Chancellor of the Exchequer, were expelled from the party.

In sum, because the gold standard regime implied the need for wage cutting, fiscal austerity and a policy of trying to revive growth through stimulating firms, the state seemed to be more favorably predisposed toward employers' than labor's demands. But, because the economic policy orientation was largely determined by the decision to institutionalize a restrictive regime, it could not make a crucial difference whether the government benches were occupied by social democrats or their "bourgeois" counterparts.

IDEOLOGICAL ADJUSTMENTS TO THE NEW REGIME

Contrary to what social democrats may have thought, the relevant question on the economic policy agenda in the years immediately following 1918 was not how to socialize the economy but how to halt inflation. While the question of socialization could be delegated to commissions for further study, the escalating inflation had to be addressed. Yet the constellation of tight labor markets and high inflation, which most countries reached around 1919, was not one that could easily be addressed within a socialist understanding of the economy. Rather than being confronted with growing and ever more wretched "reserve army of the proletariat," the developing labor market scarcity rather tended to strengthen workers' position relative to capital. Moreover, despite the political tensions between capital and labor at the end of the war, an "investment strike" or massive capital flight did not develop. Irrespective of the political tensions, employers apparently had sufficient confidence in the future to embark upon investment projects.

Although generally in favor of high wages and full employment, the labor movement had no "natural" view with respect to inflation. To take a position on inflation would require a macroeconomic theory about causes and effects of monetary factors, and that was an area that, due to the focus on conflicts of interests between employers and workers, had traditionally been underdeveloped in social democratic analysis. If Lenin, as Keynes claimed, did indeed believe "the best way to destroy the capitalist system was to debauch the currency," [168] those social democrats who aspired to a socialist society may have been expected to greet inflation. Following Marx's lead that monetary phenomena are epiphenomenal to the workings of a capitalist society, one could surmise that social democrats would be indifferent with respect to inflation. Given that it undermines the value of real debt, social democrats could even have welcomed inflation because it stimulates investment and employment without requiring wage reductions while at the same time undermining the income of the rentiers. But to the extent that nominal wages failed to adjust to inflation, social democrats would object to inflation as a mechanism of wage reduction. The emergence of widespread financial speculation and the presence of "inflation profiteers" also constituted a source of irritation for the working class, as some people apparently could get rich easily on the stock exchange while "honest hard work" was not so rewarded.

As argued earlier, social democrats generally came to support deflationary policies mainly because inflation undermined real wages, because they thought that the increase in unemployment would be short-lived, and because speculation profits constituted a major irritant. The resulting mass unemployment was interpreted not as the outcome of a specific policy regime but as the inevitable manifestations of a capitalist economy, or, in a rather more puritanical vein, as the inevitable price to be paid for the excesses of the boom period. As a result, the ideological and practical efforts at reformulating social democratic strategy during the twenties shared the common trait of, implicitly or explicitly, excluding the possibility of any viable macroeconomic alternatives.

With the acceptance of the new macropolicy regime, the range of possible ideological interpretations social democrats could give to the situation of the twenties had in fact become rather narrow. In essence, ideological adaptation to the new regime had to be defensive.

From an ideological point of view it seemed ideal for organized labor to answer calls for lower wages with an argument that made higher wages the precondition for economic recovery, thereby postulating an identity of interests between labor and society as a whole. Traditionally, this meant adherence to underconsumptionist theories. Underconsumptionist theories assume that the uncoordinated process of investment in market economies periodically leads to an expansion of the production capacity that exceeds society's ability to consume. An effective policy to combat the crisis hence requires increasing the purchasing power of workers. Such views seem to have been particularly popular in the SPD.[169] The most influential advocate of this view was probably Fritz Naphtali, who argued in 1930 that an increase in real wages by means of not reducing nominal wages to deflation would result in increased employment.[170] In the same year, the ADGB tried to convince German business that maintaining the purchasing power of wages was in everyone's interest.[171] The Swedish SAP had already pointed out in the 1890s that higher wages would both increase output through higher consumption and promote rationalization of industry by exerting pressure on profits.[172] The same view enjoyed popularity with the LO in the 1920s.[173] The Labour Party came to emphasize underconsumptionist arguments with the advent of mass unemployment in the early twenties, in a pamphlet written with the TUC called *Unemployment, a Labour Policy*.[174] In 1926, the Independent Labour Party published two reports that argued for the immediate introduction of a minimum wage plus family allowances in order to stimulate domestic demand.[175]

A closely related view interpreted the need for high wages in microeconomic, instead of macroeconomic, terms. High wages were economically beneficial, not so much because they increased aggregate demand, but because they barred the cost-cutting road to competitiveness, thereby forcing industry to innovate and improve productivity. The focus on increased productivity through rationalization, adoption of new technologies, and so forth, allowed the role of labor to be redefined from an obstacle to competitiveness to a crucial partner in productivity.[176] The "craze for rationalization" (i.e., the view that closer firm-level cooperation between capital and labor promoted a more rational and more efficient capitalism) also strongly affected social democratic parties and trade unions in the twenties.[177] As against the accusation of betraying socialist concepts of capital-labor antagonism and class struggle, closer firm-level cooperation between capital and labor could be ideologically interpreted as a step toward "industrial democracy."[178] Rather than constituting a rejection of the class struggle, these supply-side policies could be presented as an encroachment on traditional prerogatives of capital.

But however attractive ideologically, in practice such views were stillborn. Under conditions of mass unemployment, when trade unions frequently lacked the strength to prevent a reduction in real wages, the aggressive wage policies that underconsumptionist theories called for were utopian.[179] In practice, social democrats often found it difficult to resist the conclusion that lowering (wage) costs would indeed be the best way to improve (export) competitiveness and safeguard jobs in the short term. As, for example, Leif Lewin (1967: 52) points out, the SAP would tend to oppose wage cuts when in opposition while accepting them when in government. Also, the SDAP admitted that wages were too high.[180] Cooperative microlevel relations with the purpose of improving competitiveness remained largely confined to modern, less labor intensive export industries like chemicals and metalworking. And even there the pressures exerted by gold standard policies would always make such cooperation fragile.

A perhaps more important ideological effect of the de facto absence of a viable social democratic alternative was the revival of the concept of an inevitable historical progress of society toward socialism. That social democratic parties that were starting to shed their socialist ideology would temporarily come to more strongly emphasize the Marxist concept of historical inevitability might seem a logical development, irrespective of the reigning macroregime. Dissociating the goal of socialism from practical policies by relegating it to the long term of historical inevitability would seem an attractive solution for a party that wanted to exploit the opportunities for reform within a market economy, but did not want to increase internal tensions by a sudden reorientation of official policy goals. Yet, during the twenties the reference to historical inevitability had to take on an additional task. Stressing that the advent of a socialist society, in which all demands of labor would be fulfilled, would be the inevitable outcome of the progress of history was a useful rhetorical device to maintain the spirits of the constituency and not to abandon all its ideals in a period when economic policies threatened the interests of labor and when social democrats frequently could not identify alternatives to the reigning policy regime.

Lewin (1989: 168) has pointed out that for the SAP in the twenties the reference to the inevitable march of history toward socialism functioned to maintain a distinct social democratic interpretation in spite of the SAP's lack of alternative to most of the economic policies pursued by the bourgeois parties. The Norwegian DNA was a reformist party before the war but became a member of the Comintern in 1919, and, in terms of its official ideology, it remained a revolutionary socialist party throughout the twenties. But, just as was the case for the SAP, the persistence of the verbal radicalism of the DNA during the twenties may, as Tore Andersen (1978: 84) has pointed out, be seen as a way to maintain internal coherence and defend the movement from outside attacks in a period during which no effective policies against the economic crisis seemed to be available. And once an alternative did become available in the thirties, the DNA had no problems with fully and rapidly embracing "reformism" despite more than a decade of revolutionary rhetoric.

Of the parties considered here, Labour was the least affected by Marxist ideas. Nevertheless, Labour and MacDonald had traditionally stressed the inevitable progress toward socialism, but understood as a gradual process rather than a revolutionary upheaval. The ideas on contracyclical macromanagement contained in *Labour and the New Social Order* of 1918 provided the party with a basis for a practical policy program. However, as the twenties progressed, discretionary macromanagement was increasingly deemphasized on the grounds that it did not remove the root cause of economic crises, namely, the unplanned character of production.[181] And given that socialization was to be a very gradual step, in practice not much was left for a Labour government to do than to defend the gold standard.

At this point Labour met with the SPD, the party that had been most influenced by Marx. Especially in the first years after the war, references within the SPD to the historical inevitability of socialism served to defend reformist practices against internal criticism of a lack of revolutionary policies. In its policy platforms, the SPD instead deemphasized Marxist concepts as long as there seemed to be a distinct possibility for a reformist government with the SPD's participation. The Görlitz program of 1921, for example, avoided Marxist terminology in order to present the SPD as a broad people's party. But as the prospect for reform seemed to disappear in late 1923, Marxist terminology reappeared in the Heidelberger program of 1925, which accepted the concept of organized capitalism, as the official ideology.[182] According to Rudolf Hilferding, the father of the theory of organized capitalism, economic development was marked by a secular progress toward socialism as increasing cartelization and monopolization would gradually replace the market with planning. On the one hand, this program discerned a clear historical task for a social democratic party: to eventually take over the instruments of planning that had arisen in the old order so as to place them at the service of society as a whole. On the other hand, such a concept placed little demands on concrete short-term policies.

4

THE CREATION OF THE SOCIAL DEMOCRATIC CONSENSUS

Unlike the crises of the early twenties, and the seventies and eighties, the Great Depression caused the center of gravity of the political system to shift in a social democratic direction. Liberal, conservative, and Christian democratic parties alike came to accept, and often spearhead, the need for economic policy interventionism and the political correction of market outcomes. Initially, it seemed that Western European economies would travel sharply divergent trajectories.[1] While Scandinavian social democrats came to establish political and ideological dominance, the Nazi dictatorship destroyed organized labor in Germany. In Britain and the Netherlands, the liberal regime seemed to have survived with only minor alterations. Yet, despite the vastly different political fate of social democratic parties in the thirties, the new policy regimes all shared a basic rejection of the "liberal" political economy of the twenties. As Peter Temin has argued, "The Depression ushered in an age of moderate socialism, albeit in many variations."[2] And after the defeat of the Nazi regime, political convergence was added to convergence in economic policies.[3]

In the eyes of many contemporaries the thirties marked a change from a regime based on the trust in the forces of the free market to a regime that recognized the inherent deficiencies of markets and assigned the state the task of correcting market outcomes. That the goal of internal equilibrium instead of a fixed exchange rate now achieved priority seemed the logical, if somewhat belated, consequence of general suffrage. In a democratic polity, the desires of the broad electorate rather than the prejudices of *haute finance* would have to inform economic policy making.

Proclaiming the primacy of the political, however, conflicted with the core assumption of neoclassical and Marxist theories alike that political interventionism at best was futile and at worst would lead to serious economic disturbances. How could the alleged reassertion of the primacy of politics during the depression have ushered in the longest boom in modern history? Why did the decline of the gold standard, the balanced budget dogma, and independent central banking not produce the inflationary chaos they were seen to have produced one decade earlier? Why was it that in the middle of the depression governments embarked on policies that increased public control over the economy and de facto strengthened the wage bargaining powers of the trade unions without being confronted with serious opposition from employers?

The fascist reaction to the Great Depression seemed to lend itself most easily to interpretation within the old zero-sum framework. Marxists were not alone in arguing that by destroying labor organizations, fascism accomplished the radical reduction in real wages that business had found impossible to obtain within a democratic polity.[4] However, this interpretation ran afoul of the Western European democracies and especially of those countries where social democratic parties came to power. In the latter countries, economic recovery proved to be possible while the political and economic influence of labor was actually strengthened. Capitalism obviously did not require the radical suppression of the working class in order to survive.

Yet, it might still be possible to understand the new policies in the old zero-sum framework by arguing that the different fate of European countries in the thirties reflected different political preconditions for reducing the claims of organized labor. In this interpretation, Scandinavian social democracy was successful because it induced labor to accept the wage cuts that conservative parties had found impossible to bring about. As Bo Gustafsson (1974: 141) has argued with respect to the policies of the SAP since 1932, "The 'new' policies were first of all a new form of wage cuts."[5] In the Weimar polity, however, it might be argued, such a policy could be implemented only under dictatorship. As, for example, Charles Maier (1987: 104) argued: "Now it did not require fascist institutions to contain wage pressure; in Great Britain wages remained low despite major union offensives. But in Italy and Germany the 'opening' of the political system in the postwar period and the tumultuous advent of mass political parties and powerful unions seemed to preclude similar stabilization. Fascism seemed to provide the necessary political framework."[6]

Eventually the standard analysis of the regime change came to postulate the discovery of a new economic paradigm: Keynesianism. Social democrats interpreted the Keynesian hypothesis that only discretionary macromanagement could guarantee full employment as a confirmation of their view that capitalism needed to be tamed by the state. Neoclassics could embrace the new orthodoxy only after they had integrated it into their framework by attributing the possibility of an unemployment equilibrium to stickiness of nominal wages (see Chapter 2). Even Marxists came to make peace with a theory that argued that government interventionism could rid capitalism of its crisis tendencies. Jürgen Habermas (1973) maintained the idea of the inevitable decline of capitalism by arguing that Keynesianism would necessarily transfer class antagonism to the political sphere. Michael Kalecki, in turn, predicted that the economic possibility of growth and full employment by means of expansionary macroeconomic policies would remain politically stillborn. As continued full employment strengthened the working class, business would – somehow – engineer a crisis so as to reinstate unemployment as an instrument of discipline.[7]

Yet, these interpretations were inaccurate. In essence, the problem of the Great Depression was one of deflation. This was not a crisis that could only be resolved by radically changing the distribution of the gross domestic product between the major social groups. The core problem was not that wages were too high to allow for profitable production (classic unemployment) or too low for output to be absorbed (underconsumptionist theories). The historical task governments faced during the Great Depression was to introduce downward rigidity of prices in a system that was being ruined by deflation.

It was the deflationary constellation that determined the character of the new regime. Notwithstanding wide cross-national variations, the new regime came to rest on three pillars: (1) a proliferation of institutional devices designed to promote downward nominal rigidity, in particular agricultural price stabilization agreements and industrial cartels backed up by tariffs, and, in some countries, a deliberate effort to strengthen the wage bargaining power of the trade unions; (2) abandoning the gold standard and stabilizing (or reflating) the domestic price level instead of the exchange rate; and (3) cheap money policies aimed at stimulating private investment.

The new regime did not emerge in response to a well-conceived master plan. Instead, most of the policy measures making up the new regime were introduced as short-term emergency measures. Governments moved to regulate agricultural markets when major parts of the sector seemed to be on the verge of total collapse. The gold parity was abandoned when speculation against the currency could no longer be stemmed. The rules of orthodox monetary policy were broken when banking systems started to collapse. It was therefore only in retrospect that the coherence of the new regime came to be discerned.

In a sense, the economic policy assignments of the gold standard period were inverted in the wake of the depression. Stimulating growth and employment now came to be a task of macropolicy whereas the concern for price stability was delegated to a large degree to microlevel measures. The view that unemployment primarily was a problem of excessive wage costs or insufficient rationalization fell victim to the Great Depression. Unemployment gradually came to be seen as a problem that governments could and should combat by means of macroeconomic policies. By the beginning of World War II, the view that monetary policy should be conducted in isolation from the government and in disregard of the developments of the real sector had also been discarded. The deflation convinced most politicians, on the left and the right, that monetary policies, far from being neutral, did exert a powerful influence on growth and employment and thus should not be conducted independently but rather should be subjected to the government's overall policy goals.

By abandoning the gold standard and institutionalizing a regime that did

not need to (threaten) continuous macroeconomic restriction in order to maintain the parity or stabilize the price level, the groundwork was laid for a
dramatic increase in growth and investment. Consequently, the next four decades would utterly embarrass predictions of an inherently crisis-prone or stagnant capitalism. In large part as a result of rapid growth, social welfare systems
could be vastly expanded during the next decades. Most important perhaps, the
thirties inaugurated a radical change in the relationship between the state and
interest groups. Under the gold standard regime, states necessarily had considered collective organizations of economic interests that obstructed downward
price flexibility as a potential threat to their macroeconomic goals. Now, however, such organizations came to be seen as playing an important role in
fostering economic as well as political stability. Macrocorporatist tendencies,
which had been doomed to failure under the gold standard, now increasingly
came to characterize European polities. For the same reason, it now also became
possible for social democratic parties to broaden their appeal beyond the traditional industrial working class and present themselves as a true people's party.
As a result of all these developments, the political accommodation between
labor, capital, and the state, which European societies had sought in vain since
1918, could be achieved.

   Not all social democratic parties could initially draw political advantage
from the new regime. In Britain, the debacle of the second Labour government
in 1931 split the Labour Party and made it a noncontender for government
participation for the next decade. In Germany, a price stabilization regime could
not be implemented in time to prevent the disaster of Nazi rule. Despite a
fundamental change in views concerning economic policies, the traditional
aversion of the "confessional" parties to social democracy kept the Dutch SDAP
out of government until 1939. The Scandinavian parties, in contrast, managed
to enlist the support of the farmers' parties and entered government in the
1930s.

   In the short term, it was mainly a combination of the specific domestic
political constellation and sheer luck that determined whether social democratic
parties could profit from the change in regime. Yet, in the long run the advent
of the new regime could not fail to promote the ideological dominance of social
democracy. As the conservative and liberal parties had to abandon their emphasis on downward nominal adjustment as the only appropriate policy, the liberal
orthodoxy forfeited its chance for ideological and political preeminence. No
matter that the regime of the twenties had in fact been very discretionary; the
conservatives and liberals now had to pay the price for equating nominal
downward adjustment and the gold standard with the free play of the market
and laissez-faire. In 1945, the British electorate awarded Labour an absolute
majority in Parliament. After the 1945 and 1940 elections, respectively, DNA
and SAP also commanded a parliamentary majority. In the Netherlands the
Catholic party overcame its aversion and formed a government in 1939 with
the SDAP. Only the SPD would not manage to enter government until 1966.

THE CREATION OF THE GREAT DEPRESSION

The Great Depression was a policy-induced crisis, the emergence of which can only be understood in the light of the inflation of the early twenties.[8] By assigning macroeconomic policies the sole task of preventing renewed inflation and by rigidly linking currencies by means of the gold standard, the stage was set for a disaster in which restrictive policies would cascade through the international economy. What gave the depression its particularly catastrophic character was that the decade of the gold standard had seriously weakened those institutions that could provide a safeguard against excessive downward nominal flexibility. The bargaining position of most trade unions was seriously undermined by a decade of mass unemployment and deflationary policies. Similarly, a decade of recession and deflation served to undermine agriculture. Finally, the policies of the twenties had also weakened the banking sector. Many countries already experienced bank failures during the deflation of the early twenties, and the policies of the rest of the decade were not conducive to a recovery. In short, the resurrection of the gold standard on the basis of a restrictive policy regime meant that the threat of a cumulative cycle of deflationary policies was ever present. The disaster was waiting to happen and it did so with the Great Depression.

The downward slide of the world economy was initiated by restrictive policies in Germany and the United States during 1927–28.[9] Since 1927, Reichsbank president Hjalmar Schacht had aimed to discourage long-term capital import.[10] The Reichsbank increasingly worried about large capital inflows into Germany, in particular because the favorable balance-of-payments situation undermined Germany's claim that it could not pay reparations.[11] Reparations agent Seymour Parker Gilbert agreed with Schacht but for the opposite reasons. In Gilbert's view, reduced capital inflows would force German authorities to pursue more restrictive policies and this would lead to fewer imports and an improved trade balance. Accordingly, Germany would be better able to pay reparations.[12] Together Gilbert and Schacht managed to close the American capital market to German borrowing for some time.

Whereas the quarterly average value of Germany's bond flotations abroad had still been RM 578 million from the third quarter of 1927 to the second quarter of 1928, it fell to RM 75 million in the second quarter of 1929.[13] Being unable to borrow substantial amounts abroad, Germany would have to run a substantial trade surplus if it were to pay reparations. Since both the provisions of the Dawes Plan and Germany's own fear of inflation ruled out devaluation, improvement of the trade balance had to be achieved by means of a domestic recession.[14] The immediate result of reduced capital inflows was a sharp reduction in public investment. Since public investment exceeded private investment in the latter part of the twenties,[15] this was a major blow to the economy. At the same time, the Reichsbank's policy of high interest rates and credit contraction discouraged private investment.

In the United States the Federal Reserve worried about domestic speculation and engineered its own monetary contraction. The result was a radical reduction of capital outflows beginning in the second half of 1928, which forced other countries into restrictive policies if they wished to maintain the gold parity of the currency. Britain tightened monetary policies in mid-1928, but sterling remained weak until it was floated in 1931. Accordingly, the recently elected Labour government under Ramsay MacDonald actually had to meet the crisis with high interest rates and drastic fiscal cuts, instead of expansionary policies to cut unemployment.

As restrictive policies proliferated through the international system the Great Depression took shape. By 1931, banking systems started to collapse under the pressure of deflation. The first was the Austrian, precipitated by the failure of the Creditanstalt, closely followed by the German one. In March 1933, newly elected president Franklin Roosevelt had to declare a bank holiday in the United States.

DEFLATION AND UNEMPLOYMENT

After a period of relative price stability from the midtwenties, a renewed deflation set in around 1928. Within a span of three years, wholesale prices fell at least 15 percent from their 1928 level (see Figure 4.1). The decline was most pronounced in the Netherlands. Between 1928 and 1932, prices fell by approximately 38 percent, and continued to fall, albeit at a slower pace until reaching 60 percent of their 1928 level in 1935. Despite Heinrich Brüning's ferocious deflation policies, Germany did not manage to match the Dutch deflation. Here the bottom was reached in 1933, when wholesale prices stood at about 69 percent of their 1928 level. Reflation set in soon after the coming to power of Hitler's NSDAP (National Sozialistische Deutsche Arbeiterpartei). Countries that abandoned the gold standard in September 1931 managed to contain the extent and duration of deflation. In Norway, prices were already stabilized in 1931 at around 79 percent, and by 1937, the 1928 level had been reached again. The Swedish wholesale price index kept falling after 1931, albeit at a slow pace, to reach bottom in 1933 at about 72 percent. In Britain, deflation of wholesale prices was halted in 1932 at around 72 percent of the 1928 level.

In terms of consumer prices a similar picture emerges (see Figure 4.2). Again, the extent and duration of deflation were most pronounced in Germany and the Netherlands. Dutch consumer prices fell continuously until the guilder was cut loose from gold in 1936. At that point the consumer price index stood at about 77 percent of its 1928 level. In Germany, stabilization already took place in 1934 when the consumer price index bottomed out at about 81 percent. Deflation was much less pronounced in the remaining three countries, and recovery took place earlier. Norwegian and British prices fell by about 15 percent and stabilized in 1933. The Swedish index stopped falling in the same

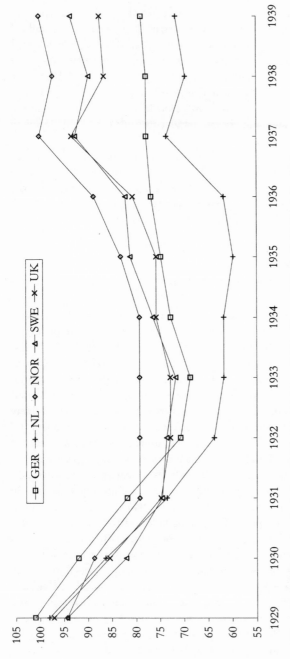

Figure 4.1. Wholesale price index, 1928–39 (1928 = 100). (Source: Mitchell 1992: 841–44.)

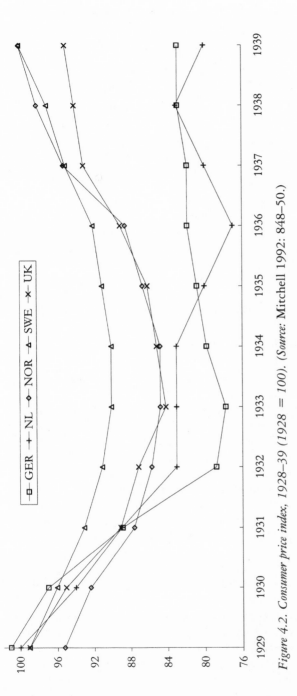

Figure 4.2. Consumer price index, 1928–39 (1928 = 100). (Source: Mitchell 1992: 848–50.)

Table 4.1. *Index of national product, 1930–39 (1930 = 100)*

	Germany	Sweden	Norway	Netherlands	Britain
1931	89.1	90.5	92.0	94.1	94.9
1932	84.7	88.1	96.8	90.7	94.6
1933	96.1	89.3	99.0	88.0	96.4
1934	105.7	97.9	102.6	87.5	102.8
1935	119.0	102.8	107.8	89.5	106.8
1936	134.4	110.2	115.0	91.9	110.1
1937	148.4	117.5	120.0	97.7	114.2
1938	165.0	121.8	122.8	99.3	117.5
1939		128.5	128.7	101.9	121.3

Note: Sweden, Norway GDP at constant prices. Netherlands, Germany, NNP at constant prices. Britain, GNP at constant prices.
Source: Mitchell 1981.

year at about 90 percent of its 1928 level. Reflation also was more pronounced in these three countries. In Germany and the Netherlands, the consumer price index stood at about 80 percent at the end of the decade, whereas Britain, Norway, and Sweden had roughly reached the 1928 level again.

The fall in national product roughly matched the deflation picture (see Table 4.1). Hardest hit were Germany and the Netherlands. But while recovery set in in Germany around 1933, the Netherlands had to wait three more years. Moreover, the Netherlands were the only country where the national product by the end of the decade failed to substantially exceed its 1930 level. The recession was least pronounced in the United Kingdom and Norway, although the latter country had started the decade with a quite depressed economy. Sweden recorded a comparatively strong recession but German levels were not reached. As in Germany recovery in Sweden began in early 1933.

Table 4.2 gives an indication of the extent of unemployment. As B. R. Mitchell (1992: 166) cautions, cross-country comparisons are difficult on the basis of these indicators because Swedish and Norwegian data refer to unemployed trade union members, whereas for Germany (after 1929), the Netherlands, and Britain, registered unemployed are measured. Since trade unions were overrepresented in industry, where the crisis hits hardest, the Scandinavian figures probably somewhat exaggerate the extent of unemployment. Nevertheless, Table 4.2 gives a fair indication of the catastrophic impacts of the Great Depression. Germany recorded the most dramatic increase from 8.6 percent in 1928 to more than 40 percent in 1932. But Germany also showed the most dramatic recovery: by 1937 unemployment had fallen below its 1927 level. In the Netherlands, unemployment kept rising until the gold standard was aban-

Table 4.2. *Unemployment rates, 1927–37*

	Germany	Netherlands	Norway	Sweden	Britain
1927	8.8	7.5	25.4	12.0	6.8
1928	8.6	5.6	19.1	10.6	7.5
1929	13.3	5.9	15.4	10.2	7.3
1930	22.7	7.8	16.6	11.9	11.2
1931	34.3	14.8	22.3	16.8	15.1
1932	43.8	25.3	30.8	22.4	15.6
1933	36.2	26.9	33.4	23.3	14.1
1934	20.5	28.0	30.7	18.0	11.9
1935	16.2	31.7	25.3	15.0	11.0
1936	12.0	32.7	18.8	12.7	9.4
1937	6.9	26.9	20.0	10.8	7.8

Note and Source: See Table 3.3.

doned. Consequently, mass unemployment was still rampant at the end of the decade. The effects of Norges Bank's parity policy are shown by the very high unemployment rate in 1927. After a brief recovery between 1928 and 1930 unemployment started to rise again dramatically in 1931. Despite its stronger fall in national product, unemployment in Sweden was lower than in Norway. Recovery set in in both countries around 1933–34. With a peak of 15.6 percent, reached in 1932, British unemployment was the lowest of the countries examined here.

FISCAL EXPANSION AND THE GREAT DEPRESSION

The Great Depression has come to be understood as a historical divide that ushered in the age of Keynesianism. As the seemingly endless post-1945 boom appeared to confirm the correctness of Keynesianism, whether and when social democrats had embraced fiscal expansion came to appear as the most crucial decision of the Great Depression. Accordingly, the reluctance of the SPD and Labour to embrace the (proto) Keynesian proposals advanced by the ADGB trade union in Germany, and Keynes and the Liberal party in the United Kingdom, seemed a tragic mistake.[16] Robert Skidelsky (1967), for example, has argued that the British Labour Party's attachment to "utopian socialism" and its consequent failure to adopt "interventionist capitalism" in the thirties constituted the major missed opportunity of interwar British economic policy. The SPD in particular has been harshly criticized. While the SPD rejected the Keynesian WTB Plan of the ADGB trade union (named after its authors,

Woytinski, Tarnow, and Baader), Gregor Strasser embraced work-creation programs in his famous speech to the Reichstag on May 10, 1932. Works creation proved to be a point of electoral appeal for the NSDAP. For this reason, it has been argued that if the SPD had accepted the WTB plan, it might have weakened the NSDAP and possibly prevented the advent of the Third Reich.[17] Wladimir Woytinski, for example, the main driving force behind the WTB plan, complained bitterly that the SPD, and in particular former minister of finance Rudolf Hilferding, proved to be quite unreceptive to the proposals for a new policy.[18] Robert A. Gates (1973) followed Woytinski's interpretation, arguing that the SPD in fact promoted the downfall of the Weimar Republic because of its support for Brüning's deflation policies and its rejection of the WTB plan.[19] Because of the spending package it passed in 1932, the new Swedish labor government, in contrast came to be hailed as the first example of how undogmatic social democrats could find the solution that had eluded everybody else. As Adam Przeworski and Michael Wallerstein (1985: 208) put it: "But in Sweden the Social Democratic Party, having won the election of 1932, broke the shell of the orthodox monetary policy. As unemployment climbed sharply with the onset of the Great Depression, they stumbled upon *an idea that was truly new:* instead of assisting the unemployed, the Swedish social democrats employed them."[20]

Despite the huge amount of political and academic energy expended on it, the issue of fiscal expansion was fairly irrelevant during the Great Depression and after. It was the choices in monetary and exchange rate policies that determined the political and economic dynamics of the depression. That some parties advocated "Keynesian" policies while others were more hesitant was of little relevance for the policies pursued. The gold standard regime at the same time provoked the reemergence of proposals for fiscal expansion and made them unworkable. As the supply-side measures devised in the twenties, quite naturally, failed to have any noticeable impact on unemployment and "tinkering" with monetary policies was taboo,[21] fiscal policies were the only straw left to grasp at for those desperately needing to find a remedy for the collapsing economies. Yet as long as the conviction prevailed that tight money – with or without a commitment to a fixed exchange rate – was necessary in order to prevent inflation, fiscal expansion had to remain unworkable. Once the European currencies were allowed to float and cheap money came to be accepted as an instrument for promoting growth, fiscal expansion was rather unimportant both in theory and in practice.

THE REEMERGENCE OF KEYNESIANISM

Despite having been shelved in the early twenties, proposals for deficit spending reemerged again toward the end of the decade. The first to introduce such proposals was David Lloyd George in Britain in his so-called *Yellow Book* and the pamphlet *We Can Conquer Unemployment* of 1928. He proposed additional annual spending of £100,000,000 on infrastructrural projects, to be financed by loans and the savings that would result from lower unemployment. Keynes came out strongly in favor of Lloyd George's proposals.[22] The Labour Party also was sympathetic. As Charles Loch Mowat (1963: 350) has pointed out, in the election campaign of 1929, Labour "simply annexed Lloyd George's program, claiming that it could carry it out better than he." One year later the Swedish SAP proposed additional spending of SEK 20 million. By 1933, proposed spending had risen to SEK 195 million. The SAP aimed to finance the program primarily by borrowing.

Its Norwegian sister party followed the example in 1932 in a brochure titled *Det Arbeidende Folks Krisekrav* (The crisis demands of the working people).[23] The spending proposals were rather modest, however, and could hardly be said to be Keynesian in character. Increased spending was to be financed by cuts in other areas and higher taxes. Loan-financed spending was first proposed in the so-called Three-Years Plan[24] of 1933 and the budget proposals of January 1934. Moreover, fiscal spending was a relatively minor point in a program that strongly emphasized the need for more planning and social control of money and credit.

The Dutch *Plan van de Arbeid*[25] (Plan for work) was presented by the SDAP and the NVV in late October 1935. As far as fiscal policy was concerned, the plan proposed additional annual spending on infrastructural projects to the amount of NLG 200,000,000 for three years in a row. The plan was to be financed by borrowing on the capital market. In contrast to the work-creation policy pursued by the Colijn government, wages at public works projects should be equal to normal market wages. To further reduce unemployment the plan also proposed shorter working hours and early retirement. However, the plan did not envisage a budget deficit on the current account. Only for the purpose of investment projects (i.e., the capital account) was loan-financed expenditure acceptable. In order to balance the public sector's current accounts, a combination of cutting expenditures and raising revenues was proposed.[26]

That social democrats in the early thirties rediscovered fiscal spending was largely due to the parties' need to increase their electoral appeal, and to trade unions' demands for effective short-term measures against unemployment. Far from being convinced that discretionary fiscal policies would constitute a sufficient means to maintain full-employment and improve wages, social democrats, until long after the Great Depression, held on to their view that a durable cure for the maladies of capitalism required far-reaching microeconomic planning. Given the staunch defense of individual property rights mounted by the parties to their right, and the lack of enthusiasm in their own ranks for socialization in the midst of a crisis, mustering a political majority for such a program was utopian. Yet, social democrats could no longer be content with denouncing capitalism and the policies of the parties in government while simultaneously arguing that an amelioration of the situation would have to await that mythical time when conditions were ripe for socialism.

Within the SAP especially, younger social democrats felt that there was a painfully wide gap between the party's socialist principles and its practical policies.[27] In the early thirties, the SAP leadership was well aware that socialization was not economically feasible but rather was a policy that would serve to undermine the electoral popularity of the party. With respect to socialization, board member Sköld argued, "It is better to sit with arms crossed than to do something crazy."[28] Deficit spending filled the void in the SAP's economic policy program. As future prime minister Tage Erlander (1972: 178) argued, the new policies marked the liberation from the dilemma of not having a feasible policy to address unemployment.

The policy reorientation of the Dutch SDAP was prompted by the disappointing election results of 1933. In the first meeting of the party leadership after the election, chairman Johan Willem Albarda argued that the party needed to advance concrete proposals against the crisis and that the policies proposed hitherto were too negative and too vague. In early 1934, after the publication of the Belgian *Plan de Man,* Albarda argued that the party needed a set of proposals similar in form to the Belgian ones. On April 7, 1934, the SDAP then decided to commission what was to become known as the Plan van de Arbeid.[29]

In addition to such electoral concerns, labor parties were subjected to strong pressures from trade unions for immediate measures. The mass unemployment of the twenties had considerably weakened the unions' bargaining position. Trade unions often seemed to have no choice but to acquiesce to demands for lower wages in order not to jeopardize the employment of their members. Cuts in unemployment allowances further added to the pressure on wages. In addition, the need to enforce deflation necessarily meant that governments had to be unsympathetic to trade unions' attempts to halt wage reductions. The unions were already weakened by a decade of mass unemployment, and the depression threatened to completely destroy their ability to function as an interest organization of labor.

At this point the social democratic inability to propose alternatives to the restrictive policies became intolerable for trade unions. Because trade unions were under more pressure as a result of the crisis, they were less concerned with theoretical debates about the long-term consequences of alternative economic policies. Deficit spending seemed an obvious solution as it promised to mitigate the pressures for wage cuts while not imposing any additional costs on industry. The argument that fiscal expansion *in the long run* would merely replace private with public unemployment could not exert a convincing force in an acute crisis situation. As Sidney Pollard (1973: 246) has observed, German trade unions in the early thirties "now concentrated on ending the scourge of depression and unemployment; they were a pressure group more directly concerned with this than any other, as the economic consequences of the depression threatened to undermine their whole power and influence, and, when men are driven to the wall, they discover merit in ideas that will assist them to fight even if their logic seems weak to others." Trade unions, therefore, became the force behind the policy reorientation of the social democrats.

Indeed, in Germany it was the ADGB, that developed deficit spending proposals. The ADGB started to develop its plan for public works after the radical cuts in unemployment insurance began in 1930. As ADGB economist Gerhard Colm noted: "We [the ADGB] cannot wait for a reconstruction of the economy in order to be able to reduce unemployment; rather the concern of the moment is to restore the functioning of the capitalist economic process with all its defects."[30] The famous WTB Plan advocated deficit-financed public works to the amount of RM 2 billion. It was accepted by the ADGB in April 1932[31] but eventually rejected by the SPD. The plan was to be financed by loans, savings on unemployment insurance, and, if necessary, by money creation.

In Sweden, the pressure of the LO was decisive for the adoption of the SAP's "new" policy in 1930. Initially, the LO had concentrated on measures that might reduce pressures on wages by improving the income of the unemployed. Most important, in this respect, was its demand for comprehensive unemployment insurance. Moreover, since 1928, the LO had demanded that work-creation programs pay market wages.[32] But when it became clear in 1930 that the SAP's plan for a comprehensive unemployment insurance scheme would not find a parliamentary majority, the LO rediscovered the policy of job creation by means of fiscal spending. The Dutch plan was written jointly with the NVV trade union, which, in the early thirties had started campaigning for work-creation programs to be financed by a tax on higher incomes, and against further cuts in wages and unemployment benefits. The Norwegian plan was a coproduction of the party and the LO union.

FISCAL POLICIES AND THE GOLD STANDARD

But whereas deficit spending may have seemed the solution to overcoming the deadlock between capital and labor, such policies were incompatible with the gold standard regime. As long as social democrats did not openly advocate abandoning gold, fiscal expansion was not viable either, because deficit spending was likely to undermine confidence in the currency. A loss of confidence in the currency, however, was generally considered to have disastrous consequences. Capital outflows and the loss of creditworthiness might easily bankrupt the state and the economy. In addition, a floating exchange rate, in the eyes of many politicians, raised the specter of inflation again.

Indeed, from the perspective of the 1990s, the refusal of politicians like Hilferding and Snowden to embrace fiscal expansion would seem fully understandable, if not inevitable. That governments that faced large and growing budget deficits as a result of the economic collapse were under constant threat of capital outflows, had to cope with a restrictive international environment, and were tied to a fixed exchange rate had little choice in macroeconomic policies seems rather obvious to many. Moreover, the proposition that a floating exchange rate creates a real danger of inflation enjoys a wide following in the 1990s. What set apart the SPD and Labour from the DNA and SAP was not so much the former's refusal to shed some of their antiquated ideological ballast as their unwillingness or inability to ignore the inconsistency of a position that advocated fiscal expansion while declining to abandon the gold parity.

The Norwegian labor party did not have to confront a potential contradiction between increased spending and exchange rate stability. The DNA developed the first plans for increased public spending – taking up proposals from the 1922 crisis program – only after the krone was floated.[33] But it is unlikely that the DNA would rather have abandoned gold than pursue restrictive policies in defense of the parity, had it been in government in 1931. *Arbeiderbladet,* the party's main newspaper, made the point quite clearly: "That the krone's convertibility with gold has now been suspended must actually be considered a disaster, brought about by external circumstances."[34] In particular, Norwegian labor, which had experienced the effects of deflation more severely in the twenties, might have been expected to greet the demise of the gold standard. But instead of reading "An End to Deflation?," *Arbeiderbladet* opened with the headline "Ferocious Price Increase on the Way?" on September 28.[35] Although the increase in the discount rate following the float was bemoaned,[36] the fear of inflation continued to dominate the social democratic press's comments during the following days. On September 28, Hornsrud argued that a strict control of prices was the most important task of the moment.[37] Agricultural price stabilization schemes, however, were not considered to add to inflation. On the contrary, *Arbeiderbladet* argued that price regulations would actually prevent the rise in bread prices, which would otherwise surely have followed depreciation.[38] Furthermore, it was feared that the krone would now be subjected to speculation, which would further add to inflationary pressures.[39] In addition, the uncertainty resulting from a floating currency was argued to be detrimental to the economy.[40] Member of Parliament Alfred Madsen was one of the few to hint in the early days that reflation might stimulate production, yet he simultaneously warned strongly against the dangers of inflation.[41]

From the safety of the opposition benches, the SAP simply avoided addressing the choice between fiscal expansion and a fixed exchange rate. The motion to the First Chamber No. 1930: 108, which contained the party's first deficit spending proposal, generally is seen to have marked the conversion to Keynesianism. Yet, it is rather doubtful that the SAP also would have had the courage to implement such a policy if it had had a chance to do so *before* the krona was floated. The SAP did not perceive the gold standard as a policy decision that could be altered at will. It never spoke out publicly in favor of abandoning gold. As the protocols of its meetings show, from the early twenties to September 27, 1931, the day when the krona was floated, the board of the SAP never discussed exchange rate policy as an instrument which might be employed to further social democratic goals. In fact, there is virtually no mention of the gold standard at all.

The SAP also viewed the gold standard as a bulwark against inflation. Accordingly, after September 27, it initially feared inflation. Gustav Möller, board member and future minister of social affairs, explained on May 7, 1932, in a parliamentary debate about exchange rate policy: "It must be considered completely self-evident that at the moment Sweden abandoned the gold standard, and in the period right after it, inflation was the danger present."[42] In order to counter this perceived threat of inflation, the Riksbank, on the day the krona was floated, increased the discount rate from 6 percent to 8 percent. Both the SAP and the LO agreed with this policy.

On September 28, the SAP board was asked to attend a meeting with the leadership of the Riksbank in order to discuss the new situation. Following this meeting, Möller, on behalf of the SAP board, wrote a letter to social democratic journalists that was to serve as a guideline for the reporting about exchange rate policy.[43] Möller argued that a wait-and-see attitude should be taken. "Whether we should go back to the gold standard, whether we should attach to gold again where we left it or at another value, whether it would be right to make all efforts to maintain the internal purchasing power of the krona, all these should be, for the time being, open questions." Möller implicitly admitted that maintaining the gold standard would have required further wage cuts: "It was felt that the party press, as already happened in the great majority of newspapers, should underline that the basis for a wage reduction policy of the employers has disappeared." Yet in the seven years Sweden was on the gold standard, the SAP never argued that it should be abandoned because it required wage cuts.

Most important, Möller argued that the papers should not write anything that might contribute to some kind of panic. "The economic condition of the country, overall, is quite healthy. The state budget is in a more satisfactory condition than in the majority of countries." But if Möller thought that a country with an unemployment rate in excess of 20 percent was overall quite healthy, and that large budget deficits would have implied an unhealthy economy, then it is unlikely that the SAP would have found the courage to abandon gold itself.

In line with what happened in other countries, the SAP only realized that the end of the gold standard did not imply inflation but the possibility to pursue more expansionary monetary policies and to terminate a highly destructive deflation after a few months of experience with a floating currency. In May 1932, the SAP agreed with the Riksdag banking committee and the majority of the Riksdag to bring about a moderate *reflation* of the wholesale price level. It was at that point, rather than with the publication of motion No. 1930:108, that the party shed its economic policy views of the twenties. Since in May 1932 the overwhelming majority of the Riksdag had accepted the need for reflation and more expansionary monetary policies, the new SAP government of the fall of 1932 faced radically different preconditions for fiscal policy making. On the basis of a now generally recognized need to reflate rather than deflate, the compromise between the agrarian party and the SAP along the lines of support for agriculture plus deficit spending became possible. The return of the SAP to government in 1932 did contribute significantly to the rapid recovery of Sweden: first, because it signaled the decisive defeat of the old regime; second, because, unlike British policies the SAP was willing to make extensive use of the room for maneuvering that had become available after September 1931, both by monetary and fiscal policies. Yet the economic and political success of the SAP ultimately depended on a decision it did not dare to take itself.

The Dutch labor party, which was in opposition until 1939, simply avoided discussing the exchange rate consequences of its spending proposals. Up to 1934, the party and the NVV trade union unanimously supported Prime Minister Colijn's exchange rate policy.[44] W. H. Vliegen's brochure of March 1934, *From Word to Deed,* which according to Jos Perry (1994: 391) was hailed in the SDAP as the first constructive contribution to combating unemployment, did not mention abandoning the gold standard. In response to the favorable experiences abroad, some open opposition against the gold standard emerged within the SDAP in 1934. Since neither the SDAP nor the NVV could now internally agree on the desirability of abandoning the gold standard, the whole issue was studiously avoided.[45] *The Plan van den Arbeid* of 1935 did advocate an extension of credit, but it did not advocate abandoning gold, nor did it discuss the monetary policy consequences of the proposed extra spending. Even within the SDAP, some doubted openly whether the plan could actually be realized without devaluation.[46] Prime Minister Colijn's response to the plan seized upon exactly this weakness. His main objection was that the plan might hamper the downward adjustment of domestic prices. The latter, however, was considered crucial in order to maintain both gold and the competitiveness of Dutch industry.[47] According to the economic spokesman of Colijn's ARP (Anti-Revolutionaire Partij), P. A. Diepenhorst, the additional spending envisaged in the plan might perhaps lead to a limited recovery, yet it was also quite likely that the deficit would disrupt business confidence and worsen the situation instead.[48]

The Labour Party, unfortunately perhaps, was in government when sterling came under pressure in the summer of 1931, and hence had to address the issue of exchange rate stability. Lloyd George's and Keynes's spending programs were not viable alternatives as long as the gold standard was maintained. Lloyd George himself did not advocate abandoning gold.[49] And Keynes endorsed this view, possibly because he did not wish to disqualify his fiscal policy proposals by linking them to the taboo subject of devaluation. Keynes considered fiscal spending a second best alternative that became relevant because low interest rates were ruled out by the need to defend the exchange rate.[50] Accordingly, the pre-September 1931 debate between the Treasury, Lloyd George, and Keynes came to focus on the question whether it was possible to expand aggregate demand without an expansion of the money supply. Keynes answered in the affirmative. Even without monetary expansion, financing for an increase in aggregate demand could be found if the velocity of circulation increased – or, put differently, if wealth holders could be induced to reduce the amount of liquid assets in their portfolio. According to Keynes, funds had accumulated in the commercial banks that were not put to productive use, the so-called idle balances. These funds might be employed by loan-financed public works.

Now, it might be possible that wealth holders would reduce their liquidity in response to an offer of public debt, which obviously had to be considered safer in the depression than private debt. There were two practical problems. First, if the increased public demand did not spark an increased willingness to invest in private industry, the reduction in unemployment could only be sustained at the price of continuous budget deficits. Keynesians would hence have to trust in the exogenous recovery of the economic cycle in order to avoid permanent deficits. Given a monetary regime devoted to restrictive policies, such a recovery of optimism was hardly likely. Second, and more important, openly abandoning the balanced budget doctrine, one of the pillars of the gold standard regime, might easily disrupt the confidence of international financial markets. At that point even more restrictive monetary policies would be required in order to stabilize the currency and find subscribers to public debt.[51] It was this practical fear of the loss of credit, rather than a dogmatic adherence to budget balanced, that informed Labour minister of finance Snowden.[52] During 1930 and 1931, the Treasury increasingly came to stress the possible loss of confidence in the pound, as the decisive argument against proposals for fiscal expansion.[53] A policy of debt-financed fiscal expansion in combination with adherence to the gold standard was impossible as the priority of the exchange rate mandated more fiscal and monetary restriction rather than expansion.

In practice, this was exactly what happened. Initially, prospects for fiscal expansion looked good given that the Labour Party had accepted much of Lloyd George's proposals in its 1929 election platform, and moreover, had to rely on the Liberal Party for a parliamentary majority. By mid-1930 the Labour government did indeed increase spending on public works schemes.[54] In addition, the rapid increase in unemployment caused an automatic deterioration of the budget. But, given the unwillingness to raise interest rates radically[55] or to float the pound, budget cuts were inevitable once sterling came under pressure again.

It is significant that Keynes himself was not willing to solve the dilemma by clearly advocating a break with gold. On the one hand, he rejected a policy of consistent deflation, but, on the other hand, he indicated that budget cuts might be required in order to defend sterling. At the April 16 meeting of the Economic Advisory Council, Keynes warned that a call for internationally coordinated reflation might be interpreted as a sign of British weakness. He also rejected Ernest Bevin's (TUC) suggestion to abandon gold because it would have detrimental effects for the City.[56] On July 13, 1931, the MacMillan Commission, an official inquiry into British monetary policy that has become famous for its confrontation between Keynes and the Treasury and BoE, published its report. It clearly rejected devaluation. Addendum I to the report, of which Keynes was a coauthor, concluded that the disadvantages of devaluation would greatly outweigh its benefits.[57]

By early August 1931, Keynes had come to regard devaluation as inevitable. As he wrote in a letter to Prime Minister MacDonald, dated August 5, 1931: "it is now nearly *certain* that we shall go off the existing gold parity at no distant date. Whatever may have been the case some time ago, it is now too late to avoid this."[58] One week later he seems to have changed his mind somewhat, as he argued in another letter to MacDonald, dated August 12, 1931: "I believe that it is still possible for us to keep on the gold standard if we deliberately decide to do so but, if this is the case, we should have to conform our whole policy accordingly. Personally I should support for the time being whichever decision we made, provided the decision was accompanied by action sufficiently drastic to make it effective."[59] After the fall of the Labour government Keynes did not contend that an expansionary policy aimed at combating the crisis would require freeing sterling from its golden fetters. As late as September 16, 1931, he maintained that devaluation was just one of the three policy alternatives the government should consider, the other two being import controls and an international conference "for giving the gold standard countries a last opportunity."[60] As Skidelsky (1992: 394) has noted, Keynes's hesitation on the matter confirmed MacDonald in his policy of defending the parity.

From within the labor movement, only Ernest Bevin and Walter Citrine of the TUC and Oswald Mosley[61] of the Independent Labour Party unequivocally advocated abandoning gold. Mosley was fairly uninfluential, but Bevin and Citrine wielded considerable power. Despite the TUC's refusal to accept the August 1931 spending cuts, Bevin and Citrine did not propose floating during the talks with MacDonald on August 20, 1931. It was only at the TUC conference of September 7–8, hence after the formation of the national government, that Bevin proposed to abandon gold.[62]

The German SPD had been in opposition since March 1930, but it, nor the authors of the WTB Plan, could not avoid the crucial issue. Given the recent experience of hyperinflation, any policy proposal had to address the monetary consequences. Moreover, given the collapse of international lending and the sorry state of German capital markets, Woytinski et al. felt that it might not be possible to secure the necessary loans to finance deficit spending. In that case, the Reichsbank should help out by financing part of the program by printing money. The WTB Plan, in other words, was a proposal for fiscal *and* monetary expansion.

Like its sister parties, the SPD lacked the courage to take the initiative for a reorientation of monetary policies. But also like its sister parties, it *did not* reject additional fiscal spending. The SPD certainly did not share the British Treasury's view that additional public spending would merely lead to a reduction in private activity. As was shown in Chapter 3, in the crisis of 1926 Hilferding himself proposed public works programs. Given that the spending program of 1926–27 seemed to have saddled the state with a higher budget deficit without having sparked economic recovery, the SPD had good reasons to be skeptical. Yet, in the desperate economic situation of 1932 it *did* propose loan-financed public works programs. In the summer of 1932, an agreement on work-creation programs was reached between the SPD and the ADGB that was presented in a series of motions to the Reichstag in August and September 1931. Instead of the WTB's RM 2 billion, only RM 1 billion was to be spent on work-creation programs. The proposals were to be financed by means of loans, taxes, and reduced spending in other areas. The proposals were first submitted to the Reichstag in May 1932. They were resubmitted in August–September 1932, but this time a forced loan was anticipated.

What the SPD did not want to propose was monetary financing of deficits. The proposal presented in May and August–September 1932 did not mention the money creation included in the WTB Plan. The majority of the SPD leadership, as did many in the ADGB, feared that a return to the principle of financing spending by the printing press would mean a return to inflation.[63] For Woytinski it was quite difficult to allay fears of inflationary consequences, because he had earlier been quite vocal that reflation was crucial in bringing about recovery and that central banks should do so by expanding the money supply. And although he argued in response to the criticism that the effects on the price level would be negligible, he failed to convince. [64]

The fear of the SPD was not so much that, say, a 5 percent increase in the money supply would cause a 5 percent increase in prices. In such a case, the SPD might have been willing to take the risk. Rather, its main fear was that money expansion would set off an uncontrollable inflationary process.[65] Also the SPD had experienced the inflation of the early twenties, not in the neoclassical fashion as a mechanistic process determined by the change in money supply, but as a dynamic market process that overwhelmed policy makers. Gregor Strasser of the NSDAP, in contrast, did not fear a cumulative inflationary process if the state would embark on money creation. In his Reichstag speech of May 10, he argued that a danger of inflation did not exist as long as a "clean and strong" state changed course in time.[66] The SPD, which did not plan to place the economy, including wage bargaining, under militaristic control, may have been less confident in the ability of the state to contain such a process.

In sum, the SPD did not reject the WTB Plan because of a dogmatic adherence to fiscal orthodoxy or a Marxist-inspired fatalism, but because it feared that monetary financing of spending programs would be inflationary.[67] In this, it was in full accordance with its sister parties.

THE ABSENCE OF KEYNESIAN POLICIES

Whereas fiscal expansion was unworkable as long as the gold standard mentality reigned, it was in practice rather unimportant after the gold standard had collapsed. In fact, expansionary fiscal policies to combat unemployment have

Table 4.3. *Central government expenditure and budget deficits, 1920–39*

	Total Expenditures (millions of national currency)			Budget Deficits (percentage of GNP)		
	Netherlands	Norway	Sweden	Netherlands	Norway	Sweden
1920	935	648	945		−1.06	−0.41
1921	1032	746	1116		−5.44	−3.62
1922	1123	585	983		−4.14	−3.60
1923	807	550	778	−5.78	−4.46	−2.98
1924	737	478	775	−1.19	−2.84	−1.27
1925	699	486	714	−0.49	−1.86	−0.68
1926	689	445	758	0.62	−1.53	−1.15
1927	645	395	810	1.42	−0.73	−1.45
1928	698	397	740	1.66	−0.78	−0.35
1929	729	387	792	0.50	−0.81	−0.58
1930	738	376	811	0.22	−0.44	−0.31
1931	865	374	819	−0.34	−1.11	−0.40
1932	883	361	894	−3.86	−1.09	−1.83
1933	993	309	1067	−5.35	−1.24	−3.85
1934	932	302	973	−6.00	−0.57	−2.04
1935	989	341	1148	−2.58	−1.05	−2.45
1936	935	384	1113	−3.33	−0.66	−1.85
1937	938	422	1199	−2.22	−0.15	−2.10
1938	1045	472	1372	−1.20	0.03	−2.41
1939	1182	567	1578	−2.77	−0.51	−2.45

Source: Drukker 1990: 339–43.

been a rare species that has mainly thrived within the confines of textbooks. Keynesian policies were absent in response to the Great Depression and largely irrelevant during the so-called Golden Age from the midforties to the early seventies. As Peter Temin (1989: 108), analyzing the policies of France, Germany, the United Kingdom, and the United States, argues: "The 1930s were not a test of Keynesian theory because Keynesian policies were not used." In effect, Keynesian contracyclical demand management policies were only pursued in Germany during 1926,[68] and, on a broader scale, during the seventies. In both cases, such policies proved largely unsuccessful and short-lived.

Table 4.3 gives the figures for central government expenditure and budget deficits for the three small countries during the interwar years. High budget deficits were most frequently the unintended outcome of recession rather than the result of discretionary contracyclical policies. All three countries suffered high budget deficits during the early twenties as well as during the early thirties, while deficits were reduced during the late twenties and thirties until armament spending took off. The deficits of the early and midtwenties were the outcome of the stabilization crisis. The high deficits of the early thirties, of course, reflect the onset of the Great Depression. In neither country did the ascendancy of governments who broke with the old economic policy orthodoxy lead to a decisive fiscal stimulus.

Strongly supported by the social democrats' reading of their own history,[69] Sweden has long been considered the best example of a shift to the new Keynesian strategy. After the SAP came to power in 1932, the doctrine of balanced budgets was replaced with the view that budgets should balance over a business cycle. In order to reduce unemployment, a loan-financed public works program was implemented. By now, however, it has become almost commonplace to note that the fiscal stimulus was too small and came too late in order to be able to explain the recovery from the Great Depression.[70] Compared to the first three years of the social democratic government, budget deficits were larger during the depression of 1921–23, when the doctrine of balanced budgets still reigned supreme. After the strong increase in 1933, budget deficits were gradually reduced again. The original intention was to amortize the debts incurred for the fiscal program in seven years, but the SAP government did so in three years. Despite high unemployment, "amortization payments surpassed expenses already during the budget year of 1935/36."[71] When looking at total rather than central government expenditures, the fiscal stimulus looks even less impressive. According to the figures given by Villy Bergström (1969: 43, 129), the total deficit for the fiscal years 1933–34 was not significantly larger than for the two preceding years, whereas the total budget for the years 1936–38 showed a surplus again.[72] Hence, one might argue that the real difference in fiscal policies was related to the terms in which governments justified policies rather than to the substance of policies.

For Norway, there are even less indications of a dramatic change in fiscal policy. Budget deficits during every year from 1921 to 1926 were considerably higher than during any other year of the interwar period. Although these deficits to a large extent reflected the collapse of revenues, the catastrophic situation of the economy did prompt governments repeatedly to approve relief programs (especially for agriculture). After the krone had returned to gold in 1928, the budget situation improved and fiscal policies reverted to a more consistently restrictive course in order to allow for the repayment of debts. The renewed increase in deficits during the Great Depression was much less dramatic than compared to the twenties. The so-called cow trade between the DNA and the farmers' party, which enabled the social democrats to build a government with majority support under prime minister Johan Nygaardsvold, took place in 1935. Yet, it did not give rise to more deficit spending. Although the advocation of loan-financed deficit spending by the DNA since 1934 represented a significant change in discourse, it can be maintained that in practice the DNA governments in the thirties adhered more strictly to the doctrine of balanced budgets than had been the case for the conservative governments of the twenties. Nygaardsvold could only implement 76 million of the proposed 140 million kroner program. Since most of these in turn were financed through taxes, the expansionary effect was negligible.[73] Consequently, budget deficits actually declined after 1935.

In the Netherlands, the view that the recovery from the Great Depression was due to the changing character of fiscal policies has been absent. Although budget deficits were generally higher in the thirties than was the case for the Scandinavian countries, this reflects the longer duration of the crisis as the Netherlands desperately clung to the gold standard until 1936. Despite the enormous emphasis Christian democratic prime minister Hendricus Colijn placed on the importance of a balanced budget, he was largely unsuccessful.[74] Under the pressure of very high unemployment rates, Colijn even implemented a modest work-creation program in 1934, which, in contrast to the Scandinavian programs, paid below market wages. When the gold standard was finally abandoned in 1936, the doctrine of balanced budgets had survived unscathed.

It is generally accepted that also after September 1931, British governments were unwilling to resort to deficit financing. The national government saw maintaining a modest budget surplus as a contribution to creating the optimistic expectations that were required to bring about economic recovery. Budget deficits might be interpreted as a commitment to inflation and hence might cause undue pressures on the pound, thereby jeopardizing the cheap money policy. In addition it was argued that fiscal expansion would only contribute to employment growth if it was accompanied by an expansion of the supply of money. However, the cheap money policy pursued by the national government in itself would stimulate private activity, and it was therefore unnecessary to take the circuitous route of budget deficits.[75] As Table 4.4 shows, the British central government accounts were generally in surplus during the twenties and thirties. Only in the run-up to World War II, when the need for rapid rearmament was allowed to override fiscal caution, did sizable deficits appear.

In Germany the Nazi regime clearly abandoned the balanced budget principle. The work-creation program approved in June 1933 provided for limited tax reductions and additional spending on housing and road construction. In total, the Nazis spent about RM 5.1 billion on such programs during 1933–34.[76] However, this amounted to about 1 percent of gross national product and was therefore too small to explain the rapid recovery.[77] Spending on armaments, in contrast, increased from RM 700 million in 1933 to RM 3.5 billion in 1934 and RM 5.2 billion in 1935.[78]

It would be difficult to equate the Nazi program simply with Keynesianism.[79] Rather the deficit spending program was part of a much wider and "un-Keynesian" change in economic policy regime. As was argued earlier, deficit spending had occurred at several times in the twenties but generally failed to be successful (see also Table 4.5). That the deficit spending by the Nazis

Table 4.4. *British central government accounts, 1920–38*

	Total Receipts	Total Expenditures	Deficit (−)
1920	1053	964	89
1921	1020	982	38
1922	934	865	69
1923	859	783	76
1924	803	769	34
1925	816	794	22
1926	812	820	−8
1927	841	789	52
1928	857	804	53
1929	864	838	26
1930	872	882	−10
1931	874	906	−32
1932	912	886	26
1933	881	836	45
1934	878	828	50
1935	890	867	23
1936	921	907	14
1937	987	989	−2
1938	1036	1145	−109

Note: In millions of pounds.
Source: Howson 1975: 155.

coincided with rapid economic recovery is most likely to be attributed to the ensemble of policy changes. The program coincided with a radical reorientation of monetary policy in which the gold standard emphasis on deflation and tight money was decisively rejected. It is the rejection of the gold standard type of monetary policy that was of greater importance than deficit spending and, in fact, allowed deficit spending to exert positive effects on the economy.

THE DEMISE OF THE GOLD STANDARD: POLICIES TO PROMOTE NOMINAL RIGIDITIES

While social democrats were groping their way toward short-term crisis measures that would leave private property rights intact, the parties to their right overtook them from the left. Beginning in the late twenties, conservative, liberal, and farmers' parties, with differing degrees of enthusiasm, engaged in

Table 4.5. *German public finances, 1926/27–1932/33*

	1926/7	1927/8	1928/9	1929/30	1930/1	1931/2	1932/3
Total revenue	18,412	21,307	22,816	23,205	23,104	20,694	16,684
Total expenditure	20,397	22,460	25,043	25,736	25,400	21,971	18,168
Balance	−1,985	−1,153	−2,227	−2,531	−2,296	−1,277	−1,484
Increase in public debt	1,742	1,075	3,561	3,159	2,704	155	170
Total expenditure as % of GNP	26.9	26.8	28.4	29.6	32.1	33.3	31.8
Increase in debt as % of GNP	2.3	1.3	4.0	3.6	3.4	0.2	0.3
Budget balance as % of GNP	−2.6	−1.4	−2.5	−2.9	−2.9	−1.9	−2.6

Note: In millions of reichsmarks.
Source: Computed from James 1986: 52.

far-reaching microlevel regulation of product markets, giving the state and private-interest groups the right to set prices, control production, monopolize foreign trade, and force individual producers to join collective regulation schemes. With little respect for the property rights of producers, the state promoted encompassing cartels in a host of markets so as to suppress the mechanism of supply and demand. Ironically, their justification for doing so was diametrically opposed to the thinking of social democrats. Social democrats believed that in the long run market forces would have to be suspended in order to achieve genuine progress, while some short-term relief could be obtained through fiscal measures. The parties to their right instead argued that, while in the long run free competition was the only guarantee for prosperity and democracy, short-term relief required the temporary suspension of free competition.

Commonly, price stabilization measures were introduced in the agricultural sector first. Because of their substantial seasonal demand for credit, farmers were very sensitive to the increasing real indebtedness resulting from deflation. The standardized character of their products and the presence of a large number of independent producers also made agricultural markets more susceptible to price competition. Moreover, unlike business, small farmers in particular lacked the possibility of trying to recoup the costs of rising real indebtedness by reducing wages, and accordingly the state was the only possible addressee for their grievances.

Policies to prevent the downward flexibility of prices commonly spread from the agricultural sector to industry and wages. As the depression progressed, industry came to realize more and more the desirability of stabilizing the price level. The term commonly used by the business community to convey the destructiveness of a deflationary constellation was "ruinous competition." Ruinous competition referred to a market constellation in which each individual firm's efforts to maintain demand for its products by lowering prices led, because pursued by all firms, to more economic difficulties for all firms. The logic of deflation also implied that stabilization of nominal wages would be beneficial to the economy. As long as labor in individual firms was willing to accept lower wages to safeguard employment, stabilization of industrial prices would be difficult. Whether business realized it or not, in a deflationary constellation its interests were served by a labor movement that had the ability to put a floor under nominal wages.

In sharp contrast to the inflationary constellation of the early twenties, the effect of deflation thus was to exert powerful pressures for closer cooperation between the state and economic interest organizations. Most important, because the demands of business, agriculture, and labor for stable prices/wages were not incompatible with each other, such closer cooperation between state and civil society would promote rather than hinder social accommodation. Most social democrats initially were skeptical about the spread of price stabilization agreements, as they seemed to imply a coalition of farmers, business, and the state aimed at increasing the cost of living. Yet at the same time the spread of state intervention to stabilize markets could not fail to strike an ideological chord with them. This ambiguity about the new regime, however, would soon make way for acceptance as it became clear that the new policies did not imply solving the crisis at the expense of workers, but rather contributed to a general improvement in economic conditions.

PRICE STABILIZATION IN AGRICULTURE

Intervention to stabilize agricultural prices displayed a similar logic everywhere. Tariffs and import quotas frequently constituted the first break with the principle of market formation of prices. Imposing a tariff or quota had the double advantage of placing no additional burdens on the budget and avoiding direct intervention with production or marketing. These two features made such measures more palatable to liberal parties. Yet, in the face of fierce competition between domestic producers, restricting imports proved insufficient to halt deflation. Moreover, in the case of agricultural exporters, the spread of trade restrictions served to increase domestic deflationary pressures as the loss of export markets outweighed the gains from restricting imports. Halting deflation in agricultural markets, therefore, required direct intervention with domestic price setting, production, and marketing. In many instances domestic producers attempted to stabilize prices by means of voluntary schemes, but failed due to problems of free riding.[80] At that point the state stepped in.

Table 4.6 summarizes the main measures.

The pattern for agricultural intervention in Norway was set in June 1930, when the second liberal Mowinckel government passed the Marketing Act. The act was a response to the failure of cooperatives to stabilize prices on a voluntary basis and was aimed at promoting the centralized marketing of agricultural products.[81] During the following months centralized marketing schemes for pork and, most important, milk were created. The milk marketing board sold milk at uniform prices and was granted the right to collect contributions, even from nonmembers. Toward the end of the decade, similar principles were applied to the fishing industry, which had also proved unable to organize a viable cartel without legal enforcement.

Prime Minister Colijn, who dominated Dutch economic policy from 1933 to 1939, was a convinced liberal, although, like other liberals, he did not advocate laissez-faire monetary policies.[82] However, as his tight monetary policies could only aggravate the crisis, Colijn felt forced to relegate the superiority of liberal supply policy to the long run and promote direct intervention in markets. The policy of price stabilization in agriculture had already started in 1930 under Colijn's Catholic predecessor Ch. J. M. Ruys de Beerenbrouck. Legislative activity speeded up after the devaluation of the pound. On October 29, 1931, Minister of Trade T. J. Verschuur presented a law that would allow for the imposition of import quotas. Yet, protection of the domestic market would not be sufficient for export-oriented Dutch agriculture. Moreover, guar-

Table 4.6. *The main agricultural price stabilization measures*

Year	Britain	Germany	Netherlands	Norway	Sweden
1929		Gliding tariff on wheats, rye, oats, and barley		Eggs Marketing Scheme	
1930				Marketing Act	Milling and blending quotas for wheat and rye
1930				Horticultural Products	Guaranteed minimum price for grain. Grain import monopoly
1931	Agricultural Marketing Act	Osthilfegesetz (March)	Wheat Act	Milk Marketing Scheme	
1931	Horticultural Products Act		Crisis Import Act	Butter Act	
1931				Pork Marketing Scheme	
1932	Wheat Act		Crisis Dairy Act		Milk regulation
1932	Import Duties Act		Crisis Pigs Act		Sugar regulation
1932			Crisis Land-Lease Act		
1933	Agricultural Marketing Act (expanded)	Government monopoly in oils and fats	Agricultural Crisis Act		Import monopoly for dairy products

Table 4.6. (*Cont.*)

Year	Britain	Germany	Netherlands	Norway	Sweden
1933	Sea-Fishing Industry Act	Act Concerning the Provisional Organization of the National Corporation of Agriculture and the Measures for Regulating the Market and Prices of Agricultural Products	Crisis Import Act (expanded)		
1934	Cattle Industry (Emergency Provisions) Act			Meat and Pork Marketing Scheme	
1936	Sugar Industry (Reorganization) Act				
1937	Livestock Industry Act				
1938				Raw Fish Act	

anteeing minimum prices would eventually also imply a need for the regulation of quantities produced. A new stage was reached with the Crisis Dairy Act of 1932. The act guaranteed farmers a subsidy per liter of milk to be financed by a surcharge on fats. The Agricultural Crisis Act of August 1933 constituted a further intensification of price stabilization, as it integrated the separate measures into one centralized framework. At the same time, it marked the government's realization that intervention in agricultural markets would be of a more permanent nature than originally expected. In the end, the Colijn government found itself guaranteeing minimum prices and regulating production for most agricultural products, while in some cases even trade was monopolized.

With Heinrich Brüning of the Catholic Center Party, Germany got a chancellor in 1930 who placed as much emphasis on deflation as the solution to economic problems as Colijn did in the Netherlands. In particular, after Britain and many smaller countries had floated their currencies, reduction of the domestic price level became crucial so as not to jeopardize the export competitiveness of the German economy.[83] For such policies, Brüning could not find a parliamentary majority. In response, he dissolved the Reichstag and went on to govern by presidential decree. The emergency decree of December 8, 1931, provided, for example, that all existing collective wage agreements be reduced to their level of 1927. In addition, all housing rents and many prices were to be reduced by 10 percent while long-term interest rates up to 8 percent were lowered to 6 percent and higher rates cut proportionally.

Brüning did not, however, advocate deflation for the agricultural sector.[84] Already under the previous government, agriculture had received an increasing amount of support. Under Brüning's chancellorship, the programs were expanded massively. Originally the subsidies were mainly intended for agricultural areas in East Prussia but were extended to all the regions east of the Elbe in 1931. In addition, measures to reduce the debt burden of agriculture became an important part of Brüning's policies. Local authorities were given the right to selectively reduce interest rates on outstanding loans to agriculture, postpone repayment, or even reduce the principal. But despite extensive financial support, deflation of agricultural prices was not halted. Hitler accomplished this.[85]

In the democratic countries, a comprehensive system of agricultural price support emerged in a piecemeal fashion. The ideological resistance of liberal and conservative governments to such measures meant that price regulation was generally only introduced when the economic survival of producers seemed acutely threatened. The NSDAP did not need to overcome reluctance with respect to microlevel regulation. With the Act Concerning the Provisional Organization of the National Corporation of Agriculture of September 13, 1933, they devised a nationwide system of regulation that was to cover all aspects from prices and quantities to distribution, marketing, wholesaling, and retailing. As in other countries, the authorities charged with price setting would also have the right to enforce compliance by individual producers.[86]

In Britain, legislation aimed at stabilizing agricultural prices was not without precedent. The Corn Production Act (1917) and the Agriculture Act (1920) guaranteed minimum prices and wages. But, in the early twenties, stabilization of agricultural prices and wages had to be abandoned in the face of the return to the gold standard.[87] State-assisted price stabilization was reintroduced with the Labour government's Agricultural Marketing Act of 1931, which was presented in response to the failure of voluntary cooperative organizations. Under the act, the formation of collective marketing schemes was encouraged by enabling the government to make such schemes binding on all producers.[88] The conservative governments that followed Labour's collapse in 1931 developed these policies further. The conservative approach differed from Labour's in that, to allay farmers' fears of state domination, it reduced the powers given to the minister of agriculture in favor of a more important role for interest organizations.[89] The revision of the Agricultural Marketing Act in 1933 allowed producer organizations to control prices and production and enabled the government to promulgate tariffs and quotas in support of such schemes.[90] The Wheat Act of 1932 followed a different route as it introduced direct subsidization with government funds in order to guarantee a minimum price.

In Sweden deflation led to a proliferation of direct interventions. In 1930, the conservative government resolved to subsidize growers of sugar beets. In order to maintain demand for domestic grains, importers of flour and domestic millers as of 1930 were required to use a specified minimum percentage of Swedish grain. But again, securing domestic demand proved insufficient in halting the fall in prices, and a minimum price needed to be enforced. Whereas price stabilization of sugar could take place through a preexisting de facto private monopoly in sugar refining, stabilization in the grain market required closer cooperation between producers and millers. In 1931, the liberal government granted the newly formed organization of Swedish millers the import monopoly in return for agreeing to buy grain at a government-determined minimum price.

Most important was the milk regulation of 1932, passed under the liberal government. Following the Norwegian example, the solution reached consisted of giving the agricultural interest organization SAL (Sveriges Allmänna Lant-brukssällskap) the right to impose a duty on all domestic producers so as to prevent undercutting of the minimum price. Part of the proceeds was used to finance the export of excess milk. The milk market regulation was completed in 1933 under the SAP government by the creation of an import monopoly for dairy products.[91]

PRICE STABILIZATION, SOCIAL DEMOCRATS, AND LIBERALS

In a traditional power politics perspective, the advent of price stabilization policies would point to the pivotal position of agricultural interests. Agricultural price stabilization did not seem to be in labor's interest. During the twenties European social democrats generally opposed agriculture tariffs and price support because they increased the cost of living.[92] Instead, labor's preferred solution mirrored the policies it advocated for industry, namely, increased competitiveness through increased efficiency.[93] Agricultural price supports also reduced the budgetary space available for spending on public works programs. Nor would agricultural price stabilization seem to be in the interest of industry. Higher food prices were likely to promote higher wage demands. Moreover, agricultural protection might provoke retaliation in the form of industrial protection. That price stabilization nevertheless became the dominant policy would hence seem to point to the ability of agricultural interests to block a labor-business coalition.

Agriculture did indeed seem to occupy a pivotal position in many countries. In Germany, the revolution of 1918–19 had failed to dislodge the Prussian Junkers from their strong position. In the Netherlands, agricultural products traditionally accounted for a disproportionately high share of exports. Moreover, the strong organization within the agricultural sector gave farmers a disproportionate access to the Catholic and Protestant parties. In Scandinavia, the agricultural sector still employed more workers than industry during the Great Depression.[94] Moreover, Scandinavian farmers formed separate political parties, which provided the necessary parliamentary support for the SAP (in 1932) and the DNA (1935) to form a government.

It is not possible, however, to understand the specific character of the policies pursued during the Great Depression in terms of the relative power of competing political interests. It may seem self-evident that conflicts of interest should function as the starting point for political analysis, because among groups that hold no conflicting interest political bargaining would seem irrelevant. But this mode of analysis in effect implies a neoclassical model in which changes in relative prices are considered crucial while changes in absolute prices are epiphenomenal. In this perspective, labor, for example, would be indifferent to a situation in which real wages remained unchanged as all prices and wages fell at the same rate and a situation in which real wages remained unchanged and all prices were stable. The key to understanding the political outcomes of the Great Depression is realizing that those two situations were not equivalent. Continued deflation implied recession whereas price stability was a prerequisite for recovery. A political coalition based on lowering prices hence could not be durable under the Great Depression, whatever its initial political majority.

The advent of agricultural market stabilization even in Britain might have served to dispel the notion that the emergence of such policies depended on the political resources agricultural interests could muster. Agriculture in Britain was politically unimportant ever since the repeal of the Corn Laws in the nineteenth century. Nor can the Swedish and Norwegian policies be interpreted as the political price reluctant social democrats had to pay to be able to form a government and pursue their programs of fiscal expansion. Indeed, on the basis of the assumption that social democrats placed the highest priority on fiscal expansion and saw agricultural protection primarily as a threat to real wages, one should have expected the formation of a liberal/labor rather than a farmer/labor coalition. With respect to the proposed spending programs, the DNA's views were closest to those of the liberals (Venstre). DNA's 1934 crisis proposals envisaged additional spending of NOK 140 million. The liberal proposal was the next highest with NOK 42.9 million, while the farmers' party only proposed NOK 15 million. The conservative party declined to propose any concrete figures.[95] DNA proposed to finance about 60 percent of the additional budget by loans. Venstre also had come to accept the principle of loan-financed deficits but only proposed to finance about 30 percent in that way. For the farmers' party, loan-financed deficits were out of the question. Additional spending would have to be financed by increased revenues. Moreover, relations between the DNA and the BP had become quite hostile during the latter's government tenure from May 1931 to March 1933. As late as May 1933, BP chairman Jens Hunseid, in a speech to the Storting, had questioned the right of labor to organize when he argued that the tyranny of the trade unions threatened the interests of society.[96] Indeed, in March 1933 the time for closer cooperation between labor and liberals seemed to have arrived as Hunseid's BP government was toppled by the liberals with the help of the DNA because the BP proposed additional cuts in spending plus a new tax to support agricultural price stabilization. The new government under liberal Prime Minister Johan Mowinckel initiated a new public works program.

Similarly in Sweden, an agreement between the liberals (Frisinnade) and the SAP would have seemed more likely. In terms of additional spending packages, the difference between the two was negligible. The package the SAP and the farmers party agreed on in 1932 amounted to SEK 485.5 million, whereas the liberals had proposed SEK 484.5 million. Of this amount, both the SAP/farmers' party and the liberals proposed to allocate SEK 100 million to public works programs. The conservatives instead only proposed SEK 57 million.[97] Given that the spending programs were basically the same, the SAP should have preferred an agreement with the liberals because they shared a preference for free trade. And indeed, in June 1930 the liberals and the SAP had cooperated to vote the conservative government of Salomon Lindman out of office when the latter proposed higher tariffs in order to protect agriculture.

Nevertheless a liberal/labor coalition based on additional spending on public works, low food prices, and free trade did not emerge in Scandinavia. The main reason was that, due to the radical deterioration of the situation in the early 1930s, liberals and social democrats themselves came to realize that price stabilization might be the only way to stave off the total collapse of the agricultural sector. Despite its emphasis on market adjustment and increased productivity as the solution to agriculture's problems, it was the second liberal government of Mowinckel that introduced far-reaching market regulation in Norway through the Marketing Act of 1931. In Sweden, a liberal government passed the minimum price for grain and milk regulation. As Bo Rothstein

(1992) has pointed out, Swedish liberal politicians argued that the depth of the crisis required a break with liberal principles of market adjustment.

Similarly, social democrats abandoned their position that agricultural price stabilization was to be rejected because it increased the cost of living. The Great Depression generally convinced labor that the supply-side policy of rationalization could not be the solution to the unemployment problem. Instead, trade unions in particular started to push for government intervention. At that point, it became difficult for social democrats to oppose agricultural price stabilization and stick with its policy of agricultural rationalization. A strategy that aimed to overcome the anarchy of the market by means of collective organization and government intervention could hardly be rejected by a movement that held that organization and regulation were superior to markets. Put differently, the same forces that pushed social democrats to propose direct government intervention to solve the unemployment problem also pushed them to revise their views on agriculture.

The Norwegian party took this step wholeheartedly. Like all other parties in the Storting, the DNA voted for the Marketing Act of 1930. The DNA maintained that marketing boards actually served to withdraw part of production from the capitalist, profit-oriented sector. Within the Swedish SAP, the advent of crisis and more intervention initially led to a split on agricultural questions. Per Edvin Sköld, the SAP's spokesman on agriculture and minister of agriculture since 1932, had advocated rationalization as the best solution in the twenties, but he now supported price stabilization measures. Together with Ernst Wigforss and a host of other social democratic MPs, he voted in favor of the sugar subsidies of 1930. As Wigforss noted, the Riksdag's discussion about sugar "marked a step on social democracy's road away from the liberal economic policy."[98] At the same time, the sugar subsidy made clear that price stabilization might be conducive to some of social democracy's own goals. The SAP managed to pass a motion in the Riksdag that stated that since the state guaranteed the price for sugar beets, the wage of workers in the sugar beet sector should also be guaranteed.[99]

The SAP parliamentary group was also split on the question of blending in a minimum percentage of domestic grain. The SAP voted against milk regulation in 1932, but as Sköld pointed out, this was not because he was against compulsory organization. On the contrary, he argued, compulsory organization was quite correct and in accordance with what the trade unions had always argued: namely, that it was not just that organized workers fought for a better wage level that then also benefited those who refused to pay union dues.[100] Instead, his main reason for opposing milk regulation was that he feared foreign retaliation. Within the SAP, Anders Örne was the main advocate of the view that agricultural protection harmed consumers and workers, but Örne's position was contradictory as he also supported the idea of regulation in order to overcome the inherent problems of markets. As Per Thullberg (1974: 156–7) points out, his proposals for organization within the dairy sector were rather similar to those of the SAL: in sum, that the SAP's acceptance of agricultural protection in the famous "cow trade" with the farmers' party in the summer of 1933 was not primarily a tactical move inspired by the wish to remain in government.[101] Rather the change in agricultural views fitted perfectly within the general reorientation in economic policy views prompted by the Great Depression.

That the political outcome in Sweden and Norway was a labor/farmer rather than a labor/liberal coalition was largely due to the ideological problems the latter had in justifying a policy of market regulation. Social democrats could embrace the policy initiated by the liberals as fitting within their vision of a regulated economy. The liberals themselves found it increasingly difficult to justify the continuation of a policy that had been implemented as a short-term measure. The Norwegian liberals' parliamentary support for a levy on margarine and rationing of fodder in 1934 created such internal tensions that there was talk of a split in the party. A significant fraction held that the party had gone too far in pursuing nonliberal policies. The liberal government was replaced by a DNA government, with BP support, in 1935 when Prime Minister Mowinckel proposed reducing support to agriculture. Mowinckel was aware that his proposals would mean the end of his government, but he did not want to expose the party to more internal strain by pursuing interventionist policies. In Sweden, the farmers' party struck the "cow trade" with the SAP in 1933 because it had more trust in the social democrats' continued adherence to market regulation, especially so since the smaller liberal party opposed such policies, as did some within the Frisinnade.[102]

INDUSTRIAL ORGANIZATION

While agriculture may have been most sensitive to its effects, industry suffered just as well from deflation. Accordingly, recovery from the Great Depression required that industrial prices also be stabilized. Stabilization of prices, in turn, required stabilization of wages. Wage and price stabilization in industry did not give rise to as far-reaching government intervention as agricultural price stabilization. As long as the fixed exchange rate was in force, price stabilization could not be extended beyond agriculture. After the switch to cheap money, the organizational strength in the industrial sector frequently proved sufficient so that the state was not required to strengthen or even create collective organizations. Yet, in some countries governments did consciously strive to increase the degree of organization in the industrial area.

As in the case of agriculture, Hitler's regime devised the most far-reaching measures. A decree of July 15, 1933, allowed cartels to enforce prices on noncompliant producers. At the same time, the ministry of economic affairs was given the right to create compulsory cartels. The official justification for this decree was that "intensified competition and the low price level resultant therefrom . . . have brought nearer the point at which the ruin of enterprises valuable to our national economy is threatened. . . . The compulsory order, with the help of the state's sovereignty, gives the cartel a power which it could not obtain on a voluntary basis."[103]

The efforts of British governments to stabilize prices centered on promoting the collective organization of producers. Protectionist measures were a crucial tool, both by preventing price stabilization from being undercut by foreign competition, and by making their imposition contingent upon the collusion of domestic producers.[104] Such policies were started by MacDonald's Labour government with the Coal Mines Bill of 1929. Under the national, and later conservative, government the effort to organize industry increased significantly. As Donald Winch (1969: 213) notes, "Schemes for fostering combination among producers and sellers for the purpose of abridging competition, restricting output, price-fixing, and the elimination of excess capacity, were encouraged tacitly and explicitly in every major British industry in the 'thirties.' " The main targets for government intervention were coal mining, cotton, shipping, iron, and steel. The British steel industry, for example, had traditionally been characterized by a great many small producers, and therefore voluntary cartel agreements had been virtually impossible to arrive at. In return for the import duties levied since 1932, the government required the industry to centralize so as to be able to control prices and production. As a result, British industry was able to join the second International Steel Cartel in 1935 whereas it had not been able to join the first one (1926–31) owing to the lack of a domestic structure that would allow cartel agreements to be enforced.[105]

Because the Dutch government decided to maintain deflationary macropolicies for much longer, the need for microeconomic measures to halt deflation was felt perhaps more urgently here. Yet, politicians generally did not link the two phenomena. Rather than seeing government-assisted market regulation as a crisis measure that had become necessary as a result of the deflationary policy, the need for market regulation was primarily seen to arise because of inherent weaknesses of decentralized competition. Demands for the "organization of industry" materialized first in the Catholic RKSP (Rooms-Katholieke Staatspartij) but soon spread to other parties. The centerpiece of the legislation was the Cartel Law of 1935. With this law, the government acquired the right to make cartel agreements binding on all firms in a sector upon a request from industry.[106] In addition, the Firm Licensing Law of 1937 allowed governments to protect firms from competition by making the establishment of new producers dependent on a government license. Private industry was generally quite enthusiastic about acquiring the ability to prevent "murderous competition"[107] with the help of the state, although they preferred to impose regulation as much as possible through their own organizations and opposed giving union representatives a seat on the commissions that were to implement the various laws.

PROMOTING NOMINAL WAGE RIGIDITY

In the area of wage bargaining two sets of countries can be distinguished. In Britain, Norway, and Sweden, trade unions were generally still strong enough to stabilize wages on their own once the change in macroregime had taken place. The acceptance of price stabilization as an economic policy goal in these countries simply implied that the state stopped its efforts to undermine the unions' bargaining power. In Sweden, the social democratic government changed the guidelines for the SAK's unemployment policies so that they would no longer exert downward pressure on wages. The SAK was now directed to pay wages at market levels, and it was no longer permitted to direct unemployed workers to firms that were boycotted by the unions. In addition, unemployment benefits now became available for all the unemployed whereas under the previous system they had covered only about 50 percent. In Norway, compulsory unemployment insurance was introduced by the DNA government in 1935, and in Britain, the national government reversed Ramsay MacDonald's cuts in unemployment benefits in 1934.

In the Netherlands and Germany, where trade unions had traditionally been weaker, as in the other three countries, and where the depression had been much more severe, the state actually moved to strengthen the wage bargaining position of labor. Moreover, such intervention found the tacit consent of the business community.

Dutch prime minister Colijn reversed his policy of promoting downward wage adjustment in 1937 with a law that enabled the minister of social affairs to make collective agreements between unions and employers also binding on nonunion members in the whole sector concerned. The unions had campaigned for such a law ever since 1918, but fierce resistance of employers and the government's emphasis on reducing wage costs allowed for little progress. Why, then, did the government and employers change their mind in the late thirties? The Cartel Law of 1935 made it difficult for the state and employers to keep resisting a similar arrangement in the labor market. Yet, apart from considerations of social fairness the law also answered an economic need. Falling nominal wages exerted a severe strain on cartel agreements, as individual firms could obtain an advantage by reducing their wage costs. Since unions were too weak to ensure wage discipline, also employers could now see the advantage of legislation. Indeed, one of the arguments used most often in support of the law of 1937 was that it protected employers from unfair competition. Moreover, it was pointed out that the law was going to be used to raise wages and that preventing downward wage competition was beneficial, since the level of effective demand was too low.[108]

It might seem rather misplaced to claim that the Nazi regime actually strengthened the wage bargaining power of labor. The NSDAP was extremely hostile toward labor while being rather more sympathetic toward business. One of its first acts was to destroy organized labor. The Communist Party was the first target. Its chairman, Ernst Thälmann, was arrested on March 3, 1933, and five days later the parliament seats of the party were annulled. In March 1933, security forces and police occupied trade union offices. On May 2, 1933, the ADGB and the white-collar AfA (Allgemeiner freier Angestelltenbund) trade

Table 4.7. *Gross wages, Germany, 1928–36*

Annual Averages	Gross Wage Income				Cost of Living
	Nominal		Real		
	Hourly	Weekly	Hourly	Weekly	
1929	129.5	128.2	104.7	103.6	123.7
1930	125.8	118.1	105.7	99.2	119.0
1931	116.3	103.9	106.4	95.1	109.3
1932	97.3	85.8	100.7	88.5	96.9
1933	94.6	87.7	99.8	92.5	94.8
1934	97.0	94.1	99.7	96.7	97.3
1935	98.4	96.4	99.6	97.6	98.8

Note: 1936 = 100.
Source: Siegel 1982: 104.

unions were effectively destroyed by the NSDAP. After some months of terror, the SPD was declared illegal on June 22, 1933.

The NSDAP's hostility toward labor has led to the interpretation that its economic policies aimed to bring about a radical drop in real wages. Nevertheless, the figures for real hourly wages in Table 4.7 do not bear out this contention. Real hourly wages rose slightly from 1929 to 1931, but declined significantly in 1932. During the first three years of the Nazi regime, they remained virtually unchanged. Real weekly wages fell steadily from 1929 to 1933, reflecting a reduction in hours worked per week. During the first three years of the Nazi regime, the real weekly wage increased continuously.

The real wage cuts that took place during the Great Depression therefore occurred before the coming to power of Hitler. Moreover, in contrast to what standard economic theory claims, real wages are not really a good indicator of the bargaining strength of the unions. Wage contracts are negotiated not in terms of baskets of goods but in money terms, and because trade unions do not set the price level, they cannot directly control the real wage. Given the radical increase in unemployment and Brüning's deflationary policies, it would be difficult to argue that the years 1929–31 witnessed a strengthening of the trade unions. Indeed, if one looks at nominal hourly wages, the variable over which unions have a direct influence, one sees a rather significant drop. During 1929–31, deflation simply outpaced nominal wage reductions.[109] Increasing real wages were a symptom of a deflationary constellation, and as long as deflation continued, investment would continue to collapse. It was exactly this cause of the depression that the Nazis removed.

Hitler's law on labor market relations of May 19, 1933, replaced wage bargaining with a so-called board of trustees, which was to unilaterally determine wage contracts. In contrast to the collective agreements of the Weimar Republic, the wage decrees of the board of trustees were conceived as floors; that is, employers were allowed to pay higher but not lower wages. In addition, firms with more than twenty employees were required to create a works council that was to have the right to take the employer to court if he or she paid wages below those decreed by the trustees. The system of labor trustees thus institutionalized and enforced binding sectorwide wage levels. This, however, stood in sharp contrast with the previous years. Under Chancellor Franz von Papen, employers were actively encouraged to underbid the existing wage contracts. In contrast to Brüning's policies of lowering wages by decree, the board of trustees, during the first years of the regime, prolonged existing contracts. As Table 4.7 shows, this system succeeded in stabilizing wages. Hourly nominal wages, after a radical decline during the later years of the Weimar Republic, started to move upward after 1933.[110] For weekly wages this trend is more pronounced as a result of an increase in hours worked per week.

The official justification for the law of May 19, 1933, was that a board of trustees was necessary in order to "avoid the social and economic dangers which might result from an abuse of power by the employers."[111] Nevertheless, the new system was not unwelcome to employers. As Arthur Schweitzer (1964: 400–1) has argued:

> During the Depression declining wage rates enabled employers to reduce their prices. Price competition disintegrated cartels, since some of the members became outsiders. In small business, the level of prices shifted downward for whole industries when independent unions were suppressed, and wage rates tended to fall to the level of unemployment compensation. Many employers suddenly discovered that unionized wage rates had put a floor under the prices of their products. . . . Thus, instead of realizing an advantage from the abolition of unions producers experienced extreme price competition in product markets.

The massive unemployment of the last years of the Weimar Republic, plus Brüning's wage decrees, had already severely weakened the unions. The victory of the NSDAP removed the last dikes. The result might easily have been more deflation and increased pressure on business cartels. The system of sectorally binding wage decrees hence fitted well with employers' policies in the cartelized sector. The attitudes of employers in the small noncartelized sectors were more similar to the views found, for example, in Swedish dairy farming. In these sectors, employers lacked the ability to stabilize prices on a voluntary basis. But because they saw "cutthroat competition" as the main threat, they exerted pressure on the state to enforce price stabilization on unwilling members.[112] The situation changed radically around 1936 when full employment was reached. The main task of the trustees now was to prevent an escalation of wages. From this point on there is no doubt that the Nazi regime significantly weakened labor's bargaining strength.

In sum, it seems hard to understand the economics of Nazism in the traditional distributional framework. The enmity of the NSDAP toward organized labor was political rather than economic in nature. Both the SPD and the trade unions had been the staunchest defenders of the hated Weimar Republic. In March 1933, the SPD voted against Hitler's enabling act. Moreover, a dictatorial movement like the NSDAP by its very nature cannot tolerate different worldviews. While it was an urgent concern for the NSDAP to eliminate labor as the most powerful rival political organization, it was an equally urgent concern to gain the allegiance of the broad majority of workers. Partly because of the lessons he had drawn from the collapse of the empire in 1918, Hitler was very anxious not to provoke labor unrest with a dramatic decrease of living standards. Moreover, for some time the NSDAP feared a general strike, like the one that had doomed the Kapp-Lüttwitz putsch of 1920. The deflationary constellation of the Great Depression allowed the NSDAP's dual policy of destroying the political organizations of the labor movement while trying to gain the allegiance, or at least tacit toleration, of the working class to succeed.

CEMENTING THE NEW REGIME I: CHEAP MONEY

Instead of being abandoned by direct political decision, the commitment to the gold standard and the quantity theory was hollowed out from the inside through the spread of microeconomic policies to halt deflation. The outer shell instead was smashed by international financial markets, and in some cases by the threat of the collapse of the domestic banking system. Only after the currencies had been floating for some time did most governments find the courage to employ monetary policies in order to stimulate growth.

THE COLLAPSE OF THE GOLD STANDARD

The mounting conflict between the unwillingness (1) to abandon the parity and (2) to pursue consistent policies required to defend the parity could not fail to arouse the suspicion of financial markets. The first victim was sterling, which was forced off gold in September 21, 1931, after intense capital outflows. Worn out by a decade of crisis, the BoE declined to mobilize its defenses and finally let the pound float. Initially, Norway and Sweden were determined to maintain their parity. Due to massive capital outflows the foreign exchange reserves of the Swedish Riksbank shrank rapidly from SEK 127 million at the end of August to SEK 38 million on September 21.[113] In order to continue its defense of the krona the Riksbank tried to raise a foreign loan but failed. On September 27, the currency was floated.

In Norway, foreign exchange reserves dwindled as a result of speculation on an impending depreciation.[114] And the Norwegian central bank was as hapless as the Riksbank in its attempt to obtain foreign funds. Immediately following the devaluation of the pound, Norges Bank conducted talks with representatives from government, parliament, and business. Among all these groups there was a strong feeling that the krone should follow the pound. The Norwegian association of bankers shared this view. Although the government still was not willing to instruct the bank to float, Norges Bank realized that even tighter monetary policies to defend the currency were by now politically impossible. Once the Swedish (and Danish) decision to float became known, Norges Bank felt it had no other choice but to follow suit.

The Netherlands were rather unfortunate not to have shared in the distrust with which international financial markets eyed the declarations of the British, Norwegian, and Swedish governments to maintain the parity. Based on its long-term reputation as a hard currency and the domestic political stability of the Netherlands, the guilder instead became a safe haven for hot money flows. In the week following September 21, 1931, private capital inflows swelled the gold reserves of the Nederlandsche Bank from roughly NLG 450 million in the second quarter of 1931 to about NLG 900 million by the end of the year and to more than NLG 1 billion by the third quarter of 1932.[115] As international financial markets failed to present the Dutch with a fait accompli, it was up to the government to decide whether to follow the example of other countries or to intensify domestic deflation. However, neither the government nor the opposition could muster the courage to abandon their self-imposed external constraint.

Prime Minister Colijn of the Protestant ARP had no doubt that the postwar inflation had been caused by the government's attempt to buy social peace by means of public spending.[116] Accordingly, balanced budgets and the discipline of the gold standard were indispensable. Nor could the competitive advantage that other countries had gained by floating be a reason for the Netherlands to follow suit. Colijn was convinced that inflation would follow on the heels of depreciation, thereby undoing any competitive advantage. Moreover, he had great confidence in the ability of the Netherlands to depress the domestic price level.

But even after it became clear that not inflation but recovery accompanied floating, abandoning the parity was not seriously contemplated. After Belgium left the gold standard on April 1, 1935, the Catholic minister of economic affairs advocated a similar step for the guilder, but he failed to obtain a majority in the cabinet and resigned. In his answer of April 15, 1935, Colijn maintained that abandoning gold would create "complete chaos in the monetary field."[117] In the end, it would take almost five years from the British devaluation before the guilder was cut loose from gold. On the night of Sunday, September 26, 1936, the Dutch government finally gave in, one day after the French and Swiss devaluations had left the guilder as the only remaining currency on gold.

Germany never officially abandoned the gold parity. But since the burdens of deflation soon became intolerable, the refusal to float the currency meant that the gold standard policies had to be abandoned by means of another route, namely, by administratively isolating German financial markets from foreign pressures. By 1931, the economic crisis had reached such proportions that German business was not only undertaking no more new investment projects but even failed to compensate for the depreciation of the capital stock. The massive wave of debt defaults, which accompanied such a contraction, created suspicions with respect to the solidity of German banking. The Reichsbank did its best to add to the problems of the German banks.

The increasing distrust of domestic as well as foreign depositors put the Reichsbank under double pressure. On the one hand, the increased liquidity preference implied a reduction of the velocity of money and a higher demand for cash. On the other hand, capital outflows reduced the bank's gold and foreign exchange reserves. Increasing demand for notes and decreasing foreign exchange reserves soon threatened to push the gold and foreign exchange coverage of the note issue to below the 40 percent stipulated in the Dawes Plan of August 1924.

The sensible thing for the Reichsbank to do in the spring and summer of 1931 would have been to restrict capital outflows and ignore the 40 percent limit. But, the 40 percent minimum was sacrosanct because it was interpreted as the symbol of Germany's commitment to prevent another hyperinflation. Rather than acting as lender of last resort, the Reichsbank therefore resorted to quantitative credit restrictions in the midst of a major financial crisis. The result was a run on the banks that forced the government to announce a banking holiday, on July 14, 1931, that was to last, with different degrees of severity, to September 5, 1931. At the same time, heavy exchange controls were imposed. Starting on July 15, transactions involving foreign currencies, and later also in assets denominated in foreign currencies, were centralized at the Reichsbank. As a result, the reichsmark de facto became an inconvertible currency. Moreover, in order not to drive the whole banking system into ruin, the Reichsbank was forced to abolish its credit restrictions. By December 31, 1931, the gold and exchange coverage of the note issue had dropped to 24.2 percent.[118]

However, abandoning the gold standard was not tantamount to establishing a new regime. The absence of an external constraint by itself could not force governments to abandon tight money. In the months following September 21, 1931, it seemed indeed that the floating of the currencies would not give rise to a reorientation of monetary policy. Rather than using their new freedom to relax monetary policies, governments and central banks saw a need for tight money in order to fight inflationary dragons.

On the same day the pound was floated, the BoE increased the bank rate sharply from 4.5 percent to 6 percent in order to counteract the expected inflation. MacDonald and the bank tried hard to create the impression that floating was a temporary expedient that soon would give way to a return to gold, albeit at a lower parity.[119] In Germany the desire to get rid of reparations added to the fear of inflation, preventing a clear break with the old regime. Notwithstanding the banking crisis, neither Brüning nor the Reichsbank was prepared to rethink the fundamentals of their economic policies. The experience of the hyperinflation was still too vivid to simply let the reichsmark float and make money cheap. Moreover, Brüning remained convinced that the only way to get rid of reparations was to pursue a tight policy that would clearly demonstrate Germany's inability to pay.

The sentiments in Scandinavia were not much different. Swedish finance minister Felix Hamrin declared right after the currency was floated that the new goal for monetary policy was "to safeguard the domestic purchasing power of the Swedish krona."[120] It would be tempting to interpret this as a break with the policy of deflation. In fact, the proclamation was intended to signal that inflation would not be tolerated. Even though microeconomic policies had sought to counteract deflation in individual product markets since 1930, the gold parity still appeared as the safeguard against runaway inflation. Accordingly, the proclamation of the goal of domestic price stability was accompanied by a significant increase in the discount rate from 6 percent to 8 percent, while the Riksbank asked commercial banks to exercise caution in their lending policies. At the same time, Hamrin declared that the krona would return to gold as soon as foreign conditions permitted. The Norwegian central bank followed the example of its neighbor with a similar declaration and the same increase in discount rates.

THE END OF THE QUANTITY THEORY

As the specter of inflation failed to show while the depression raged on, governments gradually came to reorient monetary policies in a more expansionary direction. If abandoning gold did not produce inflation, then perhaps the last remnant of the gold standard ideology, namely, the quantity theory, might also be abandoned without causing mayhem.

This change was clearest in Sweden. As inflation failed to materialize while the crisis progressed, deflation came to be seen as the crucial problem. Reflation was first proposed by the minister of finance in January 1932, but the matter was delegated to parliament's banking committee. The committee's report, which was submitted to the Riksdag in early May, contained a unanimous recommendation of a moderate reflation of the wholesale price level. In a complete reversal of the gold standard policy, it was now argued that the exchange rate should adjust to the desired development of the domestic price level.

Social democrats agreed. In an article in the newspaper *Social Demokraten*, Wigforss argued in November 1931 that a return to the gold parity would be unacceptable because it would require deflating the domestic price level and hence would lead to more unemployment, a weaker trade union and lower wages.[121] Five months later, right before the Riksdag debate about the banking committee's proposals, Wigforss argued in the same newspaper that, in view of the ongoing deflation, the program of moderately increasing the wholesale price level was also in the interests of the working class because it would help the economy recover without leading to a noticeable rise in consumer prices and, therefore, without causing real wage losses.[122]

Given the unanimous support in the banking committee, it was not surprising that parliament, in early May 1932, agreed to ask the Riksbank to reflate the wholesale price level. Different parties may have had different reasons to agree with this program. The conservatives may have hoped to reduce wages through reflation.[123] Social democrats instead argued that reflation of the wholesale price level would help the economy recover, while the stability of consumer prices would prevent wage cuts.[124]

While wholesale prices did indeed stop falling from June 1932 onward, a new price fall set in during the first six months of 1933. In the spring of 1932, the SAP government appointed a committee to look again at how monetary policy was best conducted. The committee reconfirmed the expansionary policy aimed at reflation. Gustav Cassel, one of Sweden's most famous economists and an advocate of deflation in the early twenties, now even suggested to help raise the price level by having the Riksbank finance the social democrats' public works program.

Because of the almost eight-year-long and rather painful struggle to return the Norwegian krone to gold, opposition against deflationary policies was perhaps more pronounced in Norway than in other countries. Central bank governor Rygg was well aware that once the currency was floated, the political tolerance for dear money would be slim. On October 8, the discount rate was lowered from 8 percent to 7 percent. Yet, initially Norges Bank tried to limit devaluation. During October, it intervened in foreign exchange markets to maintain a revaluation relative to sterling. In the face of opposition from, among others, business, this policy was abandoned by the end of the month. By the end of the year, the krone had devalued 10 percent relative to sterling. Until June 1933, when the krone, together with the krona, was tied to sterling, Norges Bank did not attempt to stabilize the exchange rate.

When DNA prime minister Johan Nygaardsvold, in his inaugural declaration in 1935, promised that the government would "as long as it stands in its power defend the economic life in the country from swings in the value of money," it was the danger of deflation that was primarily on his mind. One year later the social democratic government awarded Norges Bank the right to conduct open market operations. At the same time the upper limit on Norges Bank note issue was raised by 30 percent from NOK 250 million to NOK 325 million. According to Hodne (1983: 95), the latter decision contributed more to the recovery from the depression than the alleged Keynesian deficit spending.

Despite his dogged defense of the pound as prime minister of a Labour government, the switch to cheap money under MacDonald's national government was marked by less hesitation than elsewhere. That restrictive monetary policies might seriously depress economic activity was well known to British policy makers even under the gold standard. Ever since the resurrection of the gold standard, the conflict between the domestic and international requirements of monetary policies stood out clearly. Winston Churchill, Chancellor of the Exchequer in the second Baldwin government, protested against every increase of the bank rate. Labour's Chancellor Snowden equally was convinced of the detrimental effects of high interest rates. Yet as long as the consequences of cutting the pound loose from gold were considered potentially more disastrous, opposition to dear money could not become politically effective. But after September 21, 1931, British conservatives acted decisively to implement a regime of cheap money in which exchange rate and monetary policies came to be judged primarily with respect to their effects on domestic growth and employment, and in which the responsibility for such policies reverted to the government instead of the BoE.

Whereas sterling had been weak after September 21, by early 1932 the pound was under strong upward pressure. The government's wish to prevent a strong appreciation of the pound prompted the creation in mid-1932 of the Exchange Equalization Account (EEA), a treasury-directed fund for managing the exchange rate. Although the BoE performed the interventions, the EEA signified a clear break with previous policies as it was now established that (1) the exchange rate had to be managed in view of the requirements of the domestic economy, and (2) exchange rate policy was the responsibility of the government. However, as exchange rate management constituted the core of monetary management, formation of the EEA effectively meant that interest rate management now also became the domain of the government. Despite the reluctance of Governor Norman, who as of February 1932 would have preferred an appreciation of sterling,[125] the government pushed for and obtained a low bank rate. Between February and June 1932, the bank rate was lowered from 6 percent to 2 percent, and it would remain there until 1939. With the pound freed from gold, the government now also set out to bring about a reflation of the domestic price level. By March 1932, the treasury was advocating a rise in wholesale prices.

Unfortunately, German politicians could not muster the flexibility Mac-Donald displayed after September 21 in time to prevent the rise of Hitler. The economic failure of Brüning's deflation policies was preordained. The political victory of Nazism was not. In the midst of the Great Depression, German politicians eventually discovered that a consistent policy of price stabilization was the only solution. As the experience of other countries showed, such policies provided the opportunity to start healing the deep rifts between labor, business, and agriculture that the gold standard had provoked. Yet, in a polity so poisoned by mutual suspicion as Weimar was, it proved impossible to muster enough support for such a policy program.

Starting with the collapse of the banking system in the summer of 1931,

Brüning gradually lost industry's confidence. In the summer of 1932, he was replaced with Chancellor von Papen owing to the opposition of industry and agriculture to yet another emergency decree. The lesson von Papen had drawn from Brüning's policies was that more expansionary rather than more restrictive macroeconomic policies were required. He immediately implemented the RM 135 million work-creation program that the Brüning government had drafted in its last days and added another RM 170 million in early September. Of more importance was that von Papen also made a cautious start with more expansionary monetary policies, although it testifies to the strength of the taboo of money creation that he chose to do so more or less covertly. Von Papen issued a total of RM 1.5 billion in coupons that business could use to pay taxes in the years 1934–38. Since the tax coupons could be deposited at banks and were rediscountable at the Reichsbank, they were in fact a form of money. Reichsbank president Luther complied because, although he did not admit it, he could no longer be sure that the government was willing to respect the independence of the bank.[126] The Reichsbank had gained political independence under pressures from the Allies, who wanted to safeguard reparations payments. The Laussanne conference of July 8, 1932, effectively ended reparations, thereby again making the position of the bank a matter of national politics only. After the fall of Brüning, conservative newspapers were openly speculating about the need to replace Luther with someone who was willing to pursue a more relaxed policy. Notwithstanding Luther's explicit request, von Papen refused to include a guarantee of the independence of the Reichsbank in his speech on the end of reparations.

At the same time, however, von Papen attempted to reduce unemployment by speeding up the fall in wages. Although he did not lower wages by decree, he granted business the right to pay wages below the level agreed in collective agreements as long as the total wage sum of the firms remained the same. In this von Papen tried to directly couple lower wages with more employment. In addition, the level of unemployment benefits was reduced and employee contributions increased. The ADGB and the SPD, not surprisingly, considered von Papen's policy an attempt to shift the burden from business to labor.[127]

In November 1932, von Papen was replaced by General Kurt von Schleicher. It was under von Schleicher that German politics stumbled upon the basic recipe with which social accommodation was being brought about in other countries: stabilization of prices, including wages, and cheap money supported by some fiscal expansion. Under von Schleicher German economic policies abandoned the last remnant of the gold standard ideology, namely, that wage cuts were a precondition for increased employment. Von Schleicher certainly was not sympathetic toward the SPD or toward the idea of democracy. Instead, he had clear sympathies for the Strasser wing of the NSDAP. Yet by giving up the policy of wage deflation, he hoped to stabilize his government by seeking the support of the ADGB. Here, then, was a first glimpse of the broad political coalition that, in principle, it was possible to organize on the basis of reflationary policies. Politically, however, it was impossible for the ADGB to support a Prussian general who was so clearly hostile to the SPD. Without the necessary political legitimacy to exploit and develop the new regime, the von Schleicher government had to be short-lived. Within two months Adolf Hitler took over the chancellorship.

With Hitler came the decisive regime transformation in monetary policies. He immediately replaced Luther with former Reichsbank president Hjalmar Schacht. During the twenties Schacht had preached the gospel of the gold standard. By 1933, he apparently had completely abandoned the quantity theory. Reflecting on the Reichsbank's role in the Nazi recovery, Schacht (1950: 57, 60) wrote:

> Money is not capital but it can be transformed into capital at any time. . . . The whole automatism of the banknote system laid down by classical economists was found to be in contradiction to the real process of economic evolution. One simply could not leave a whole economy without financial and currency supply, merely because a previous currency theory had contrived such an 'automatism'. That is why the Reichsbank disregarded traditional theory and spurred on production, by generating credit in the form of newly created money, in a broadminded way. Its success proved that it was right. There was no question of any inflationary effect, for the quantity of goods increased so rapidly that it was equivalent to the increased volume of money put into circulation.[128]

In addition, while Luther still had complained bitterly that the budget deficit under Von Papen might require the Reichsbank to extend loans to the government, the Reichsbank now did not have any such qualms.

In sum, the deflation of the Great Depression cleared the way for a radical, but gradual, reinterpretation of the responsibilities of monetary policies. In a bout of political amnesia, most political parties, between the end of the depression and the late forties came to forget that, a decade before, they had clamored for a strong central bank to tie their hand to the mast in order to restore discipline to an inflationary economy. If the absence of the gold standard did not mean inflation, then the policy of defending gold apparently had unnecessarily depressed the economy. In many cases, central bankers now came to be considered the culprits who had sacrificed the prosperity of the economy in order to serve the idol of gold. As a result, central bankers lost much of their independence. Whether legally independent or not, the absolute priority given to a fixed parity meant that central banks necessarily enjoyed a high degree of power and independence. The floating of the currencies implied that much of the political initiative in monetary policy would return to governments. More important, the new interpretation of monetary policies required less independent central banks. Monetary policies again were seen to exert a powerful influence over growth and employment. If monetary policies, however, implied trade-offs between growth and inflation, then such decisions had to be taken by governments instead of independent central bankers.[129] Accordingly, independent central banks came to be considered as a foreign element in a democratic polity. As an expression of this new conviction, Norges Bank, the Bank of England, and the Nederlandsche Bank were nationalized shortly after 1945.

CEMENTING THE NEW REGIME II: AFTER WORLD WAR II

The end of World War II brought the political success social democrats had already expected after 1918. The Scandinavian labor governments of the thirties no longer appeared as exceptions but as the beginning of a decisive political trend. The Great Depression had apparently shown that liberal economic management was bankrupt, and this could not fail to have a positive effect on social democrats. Even more important for the success of the social democratic program was that the other major parties, if only in order not to make their economic policy program seem hopelessly behind the times, came to accept a good deal of it.

Yet, the end of World War II did not bring a change of regime. In 1945, the economic policy objectives of governments were rather similar to what they had been in 1918 and for largely similar reasons. Stimulating production enjoyed the utmost priority. If anything, the larger scale of destruction made this goal more urgent now. Moreover, with the experience of the interwar period in mind, governments were determined not to let economic recession threaten political accommodation. Alan S. Milward (1984: 446) summarizes it succinctly: "High and increasing output, increasing foreign trade, full employment, industrialization and modernization had become in different countries, as a result of the experience of the 1930s and the war, inescapable policy choices, because governments could find no other basis for political consensus."

Stimulating growth required expansionary macroeconomic strategies. But as after 1918, cheap money rather than budget deficits were to be the main instrument. Interest rates were to be kept low in order to stimulate private investment, facilitate the repayment of the large stock of government debt, and counteract the recession that many politicians feared would follow the postwar restocking boom within a year or two. Keynesianism, with its emphasis on fiscal policy and consumption, simply did not address the problems governments expected to be confronted with after the war. Instead of the prioritization of consumption implicit in a Keynesian strategy, governments felt that the first priority in a devastated Europe should be to rebuild the capital stock. Furthermore, given the scarcity of convertible currencies – primarily U.S. dollars – imports of consumption goods had to be curtailed to the benefit of investment goods.

LABOR IN POWER AND CHEAP MONEY

The British general elections of the summer of 1945 produced a landslide victory for Labour. For the first time since 1931, a Labour government, headed by Clement Attlee, would hold office again, but this time backed by a solid parliamentary majority. In response to the disaster of 1931, Labour had seriously rethought its economic policy positions. The annual congress of 1934 and Labour's Immediate Program (1937) rejected deflation and the gold standard and came to advocate stabilization of wholesale prices.[130] More important for postwar policy was the document *Full Employment and Financial Policy* (1944), written by Labour's economic spokesman, Hugh Dalton. Interest rates were to be kept low permanently so as to facilitate reconstruction and maintain full employment. Exchange controls were required to keep them low.

Despite the monetary overhang, Dalton, now Chancellor of the Exchequer, in 1945 therefore set out to depress nominal interest rates below prewar levels. Except for the last two, the reasons he gave for this cheap money policy were quite similar to those that led Lloyd George to spurn dear money during 1918–19:

> To save public expenditure on interest, to improve the distribution of income, to encourage investment and to make sure of full-employment. . . . I wished to help the local authorities to keep down the cost of housing programs, and thus keep down rents. I wished, most of all, to help the local authorities in the 'blitzed cities', both by special grants and by cheap loans. And I wished to prepare the way for the series of nationalisation bills which, during this parliament, we intended to pass. The higher the national credit, the lower the rate of interest, the less the annual compensation charge corresponding to a given capital value.[131]

The SAP captured 50 percent of the second chamber seats in 1944, although this constituted a setback from the absolute majority it had held since the 1940 election. In Sweden, too, stimulating private investment with the help of low interest rates was a core economic policy. In addition, low interest rates were considered crucial for the success of the SAP's program of radical expansion of affordable housing.[132] Accordingly, the Riksbank kept the discount rate at 2.5 percent and the yield on long-term government debt at 3 percent. An increase in discount rates did not occur until the Korean War boom. Rapidly increasing activity, however, exerted upward pressure on interest rates. If it were to keep interest rates low, the Riksbank would have to insert liquidity into the economy, and it did so by pursuing state debt. Between 1946 and 1948, its holdings of state debt increased from SEK 1 billion to SEK 3 billion.[133] When Ivar Rooth, the governor of the Riksbank, insisted that inflationary pressures should be combated by cuts in public spending and higher interest rates instead, he was made to step down in December 1948.[134]

The Norwegian labor party gained an absolute parliamentary majority in the 1945 election. Like the SAP, the DNA stressed low interest rates as an important instrument for bringing about more income equality. Low interest rates would mean low income for rentiers and would keep housing rents low. In 1945, Norwegian authorities then decided to lower the yield on state bonds to 2.5 percent. Norges Bank's discount rate was set at the same level and stayed there for the next five years.

Dutch social democrats were less successful. In order to create a true peoples' party that could also attract voters with religious backgrounds, the SDAP was dissolved and the Partij van de Arbeid (PvdA) created in 1946. The PvdA in effect was a merger of the large SDAP with the liberal and Protestant splinters VDB (Vrijzinnig Democratische Bond) and CDU (Christen-Democratische Unie). Yet the effort to break through traditional barriers failed. Although the PvdA captured twenty-nine seats in the 1946 elections to the second chamber, compared to twenty-three for the SDAP in the last prewar election of 1937, this was less than the share of the three constituent parties had been. Nevertheless, the PvdA broke out of its political isolation as it formed a coalition government with the Catholic party in which it occupied the crucial positions of finance and economic affairs.

The PvdA's minister of finance, Pieter Lieftinck, shared Dalton's general outlook with respect to interest rate policy. High interest rates would reduce investment. Given that the state debt amounted to NLG 22.2 billion, of which NLG 16.4 billion was in short-term floating debt, they would exert unacceptable pressures on the state budget. Moreover, Lieftinck argued, at a time when the government was pursuing a policy of strict wage moderation, rentiers should not be allowed an increase in income.[135] Accordingly, the government tried to keep interest rates within the range of 3–3.5 percent during the first years after the war. Although undesirable in principle, Lieftinck also held that some monetary financing of the budget deficit was inevitable, given the sorry state of the tax collection service and the urgent needs of the country. He even maintained that the monetary financing that did take place contributed to the recovery of the country as it allowed for more imports of capital goods.[136]

WARTIME REGULATIONS AND THE MICROECONOMIC CONTROL OF INFLATION

Given the determination to pursue cheap money policies, one might have expected a repetition of the post-1918 inflation. The restocking boom could easily lead to tight labor markets and buoyant demand, thereby setting off an inflationary spiral. The monetary overhang looming over the economy, especially in countries that had been under German occupation, assured that sufficient fuel for this inflation would be available. In order to keep interest rates low, central banks might have to provide additional fuel. Current account deficits plus low interest rates might provoke exchange rate depreciation. Even without a wage-price spiral under way, the sudden freeing of the monetary overhang could contribute to widespread speculation and price rises. Finally, the low interest rate policy might be compromised by excessive capital outflows if other countries pursued more restrictive policies.

If a cumulative inflationary dynamic had indeed reemerged, policy choices that seemed inescapable in order to achieve political consensus would have been reversed, as in the early twenties. In such an event, politicians and social scientists, with the quantity theory in hand, no doubt would have explained that a strong determination to grow cannot overcome economic realities, but only produces inflation. Social democrats, no doubt, would have lamented the failure to mobilize sufficient political resources, the betrayal of its leaders, international financial markets, or the inevitability of crises under capitalism. The right of the political spectrum no doubt would have explained that it was the irresponsibility of trade unions and labor governments that had caused inflation. Yet, nothing of the sort happened after 1945.

In principle, four different strategies could be pursued to avoid inflation:

1. The central banks could adopt a restrictive policy so as to reduce the money supply and stimulate holding liquidity.
2. Governments could try to stimulate the production of goods in order for an increasing GDP to absorb the excess liquidity.
3. The existing currency could be declared invalid and replaced by a new one.
4. Production, consumption, wages, and financial transactions could be subjected to rigid controls. This last strategy implied maintaining and even extending much of the wartime control apparatus.

The first strategy obviously was in conflict with the economic policy philosophy of the time. The second alternative had failed already after 1918. In occupied Germany the Allies pursued the third option as the reichsmark was replaced by the deutsche mark (DM) in 1948. Although currency reform obviated the need for a period of sharply restrictive monetary policies with all its consequences for the real economy, for countries other than Germany such a solution did not seem attractive because it implied a radical change in the structure of wealth holding due to the destruction of accumulated monetary assets. This left the fourth strategy.

In contrast to 1919–20, there was no bonfire of controls after 1945. The maintenance of widespread controls for a transitional period enjoyed consensus. The experience of 1918, when rapid deregulation had undermined recovery, informed the outlook not just of social democrats but also of liberals and conservatives. Although the latter may have desired more rapid deregulation than social democratic governments were willing to undertake, the need for extensive controls was not contested.[137] After 1945, trade unions, too, were convinced of the need for extensive regulations.

The Labour Party's document, *Full Employment and Financial Policy*, argued that subsidies to consumer goods in combination with direct controls on investment, prices, and finance were to be maintained in order to avoid inflation. These proposals were echoed in the government's white paper on employment policy (1944).[138] Likewise, the SAP committee on postwar economic policies concluded in 1943 that public regulation of prices, imports, and foreign exchange had to be maintained in order to prevent inflationary pressures after the war. In fact, price controls were even extended in 1947. The new generation of Norwegian economists, who would have a decisive impact on the DNA's policy, were equally convinced that the best way to avoid an inflationary spiral was to maintain extensive regulations,[139] as were Dutch social democrats and Catholics.

The direct regulations employed pertained to four main areas. First, comprehensive price controls, which had emerged during the war, were to be maintained. In Norway, for example, the law of May 8, 1945, instituted a "price directorate" with far-reaching competencies concerning prices and production. In occupied West Germany, the Allies decreed a general price stop at the end of the war. For consumer goods, postwar rationing systems were also kept in place. In addition, many governments resorted to subsidization of basic consumption goods in order to prevent a wage-price spiral. Second, strict licensing of investment was to prevent excessive demand for investment goods. Third, European governments felt that devaluation was not likely to solve the balance-of-payments problem, but rather would create an additional source of inflation. Sweden, Norway, and the Netherlands maintained their exchange rate with the pound, whereas the pound was kept stable with respect to the dollar. Instead, strict rationing of imports was used to contain trade balance problems. And in order to avoid disruptive capital flows, European currencies were protected by a tight wall of exchange controls. Apart from the abortive attempt with sterling in 1948, currencies did not become fully convertible until the late fifties. Sweden, which due to its intact productive apparatus did not suffer from trade balance problems, even decided to revalue the currency in the summer of 1946 in order to combat inflation.

Finally, efforts to moderate nominal wage increases constituted a central element in the policy of preventing inflation. Formal income policies were only pursued in the Netherlands and Norway. After the experience of the Nazi regime, both German unions and employers strongly rejected any form of state intervention in bargaining. In Britain and Sweden, the TUC and the LO considered direct government intervention in wage bargaining a threat to their role. Yet, despite the absence of formal tripartite income policies, governments could count on the support of the trade unions. Obviously, the fact that social democrats were the governing party in most countries greatly facilitated a policy of voluntary wage restraint. Coming from a government that represented the interest of labor, appeals for nominal wage restraint carried much more weight.

British Labour prime minister Attlee initially relied on exhortation to convince the TUC that a policy of wage moderation was crucial. In the spring of 1946, the National Joint Advisory Council, a wartime tripartite body, was revived as a discussion forum for wage development. Foreshadowing the corporatist exchange logic that was to become of crucial importance in many countries during the next decades, in the fall of 1947 the TUC agreed to a voluntary wage freeze in exchange for a freeze on incomes from profits and rents; food subsidies; and a levy on investment income above £2,000 per year. To further strengthen the element of equality, Attlee pressed the British business association to accept a voluntary limit on dividends. Finally, the TUC suggested exemption for the lowest wage groups and for wage increase, which would restore established wage differentials.[140] On March 24 of the next year, a majority of TUC delegates again voted in favor of a wage freeze, and this policy was reconfirmed during the next two years.

The Dutch and Norwegian governments, in contrast, came to occupy a central position in wage bargaining during the first postwar decades. The so-called Dutch guided wage policy, which started in 1945, basically implied that wages were set by the minister of social affairs after having consulted the tripartite Socioeconomic Council (SER, Sociaal Economische Raad). In 1945 wages were set at 115 percent of their 1941 level and subsequently frozen until 1948, when an increase was granted. The Norwegian government froze wages for one year after the cessation of hostilities. In the 1946 wage bargaining round, the DNA, and in particular finance minister Erik Brofoss, pressured LO to moderate wages so as not to jeopardize economic recovery. In view of increasing inflation and balance-of-payments problems the government in the summer of 1947 suggested a wage stop, and the LO agreed.[141] Up to 1952, wage bargaining took place at the national level between the LO and the NAF. In addition, all agreements were subject to permanent compulsory arbitration by the wage arbitration board, an independent body of experts appointed by the government.

IDEOLOGICAL ADJUSTMENTS TO THE NEW REGIME

The ideological outcome of the Great Depression was to establish the hegemony of social democratic ideas in economic policy making. Whereas the need to combat the post-1918 inflation confronted social democracy with a fundamental ideological dilemma, the deflation of the depression created a similar problem for conservatives and liberals.[142] As they had defined a strategy of giving priority to a fixed exchange rate, and relegating the responsibility for growth and employment to the microlevel as laissez-faire, they could not embrace the (correct) argument that the new regime constituted a change in policy assignments and goals rather than a change from noninterventionism to interventionism. Accordingly, the policy changes of the Great Depression had to appear as the bankruptcy of liberalism. Apparently, an "automatic" monetary policy tied to the defense of the parity was not a precondition for but an obstacle to prosperity. As conservatives and liberals found that they had to heed the call from agriculture and business for price stabilization, it became rather difficult to differentiate their views from the social democratic position that a market economy required extensive political steering. Moreover, once it had become accepted that price stabilization was a necessity, it became difficult to argue that this principle applied everywhere except in the case of wage bargaining.

Nevertheless, it would be wrong to claim that the depression of the thirties confirmed the original social democratic analysis. Instead, social democrats had to perform a series of reinterpretations before they found a satisfactory way of integrating the experience of the depression into their overall ideological framework. In their desperation to find policies against unemployment that could muster enough political support so as to be actually implemented, social democrats came to deemphasize the question of property rights and rediscovered the topic of fiscal stimulation, in the early thirties. Surprisingly, conservatives and liberals seemed to be moving in an opposite direction. The market regulations introduced by conservatives and liberals actually caused social democrats to take up the question of property rights again. The result was a series of plans for far-reaching political control of the microeconomy, but this time within the overall framework of a market economy. But as the new macroregime removed the causes of deflation, social democrats had to find out after 1945 that their new programs lacked political support. Apparently, the question of property rights had to be downplayed again. The end result was that the social democrats came to embrace some form of Keynesianism as their economic policy ideology in the fifties.

THE REEMERGENCE OF PLANNING

Given the urgently felt need for crisis measures that could command political support outside social democratic circles, the result of the Great Depression might have been to make the idea of microlevel planning even more irrelevant than it already was during the twenties. That the opposite happened was in large measure due to the reaction of conservative and liberal parties to the depression. Given the rapid spread of price stabilization arrangements, frequently at the behest of business and agriculture, it seemed to social democrats that the issue of planning now had been placed on the political agenda. All of a sudden it appeared that views of a planned economy could be given a concrete interpretation and that, therefore, the dualism between practical policies and the conviction of the need for a planned economy that had plagued parties throughout the twenties could be solved.

Although they subsequently came to be interpreted as the essence of the new policies, social democrats came to see the fiscal stimulation packages of the thirties as merely a first step in taming the capitalist system. Expansionary macropolicies had been necessary in the depression to combat the crisis. The longer-run task was to prevent future crises, and that could only be achieved through strongly increased public planning of production and investment. Accordingly, after 1945 most social democratic parties saw it as their historical task to bring to its logical conclusion what had started in the thirties, namely, to subject production and consumption to far-reaching public planning.[143]

In the Netherlands, the interventionist policies of Christian Democratic prime minister Colijn shifted the discussion in the SDAP away from the socialist version of laissez-faire, which argued that it was futile to try and cure the evils of capitalism within the system, toward plans for reforms within the system.[144] The shift in perspective from socialization to planning took place between the publication of the pamphlet *Socialisatie* (1933) and the *Plan van de Arbeid* (1935). The former report was a revised version of the 1920 socialization report and, after the disappointing election results of 1933, came to be seen by the SDAP leadership as lacking concrete proposals for combating the crisis. The *Plan van de Arbeid* distinguished clearly between short-term (macroeconomic) crisis measures to combat the depression and the introduction of far-reaching planning as the only long-term solution to the problems of capitalism.[145]

After 1945, the concept of planning was moved to the forefront in the PvdA's policy discussions. In an attempt to merge social democratic and Catholic views, Hein Vos, one of the authors of the *Plan van de Arbeid* and minister of economic affairs from 1945 to 1946, presented a blueprint for a corporatist organization of the Dutch economy. The economy was to be organized in roughly three dozen vertically integrated tripartite boards, so called PBOs, that were to determine investment, production, prices, and wages. The state was to have a decisive influence in these boards as it would have the right to postpone or nullify their decisions. At the national level, the tripartite SER was to advise the government with respect to its social and economic policies.

The Norwegian DNA's crisis proposals of the thirties clearly distinguished between short-term macroeconomic measures and long-term planning.[146] Because the core weakness of capitalism was its uncoordinated character, planning was necessary to solve the unemployment problem. Yet, this view, which became the official party analysis, was quite different from previous views. In the twenties socialization of the economy had been considered the necessary first step toward a planned economy. From the early thirties onward, it was argued that planning could also be pursued without the abolition of private ownership of the means of production.[147] During the war, exiled members of the Norwegian trade unions gave more concrete content to such ideas by drafting proposals for future economic planning similar to the Dutch ones.[148] Many of these ideas entered the DNA's 1949 program.

The Swedish views on postwar planning were rather similar. After having successfully conquered the crisis by means of macroeconomic policies, the SAP believed it would now set out to reorganize the economy so as to prevent a repetition of the Great Depression. Its program for the postwar period called for a tripartite body for long-term investment planning, the foundation of a state bank, and the socialization of the insurance industry. Moreover, the state should establish public firms to compete with private business in those areas where private entrepreneurship was operating inefficiently.

In Germany, Hilferding had to admit in the face of the depression that his prediction of an increasingly stable "organized capitalism" was incorrect. Instead, the SPD came to interpret the turn to microeconomic interventionism under the Brüning government as a confirmation of its view that the anarchic character of capitalist production would inevitably lead toward ever more intense state regulation and a suspension of the rights of private property. In response to Brüning's policies, the SPD even went so far as to claim that the increasing political intervention meant that the "right of the state to interfere in the economy for the benefit of society as a whole had been proclaimed."[149]

Unlike other parties, the SPD did not develop such views into concrete proposals after 1945. Partly because he feared the party might waste its energies on dogmatic debates, the new chairman, Kurt Schumacher, rejected all calls for the drafting of a new program. The SPD had to distill its views on economic policies from statements by prominent members like Kurt Schumacher, Viktor Agartz, and Hermann Veit.[150] Given the experience of the Nazi period, proposals like the Dutch PBOs may have contained too many corporatist overtones for the SPD.[151] Yet the SPD's postwar views on the regulation of the economy were in many ways reminiscent of the "Umbau der Wirtschaft" plan of the early 1930s. This plan, which originated from the AfA union and was presented to the Reichstag by the SPD in August–September 1931, called for increased planning in private industry alongside nationalization of key industries and the expansion of the public sector. The state was to play the dominant role in the planning process. After 1945, the SPD stressed that recovery would be possible only on the basis of a planned economy. This did not, however, mean a nationalized economy. Only key industrial sectors were to be nationalized. As Schumacher explained in 1945, the following industries would have to be socialized: banking and credit, insurance, mining, coal, iron, steel, metalworking, and all other sectors of the economy that were monopolistic or cartelized.[152]

At first sight the Labour Party's official policy position at the end of World War II might seem to still conform more closely to the old socialist ideology than was the case for other parties. The experience of the depression seemed to have strengthened Labour's conviction of the need for a socialist planned economy. Labour's 1934 manifesto *For Socialism and Peace* advocated "full and rapid socialist economic planning, under central direction."[153] The 1945 election manifesto in turn saw nationalization of certain key industries[154] as the centerpiece of Labour's policies whereas the concept of long-term planning of private industry was largely absent.[155] Moreover, the Labour Party officially maintained its commitment to the goal of a socialist economy. However, such a conclusion would be misleading. Perhaps even more so than for other social democratic parties, a pragmatic policy of promoting growth and employment was the central concern for Labour after the war. The nationalizations that Attlee under-

took were not seen as a step toward a socialist economy, nor were the nationalized industries to be used as instruments in a centrally directed economic
strategy. Rather nationalization was primarily conceived in terms of improving
the efficiency of certain essential industries like coal where private owners were
seen to have "failed the country."[156]

By 1947, the enthusiasm for nationalization declined rapidly, partly because
doubts emerged whether nationalization really was the best way to promote
efficiency.[157] Instead, the severe current account crisis of that year gave rise to
efforts at planning similar to those pursued by other social democratic parties.
After Stafford Cripps had replaced Hugh Dalton as Chancellor of the Exchequer
in 1947, a tripartite approach to reorganization of private industry became
Labour's dominant industrial strategy. The Industrial Organisation and Development Act of 1947 provided for the creation of tripartite Development Councils that would take care of reorganizing industrial sectors. In contrast to, for
example, the Dutch PBO proposals, the emphasis here was on voluntary agreement with no central role for the state. At the national level, the process of
industrial reorganization was to be coordinated by the Central Economic Planning Staff, created in 1947, and the tripartite Economic Planning Board.

THE DEFEAT OF PLANNING AND KEYNESIANISM

The social democratic argument for planning was based on the notion that the
uncoordinated character of decision making in a market economy would necessarily lead to crises. Conscious coordination of economic decisions was to be the
remedy. Yet, the crisis of the thirties was primarily related to the process of
disposition over money and not to the uncoordinated character of firm-level
decision making. The depression had shown that a monetary economy required
a fair degree of nominal rigidity and that governments could only violate this
requirement at great costs. The new macroregime, however, had found a rather
effective answer to the destructive effects of deflation, and accordingly the
widespread postwar discussion about the need for planning in order to cure an
inherently stagnant and crisis-prone capitalism was basically addressing a non-
problem.

With episodes from the height of the deflation in mind, when business was
desperately calling for governments to protect it from the anarchy of the market,
social democrats after 1945 actually were surprised at the resistance of the
business community to their planning proposals. Under the new macroregime,
however, the private sector came to look upon such proposals as an undesirable
intrusion rather than a welcome protection against the anarchy of the market.
But, it was not only business that objected. Without a crisis in sight, trade
unions could not become enthusiastic about a system that would radically curtail
their freedom of action by replacing bargaining with state control. As the
expected postwar recession failed to materialize and center and right-wing

parties, business, and labor proved increasingly skeptical with respect to their plans, social democrats decided to shelve the construction of a planned economy.

The Dutch PvdA needed the Catholic KVP (Katholieke Volkspartij) to muster sufficient parliamentary support for its PBO plans. While Catholic thinking at the time was strongly convinced of the need for a corporatist organization of the economy, the KVP objected to the strong position the state was to have in the PvdA plans. Instead of imposing PBOs from above, the Catholics proposed to form them only after mutual agreement between the firms and workers concerned and the state. The result of the 1946 election, in which the KVP became the biggest party, was that the PvdA had to accept the Catholic proposal. Inside the labor movement, Vos's plans did not command uniform consent. The social democratic trade union NVV, in line with their Christian colleagues and the employers' organizations, rejected the original plans because it considered them a threat to its own position in the economy.[158] Given rapid growth, it was no surprise that business showed virtually no interest. Consequently, the whole PBO plan simply petered out.

The SPD remained confined to a rather unfruitful opposition role from the foundation of the Federal Republic of Germany (FRG) until 1966. In part, this was the result of its foreign policy position and its failure to shed its explicit working-class rhetoric and symbols in the early years of the FRG. A major contributing factor, however, was its continued insistence on planning and socialization of essential industries. The tight administrative regulations, which were maintained up to the currency reform of 1948, rapidly became quite unpopular. The impressive growth, which set in with the Korean War boom, meant that the SPD's insistence that economic recovery was only possible on the basis of planning rapidly outlived itself. The national elections of 1953 gave a clear indication of the unpopularity of the SPD's program. Whereas the Christian democrats polled 45.7 percent, compared to 31 percent in 1949, the SPD's share fell from 29.2 percent to 28.8 percent. Even among its core constituency of the urban working class, the SPD only managed to poll 50 percent.[159] After yet another election defeat, the SPD finally abandoned the remnants of socialist tradition by rejecting the socialization of even key industrial sectors in the Godesberger Program of 1959.

The parties who enjoyed a parliamentary majority were no more successful in implementing planning. In Sweden, the SAP shelved its proposals for planning definitively after the 1948 election, which was dominated by this issue. In the preceding three years a heated debate raged between the SAP, on the one hand, and the "bourgeois" parties and business, on the other. The SAP stressed continuously that planning was necessary to avoid the coming crisis. The opponents in this debate, in contrast, held quite optimistic views about the economic future. As these views proved to be correct, the SAP felt it unwise to risk alienating virtually all other parties, business, and perhaps even the LO, for the sake of a program that no longer seemed economically necessary.

The postwar DNA government created the institutional framework for planning, but, in practice, the impact of these councils remained negligible, mainly owing to a lack of enthusiasm on the side of business. Moreover, the party decided not to present to parliament its "rationalization law," "which would have empowered the government to reorganize private industry on the basis of 'social considerations.' "[160] As in other countries, the main reason for the DNA's decision to forsake its planning ambitions was a combination of strong political opposition from business and the "bourgeois" political parties and a continuous economic boom.[161] Perhaps more so than for other social democratic parties, the DNA had seen planning as a means to promoting growth. When its pessimism about postwar economic development proved unfounded, abandoning planning was no difficult step to take. After 1952, the term "planning" remained in the DNA's vocabulary, but now it came to stand for management of credit and budgetary policies aimed at preventing inflationary overheating in a rapidly growing economy.

The British Development Councils suffered the same fate. In the end, only four councils were started,[162] but even those did not meet with great enthusiasm from business and therefore largely remained inconsequential.[163] Jim Tomlinson captures the essence of industry's changing enthusiasm for regulation: "Initially employers were sympathetic to the idea and the intention was that these establishments should be voluntary. However, employers' attitudes changed, as it became apparent from 1947/8 that the DCs would not be needed as bases for cartels in a slump. Quickly they became viewed rather as instruments of governmental control."[164] Also in Britain, the TUC was rather skeptical with respect to planning. Economic planning would also entail that the state controlled the allocation of labor to firms. Indeed the so-called manpower budget was seen as a crucial element in the Labour Party's planning concepts. But while the TUC was willing to enter into tripartite voluntary wage restraint agreements, it did strenuously object to a system in which the unions' role in wage bargaining was to be replaced with administrative decision.[165]

The obvious irrelevance of detailed microeconomic planning for economic prosperity left a void in the social democratic interpretation of the role of the state in economic management. It was at this point that Keynesianism came to play its most important role. Keynesianism was an ideal ideological tool for social democracy. To identify an interventionist state as the guardian of economic prosperity gave social democrats an ideological advantage over political movements that had more strongly emphasized liberal concepts. Moreover, to identify fiscal stimulation as the key to prosperity allowed social democrats to credit their superior economic insights for the recovery from the Great Depression. Unlike cheap money and price stabilization, plans for fiscal stimulation did emerge primarily from the labor movement during the Great Depression. Finally, the macroeconomic character of the Keynesian recipes denied the existence of an inevitable trade-off between high wages, extensive welfare, and growth and employment. Rather than having to defensively justify welfare state arrangements as measures that protected labor against the social hardship of a market economy, they now could be interpreted as measures that not only contributed to greater social and economic equality but also increased the stability of the economic system due to their effect as automatic stabilizers.

And as the post-1945 boom did not want to end, liberals and conservatives could not afford to miss the golden opportunity of embracing an economic theory that attributed prosperity to the farsighted intervention of governments – albeit for them the money illusion interpretation of Keynesianism (see Chapter 2) was inherently more attractive. Prosperity, however, depended not on contra-cyclical fiscal policies but on the ability to combine full employment with low inflation. As the institutional preconditions for such a strategy were gradually being undermined since the late sixties, the stage was set for political parties to unearth many of their economic policy ideas that seemed to have gone down for good in the shipwreck of the Great Depression.

5

THE BREAKDOWN OF THE
SOCIAL DEMOCRATIC
CONSENSUS

> The only reason we have unemployment is that governments are using it
> to contain, or to reduce, inflation. (Richard Layard 1986: 29)

In essence, the viability of the growth regime of the post-1945 era depended on the ability to contain inflation without recourse to sharply restrictive macroeconomic policies. In practice, this meant increasing reliance on income policies, since the price and quantity controls of the immediate postwar period could not be continued indefinitely. Yet, relying on income policies is always a precarious strategy. Ultimately trade unions are organizations designed to benefit their members in wage bargaining and not to function as an additional instrument in macroeconomic policies. During the sixties the strategy of relying on microeconomic policies to contain inflation increasingly came into conflict with the organizational logic of the trade unions, especially so because many countries experienced a further reduction in unemployment rates during that decade. The wave of labor unrest that spread across Western Europe in the late sixties therefore was not the prelude to a further strengthening of the left but rather the first announcement of the end of social democracy's ideological hegemony. The disintegration of income policies as an instrument for containing nominal wages spelled the danger of an inflationary spiral. As in the early twenties, the only feasible policy in such a constellation, for social democratic and non–social democratic governments, would be to reintroduce unemployment in order to contain inflation. The defeat of the social democratic approach to economic management and the rise of neoliberalism during the seventies and eighties is primarily a story about the disintegration of the ability to contain inflation by microeconomic means.

POSTWAR PROSPERITY

ADAPTATIONS TO FULL EMPLOYMENT

As the widespread use of wage and price controls in the second half of the forties prevented an inflationary spiral and thus obviated the need for a restrictive macroeconomic regime, a different dilemma emerged: how to keep inflation low in conditions of full employment without relying on wartime controls indefinitely. Instead of giving rise to a new policy regime, which reintroduced unemployment, the inflationary pressures of the late forties and early fifties prompted three policy adaptations. First, as wartime controls were gradually abolished, bi- or tripartite income policy became the central pillar of a policy of moderating inflation. In the Netherlands, the system of guided wage policy was maintained until the midsixties when it was replaced by a more corporatist pattern of wage bargaining in which unions gained a more equal position compared to the previous system. In Norway, such a corporatist system of wage bargaining was already established in the forties.[1] In Sweden, wage and price moderation through centralized bipartite agreement became the dominant pattern for the next decades. Although the government did not directly intervene until the seventies, the crucial importance of containing nominal wage growth strongly informed both bargaining partners. Wage bargaining was less centralized in Britain, but voluntary or statutory wage moderation was a constant element in British economic policy during the next decades. The exception to this pattern was Germany. Here tight labor markets did not emerge until the sixties. This was the result not of a different macroregime but of the massive inflow of refugees from Eastern Europe, which allowed for the combination of above-average growth rates with relatively slack labor markets.

Second, fiscal policies became used more actively for *reducing* demand pressures in an economy running at full speed. The regime could not be stabilized by relying entirely on income moderation. If nominal wage moderation were to carry the main responsibility for keeping inflation down, it would have to be supported by economic policies that prevented labor markets from becoming too tight. Under sufficiently tight labor markets, a policy of wage moderation would become unworkable because it constituted a threat to the internal cohesion of trade unions. At the point where employers were willing to offer wage increases greater than those agreed upon in centralized bargaining in order to attract workers, the union leadership would have to break with a policy of moderation if it did not wish to lose all legitimacy. Sweden experienced such a situation already in 1947 when wages increased rapidly despite the fact that both the LO and the employers' association SAF (Svenska Arbetsgivareföreningen) issued urgent appeals for moderation. The unions' response was the famous Rehn-Meidner model (named after the two LO economists who invented it), which came to inform much of the macroeconomic policies of the SAP in the fifties and sixties. The model explicitly assigned short-term demand management a restrictive role to avoid overheating and to maintain the cohesion of centralized bargaining. Also, in Norway fiscal policies came to play a more active role as tight labor markets and wage drift increasingly put pressure on the system of centralized LO-NAF bargaining and permanent compulsory arbitration. From 1952 onward, bargaining became more decentralized and permanent compulsory arbitration was abolished. In the United Kingdom, this pattern emerged in 1947. The 1947 budget was the first postwar budget in which restrictive fiscal policies were explicitly conceived as a means to reduce inflationary pressures and thereby to lessen reliance on direct controls.[2] In the Netherlands, the Korean War boom saw the first application of restrictive fiscal policies.[3]

Third, demand pressures prompted an adaptation of monetary policies. Due to the persistent threat of inflationary overheating, the commitment to a rigidly low interest rate had to be abandoned. However, given the optimistic expectations about future demand and profits, central banks frequently found out that moderate interest rate changes were not too effective. Starting from a low level in relation to expected profits, moderate increases in the discount rate would not do much to deter lending to industry. At the same time, open market policies, by which the central banks sold state debt to the public to reduce liquidity, would be difficult to pursue if the public held investment in industry to be more attractive. With the option of a monetary stabilization crisis along the lines of the early twenties barred, central banks resorted to a policy that, instead of reducing the willingness to invest, sought to curtail the ability of the financial system to finance investment by means of credit rationing. Credit rationing allowed for a more direct control of the amount of liquidity in the economy by means of the (temporary) imposition of a ceiling on the amount of lending the financial system was to undertake. This meant that the commercial banks might be directed to invest in state debt, allowing the authorities to siphon off liquidity during periods of exceptionally buoyant demand. Alternatively, the central bank might simply impose a ceiling on the amount of lending by commercial banks. In the equity market, a rationing of credit could be achieved by restricting new share emissions.

In the Netherlands, quantitative credit controls were used for the first time as a temporary emergency measure by the central bank in 1950. One year later the law on the credit system codified the use of such instruments. In the same year, the Swedish Riksbank was allowed to employ credit rationing. In Norway, credit rationing was introduced in 1955 in the form of an agreement between the state and financial institutions. In the United Kingdom, limits on bank advances to industry were used as an element of monetary policy beginning in the late forties.[4]

In sum, during the early fifties a policy pattern emerged that was to become typical for the next decades. When tight labor market conditions put too much tension on the peak unions' ability to enforce wage moderation, macroeconomic policies resorted to brief periods of restriction.[5] Given the macroeconomic authorities' long-term commitment to growth and full employment, and in a constellation in which income policies could be relied on to support a macroeconomic growth orientation in the long run, these brief periods of macroeconomic restriction were interpreted as just that, rather than as a regime changes. Accordingly, they could be employed without negatively affecting the engine of private-sector growth: positive expectations about future growth prospects. In the words of James Tobin (1980: 19):

> As Keynes also knew, protracted under-production and under-utilization severely damages the marginal efficiency of capital. In mild and short-lived recessions investment is buoyed by the belief that high employment and prosperity are the long-term norm. Once this confidence is destroyed, as contemporary events again demonstrate, it is terribly difficult to revive it. The practical moral is that active policy, along with market response, is part of the social mechanism for maintenance or restoration of equilibrium.

THE IRRELEVANCE OF KEYNESIANISM

Although it became the official policy interpretation of many political parties, during the unprecedented boom of the fifties and sixties expansionary demand management in order to protect full employment was rather irrelevant. The regime's commitment to growth, and its ability to contain inflation without recourse to durable macroeconomic restriction, generally meant that private investment demand remained buoyant. The cycle of boom and recession, which Keynesians held to be an inherent feature of a market economy, simply did not appear.[6]

Even in Keynes's native Britain, deficit spending was absent and fiscal policy mainly exerted a contractive influence on consumption. Writing in 1968, R. G. O. Matthews (p. 556) concluded that "throughout the post-war period the Government, far from injecting demand into the system, has persistently had a large current account surplus. This surplus has varied in amount, but government savings have averaged about 3 percent of the national income."[7] If anything, the "Keynesian period" in Britain may be said to have lasted from 1967, when sterling was devalued and the budget deficit increased, to 1976, when the Labour government came to the conclusion that fiscal pump priming was not feasible. The first serious attempt at Keynesian policies during this century in Sweden occurred in the midseventies when policy makers tried to bridge the international recession.[8] The same applies to Norway. There, the budget showed a deficit in 1945 and 1946, but by 1949, the budget surplus amounted to 6.9 percent of gross domestic product. From 1949 until 1962, the budget was continuously in surplus with the exception of the year 1954. Also for the period 1962–73, budget surpluses were common.[9] In Germany, Keynesian concepts gained importance only since the midsixties, when inflationary pressures started to emerge from increasingly tight labor markets. Keynesianism became official policy doctrine only in 1966, when the SPD took office in a grand coalition with the CDU (Christlich Demokratische Union) and CSU (Christlich Soziale Union).[10] As in other countries, Keynesianism in Germany was initially discussed as an additional instrument to help contain inflationary pressures rather than as a policy to reduce unemployment.[11] Its first application, however, was in an expansionary direction in 1967, when it was widely credited with the quick recovery from a brief recession. In fact, the recession itself was the result of a dose of tight money administered by the Bundesbank, which felt that fiscal policy could not be relied on sufficiently. The recession was quickly overcome as the bank loosened the reins. From then on until the first oil price shock, preventing overheating was the main problem for German fiscal policies. Finally, in the Netherlands, the Keynesian view of contracyclical fiscal policies gained political acceptance only in the early sixties and also here as a means of depressing rather than stimulating demand. Discretionary deficit spending in order to alleviate unemployment was first pursued in the wake of the first oil price crisis and de facto abandoned again during the early eighties.

To be sure, those who wanted to see a Keynesian revolution could nevertheless do so.[12] Alan Booth (1984: 264) has stated that the absence of deficit spending could not be taken as proof of the absence of Keynesian policies because "there is nothing inherently 'Keynesian' about a budget deficit, either in theory or practice." Moreover, it could be argued that attempting to reduce overall demand by means of budget surpluses, after all, is an instance of discretionary management. For the Netherlands, for example, A. Knoester (1989: 95–99) interpreted the restrictive fiscal policies in 1951 and 1956 as examples of Keynesian policy making.

More than sixty years after the publication of Keynes's *General Theory* there is still widespread disagreement about the "correct" interpretation. The Keynesian label may be applied differently, but at that point the discussion ceases to be one about the character of policy making and becomes one about "what Keynes really meant." There are good reasons for questioning the centrality of contracyclical policies in Keynes's views,[13] but to claim that Keynesianism is unrelated to the proposition that contracyclical fiscal policies can safeguard full employment, given a tendency toward unemployment equilibrium, contrasts too much with both Keynes's advocation of fiscal expansion in the early thirties and the common understanding of the term among policy makers. If the term "Keynesianism" is understood in this common sense, then one must conclude that such policies were not important in the first postwar decades.

MOUNTING TENSIONS

During the second part of the sixties, rank-and-file discontent with a policy regime that required workers to abstain from fully exploiting their market strength became increasingly acute. Immediately after the war, the pronounced feeling of a national emergency and the government tenure of social democrats had greatly facilitated a policy of nominal constraint. As the problems of postwar reconstruction were overcome, extension of welfare state arrangements came to play a more important role in maintaining unions' support for the regime. Yet, such mechanisms increasingly proved insufficient, especially so as labor market conditions further tightened during the sixties. Within the unions, growing dissatisfaction with the regime was manifested in strong pressures for more local autonomy.

Within the party such opposition promoted the growth of an internal leftist opposition that called for a "more socialist" social democracy. Instead of concentrating on wage moderation, social democrats were urged to rediscover their role as representatives of the working class in the struggle with capital. Frequently, the leftist opposition to the policies of the fifties and sixties was voiced by a new generation of middle-class intellectuals who were now entering social democratic parties in large numbers.

Within the SPD the youth organization JUSO (Junge Sozialisten) came to hold increasingly socialist positions. In the Dutch PvdA, a new generation of young members organized, its own tendency, the so-called New Left. In Norway and Sweden, the increasing popularity of small leftist parties strengthened the left wing of the social democrats. Even in Britain, the tendency toward deradicalization of the party's official ideology, which has set in with the eviction of Labour from government in 1951 and was spurred on by a series of subsequent election defeats, made way for a renewed radicalization of policy positions in the late sixties.[14]

The response of social democrats to the challenge of leftist opposition was threefold. First, the extension of the welfare state was speeded up, but now frequently in the form of an explicit quid pro quo for wage moderation. Second, firm-level codetermination became an important issue. Third, social democrats sought to reduce excess profits in industry, both to limit the available room for granting wage increases and, more important, to defuse the unions' impression that income moderation was a one-sided affair. The Dutch PvdA, for example, developed plans for siphoning off excess profits during the early and midsixties. The most sophisticated proposals were the so-called wage earner funds, presented by the Swedish LO and SAP. The proposal called for a share of excess profits being paid into a union-managed fund that would acquire stock in Swedish firms. In this way, the labor movement would come to own a gradually increasing share of Swedish industry[15] while the latter would be provided with relatively cheap credits. To avoid interunion fragmentation, these funds were to be managed not on a firm-level basis but by the national level of the LO.

For some scholars[16] and more than a few social democrats, the renewed emphasis on firm-level democracy and proposals like the Swedish wage earner funds meant that social democracy was about to resume its journey to a socialist society. Walter Korpi (1978), for example, argued that the new regime of the thirties had been a class compromise as social democracy became strong enough to make employers accept strong trade unions, an extensive welfare state, and

interventionist policies, but was still too weak to dislodge capital. Toward the
seventies social democracy was seen as having accumulated sufficient power
resources to end the compromise. However, as indicated above, the new policy
regime established in the thirties cannot be understood as a compromise between labor and business. Rather, the new regime was based on a common
interest in ending deflation. Similarly, the radicalization of the late sixties and
seventies did not constitute an effort by a greatly strengthened social democracy
to complete the transformation of economy and society begun in the thirties,
but instead reflected growing problems with handling the macroregime. The
Swedish proposals for wage earner funds, for example, were a logical extension
of the Rehn-Meidner model prompted by the increasing problems the LO
experienced with fulfilling the task of maintaining moderate nominal wage
increases in a period of tight labor markets and high profits. By giving the
unions a share of the profits and stocks of private business, the LO simply hoped
to contain the increasing radicalization of wage demands at the local level.

   In the end, the significance of such leftist revolts as staged by the JUSOS
in the SPD and New Left in the PvdA amounted to not much more than a
vehicle for bringing about a generation change in the party leadership. Irrespective of the leftist outlook of a new generation of members, the direction social
democracy would take during the next decades would be determined by the
degree to which it remained able to rely on labor market institutions instead of
unemployment to contain inflation. To the extent that the leftist tendencies of
the late sixties and early seventies built on worker opposition to the arrangements of the old regime, they were not the harbingers of a new radicalization
but rather announced the decline of social democracy and the advent of the
ideological dominance of neoliberalism.

THE ADVENT OF DISINFLATION

Whereas the regime changes in the 1920s and 1930s took place within a span
of four to five years, in the seventies and eighties the transition to a new regime
took almost eighteen years to be accomplished – from the Bundesbank's turn to
restrictive policies in the summer of 1973 to the pegging of the Swedish krona
to the ECU (European Currency Unit) on May 17, 1991. In the late teens,
European countries were subjected to a common shock – the upheaval of World
War I – which elicited a common policy response. During the Great Depression,
the commitment to gold meant that policy shocks in the major countries were
rapidly transmitted throughout the system. In the seventies and eighties, a
common shock was not present. Nor were countries initially willing to adjust
their economic policies to the defense of a fixed exchange rate. The Bretton
Woods system broke apart as policy preferences came to diverge more sharply
between countries that displayed a very low tolerance for inflation and those
where inflation was more easily tolerated in order not to jeopardize full employ-

ment. In addition, institutional differences were more pronounced. The disparity between the highly centralized Swedish system of wage bargaining and the competing crafts and industrial unions in Britain, for example, did not have a counterpart in the twenties or thirties. Yet, in the end the differences in policy preferences and institutional setup only accounted for differences in timing, but did not allow for the durable coexistence of different policy regimes.

The first countries to switch to a regime of macroeconomic disinflation were Germany and the Netherlands, not because they were confronted with the most serious inflationary pressures, but because the political commitment to a growth regime was most precarious there. Yet, the German and Dutch strategy of pursuing a restrictive monetary regime and tolerating high unemployment might have been expected to remain an isolated phenomenon in a Western Europe, where most other countries pursued macroeconomic policies for growth and employment. As long as other countries were willing to let the Deutsche mark (and the guilder) revalue, emulation of the German policy regime was by no means unavoidable. Through a more flexible exchange rate management, it would be possible for countries with different macroeconomic strategies and different wage-setting dynamics to coexist in an open world economy. Once Germany had embarked on a restrictive monetary regime, maintaining a fixed exchange rate with the mark became tantamount to importing restrictive policies. Restrictive German policies would result in current account deficits, and expansionary domestic policies would serve to aggravate the problem. As long as devaluation was ruled out, such problems would eventually have to be corrected by means of restrictive domestic demand management. Furthermore, maintaining a fixed exchange rate implied that nominal wages had to be kept in line with those in Germany if export competitiveness was not to be undermined by a real appreciation.

The German and Dutch governments, in contrast, had a clear incentive to link other countries to their policy strategy by means of a fixed exchange rate arrangement. If other countries would join them in a fixed exchange rate arrangement, they might be able to combine restrictive monetary policies and nominal exchange rate stability with real depreciation, as long as they were able to keep inflation rates below those in other countries.[17] Under a flexible rate arrangement – and in contrast to the popular argument about the dominance of the Bundesbank in Western European monetary affairs – the German and Dutch strategy might easily have backfired. Pursuing a more restrictive policy than all other countries might prompt an excessive revaluation of the currency and hence cause serious problems for exports. Given the (political) weight of the exporting industry in both countries, such an outcome might easily undermine the political support for the anti-inflation course. Moreover, the demonstration effect of neighboring countries pursuing successful policies for growth and employment might have served the same purpose. In other words, Germany and the Netherlands might have suffered a fate similar to that of countries that tried desperately to cling to the gold standard even after September 1931.

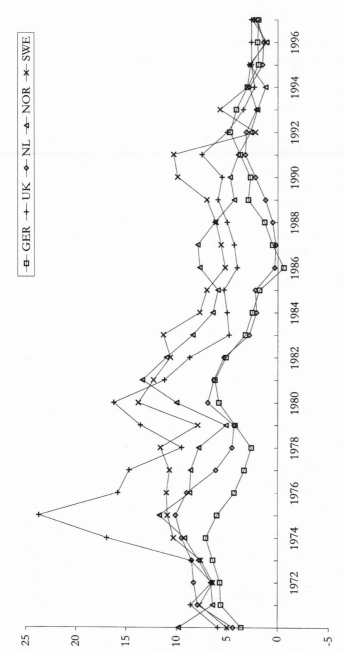

Figure 5.1. Private consumption deflators, 1970–97 (percentage change from previous period). (Source: OCED Economic Outlook.)

Initially, the end of the Bretton Woods system and the failure to recreate a fixed exchange rate arrangement in Europe indeed seemed to announce a divergence between expansionary and restrictive countries. Yet, there was a crucial difference between the Great Depression and the seventies: in the latter the problem was inflation and not deflation. Figure 5.1 shows the annual percentage increase in consumer prices since 1970. The first oil shock contributed strongly to already rising prices in all countries. The effects were comparatively moderate in Germany, however. After 1975, Dutch rates rapidly converged on the German figures. Since then, those two countries have consistently recorded the lowest inflation rates. Britain performed much worse than the other countries in the seventies, but after Margaret Thatcher assumed office, inflation fell rapidly. After 1979, therefore, the two Scandinavian countries recorded the highest inflation rates. By the early nineties, however, all counties had converged on the German level.

Given the dominance of inflationary pressures, it was not surprising that convergence of restrictive policies based on fixed exchange rates within the European Monetary System (EMS) rather than expansionary policies and flexible exchange rate management became the norm in Europe. Pursuing a soft-currency policy in order to safeguard full employment implied that the purely institutional, as opposed to economic, ability of labor market institutions to maintain nominal wage moderation attained greater importance. Without a fixed exchange rate constraint, any price level, in principle, was compatible with competitiveness. But, removing the threat of job loss and balance-of-payments crises due to excessive nominal wage increases could only serve to aggravate inflationary problems in those countries where the postwar pattern of negotiated wage moderation was rapidly disintegrating. A fixed exchange rate link to Germany instead could play the welcome role of an external anchor to the price level.

For the same reasons the fairly elaborate apparatus of exchange controls that was in use throughout Western Europe was abolished. During the late sixties and early seventies both deficit and surplus countries tightened exchange controls to prevent excessive capital outflows or inflows.[18] With the advent of disinflation, exchange controls lost their raison d'être. Countries like Germany and the Netherlands, who had suffered from extensive capital inflows, now could simply allow the currency to revalue. For weaker-currency countries the decision to give priority to disinflation implied that there was no longer any use for an instrument that was designed to isolate the domestic economy from a more restrictive international environment. Free capital flows, instead, might help stabilize the new regime as (the threat of) outflows could serve as a powerful political and economic hindrance to more expansionary policies. In addition, exchange controls now came to be seen as a source of microeconomic inefficiency and an impediment to the competitiveness of domestic financial institutions.

Whereas in the interwar period Germany (until 1933) and the Netherlands (until 1936) were fighting an already lost battle by clinging to restrictive policies, in the seventies they became the pioneers of a regime that would come to be generally accepted in the next decade. Initially, both larger countries like the United Kingdom, and smaller countries like Sweden and Norway, whose politically dominant social democracy was unwilling to accept the consequences of a disinflation strategy in terms of lower growth and higher unemployment, opted for a more expansionary macroeconomic course. Yet, having the political will to continue the old regime was not a sufficient condition if the institutional apparatus to implement such policies was progressively disintegrating. Hence the first set of countries to follow the German and Dutch lead were those, like the United Kingdom, the United States, France, Denmark, and Belgium, that displayed a pronounced political desire to continue a growth regime but lacked the microeconomic means for doing so. Britain, in particular, with its decentralized trade unions and exposed currency, was institutionally ill equipped.

Yet, even after the second oil price crisis, Norway and Sweden maintained their course of giving priority to full employment. In those countries, not only was the political will for full employment more pronounced, but the institutional preconditions seemed ideally suited for such a strategy. But eventually Scandinavian social democrats, too, had to discover that in the longer run it is not possible to give policy priority to full employment instead of price stability. Despite their higher institutional capacity for income policies, their strong emphasis on employment caused Swedish and Norwegian inflation rates to be continuously above those in countries like Germany and the Netherlands. Although inflation initially provided for an additional stimulus to the economy, widespread financial speculation soon emerged. In the face of acute labor scarcity, escalating nominal wages, and rampant financial speculation, Scandinavian social democrats had no other alternative than to stabilize their price levels by means of unemployment.

Mass unemployment was the inevitable result of the regime shift (see Figure 5.2). In 1970, open unemployment in Germany and the Netherlands was below 1 percent. Between 1973 and 1975, unemployment rose to around 3 percent. The latter part of the seventies saw stabilization, but the second oil price shock caused a dramatic increase. Toward the mideighties the situation improved somewhat, but in the early nineties a rapid deterioration set in. Despite its higher tolerance for inflation, Britain initially performed worse than Germany and the Netherlands in terms of unemployment. Margaret Thatcher's policies brought about a dramatic deterioration, but toward the late eighties unemployment seemed to fall almost as rapidly as it had emerged in the late seventies. Also in Britain, the early nineties again saw a strong increase in unemployment rates. For most of the period, Sweden and Norway instead seemed to be unaffected by the problems plaguing the other countries. The first oil price shock had hardly any effects at all on open unemployment. The recession of the late seventies and early eighties did make a noticeable dent, but unemployment started to decline soon afterward. Norwegian unemployment shot up rapidly after the regime shift in 1987 but remained lower than in the other countries.

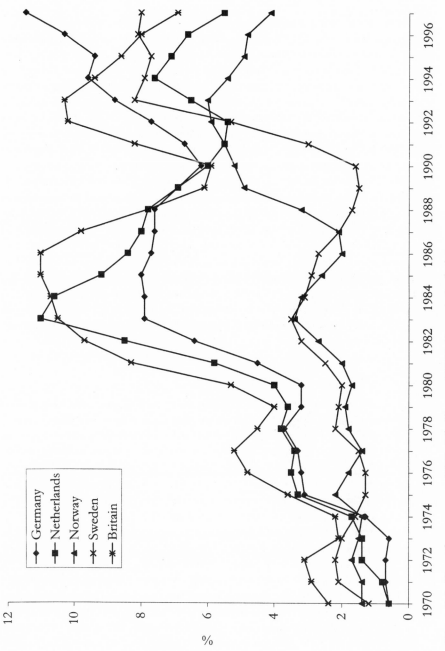

Figure 5.2. Unemployment rates, 1970–96. (Source: OECD Economic Outlook.)

Sweden instead definitely joined the high unemployment club after the regime change in 1990–91. By 1996, open unemployment amounted to 8.1 percent, a rate exceeded only by Germany.

The political dynamics of the regime change were similar to the thirties, in the sense that those parties who initiated the new regime generally were not able to profit from it electorally. Rather, the U-turns many social democratic governments made seemed to signal the correctness of the neoliberal critique that the social democratic policy model was fundamentally flawed. In Britain, the change started in 1976 under Denis Healey and James Callaghan, but it was left to Margaret Thatcher to fully develop the new regime. Also in Germany, the SPD could not thrive under a regime of high unemployment, and it found itself in opposition from 1982 onward. Except for a brief interruption in 1981, the Dutch PvdA sat on the opposition benches between 1977 and 1989. Only Scandinavian social democrats fared better in electoral terms. The SAP was voted out of office after it initiated the new regime, but the even more rapid rise in unemployment during the conservative government allowed it to return in 1994. The Norwegian labor party also came under strong pressure after the regime change but managed to stay in power mainly because the abundant oil income allowed it to turn to highly expansionary fiscal policies in the late eighties and because the opposition parties failed to agree among themselves about the contours of an alternative government.

NEW (OLD) ORTHODOXIES

Quite similar to the developments of the early twenties, the increasing intractability of inflationary problems caused the doctrine of the neutrality of money to return to the political stage. Whereas Milton Friedman had been outside mainstream economics during the fifties and sixties, since the early seventies more and more governments converted to monetarism. But as in the 1920s, conversion to monetarism in no way implied the advent of nondiscretionary or rule-bound monetary policies; quite the contrary. Also in this period, the prediction that monetary contraction would only have short-term effects failed to come true. When it did not disappear after the stabilization crises, durable mass unemployment again became interpreted in microeconomic terms, in particular as the result of the failure of trade unions to allow market forces to operate so as to clear the labor market. As a consequence, supply-side economics followed on the heels of monetarism, attributing the enduring recession to (policy-induced) market distortions.

Because of the long duration of the policy transition, the change in orthodoxies was much more drawn out than in the twenties. At some point during the late seventies and early eighties, it seemed that rather than converging, economic policy strategies were diverging between more expansionary social democratic policies and restrictive neoliberal regimes.[19] Keynesians sought to explain this divergence in national policy strategies by incorporating the concept of corporatism into their analysis.[20] Although macroeconomic policies were still held to be effective, governments could maintain full employment only if trade unions exerted nominal wage moderation to prevent high inflation. Such a policy assignment, however, could be executed only under a corporatist policy pattern of tripartite negotiations between the government and highly centralized trade unions and employers associations.[21] However, as even the corporatist showcases of Austria, Norway, and Sweden submitted to high unemployment and restrictive policies, such an interpretation became untenable. At this point, the argument that restrictive policies had been forced on reluctant social democratic governments by external constraints, in particular by internationally mobile financial capital, became well-nigh irresistible for Keynesians. This argument allowed them to maintain that macropolicies were still effective (thereby not having to admit to a theoretical error), whereas the restrictive policies pursued could be attributed to force majeure (thereby exempting social democrats from having to admit policy mistakes). At the same time, this view allowed them to arrive at the same policy conclusions as their opponents, namely, that expansionary macroeconomic policies were unavailable and that the key to renewed prosperity had to be sought on the microlevel. Not surprisingly, this time the left sought to counter the offensive of neoliberal supply-side policies with its own version, in which strong unions were seen to promote productivity and hence competitiveness.

THE FORERUNNERS: GERMANY AND THE NETHERLANDS

When Willy Brandt assumed the chancellorship of the Federal Republic in 1969, he was the first social democrat to do so since Hermann Müller had stepped down in 1930. That Brandt succeeded was to no small extent due to his minister of economics, Karl Schiller. As even the reputed father of the postwar economic miracle, Ludwig Erhard, felt forced to consider a more activist type of macroeconomic management, the liberalism of the fifties suddenly seemed outdated. Schiller's Keynesian concept of discretionary macromanagement instead appeared to hold the key to the economic problems of modern Germany. Indeed, the rapid recovery from the 1967 recession seemed convincingly to demonstrate the superiority of Schiller's Keynesianism. Whereas Schmumacher's insistence on the need for more planning during the postwar economic miracle condemned the party to stay on the opposition benches, beginning in the midsixties the SPD and not the CDU appeared to be the party that could best manage the economy. And in Germany, a reputation for successful economic management has traditionally been the single most important precondition for electoral success.

The real test of the SPD's ability to manage the economy, however, came not in 1967 but in the wake of the first oil price shock of 1973. According to

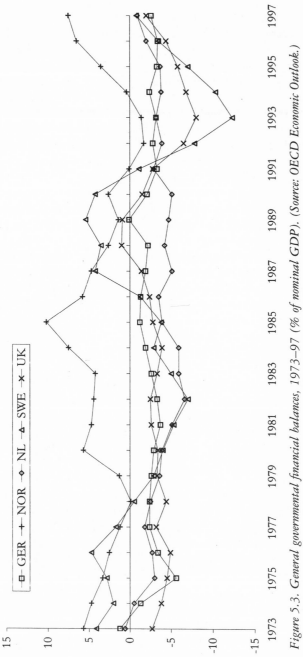

Figure 5.3. General governmental financial balances, 1973–97 (% of nominal GDP). (Source: OECD Economic Outlook.)

estimates by the Organization for Economic Cooperation and Development (OECD), the oil price increase reduced demand in the Western world by approximately $16 billion. At the same time, many Western countries had already been pursuing restrictive macroeconomic policies in response to the strong boom of the early seventies. As a result of both shocks, unemployment started to rise alarmingly throughout the Western world. In Germany, unemployment rose from 0.8 percent in 1973 to 3.6 percent in 1975. Not surprisingly, the SPD-FDP coalition immediately embarked on a program of deficit spending in the budget for 1974. Consequently, the budget turned around from a surplus of 1.2 percent in 1973 to a deficit of 5.6 percent in 1975 (see Figure 5.3).

Dutch fiscal policy reacted in a similar way. In the Netherlands, the 1973 elections led to the formation of probably the most leftist government in the history of the country. The PvdA was the largest party in the cabinet with seven out of sixteen ministers. Since the rightist CHU (Christelijk Historische Unie) did not take part, the Christian democratic part of the cabinet also showed a relatively leftist tendency. Furthermore, the PPR (Politieke Partij Radicalen) and the left-liberals (D'66) were represented in the cabinet. The new Dutch cabinet, not surprisingly, attached a high priority to full employment. When the unemployment rate started to increase rapidly from 2.2 percent in 1973 to 2.7 percent in 1974 and 5.2 percent in 1975, Keynesian deficit spending was set in motion. Expansionary fiscal measures of the den Uyl government until 1976 totaled more than 10 billion guilders. The bulk of additional spending was used for stimulating construction activity. Although less dramatically than in Germany, in the Netherlands the budget turned around from a surplus of 0.6 percent in 1973 to a deficit of 3 percent in 1975 (see Figure 5.3).

THE FAILURE OF KEYNESIANISM AND SOCIAL DEMOCRACY

Whether Keynesian deficit spending could succeed depended on the course of monetary policy. Instead of supporting fiscal expansion, both central banks were pursuing fiercely restrictive policies. German monetary policy had turned strongly restrictive after March 1973 when the Bundesbank and the government decided to float the Deutsche mark. As long as the mark was tied to its dollar parity, the Bundesbank was unable to decisively combat the inflationary pressures resulting from strong growth and tight labor markets in 1972–73. Instead of curtailing money growth, it was forced to sell large amounts of marks in exchange for dollars in order to prevent appreciation. On March 1 alone, the Bundesbank bought $2.7 billion. The oil price crisis did not cause the bank to change its course. The inflationary effects of the oil crisis did not seem to call for more relaxed monetary policies. Yet at the same time the bank also realized that any attempt to prevent an upturn in inflation in the wake of the oil price increase would have disastrous consequences. More important, the bargaining round of 1974 in which the aggressive tactics of the unions brought them large nominal wage increases convinced the bank that tight money was necessary. While the SPD-FDP government embarked on expansionary fiscal policies, the Bundesbank pursued a tightly restrictive stance.

The Dutch central bank pursued similar policies for much the same reasons. Having a reputation for low inflation like the Deutsche mark, also the guilder came under strong upward pressure during the final stage of the Bretton Woods system, thereby preventing the bank from tackling domestic inflationary pressures. The DNB also remained convinced that the wage bargaining behavior of the unions did not mandate a more relaxed stance even after unemployment had started to increase. Thus, restrictive monetary policies counteracted more expansionary fiscal policies in 1974 but the conflict eased in the second part of 1974 as the guilder was strong on international markets.

Given tight money it was not too surprising that the fiscal expansion packages failed to solve the unemployment problem. Whereas budget deficits increased rapidly, unemployment did not decrease, although it seemed to stabilize in 1976. In response, both governments resolved to reduce budget deficits in 1976. In Germany, Chancellor Helmut Schmidt approved a package of budget cuts on September 10, 1975, with the aim of reducing the deficit by about DM 23 billion during the next two years. The core of the package consisted of a reduction in benefits from and an increase in contributions to the unemployment insurance fund.[22] In the Netherlands, 1976 marked the turning point in the PvdA's fiscal policies from Keynesian stimulation to budget consolidation. Confronted with higher budget deficits, rising unemployment, and a weak guilder, PvdA minister of finance Wim Duisenberg (later to become president of the DNB) initiated the so-called 1 percent operation, which aimed to reduce the growth of the collective sector.[23] Public expenditures now came to be seen as contributing to the crisis. The generous social welfare system, it was argued, contributed to a loss in competitiveness through the high burden it placed on total labor costs. Moreover, in a highly open economy like the Dutch, fiscal spending would lead to current account deficits rather than domestic employment. The high budget deficits that would result from maintaining the system at the present level would furthermore lead to a greater need for financing and thereby promote monetary instability.

Duisenberg's turn toward fiscal austerity, however, would eventually bring about the eviction of the social democrats from government. Once the solution to the crisis was identified in terms of increasing export competitiveness by means of lowering costs, the left wing of the CDA was necessarily placed on the defensive, as were the social democrats. For the right wing, on the other hand, it seemed more attractive to form a government with the liberals, since the latter party was not as attached to the welfare state as the social democrats. Because the social democrats and liberals up to 1994 excluded each other as possible coalition partners, it had been impossible, ever since the introduction of general suffrage, to form a government without the Christian democrats.

Accordingly, the power relations within that party, rather than election outcomes, were decisive in terms of government formation. Despite a significant gain in votes, the PvdA was ousted from government after the 1977 elections as the Christian democrats decided to govern with the liberals instead (see Table 5.1).

By 1976–77, it was still by no means decided that tight money and fiscal austerity would come to be the dominant policy pattern for the next decades in Germany and the Netherlands. At least in the former, it seemed initially that the years 1972–74 might merely be an instance of a, albeit somewhat longer, stabilization recession along the lines of 1966–67. Admittedly, the switch to a policy of monetary targeting in 1974 did convey a clear signal that the bank from now on would not accept any responsibility for unemployment but would concentrate solely on price stability. However, from late 1974 onward, after it had become convinced that its restrictive policies had done enough to impress the trade unions, the Bundesbank assumed a more relaxed stance and maintained it until late 1978. And although the bank held that unemployment was the result of the failure of wage bargaining to adjust to the preannounced monetary target, such an argument was not necessarily convincing in the event its monetary policies led to a sharp appreciation of the German mark. In August 1976, the bank, under pressure from the government, intervened heavily on the foreign exchange market in order to prevent a depreciation of the currency of its second biggest trading partner, the Dutch guilder. Partly because of the support measures for the guilder, the monetary target for that year was exceeded. With the creation of the EMS in 1978, on the initiative of Chancellor Schmidt and French president Valéry Giscard d'Estaing, German monetary policies now also officially carried a responsibility for the exchange rate.

In addition, the more relaxed monetary policies were supported by a renewed turn to fiscal expansion. The disappointing results of the 1976 Bundestag elections created strong pressures within the SPD for additional measures against unemployment. In March 1977, Chancellor Schmidt approved a fiscal stimulation package in the amount of DM 14 billion, which was topped up in June. One year later, at the Bonn summit of July 1978, Schmidt agreed with the other major OECD economies that, given its large and persistent current account surpluses, Germany should now assume the role of a "locomotive" that was to help pull the world economy out of the recession by means of additional fiscal spending. The Bundesbank ended up supporting the government, although its president, Otmar Emminger, was reluctant.

By 1977–78 then, the stage seemed set for a strategy of concerted macroeconomic expansion in which not only the Bundesbank and the government, but also all major OECD economies, would pull in the same direction. Soon, however, Schmidt's fiscal expansion hit the wall of an ever more restrictive monetary policy. This time the impulse for the Bundesbank's change in policy came from abroad. Although Britain, the United States, and France had pressured Germany for more expansionary policies, they themselves lacked the

Table 5.1. *Dutch governments, 1973–98*

Prime minister	Year of investiture	Labor (PvdA)	Catholics (KVP)	Protestants (ARP)	Christians (CDA)	Liberals (VVD)	Left liberals (D'66)	Radicals (PPR)
Den Uyl	1973	X	R	R			R	R
Van Agt	1977				X	R		
Van Agt	1981	R			X		R	
Lubbers	1982				X	R		
Lubbers	1986				X	R		
Lubbers	1989	R			X			
Kok	1994	X				R	R	
Kok	1998	X				R	R	

Note: See Table 3.1.

institutional preconditions for such a strategy. By the winter of 1978, the Labour Party's policy of a "Social Contract" with the TUC exploded in rampant industrial unrest and escalating inflation. Soon after, Callaghan was voted out of office, and his conservative successor, Margaret Thatcher, embarked on a monetary shock therapy. Of more importance was that the U.S. Federal Reserve turned to a sharply restrictive monetarist strategy on October 6, 1979. Finally, the second oil price crisis of 1979 produced an additional negative demand shock combined with inflationary pressures. Germany, in fact, was now pursuing more expansionary policies than most of its trading partners. As a result, the current account surplus made way for a deficit and the mark came under strong downward pressure. In 1980, a crisis of confidence in the mark erupted. At first, the Bundesbank tried to stem the outflow of funds by a combination of intervention on the currency markets and increasing the discount rate. After it lost about one-quarter of its reserves between October 1979 and April 1980, it decided to move to a fully restrictive policy. Monetary policy was progressively tightened over the next year, especially in February 1981. The Bundesbank admitted that from the viewpoint of the domestic economy the restrictive policy could not be justified, but it argued that such policies had to be pursued due to external pressures – that is, the Federal Reserve's policy.[24]

Given the Bundesbank's stance, the policy of fiscal expansion had to become a heavy burden on the budget. The deficit increased from 2.4 percent of gross domestic product in 1977 to 3.7 percent in 1981, while unemployment also increased from 3.3 percent to 4.5 percent. Many now came to see fiscal spending as the problem rather than the solution. In order for public finances not to get out of hand, taxes would have to be raised or spending cut. Moreover, fiscal expansion also seemed to contribute to inflation as it had contributed to the current account deficit and the downward pressures on the Deutsche mark. Given that fiscal spending was ineffective, cutting spending, rather than increasing the burden on German industry by raising taxes, seemed the more promising route. In addition, many high-ranking social democrats in the government and the ministries felt that a turn to fiscal austerity was inevitable. The decisive pressure came, however, from the liberal coalition partner, the FDP. Because the FDP catered mainly to a well-off audience, it preferred a strategy of social security cuts combined with tax reductions for business. Since the party occupied a pivotal position in parliament, it could easily blackmail Chancellor Schmidt, which in turn brought him the wrath of many within his party. Nevertheless, the Christian democrats now seemed a much more attractive coalition partner for the FDP than an SPD that was deeply split on the issue of fiscal austerity. In the fall of 1982, finally, the FDP withdrew from the coalition and joined a Christian democratic government under Chancellor Helmut Kohl because the SPD, not unlike the Müller government in 1930, felt that it could no longer go along with a policy of cutting labor market programs and unemployment benefits while business was to receive tax breaks.

In the Netherlands, the deep recession that set in around 1979 initially

Table 5.2. *German governments, 1966–98*

Chancellor	Year of investiture	Labor (SPD)	Christian (CDU)	Bavarian Christian (CSU)	Greens	Liberals (FDP)
Kiesinger	1966	R	X	R		
Brandt	1969	X				R
Brandt	1972	X				R
Schmidt	1974	X				R
Schmidt	1976	X				R
Schmidt	1980	X				R
Kohl	1982		X	R		R
Kohl	1982		X	R		R
Kohl	1987		X	R		R
Kohl	1991		X	R		R
Kohl	1995		X	R		R
Schröder	1998	X			R	

Note: See Table 3.1.

seemed to strengthen the position of the social democrats. Under the pressure of the rapid increase in unemployment, from 5.4 percent in 1979 to 8.5 percent in 1981, the labor-oriented wing of the Christian democrats managed to convince the party of the need for a coalition with the social democrats. In the new coalition government, which was formed in 1981, the post of a "superminister" charged with reducing unemployment was specially created for former PvdA prime minister Joop den Uyl. But, the coalition was doomed from the outset. Although the Christian democrats agreed that measures against unemployment were urgently needed, they were not willing to tolerate higher budget deficits, and the willingness to implement fiscal stimulation packages decreased further as the recession by itself led to a rapid deterioration of the budget deficit from 3.6 percent of GDP in 1979 to 5.3 percent in 1981. Den Uyl, in turn, did not see how he could accomplish his assigned task while having to cut rather than increase spending. The coalition broke up again in 1982, and the Christian democrats returned to govern with the liberals.

The new government under Ruud Lubbers then moved to terminate the corporatist pattern of negotiated bargaining, which was seen to have become an intolerable burden on the budget.[25] Since unemployment increased to more than 10 percent in the early eighties, wage moderation could be left to the market, possibly aided by government wage decrees if the results were not satisfactory.

Indeed on November 19, 1982, unions and employers signed the so-called agreement of Wassenaar, which mainly exchanged wage moderation for a promise from the employers to reduce working hours. As the leader of the Christian union, Harm Vermeulen, stated afterward, he was so afraid of the possible invocation of decree laws by the new government that he decided to support the agreement.[26] For more than a decade the agreement did nothing to reduce unemployment. When unemployment started falling since the midnineties, however, it increasingly came to be seen as the main reason for the Dutch success.

By 1981–82, the new economic policy regime had stabilized in both countries. Keynesianism now was definitely abandoned. But as cost cutting rather than fiscal expansion was identified as the only promising economic strategy, social democrats became unattractive coalition partners for the German liberals and Dutch Christian democrats. Nor could expansionists in both countries any longer hope for support from lax monetary policies abroad, which would cause the currency to appreciate faster than the unions could cut wages. Instead, Western European countries increasingly came to accept the lead of the Bundesbank in monetary policies.

STRONG CENTRAL BANKS?

There was an alternative. If fiscal policies were not available, then the fight against unemployment would have to rely on an expansionary monetary policy. And if other countries were unwilling or unable to pursue similar policies, then any fixed exchange rate commitment would have to be abandoned. As we shall see later, the Swedish SAP prevented the mass unemployment that came to characterize nearly all other Western European countries by such a strategy. Admittedly, the Swedish social democrats had to abandon this approach in the late eighties because it placed excessive demands on labor market institutions. But, this was obviously not known in the early eighties. The question, then, is why German and Dutch social democrats did not try by this means to prevent the conflict between fiscal and monetary policies, which eventually got them ousted from office.

In the case of Germany, a popular answer has become that such a strategy would have been impossible because of the political independence of the Bundesbank. Article 3 of the Bundesbank law states that the bank shall regulate the supply of money and credit to the economy with the goal of safeguarding the currency. Article 12 states, furthermore, that the government does not have the right to issue directives to the bank and that the bank is required to support the general economic policy of the government only insofar as this is compatible with the goal of safeguarding the currency. The indirect channels of influence, which the federal government can use, are quite limited as it can appoint only ten out of twenty-one members of the central bank council. All members are appointed for a fixed (renewable) term of eight years. The only immediate means of influence at the disposal of the federal government is the right to postpone decisions of the Bundesbank for a period of up to two weeks.

Given a politically independent central bank, a regime that delegates the concern for price stability mainly to labor market institutions would seem institutionally impossible. As Fritz W. Scharpf (1987) has shown in a game-theoretical analysis, for a central bank whose primary concern is low inflation, the optimal strategy is to pursue restrictive policies that will maintain a sufficiently high level of unemployment rather than to rely on the cooperation of the trade unions and thereby risk failing to achieve its goal. Yet, it would be incorrect to argue that the new policy regime was imposed upon the German government by the Bundesbank.

From a legal point of view, the independence of the Bundesbank is not as watertight as it may seem at first sight. First, despite the absence of the right to give directives to the central bank, the decision-making process on monetary policy is legally a matter for both the government and the bank, because the government has the right to decide on exchange rate arrangements. Chancellor Schmidt, for example, could have committed Germany to a fixed exchange rate with, say, the French franc in the midseventies, thereby forcing the bank to conduct potentially unlimited foreign exchange intervention in the case of a threatening appreciation. The result would have been that the SPD, via the route of an expansion-minded Banque de France, could have pursued more relaxed monetary policies while leaving the Bundesbank law intact. Such a policy would not necessarily have conflicted with article 3 of the Bundesbank law, since it does not distinguish between external and internal stability of the currency. Hence, it is legally not entirely clear whether this article does indeed direct the Bundesbank to give absolute priority to low inflation. With respect to a similar formulation that parliament had asked him to insert in the 1948 law on the DNB, Dutch finance minister Pieter Lieftinck (1989: 166) remarked: "The currency has both an internal value, expressed in the domestic price level, as well as an external value, expressed in the exchange rates. Frequently, stabilization of one value excludes stabilization of the other. The formulation desired by parliament, in my eyes, was therefore rather inconsequential."[27] Finally, the independence of the Bundesbank is not anchored in the constitution; a simple parliamentary majority is sufficient to abolish it.[28] Dutch social democrats confronted none of these problems, as the DNB is not politically independent. In 1948, the bank was nationalized and the new central bank law explicitly gave the minister of finance the right to issue directives to the DNB.[29]

A more serious hurdle for any German government wanting to change the course of monetary policies is the strong public support for an independent central bank. It is generally accepted by the German public that credit for the relatively low inflation since the early fifties, compared to the monetary misman-agement of the early twenties and the Nazi period, goes primarily to the independence of the Bundesbank. Any government attempting to override the bank hence easily incurs the suspicion of wanting to bring about another hyperinflation. Such an interpretation of German monetary policies was by no means inevitable, however. As was argued in Chapter 3, the hyperinflation was not due to the lack of an independent Reichsbank. Nor does it seem likely that Hitler would have allowed an independent central bank to frustrate his armament program. Given the disastrous economic and political consequences of the deflationary policies of the independent Reichsbank under Hjalmar Schacht and Hans Luther, it is just as conceivable that an independent central bank would have been seen as a threat in the Federal Republic. That it was not is mainly attributable to the historical and institutional peculiarities of the early Federal Republic.

The Bundesbank and its predecessor, the Bank deutscher Länder (BdL), were certainly not born as monetarist-minded institutions. As in other countries, German monetary policies were growth oriented during the fifties and sixties. Indeed, the phenomenal economic growth rates of the Federal Republic would not have been possible without such policies. In fact, a major reason why the Bundesbank was granted a large degree of political independence when it was created in 1957 was that the policies of the equally independent BdL were judged to have been quite conducive to growth.[30] Except for a minor collision between Chancellor Konrad Adenauer and the BdL in 1956, a conflict between growth-oriented economic policies and a central bank intent on keeping a stable price level did not materialize. At times, the BdL seemed even more expansion minded than the government. For example, during the discussions of the mid-fifties about the institutional setup for a new central bank that was to replace the occupation-era BdL, the latter resisted legal limits on money creation. Economics minister Ludwig Erhard's draft of a Bundesbank law of October 25, 1955, contained the provision that the bank be allowed to increase the currency in circulation only up to a maximum of DM 1 billion at a time. Moreover, the bank would only be allowed to do so if the government agreed. The BdL, however, opposed this provision because increases of the amount of currency in circulation were the symptom rather than the cause of inflationary developments.[31] Until the early seventies, the Bundesbank pursued a growth-oriented policy of its own accord and not primarily because it had no choice under the Bretton Woods regime. As former Bundesbank president Emminger (1987) remarked, during the fifties and sixties the bank did not yet recognize the existence of a possible contradiction between the requirements of external exchange rate stability and domestic price stability.

If Germany had been confronted with tight labor markets in the fifties, then the choice between restrictive monetary policies that maintained price stability at the price of creating unemployment, and a growth-oriented policy combined with negotiated wage moderation, would have had to be addressed from the beginning. Not only because of the union's very moderate stance but, more important, because of a large influx of labor from Eastern Europe, rapid growth did not create inflationary pressures. Despite the roughly five million

German war casualties, the population of West Germany increased from 43 million in 1939 to 54.3 million in 1958.[32] The bank could thus argue convincingly that a monetary policy aimed at price stability and conducted by an independent central bank was, in fact, very conducive to growth.

Starting in the late fifties, German labor markets became tight, but the Bundesbank, instead of periodically assisting the unions by a dose of restriction, generally continued its expansionary course. During this period, the bank seems to have been most concerned with the prosperity of the export industry. Given its massive current account surplus and its low inflation, the German mark was a perennial candidate for revaluation, but the Bundesbank adamantly refused and hence was frequently forced to loosen the monetary reins even more.

The conflict became manifest for the first time in 1960. In response to tightening labor market pressures and mounting inflation, the Bundesbank did initially decide to steer a more restrictive course in June. One week later, however, the U.S. Federal Reserve lowered its interest rates and large amounts of foreign funds flowed into Germany. The conflict might have been easily solved by letting the mark appreciate. Yet, at a meeting with Chancellor Adenauer on August 4, 1960, such a solution was rejected. As Emminger (1987: 111) reports, Bundesbank president Karl Blessing fully supported this decision. Instead, the bank called upon the federal government to increase capital outflows, for example in the form of development aid, in order to reduce the upward pressure on the mark. Also in 1961, the Bundesbank, strongly supported by the CSU minister of economics Franz-Josef Strauss, adamantly opposed the government's suggestion of a revaluation in order to correct the massive current account surplus. Blessing even threatened to resign, although he eventually decided not to carry out his threat when the government gave in to pressures and revalued nevertheless.[33] The Bundesbank, admittedly, did support SPD economics minister Karl Schiller when he, against the wishes of the Christian democratic cabinet majority, proposed to revalue the mark in 1968. This episode did not, however, mark a decisive change in Bundesbank thinking. Three years later, Schiller and Bundesbank president Karl Klasen found themselves in opposite camps. In accordance with the views held by the majority of banking and industry, Klasen strongly opposed Schiller's decision to temporarily float the mark and proposed exchange controls instead.[34] According to Emminger (1987: 230), the Bundesbank council itself was split on the issue. Whereas the majority supported Klasen, a minority of seven members advocated floating. One year later (1972), the debate was repeated, but this time Klasen prevailed.

The consistent refusal to revalue was a contributing factor to the breakdown of wage moderation, which occurred in the late sixties and early seventies. Indeed, Schiller proposed revaluation in 1968 and floated the mark in 1971 because he feared the tight labor market would threaten the ability of the main union, DGB (Deutscher Gewerkschaftsbund), to maintain its policy of wage moderation. But given the experience of the fifties and sixties, it was fairly easy for the bank to convince the public that the problem lay solely with the trade unions and that a restrictive policy aimed at breaking inflation was, in fact, a precondition for a return to the postwar growth rates. At the same time, Germans were also generally convinced that a current account surplus contributed crucially to growth and employment. If the mark had appreciated strongly in real terms, the Bundesbank still might have been challenged, but, because higher inflation abroad frequently overcompensated for nominal appreciation of the mark, and because more and more countries came to use the mark as an inflation anchor, this did not happen.

WEAK LABOR

Public support for the Bundesbank seems insufficient as an explanation of why the SPD tolerated monetary policies that caused its downfall. If social democrats had perceived a viable alternative, they would certainly have advocated it, even if, from a political point of view, it were not immediately feasible. In fact, Chancellor Schmidt mostly supported the policies of the bank, and Dutch social democrats never proposed directing the DNB to change course.

The Bundesbank's change to restrictive policies in 1973, as well as the switch to monetary targeting in 1974, was clearly supported by the government. Although there is some dispute as to where exactly the idea of monetary targeting originated in Germany – within the Bundesbank, the Council of Economic Experts, or with Helmut Schmidt – it is clear that the SPD government did not object to this new policy.[35] After the escalating wage bargaining round in 1974, and especially after the embarrassing defeat of the government in the negotiations with the public-sector trade union ÖTV (Gewerkschaft Öffentliche Dienste, Transport und Verkehr), monetary targeting was to Chancellor Schmidt a welcome device that could restore discipline in the labor market. The Bundesbank and the government remained in agreement about monetary policies until early 1979. The tighter policies of the Bundesbank as of early 1979 did, however, prompt an open conflict between the bank and Schmidt. Schmidt complained bitterly about unnecessarily high interest rates in 1981, and it was even rumored that he was preparing to change the Bundesbank law.

It is quite doubtful, however, that Schmidt was actually calling for a regime change whereby the fight against inflation should again be delegated to the labor market institutions so that the Bundesbank could concentrate on stimulating the economy. As Schmidt stated in late 1979:

> We were also the first [government] to understand that you cannot cure the world's economic structural crisis by printing money. We'll not give up our conviction in that field. Others are on the verge of giving it up,

some don't have the strength to do it although they understand its being necessary. No, we will not accept wrongly so-called Keynesian recipes for a totally non-Keynesian situation.[36]

Schmidt also agreed that the mark should not be allowed to devalue like the yen; he merely believed that the exchange rate could be stabilized at somewhat lower interest rates. Whether his policy could have succeeded is difficult to say, but it is clear in any case that as long as it was accepted that the Bundesbank should follow the Federal Reserve, economic developments would not have been much different in Germany even if Schmidt had had his way in 1981. A Swedish-style strategy was advocated by only a tiny minority of social democrats. Hans-Jürgen Krupp, former president of the German Institute for Economic Research and main economic adviser of the SPD, was one of them. Another one was Alois Pfeiffer of the DGB board, who suggested that the Bundesbank let the mark devalue, and he pledged that the trade unions would exert moderation in order not to increase inflationary pressures.[37]

In the Netherlands, there are no indications that the PvdA ever seriously advocated a Swedish strategy of flexible exchange rate so as to prioritize full employment in a restrictive international environment. Conflicts between social democrats and the bank have been few and unimportant. During and shortly after the social democratic–Christian coalition of 1973–77 some criticism was voiced with respect to the exchange rate policy of the DNB. Because the policy of maintaining the parity with the mark, especially during 1977 and 1978, implied a revaluation with respect to many other countries, some social democrats argued that the DNB was counteracting the policy of improving competitiveness by means of wage moderation, and thereby was in fact preventing a reduction in unemployment.[38] On April 13, 1978, during a parliamentary debate about exchange rate policies, PvdA member Thijs Wöltgens did suggest that the DNB should take a more independent position from the Bundesbank, but he was not willing to draw the logical conclusion and advocate devaluation. In a similar debate on September 24, 1979, PvdA member Hans Kombrink encountered a similar problem with his statements. He maintained that the policy of the DNB neutralized the positive effects of wage moderation. In response to criticism from the government, however, he explained that he did not advocate devaluation, but thought that the guilder should not appreciate. As the DNB pointed out, that was a contradictory position because, given the depreciation of the dollar during the previous years, a policy of maintaining the real exchange rate would have required devaluations within the EMS framework.[39] In 1989, Wim Kok, chairman of the FNV trade union under the PvdA Christian coalition, minister of finance from 1989 to 1993, and currently prime minister, even explained that the difference in monetary policy was one of the crucial reasons why Sweden could pursue a successful policy of full employment whereas the Netherlands could not: "Sweden has created for itself space in monetary policy that, in a not unimportant way, made it possible to give priority to employment instead of to reducing inflation and maintaining the value of the currency."[40] This was quite true. Unfortunately, Kok never advocated such a strategy for the Netherlands.

Social democrats in both countries were convinced that their central bank presidents were right when they argued that a devaluation strategy would simply provoke a renewed price-wage spiral. The outlook of both parties was, and to no small extent still is, shaped by the historical failures in income policies that they both experienced in the sixties and early seventies. The wage explosions of those periods did not necessarily indicate a durable breakdown of the unions' capacity for wage moderation. Indeed, the strong focus on relative wage differences, which increasingly came to frustrate British and Swedish unions' policies of nominal moderation, was much less pronounced in Germany and the Netherlands. Because the reemergence of mass unemployment had made a deep impression on both unions, a Swedish-style strategy might also have been workable in the early eighties in Germany and the Netherlands. But the links between the unions and the party in both countries were too weak to make such a policy an unavoidable choice. Due to the lack of experience with negotiated wage settlement involving the state, for most of the fifties and sixties, the amount of mutual trust required for a Swedish-style policy was lacking in Germany. The same was the case in the Netherlands, but for quite different reasons. After the breakdown of government-dominated wage setting in the sixties, politicians found it difficult to come to terms with emancipated, though in principle still rather moderate, unions.

In addition, the structure of the unions itself militated against a strategy that placed the fate of social democratic economic policies entirely in their hands. That unions should bring sacrifices in order to keep a social democratic government in office is a generally accepted principle in Scandinavia, although it does not always work out in practice, simply because the unions and the party are considered different wings of the same movement.[41] This is not the case in Germany and the Netherlands. Although the majority of the DGB's leaders and members may have clear sympathies for the SPD, the unions are politically neutral and do have a strong segment of Christian democratic workers. In the Netherlands, unions were split along Catholic, Protestant, and social democratic lines up to the late seventies, when the Catholics and social democrats merged. Conversely, the need of Dutch and German social democratic parties to form coalition governments and the continuous presence of a viable non–social democratic government alternative also make it more difficult for even social democratic unions to trust that its sacrifices for a social democratic government will not be in vain in the end.

German Tarifautonomie

After the experience of the Weimar Republic and the Third Reich, the German trade unions came to consider the principle of government abstinence from wage bargaining (*Tarifautonomie*) as one of their most sacred achievements.

With the increasingly tight labor markets of the sixties, however, the German government came to perceive an increasing need to influence wage bargaining.[42] Christian democratic economics minister Ludwig Erhard was, in principle, quite opposed to giving organized interest groups access to political decision making. For Erhard, the competing demands organized interests made on the state were detrimental to the economy. Yet, under the conditions of the sixties, this aversion could not give rise to a "liberal" style of policy making, which kept such organizations at arm's length. Similar to British conservative prime minister Edward Heath's U-turn from neoliberalism back to corporatism in the early seventies, Erhard had to seek closer relationships with organized interests as long as he was not willing to tolerate either mass unemployment or high inflation. Accordingly, he called for a stronger direct influence of the state over the organizations of civil society. As distributional struggles intensified, Erhard argued, the liberal stage, inaugurated by him, should now make way for a more structured polity.[43] The concept of the *formierte Gesellschaft* (structured society), which Erhard presented in his inaugural speech as federal chancellor on November 10, 1965, envisaged stronger corporatist elements that would allow the state to dominate organized interest groups.

In response, Karl Schiller of the SPD advocated a corporatist solution in which interest groups and the state were to interact on a more equal footing.[44] Schiller's "Concerted Action," a tripartite meeting for the purpose of coordinating economic policies, was part of the introduction of Keynesian concepts of discretionary fiscal policy aimed at influencing short-term demand conditions; it met for the first time on February 14, 1967. In fact, Schiller only implemented his Keynesian response to the recession of 1967 after he had convinced the unions of the need for moderation. But, as Scharpf (1987: 157) notes, by the midseventies the Concerted Action had degenerated into a mass meeting at which the leaders of the participating groups read prepared statements to the press.

Both the trade unions and the government would come to look back with bad memories on this period of informal income policies. The boom that started in the summer of 1967 was unexpectedly strong, as were productivity increases in industry. In the first 1967 sessions of the Concerted Action, the DGB had agreed to wage increases of 4–5 percent but productivity in industry increased by 8.6 percent in 1968.[45] As profits exploded while the unions pursued wage moderation, Germany experienced a wave of wildcat strikes in 1969, which was followed by a "wage explosion" in the bargaining rounds of 1970–72. In the summer of 1973, another wave of wildcat strikes occurred, albeit less widespread than in the fall of 1969, as workers tried to obtain compensation for high inflation. The culmination came in 1974 in the form of a humiliating defeat for the government in the wage bargaining round with the public-sector trade union ÖTV. In the previous year, the ÖTV had accepted the government's demand for a "stability sacrifice." As prices rose much faster than expected, the rank and file grew restless, which forced the ÖTV leadership to take quite an aggressive stance in the 1974 round. Chancellor Brandt suffered a serious loss of prestige when he had to give in to the ÖTV after having declared publicly that he would stand firm. It was mainly this experience that made Helmut Schmidt reluctant to advocate a Swedish-style strategy.

The Emancipation of Dutch Unions

The system of income policies that developed in the Netherlands after the war was the most rigid of any country. Rather than being based on bi- or tripartite negotiations, the minister of social affairs, more or less unilaterally, determined wages. The main task of the trade unions was to secure their members' acceptance of the ordained wage level. Politically this system rested on the segmentation of society in hierarchically organized Catholic, Protestant, and social democratic pillars.

Unlike Germany, the Netherlands could not benefit from an extensive influx of labor, and the peculiar Dutch brand of Catholicism and Calvinism prevented tapping the domestic female labor supply to an extent comparable to patterns in other European countries. Inevitably, therefore, the attempt to pursue a state-directed wage policy under tight labor markets was to come in conflict with the organizational logic of the trade unions. Moreover, after having reached its peak in the early fifties, the internal cohesion of the pillars, and with it the control of the leadership of the rank and file, rapidly declined.[46]

The beginning of the end – "of guided" wage setting – came in 1963. Rapidly mounting rank-and-file resistance against state-dominated wage setting increasingly undermined the position of the union leadership and forced them to take a more independent attitude with respect to the state. In order to attract sufficient labor, employers in the meantime increasingly resorted to (illegal) wage drift. To prevent a complete breakdown of the system, the government granted two exceptionally high annual wage increases of around 10 percent. These measures calmed relations somewhat, but employers and unions by now were convinced that the system had to be abolished. In 1968, the government seemed to give in as it determined that wages henceforth should be set by means of bipartite negotiations at the sectoral level. At the same time, the government wished to reserve the right to declare a general wage freeze or even annul individual wage agreements if it deemed fit. The unions had severe doubts that the government, in fact, was willing to grant more freedom in wage bargaining and announced determined opposition to the new laws.

As in many other countries, labor market conflicts also came to a head in the Netherlands during the late sixties and early seventies. When parliament accepted the new wage laws in early 1969, the Catholic and social democratic unions took the unprecedented step of ending their participation in tripartite labor market bodies. As J. P. Windmuller, C. de Galan, and A. F. van Zweeden (1985: 224) put it, "The trade union movement more or less declared war on the government." When the new laws were first applied in 1971, all three major unions called a general strike of one hour against the government. Moreover, in

1970 a number of wildcat strikes for higher wages erupted that the unions soon felt forced to support in order not to lose control entirely. As a result, strike activity was at an unprecedented high during the years 1970–73.

Wage bargaining seemed to be entirely out of control, but matters seemed worse than they were. Despite the wildcat strikes, the union leadership had not lost its authority, nor did union leaders and members deny that wage setting had a heavy responsibility for supporting an economic strategy aimed at full employment and low inflation. In 1971, the first tripartite national-level agreement was signed, and macroeconomic considerations did play an important role in determining the room for wage increases. Two years later, a similar agreement was signed.

What had changed was that the unions now had to be offered a quid pro quo for wage moderation. In contrast to the fifties and sixties, they were no longer satisfied with the role of ensuring the implementation of government policies. The government repeatedly offered an increase in its contributions to the social welfare system as well as reductions in direct taxes in order to compensate for the fall in wages. A larger degree of income equality, a better social security system, and more expansionary fiscal policies in order to stimulate employment ranked highest on their list of priorities. The Netherlands, in short, had moved to a corporatist pattern of conflict mediation.[47]

Relations between the government and unions improved markedly in 1973 when the den Uyl government, which was clearly sympathetic to labor, was elected. Unions did not protest when den Uyl, under the weight of the rapidly deteriorating economic situation after 1973, requested far-reaching, but temporary, powers in income policies. As the economy deteriorated further, the unions agreed to a standstill in real wages for the year 1976. During the 1975 negotiations, they offered to keep wage growth below productivity, and their willingness for moderation increased in stages with the deepening of the crisis from the demand to price compensation only, to the demand for price compensation only for lower incomes, to the acceptance of general real wage reductions for everybody.

The den Uyl government seemed to enjoy favorable institutional preconditions for keeping inflation low even if monetary policies would have become more expansionary. Social democratic cabinet members, on the other hand, were deeply split over the desirability of expansionary macroeconomic policies. Keynesianism never became widely accepted in the Netherlands. Instead, the conviction that crises always called for moderation remained the most important economic dogma of the deeply Calvinist Dutch soul. During the parliamentary debates about the SDAP's *Plan van de Arbeid*, several MPs voiced the opinion that deficit spending in fact was immoral because penance (income cuts) rather than profligacy was required in a crisis. Also the boom of the fifties and sixties was mainly interpreted as the result of a policy that kept real wages below those in competing countries. The breakdown of state-dominated wage bargaining thus was widely interpreted as a disaster that eliminated the central cause of

Dutch prosperity. To be sure, the Calvinist belief in moderation as the cure for all possible economic evils was not an absolutely insurmountable hurdle, as Colijn's law on collective bargaining of 1937 showed, but it required a long-drawn-out deflationary constellation to overcome it. The inflation of the seventies, however, inevitably would reinforce it instead. Soon after the downturn in economic growth of the early seventies, Dutch economic policies, with the partial support of the social democrats, relapsed into a policy pattern reminiscent of the interwar period.

The change from government-dominated to negotiated wage setting also led important social democratic politicians to believe that cost cutting was the only feasible method of reducing unemployment. When the Keynesian measures of the den Uyl government did not have immediate effects on unemployment, but rather seemed to increase the deficit, strong opposition arose from within the PvdA. Den Uyl's most powerful opponent was social democratic finance minister Duisenberg. According to Duisenberg, fiscal deficit spending not only increased the budget deficit, it also reduced pressures for wage reductions, thereby effectively preventing a solution to the crisis.[48] A cheap money policy coupled with a depreciating currency would have the same effect of reducing pressures for wage reduction, and hence would not be an acceptable strategy either. If, on the other hand, sufficient real wage reduction could be brought about, then a devaluation or cheap money would be unnecessary.

Politically, Duisenberg's position was the stronger one because it dovetailed with the view of most Christian democrats and liberals. Within the party, Duisenberg's fiscal austerity program of 1976 was very unpopular. Yet to argue that fiscal expansion should be supported by cheaper money and hence depreciation relative to the Deutsche mark seemed too risky a strategy to most social democrats. If unions would not accept the real wage cuts resulting from devaluation, then the only result would be inflation.[49] If, instead, unions were willing to moderate wages, then devaluation would be unnecessary.

THE DEFEAT OF THE LABOUR PARTY

The British Labour Party, nor for that matter the Conservatives, not only did not display the Dutch and German reluctance to employ expansionary fiscal *and* monetary policies to combat unemployment, it also did not have to confront an independent central bank. Whereas Keynesianism was not practiced in the interwar period or the fifties and sixties,[50] it was employed frequently in the seventies. The Conservative government of Edward Heath had already turned from austerity to expansion in 1972 in response to rising unemployment. In reaction to the oil price crisis, the Labour government of Harold Wilson took further expansionary measures, although the budget had already been in deficit during 1973. Especially because many other countries did not take such measures, a sizable current account deficit developed (see Figure 5.3).[51] The emerging budget deficit did not necessarily signal the beginning of the end of social democratic government tenure as it had done in Germany and the Netherlands because Labour and the Conservatives were quite willing to relax the exchange rate constraint if necessary to defend domestic employment. Indeed, that monetary policy should be subordinated to growth and employment rather than to a rigidly fixed exchange rate was one of the major lessons the Conservatives and later Labour drew from the unhappy experience with the interwar gold standard. At the first signs of more serious employment problems, Heath and his chancellor Anthony Barber decided to float the pound on June 23, 1972, in order not to compromise the fiscal stimulation package and to protect competitiveness despite above-average inflation rates.

Under expansionary fiscal and monetary policies, the fight against inflation had to rest on price and income policies. However, due to the general outlook of the trade unions as well as their high degree of decentralization, conditions were very unfavorable for such a policy. The decentralization and militancy of British trade unions already were a major problem for the Labour government of Harold Wilson (1964–70) during the later years of its tenure. Wilson felt that wildcat strikes at the local level were a primary cause of the high wage drift that was undermining his statutory income policies. To remedy the situation, the white paper *In Place of Strife* (1969) proposed that the government be given the right to impose a twenty-eight-day cooling-off period in the event of wildcat strikes. In the face of massive opposition from the TUC and the Labour Party, Wilson had to abandon his plans. Also largely in response to trade union opposition Wilson de facto abandoned income policies. The result was a wage explosion. In 1970, nominal wages increased by about 14 percent despite rising unemployment.[52] The Conservative government under Edward Heath, who succeeded Wilson in 1970, was even less successful. Similar to Thatcher in 1979, one of Heath's central campaign pledges had been not to resort to income policies. Instead, he hoped to reduce inflationary wage pressure by means of industrial relations legislation. But as the Thatcher strategy showed, a credible renunciation of income policies could only be made on the basis of the political willingness to rely on high unemployment for holding inflation in check. This, however, Heath was not willing to do. His strategy soon proved to be ineffective, and in 1972 a statutory wage policy was introduced nevertheless.[53] At the same time, price controls were strengthened. The government fell in early 1974, when the miners called a strike in protest against wage policies.

After a wage explosion in 1974–75, the new Wilson government was able to enlist the cooperation of the trade unions. Wilson put his hopes in voluntary wage restraint, the so-called social contract, which in essence was a corporatist policy aimed at achieving voluntary wage moderation in exchange for improvements in social welfare and tax cuts. In addition, he promised a "new industrial strategy" intended to promote modernization and investment in private industry. Although successful in bringing inflation rates down, the wage policies of

1975–76, to the great dismay of many within the TUC, had also reduced real wages.

Due to the fragility of income policies, the British consumer price index rose considerably faster than in the other countries between 1973 and 1978. In 1975, for example, Britain recorded an inflation rate of 23.7 percent as compared to a German rate of 6.0 percent. Without the ability to contain domestic inflation, a soft currency policy had to end in an uncontrollable run on the pound. As the government seemed unable to hold prices down, a depreciation of the currency had to be interpreted as a sign that a policy that tolerated the devaluation of monetary assets would be tolerated in the future. Given fairly open financial markets, the resulting flight out of the currency manifested itself as a flight out of the pound and into foreign currencies. The beginning of the end of Labour came in 1976 when, after another devastating run on sterling, the government was forced to take the rather humiliating step of applying for assistance from the International Monetary Fund. Later that year Labour prime minister James Callaghan declared Keynesianism a failure in a widely noted speech at the party's annual conference in Blackpool. In December 1976, the Labour government started the practice of preannouncing money growth targets (for £M3) as a way of directing monetary policies solely to the fight against inflation. Although Chancellor of the Exchequer Denis Healey held that a low sterling exchange rate was good for British industry, he allowed the pound to float upward after the crisis of confidence had passed in order not to compromise the restrictive monetary policy that he held necessary to combat inflation.

Unable to reach an agreement with the unions on voluntary restraint, Wilson introduced statutory policies for the 1977–78 bargaining round. Initially, it seemed that the shock of 1976 had impressed the labor market parties sufficiently so as to give Labour's economic strategy a chance of survival. The government's policy of a tripartite "social contract" now seemed to work rather successfully. The inflation rate came down from 14.7 percent in 1977 to 9.5 percent in 1978, which put the figure below the Swedish rate of 11.6 percent (see Figure 5.1).

Yet, the social contract caused severe strains within the unions. Many union members saw income policies as measures to increase profits and hold back wages. By late 1978 wage moderation completely collapsed as the fragile centralization, which the TUC had achieved under the voluntary income policies of 1975–77, disintegrated. In the "winter of discontent" rank-and-file opposition to wage moderation exploded in a wave of strikes that disabled much of the British economy during late 1978. Also here the public-sector union (NUPE, National Union of Public Employees) played a crucial role in the breakdown. NUPE members overwhelmingly came from the bottom end of the pay scale, and in comparison even to other British unions, the NUPE leadership had fairly little control over the grass roots. According to Healey (1989: 467): "The winter of discontent was not caused by the frustration of ordinary workers after a long

Table 5.3. *British governments, 1945–97*

Prime minister	Year of investiture	Labour	Conservatives
Attlee	1945	X	
Attlee	1950	X	
Churchill	1951		X
Eden	1955		X
MacMillan	1957		X
Douglas-Home	1963		X
Wilson	1964	X	
Wilson	1966	X	
Heath	1970		X
Wilson	1974	X	
Callaghan	1976	X	
Thatcher	1979		X
Thatcher	1983		X
Thatcher	1987		X
Major	1990		X
Major	1992		X
Blair	1997	X	

Note: See Table 3.1.

period of wage restraint. It was caused by institutional pressures from local trade union activists who had found their roles severely limited by three years of income policies agreed by their national leaders."

In a last attempt to stem the tide, the government convinced the TUC to sign a joint declaration, published in mid-February 1979, in which the latter accepted the objective of reducing inflation to below 5 percent within three years. The TUC also agreed to a so-called national economic assessment, which was to determine the available room for pay increases. At the same time, the TUC issued guidelines concerning industrial disputes that were aimed at reducing secondary picketing and keeping up essential services, and which called for a ballot to precede every strike. Yet by this time, the influence of the TUC over its grass roots was rather limited and strikes continued to escalate.

Unable to implement any form of effective income policies, the Labour Party did not have an alternative anymore to a regime of macroeconomic disinflation and high unemployment. British voters nonetheless spared the party the additional humiliation of having to implement such a regime itself. As a direct result of its inability to handle the industrial relations crisis, Callaghan's government fell over a vote of no confidence on March 28, 1979. In the ensuing general elections of 1979, Margaret Thatcher's Conservative Party won a landslide victory. Labour was dismissed to the opposition benches, where it spent the first years discussing some highly illusory plans of how to regain prosperity by means of turning Britain into a siege economy.

While the basic shift in policy assignments had already taken place before 1979, it was left to Margaret Thatcher to develop the new regime. In 1979, her government embarked on a ferocious policy of high interest rates and fiscal cutbacks. At the same time exchange controls were abandoned, and, partly as a result of North Sea oil, the pound started to appreciate rapidly. In consequence, Britain experienced its worst economic crisis since the war. Nevertheless, the resulting mass unemployment offered no opportunities for an improvement of Labour's electoral fate. The fact that the last Labour government had seen no choice but to reorient policies in a Thatcherite direction made the prime minister's continuously repeated argument that there was no alternative to her policies quite credible.

THE DISINTEGRATION OF SCANDINAVIAN SOCIAL DEMOCRACY

> If we fail and push inflation up again we ourselves must bear the consequences − a lower standard of living, less employment, and less space for an active reform policy. In that case we might have to start to travel the same dark road as many other countries in Europe. (Kjell-Olof Feldt 1986; quoted in Feldt 1991: 295)[54]

In Sweden and Norway instead, the political and institutional conditions seemed ideal for keeping inflation low despite full employment. Although as we have seen, Keynesian policies played a minor role, the principle that recession should be combated by means of deficit spending had become one of the core economic policy convictions of both social democratic parties since the Great Depression. Monetary policies could be counted on to support an expansionary fiscal strategy. Ever since the interwar gold standard was abandoned, the ministry of finance had had the last say in matters of monetary policy. As in Britain, monetary policy could hence be closely coordinated with the government's overall policy strategy. Open financial markets, which the present orthodoxy holds to be the main culprit for the demise of the social democratic program, also would not seem insurmountable. In line with most other countries, Norway and Sweden had implemented far-reaching exchange controls in the years leading up to World War II. In the postwar period, however, the policy of controlling cross-border financial flows was extended and refined with the result that by the midseventies the isolation of domestic financial markets from developments abroad was probably stronger in Norway and Sweden than in any other developed industrial nation.

Labor market institutions seemed very well adapted to supporting expansionary macroeconomic policies by means of nominal wage moderation, and the presence of a dominant and highly centralized trade union greatly facilitated coordination between macroeconomic policies and wage setting. Centralization in itself was not enough, though; wage earners at the local level always faced the incentive to free ride on the moderation of others by defecting from central agreements. Of more importance, perhaps, for ensuring the control of the LO leadership over its members were the traditionally strong paternalistic elements in Scandinavian society and the close ideological links between party and union.

Nonetheless, durable full employment also proved difficult to handle for Scandinavian social democrats. In essence, social democrats stumbled over the same problem that had caused the Swedish Branting government to resign in 1920: full employment set in motion an inflationary spiral that eventually left no choice but to abandon the regime. As the former SAP finance minister Feldt summarized in retrospect, the policy of stimulating growth and defending full employment had been too successful (1991: 303–4): "We had speeded up Sweden to such an extent that both firms and households became too optimistic, too confident in the future. Because of that, wages and prices were increased too strongly and people consumed too much and saved too little. Moreover, the fight against unemployment had been so successful that we now suffered from a serious labor scarcity in several areas."[55]

In Sweden, the official end of the full employment policy was announced by SAP finance minister Allan Larsson in the budget proposals for 1991: "In the long run it is not possible to safeguard employment in an economy that has a higher inflation rate than the surrounding world. In order to protect employment and prosperity, during the next few years economic policies, with all their strength, will have to aim for a permanent reduction in inflation. This task must take priority over all other ambitions and demands."[56] Monetary policies now were assigned the task of breaking inflation while fiscal management had to try to contain the resulting budget deficits. In order to create an external anchor for domestic prices and policies, the krona was pegged to the ECU on May 17, 1991. That the ECU would function as an anchor was assured by the abolition of all foreign exchange controls, which had already been completed by September 21, 1989. Larsson's goal was indeed met: the inflation rate dropped from 9.9 percent in 1990 to 1.2 percent in 1996 (see Figure 5.1). The price to be paid was mass unemployment and huge budget deficits. The open unemployment rate alone (i.e., not counting labor market programs) rose from 1.6 percent in 1990 to 8.1 percent in 1996 (see Figure 5.2). The budget turned around from a surplus of 4.2 percent of gross domestic product in 1990 to a deficit of 10.3 percent in 1994. By 1996, however, a policy of consistent fiscal austerity had reduced the deficit to 3.3 percent.

In the face of escalating inflation and seemingly uncontrollable wage growth, the Norwegian social democratic government had already decided to embark on an austerity course in 1986. Here the centerpiece was a reorientation of monetary policies toward breaking inflation, coupled with fiscal austerity. A foreign anchor for prices and policies was installed somewhat later. On July 1, 1990, the last remaining exchange controls were abolished, and on October 19 of the same year, the Norwegian krone, too, was pegged to the ECU. As a result, open unemployment tripled from 2 percent in 1986 to 6 percent in 1993 (see Figure 5.2). Inflation, on the other hand, fell from 7.9 percent in 1987 to 1.2 percent in 1994 (see Figure 5.1). In a country awash with oil, the budgetary consequences of the new policy strategy were less severe: the surplus declined from 10.2 percent of GDP in 1985 to 0.1 percent in 1991 (see Figure 5.3).

FLEXIBLE EXCHANGE RATES AND THE DEFENSE OF FULL EMPLOYMENT

In Sweden the first oil price crisis occurred during a period when the government had been pursuing rather tight fiscal and monetary policies in order to contain domestic overheating. Almost immediately, the SAP government changed course and temporarily reduced the value-added tax in order to stimulate demand. In addition, subsidies to shipbuilding and the steel industry were stepped up, and industry was offered assistance in financing larger inventories. Soon, however, it seemed that fiscal policy had overreacted, as the demand effects of the oil price crisis were rather small. From 1973 to 1976, unemployment actually fell (see Figure 5.2). Accordingly, it was possible to again increase the budget surplus to 4.7 percent in 1976 after it had fallen from 4.1 percent in 1973 to 2 percent in 1974. Yet, the years 1974–75 merely marked a delay. In 1976, Sweden started to experience the effects of the recession abroad, but at that time the SAP had already been replaced by a bourgeois coalition under the leadership of liberal prime minister Thorbjörn Fälldin (see Table 5.4). Yet, the change in government did not signify a change in fiscal policy philosophy. If the first non–social democratic government since the Great Depression had coincided with the first serious increase in unemployment since the thirties then, the bourgeois parties feared, they might soon look forward to another couple of decades on the opposition benches.[57] Fiscal expansion was stepped up dramatically, in particular, subsidies for ailing industries. Consequently, the budget deteriorated rapidly to reach a deficit of 7 percent at the end of the bourgeois coalition in 1982 (see Figure 5.3). The most important contribution to the low unemployment rates probably came from the increase in public-sector employment from 26.1 percent to 31.7 percent of total employment between 1976 and 1982 (see Figure 5.4).

In Norway, where the bourgeois parties were less successful politically, similar policies were pursued by the social democrats. Despite a rapid increase in revenues from oil production, the budget turned around from a surplus of 4.7 percent in 1974 to a deficit of 0.1 percent in 1978. Oil revenues certainly influenced the extent to which the government was willing to spend, but the policy strategy started in 1975 was by no means predicated on the oil wealth.

Table 5.4. *Swedish governments, 1974–98*

Prime minister	Year of investiture	Labor (SAP)	Conservatives (Moderaterna)	Peoples Party (FP)	Farmers (CP)	Christian Democrats (KDS)	Percentage of parliament seats
Palme	1974	X					44.6
Fälldin	1976		X	R	R		51.6
Ullsten	1978			X			11.2
Fälldin	1979		X	R	R		50.1
Palme	1982	X					47.6
Palme	1985	X					45.6
Carlsson	1986	X					45.6
Carlsson	1988	X					44.7
Bildt	1991		X	R	R	R	48.7
Carlsson	1994	X					46.1
Persson	1996	X					46.1
Persson	1998	X					37.5

Note: See Table 3.1.

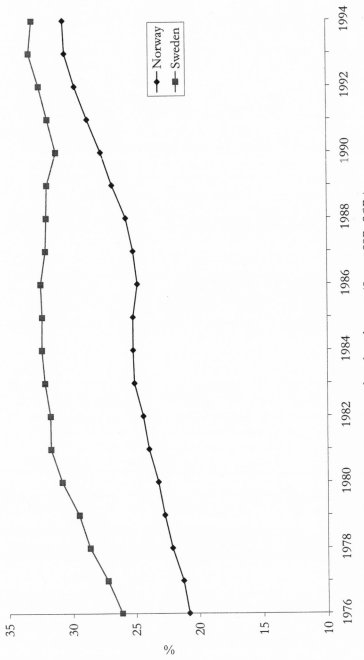

Figure 5.4. Public-sector employment as a percentage of total employment. (Source: SSB, SCB.)

In the opinion of labor's finance minister Per Kleppe, "Even without prospects of oil incomes, Norway, like Sweden, should have pursued the same general policy, namely, to maintain activity and employment despite recession abroad."[58] In addition, the labor party faced strong political incentives to increase spending. Whereas the leadership of the DNA and the LO, in a rather autocratic manner, had decided that the labor movement should vote yes in the referendum on membership in the European Economic Community held in September 1972, not only a majority of Norwegians but also a majority of DNA and LO members voted no. In an effort to regain lost sympathies, the DNA government targeted spending programs at those groups that it held crucial for its electoral success – public-sector workers, blue-collar workers in industry, and the farmers and fishermen who supported its ally, the farmers party. Subsidies to ailing firms were rapidly expanded, and in 1975 the government resolved that the average income in agriculture was to be raised to the average income of industrial workers within three years. Meanwhile, public-sector employment rose from 18.7 percent of total employment in 1973 to 25.1 percent a decade later.

Wage bargaining in both countries assumed a decidedly tripartite character in the seventies. In contrast to the pattern of the fifties and sixties, when the state influenced bargaining by means of (in)formal consultations, it now entered the arena as a third partner, offering tax cuts, subsidies, and social security improvements in exchange for moderation. The intensified coordination between fiscal and income policies was prompted by three related developments. First, actual bargaining outcomes increasingly deviated significantly from the intentions labor market partners expressed. Tripartite bargaining for the state hence constituted an attempt to gain more control over actual outcomes.[59] Second, the sixties had generally given rise to increased ambitions in employment policies. After more than a decade of boom conditions, governments' confidence in their own ability to fine-tune the economy had grown significantly. Ever lower unemployment rates and higher participation rates naturally implied stronger wage and price pressures. Third, the economic constellation after 1973 implied the need to rely to a greater extent on income policies. Whereas strong inflationary pressures in the fifties and sixties generally coincided with tight labor markets, which allowed for brief periods of macroeconomic restriction, the oil price crisis simultaneously increased inflationary pressures while reducing demand. In a constellation in which fiscal and monetary policies needed to be expansionary in order to avert the threat to full employment, income policies necessarily had to play a greater role.

In Sweden, such corporatist policies were initiated with the so-called Haga settlements of 1974–76, in which tax cuts and increased transfer payments were offered in exchange for wage moderation. The SAP did not survive in office long enough to develop them fully, however. In Norway, tripartite bargaining was introduced under the bourgeois government of Lars Korvald in 1973. But, in the eyes of the LO the wage moderation in 1971 and 1972 and the tripartite agreement of 1973 were not a success, because due to higher than expected inflation,[60] real wages decreased in 1972 and only marginally increased in 1971 and 1973. At the same time, the economy was booming and profits were high. Accordingly, resistance against centralized tripartite bargaining also grew within the LO. Opposition against income policies was further fanned by the increasing popularity of the Socialist Left Party (SV, Sosialistisk Venstreparti) among LO members. For the SV, income policies constituted an attempt to rob workers of wage increases.[61] As several large member unions rejected centralized bargaining, the LO leadership, in December 1973, for the first time since 1961 reluctantly decided in favor of industry-level bargaining.

Tight labor markets, high profits, stagnating real wages during 1970–73, a strong leftist opposition within the LO, a weakened leadership and high (expected) inflation – all contributed to a veritable wage explosion in 1974. In industry, nominal wages rose by more than 25 percent, 17.2 percent being due to contractual increases and the rest to wage drift. But in this case, too, the LO and the employers had received government assistance to help them reach an agreement. After a request from the LO, Minister of Finance Kleppe on March 29, 1973, presented a package of subsidies, tax reductions, and increased social welfare.[62] The package was an attempt to prevent the members of the crucial metalworkers union from rejecting the wage agreement of that year.[63]

In response to the experience of 1974, Kleppe now pushed for explicitly tripartite bargaining in order to bring down inflation without a change in macroeconomic policies:

> The government does not wish to combat price and cost increases at home with methods that will exacerbate the employment problem. It has, on the contrary, maintained domestic demand. In such a situation, however, domestic cost increases can lead to weakened competitiveness relative to foreign firms and thereby endanger jobs in the longer run. Partly because of this background there was a need for untraditional solutions with the index settlement in the fall.[64]

The employers association shared Kleppe's view on the desirability of tripartite bargaining. After the extremely high increases in 1974, a return to centralized bargaining held the promise of more moderate agreements. Furthermore, state participation implied that the NAF would have to shoulder less of the burden of any agreement reached. Support among the LO was more tenuous. On the one hand, the leadership realized that a repetition of the 1974 wage explosion would have negative consequences for employment and the economy in general. On the other hand, the LO leadership had to heed the internal opposition, especially from the higher-paid unions and SV sympathizers. That the LO leadership could agree on tripartite bargaining without provoking serious opposition was mainly because (1) the government in 1975 before the start of negotiations guaranteed a real wage increase of 3 percent, and (2) no provi-

Table 5.5. *Norwegian governments, 1971–97*

Prime minister	Year of investiture	Labor (DNA)	Conservatives (Høyre)	Christians (KrF)	Farmers (SP)	Liberals (Venstre)	Percentage of parliament seats
Bratteli	1971	X					49.3
Korvald	1972			R	R	X	31.3
Bratteli	1973	X					40.0
Nordli	1976	X					49.0[a]
Brundtland	1981	X					49.0
Willoch	1981			X			34.2
Willoch	1983		X	R	R		51.0
Brundtland	1986	X					45.8
Syse	1989		X	R	R		40.0
Brundtland	1990	X					40.6
Brundtland	1993	X					40.6
Jagland	1996	X					40.6
Bondevik	1997			X	R	R	25.5

Note: See Table 3.1.
[a] 40% before 1977 election.
Source: Furre 1992: 504–5

sions on limitations to wage drift were included. For the next three years (1975–77), wage bargaining in Norway took place on a tripartite level with the state shouldering about 50 percent of the costs of the LO-NAF agreements.[65]

Despite concerted efforts at wage moderation, however, neither country managed to bring inflation rates down to the German level. The higher domestic inflation rate, combined with participation in Europe's fixed exchange rate arrangement, the so-called Snake, therefore, implied a real appreciation of both currencies. In terms of a trade-weighted exchange basket the Swedish krona, for example, revalued about 11 percent between 1974 and 1976.[66] Unwilling to adjust their economic policies in a restrictive direction, the exchange rate had to give way. Both countries left the Snake and refused to join the EMS.

In Norway, the potential conflict between membership in the Snake and the commitment to full employment was not expected. After the unprecedented growth period during the Bretton Woods system, the move to more flexible exchange rates was interpreted as a threat to international trade and growth. The Norwegian government even considered the doubling of the bandwidth within which currencies were allowed to fluctuate that accompanied the replacement of the Bretton Woods agreement by the Smithsonian agreement to contribute to uncertainty. It welcomed the narrower bands of the Snake. Initially, participation in the Snake seemed to pose a threat to the ability to pursue restrictive policies domestically. With low unemployment, high price and wage increases, and the North Sea oil wells coming on-line in the midseventies, large current account surpluses and strong domestic demand were expected. Against the majority of business, but with the support of the LO, the government, on November 15, 1973, decided to revalue the krone by 5 percent. The most important factor in this decision was the desire to dampen domestic inflation.[67]

By 1977, however, the time had come to depreciate. The Norwegian krone was devalued both in April and August of 1977, and in 1978 it officially left the Snake. From 1978 to 1986, five more devaluations took place. The parliamentary debates about EMS membership in November 1978, initiated by the DNA, produced a majority against joining. The main arguments were that EMS membership meant that economic policies would be dominated by Germany; that it would lead to an appreciation of the currency; and that it implied a move toward EC membership. Norges Bank also voted against membership. The bourgeois coalition in Sweden had left the Snake in August 1977, on the ground that fixed exchange rates were not compatible with Swedish economic policies. In total, the bourgeois governments implemented four devaluations between October 1976 and September 1981.

DEFICIT REDUCTION

The policy of bridging the recession by means of fiscal spending involved the typical Keynesian mistake of treating private investment activity as an exogenous cyclical factor rather than an endogenous factor determined by the nature of the policy regime. The international downturn of the seventies, and in particular the recession of 1979–82, was not cyclical but rather the result of the decision of the majority of OECD countries to stamp out inflation. The expected international upswing thus did not take place, and the bridge-building policy had to fail in the medium term. Subsidizing ailing firms was no long-term solution. If the international economy failed to revive, even a flexible exchange rate policy that compensated for the appreciation due to higher domestic inflation rates could not reignite private-sector growth. And without an upturn in private-sector growth, a policy of keeping unemployment low by means of a rapid expansion of the public sector eventually had to shipwreck on excessive budget deficits or intolerably high tax rates.

In Norway, the social democratic government switched to a more austere fiscal course in late 1977. Minister of Finance Kleppe had called early on for a turn to austerity, but he failed to convince the government until after the 1977 elections. The policy of generally subsidizing business was abandoned for a policy of supporting only those with a good chance of survival. More important, fiscal expansion had also failed to keep down nominal wage increases. Whereas tripartite bargaining gave the government greater control over the policies of the peak associations, it simultaneously had the effect of weakening the hold of the peak organizations over their membership. In 1977–78, wage drift reached record proportions as it accounted for more than double the contractual wage increases (see Table 5.7). Instead, the government resorted to a price and wage stop, which lasted from September 1978 to January 1, 1980. Agreement was reached beforehand with the LO and employers, and in effect the price and wage freeze temporarily solved an internal coordination problem within the LO. Whereas the leadership and the low-paid unions realized that wage drift had become unacceptable, agreement on limitations to wage drift would have put too much strain on the internal cohesion of the LO. A government-proclaimed wage freeze, however, although not popular with many LO members, could be more easily accepted. In August 1978, moreover, the krone was devalued by 8 percent in an effort to improve competitiveness. The austerity policy played a role in the disappointing electoral result of 1981 and the formation of a bourgeois government under Kåre Willoch. Willoch was not intent on changing course, however. Austerity combined with the restrictive policies in the rest of Europe resulted in more than 3 percent unemployment in 1983.

For much the same reasons as Norwegian social democrats, the Swedish bourgeois government concluded in 1979 that a change of course in fiscal policies was required. In Scandinavia, however, restrictive policies are best administered by social democrats. While at least the powerful LO might have displayed more tolerance for similar policies pursued by a SAP government, the fiscal cutbacks caused a major confrontation with the unions. In the spring of 1980, Sweden experienced the most dramatic labor conflict since the war. Although the government eventually gave in, it was voted out of office in 1982. Now it was up to the SAP to reduce the budget deficit.

A SWEDISH THIRD WAY AND NORWEGIAN OIL

The new SAP government, and in particular its finance minister Kjell-Olof Feldt, was convinced that a change of course in fiscal policies was inevitable. However, if fiscal retrenchment was not to cause high unemployment, a way had to be found to stimulate private investment rather than compensating for its sluggishness by means of subsidies and public-sector expansion. Given the policies of the rest of the OECD countries, such a strategy would imply giving domestic industry a decisive advantage, both in order to prevent the restrictive conditions in the international environment from dragging down the domestic economy and to reduce current account deficits. Although the SAP had avoided the issue during the election campaign, its economic advisers had come to the conclusion that the only way to accomplish this was by means of a massive devaluation, which unlike the previous ones, would not merely compensate for higher Swedish inflation rates, but would also give export demand a real boost.

At his first day in office Feldt began his strategy of traveling a "Third Way" between the monetarism of Thatcher and the Keynesianism of François Mitterrand with a devaluation of 16 percent. In order to prevent devaluation from merely leading to more inflation, the government proclaimed a wage stop. More important, the government reached an agreement with the unions not to seek compensation for price increases in the next bargaining round. While the unions accepted a cut in wages, business had to accept the abolition of the extensive system of subsidization that had grown up under the bourgeois governments. At the same time, the growth of the public sector was to be curtailed. And, indeed, after 1982 the growth of public-sector employment flattened out in Sweden (see Figure 5.4).

During the first years, it seemed that with this strategy the Swedish SAP had indeed found a sustainable way of avoiding the mass unemployment that many other Western European social democrats had increasingly come to consider inevitable. Unemployment fell from 3.2 percent in 1982 to 1.5 percent in 1989, even though job-creation programs were drastically cut back. In contrast to traditional Keynesian strategies, the reduction in unemployment was not bought at the price of rising budget deficits. Feldt's strategy instead managed to eliminate the deficit of 7 percent inherited from the bourgeois governments in 1982 and turn it into a surplus of 5.4 percent by 1989. Because the private sector was now again creating jobs, the virtual standstill of public-sector employment did not pose a threat to full employment. Moreover, the Third Way strategy did not seem very vulnerable to external economic pressures. Immediately preceding the election campaign of 1982, the krona had come under heavy downward pressure, and after the SAP victory was announced, capital outflows increased dramatically to about SEK 1 billion per day.[68] The devaluation, however, restored confidence in the krona and capital started flowing back in again. Apparently, there was an alternative to Mitterrand's solution of reacting to downward pressures on the currency with the termination of domestic expansion. Moreover, although its centerpiece was a huge devaluation, the Third Way in fact was not a beggar-your-neighbor strategy whose success depended on other countries not pursuing similar policies. The devaluation had become necessary because Sweden wished to pursue an expansionary strategy in a highly restrictive international environment. If most other countries had had the same policy preferences as the Swedish social democrats, the devaluation simply would not have been necessary to start with. If, instead, Swedish policy makers had not devalued in 1982, they would have had no alternative but to resort to restrictive economic policies in order to reduce pressures on the krona and improve the current account balance. Such policies would have further contributed to the international recession, though the effect would have been minor, given the size of Sweden.

The Norwegian economy found itself in a rather different situation. Whereas the first oil price crisis had made the exploitation of Norwegian reserves profitable, the second one implied a substantial positive demand shock for the Norwegian economy. What Feldt had to accomplish by means of devaluation, the OPEC countries hence did for the bourgeois government in Norway. In addition, the well-filled state coffers made it impossible for conservative prime minister Kåre Willoch to continue his policy of fiscal austerity. For the Christian democrats and farmers, on whom Willoch depended for a parliamentary majority, the new oil wealth was an excellent opportunity to increase public transfers to their mainly rural electorate. At the same time, the LO protested vigorously against restrictive policies at times of increasing unemployment. During the budget debate in the fall of 1982, it organized a political protest strike in which 650,000 members participated.[69] The LO also advocated a more expansionary monetary policy. In early 1983, LO chairman Tor Halvorsen suggested a substantial reduction in interest rates in order to stimulate investment. In 1983, Willoch gave in to the pressures and formed a new government with the Christian democrats and farmers on the basis of a more expansionary policy platform. Because of the oil price crisis and the more expansionary policies, Norway avoided mass unemployment. From its peak of 3.4 percent in 1983, unemployment dropped to 2.1 percent in 1986. Despite the pressures for fiscal expansion, the reduction in unemployment resulted mainly from job creation in the private sector. Between 1983 and 1986, public-sector employment stagnated (see Figure 5.4).

THE INFLATIONARY SPIRAL

Behind the facade of the Scandinavian economic miracles of the eighties, tensions were building up. Whereas the regime changes in other Western European countries put a decisive end to the expectation that inflation would continue to rise in the future, the decision of Sweden and Norway to maintain the absolute priority of full employment indicated that the fight against inflation would have to take a backseat. The boosts given to both economies in the early eighties hence implied that market participants not only could be confident about high

demand in the future, they also would not have to fear any decisive macroeconomic measures against inflation. Not unlike the experience of the late teens
and early twenties, though much less dramatic and sudden, such a constellation
nurtured a low liquidity preference and the conviction that the best way to
defend and augment accumulated wealth was to engage in financial speculation.

Research about wage bargaining has recognized that, whereas centralization
of wage bargaining might indeed considerably improve the inflation-
unemployment trade-off, the capacity of centralized unions to direct wage
bargaining exists only within a specific range of labor market constellations.[70]
Once labor markets become so tight as to induce local employers to offer wages
considerably in excess of the central agreements, centralized bargaining will
effectively break down. A similar conclusion holds if unemployment rises to
such levels that local employees are willing to accept lower wages in order to
secure their job. What has been less well recognized, however, is that the central
bank too can be considered a peak association that can effectively control the
supply of credit to the economy only if its policies are not in strong contradiction to the incentives its constituents – commercial banks and wealth-holders
in general – face.[71] In contrast to the trade unions, the disintegration of the
steering capacity of central banks, is marked not by excessive unemployment or
labor scarcity but by the widespread expectations of deflation or inflation.

To the extent that a reduced liquidity preference increased pressures on the
labor market, a vicious circle emerged at the end of which stood the disintegration of the Scandinavian model. The main mechanisms are detailed in Figure
5.5.

The interaction between monetary policies and wage bargaining constitutes
the core of the cycle. As both central banks increasingly failed to keep credit
growth in check, inflationary pressures in the labor market increased, thereby
promoting a reduced liquidity preference. However, abundant money and tight
labor markets also made fiscal austerity increasingly illusory. Economically tight
labor markets necessarily served to increase the public-sector wage bill. Politically a tight fiscal policy was difficult to defend as it implied "sacrifices" from
public-sector employees and welfare state beneficiaries, whereas the well-off were
allowed to become even richer by means of financial speculation. In particular,
the communes were reluctant to pursue fiscal austerity at a time when a
booming economy kept the revenue coffers well filled. The failure of fiscal
austerity further increased demand pressures. Instead of falling behind the
private sector, public employment in both countries expanded at a similar rate.
Moreover, it now became harder to repeat a common practice of the fifties and
sixties, namely, using high budget surpluses as a means of cooling off demand
pressures.

The Disintegration of Financial Markets

As argued earlier, the Scandinavian system of credit rationing emerged in
the fifties in order to contain inflationary pressures. By restricting the amount
of lending financial institutions were allowed to undertake during periods of

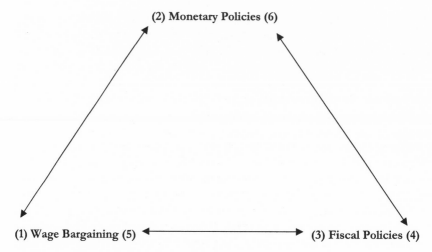

Figure 5.5. The unraveling of the Scandinavian model.
(1) The failure to check the growth of credit to the economy contributes to labor scarcity and high profits, which in turn increase the incentives of local wage earners as well as employers to defect from centrally negotiated wage bargains. Furthermore, the emergence of a "speculation economy" with high profits and wages in the financial sector makes especially blue-collar trade unions less willing to support wage moderation.
(2) Inflation due to high wage settlements in tight labor markets increases the overall demand for and supply of debt and increasingly makes both the credit rationing system as well as more market-based monetary policy instruments ineffective.
(3) Labor scarcity and high wage increases in the private sector make it difficult to contain wage demands in the public sector and thereby lead to increased public spending.
(4) Strong monetary growth makes it increasingly difficult to find political support for fiscal retrenchment. Particularly public sector unions are increasingly reluctant to support cuts in public spending at a time when high incomes are earned in the "speculation economy."
(5) The failure to check fiscal spending contributes to labor scarcity and high profits, which in turn increase the incentives of local wage earners as well as employers to defect from centrally negotiated wage bargains.
(6) Pressures for fiscal spending makes a policy of reducing monetary growth by means of high budget surpluses harder.
(*Source:* Notermans 1997.)

strong demand pressures, the economy cooled down without the need for a radical increase in interest rates. Politically, the system of credit rationing had the advantage that it allowed the social democrats to selectively protect certain groups from monetary restriction. Yet the system could only serve satisfactorily as long as expectations of continued inflation did not make holding money unattractive, whereas borrowing promised an easy return because debts could be repaid with devalued money. In such a case, the increased velocity of money, as manifested, for example, in falling savings ratios, would result in rapid credit growth as soon as restrictions were relaxed. During the late seventies, such a constellation started to develop. The high inflation of the preceding decade plus the political priority placed on full employment made it reasonable to expect inflation in the future. Moreover, as a result of the combined effects of inflation and tax deductibility of loan repayments, real posttax interest rates frequently turned out to be negative. In response, credit-rationing measures now were in force almost continuously. However, given that the factors causing a high demand for debt remained present, evasion increased rapidly.

The first response to the increasing emasculation of the traditional framework was tighter regulations, but those measures proved fairly ineffective. Full control of credit allocation would imply that the authorities assumed responsibility for the microeconomic decisions about which investment projects were to be financed and which were not. In other words, controls could not remain confined to the financial sector but would have to extend to the real sector as well. The problem manifested itself even more directly when large industrial firms increasingly started to operate financial divisions. For example, consistent credit rationing might have implied that the Swedish central bank would have to decide whether a projected real estate purchase by Volvo's finance division was mere financial speculation or was required for the prosperity of the car-making division. Such an extent of regulation, however, was neither administratively nor politically tolerable. Accordingly, since the early eighties both central banks, in agreement with commercial banks, started to push for the replacement of the credit rationing system with a system in which the central bank controlled the money supply through its interest rate and open market policies.

In Norway, the process was set under way in 1978 as the central bank tightened quantitative restrictions on bank lending in order to slow the credit supply while avoiding a sharp rise in interest rates. Given the strong demand for credit, this prompted the rise of a so-called grey market of nonbank financial institutions.[72] The following four years saw an accelerating process of increasingly strict and detailed controls and new ways of circumventing them. The election of a conservative government in 1981 initially did not imply a change in the policy of tighter regulations, although deregulation was an important issue in the conservative election platform. But the increasing ineffectiveness of the system could not fail to have its effects. By 1984 not only the central bank and the financial institutions, but also the government and the opposition social democrats, concluded that the old system had had its day. However, the change of mood was due not only to the futility of controls but also to mounting political pressures. At a time when large speculative gains could be made, the credit restrictions were also unpopular with a wider audience.

The miscalculation was that, without a strongly restrictive monetary policy to break the underlying demand for credit, deregulation could only spell further chaos. Between 1985 and 1987, the central bank virtually lost control over the economy. The actual credit supply exceeded the bank's targets by more than 100 percent each year; the household savings ratio became negative in 1986 and real estate prices rose almost by 250 percent between 1980 and 1987. At the same time, the Oslo Stock Exchange Index seemed to reach record highs almost every day.

In 1986, sentiments turned against the krone as the fall in oil prices led to a dramatic worsening of the current account. The DNA government that took office on May 9 found itself in a position similar to the SAP in 1982. The reduction in oil revenues meant that Norway would have to confront the problem of a current account plus budget deficit. In order not to jeopardize full employment despite the need for fiscal retrenchment, a big devaluation might seem the solution. Financial markets also had apparently come to this conclusion, as the shift from the Willoch to the second Brundtland government was accompanied by heavy pressure on the krone. On May 11, the government did indeed announce a 12 percent devaluation. As was the case with the 16 percent devaluation of the krona in 1982, 12 percent was larger than expected by many. Monetary policies meanwhile remained accommodating although a largely unsuccessful effort was made to reregulate parts of the domestic credit market on a voluntary basis. In accordance with the Swedish Third Way, fiscal policies became more restrictive. Having played the main role in bringing Willoch's government down by voting against his proposal for fiscal cutbacks, Prime Minister Brundtland now presented a rather similar package. Whether the Norwegian version of the Third Way would be successful depended, as in Sweden, on the ability of the labor market partners to keep nominal wage growth in check.

Developments in Sweden were very similar, although there the cycle developed about three to four years later. Evasion of credit restrictions had spread rapidly since the late seventies. By 1984, it was estimated that about 20–25 percent of lending was taking place in unregulated "grey" markets.[73] In response, the Riksbank started to tighten its regulations beginning in 1980. During the first three years, these measures were fairly ineffective. Only in 1984 did regulations finally seem to have the desired effect. This success was more apparent than real, however, because the increasing strictness of controls redirected financial flows in new and as yet uncharted channels.

By 1985, the Riksbank came to openly advocate the complete abolition of the old system, and it met little resistance. Commercial banks wholeheartedly agreed because the strong growth of the unregulated market disturbed the de facto cartel of Swedish banks. Social democratic finance minister Feldt could not see much sense in keeping a system that had proved increasingly ineffective. Moreover, regulations were rather unpopular with both industry and consumers; not even the LO protested at the time.

On November 21, 1985, the Riksbank abolished all lending ceilings. Given what had happened in Norway, the bank was very much aware that deregulation might by followed by an even faster expansion of credit. The bank interpreted the Norwegian credit explosion as the result of an inconsistent policy that, on the one hand, wanted to rely on so-called market-based instruments by deregulating the domestic credit market while, on the other hand, being unwilling to accept a rise in interest rates sufficient to deter credit growth. The bank assured Feldt that it would be able to prevent a Norwegian type of credit explosion by means of a so-called interest rate stair (*Räntetrappen*) that made the interest rate at which each individual commercial bank could have recourse to the central bank dependent on its debt position at the bank. The *Räntetrappen* gave the Riksbank the ability to apply different rates to different borrowers while the average discount rate would increase automatically in the event the commercial banks expanded their amount of rediscounting overall.[74] This system still did not imply a complete abandonment of low interest rate policies as the "staircase" did not lead endlessly upward but had a maximum rate.

However, as long as the underlying regime remained intact, a substantial increase in interest rates could not decisively change the expectations of the market. Accordingly, in Sweden deregulation was followed by a credit explosion. As Alexander Nilson (1988: 25) stated in the Riksbank's review:

> The massive borrowing by households on the organized credit market has coincided with a steep rise in real interest rates after tax. . . . Instead of being appreciably curbed by the positive real rate of interest, the borrowing propensity of households seems to have been influenced by earlier experience of markedly negative real rates after tax and this experience may continue to dominate for some years.

The Disintegration of Trade Unions

Under the type of boom that developed in both Norway and Sweden, wage moderation eventually had to collapse. At a time where large gains could be made on the stock market and by speculating with real estate, wage moderation became unacceptable for many members. But even the developing labor scarcity by itself would probably have been sufficient to provoke a breakdown in wage moderation. In a situation where business enjoyed exceedingly good profits and unemployment dropped below 2 percent, even the highly centralized unions of the fifties and sixties would have been overburdened by a policy of wage moderation.[75] But by the eighties both peak unions had considerably less authority over wage setting than in the fifties and sixties. The main reason for the waning influence of the LO leadership was increasingly sharp disagreement about the relative wage structure between employees. The structural decline of the number of blue-collar jobs has contributed to these tensions to the extent that industrial labor increasingly resists the narrowing of wage differentials to the now increasingly important sector of lower-paid public-sector jobs. Higher-paid white-collar sectors, in turn, formed their own unions outside the LO in order to prevent further equalization of its wages to blue-collar jobs. There are strong indications, however, that within the traditional blue-collar sector wage equalization has been practiced to such an extent as to cause opposition.[76]

As the case of Austria shows, a policy of wage equalization is not necessarily a precondition for centralized bargaining. Nonetheless, for a host of historical reasons, equalization has traditionally played a strong role in justifying central-ization. Because the SAP government had already made clear in 1948 that it would step back if wage growth were not kept under control, LO(S) had to find a way of keeping its members in check. By emphasizing equalization (i.e., equal pay for equal work) as a central norm of the labor movement the LO found a potent internal justification for wage moderation. Workers who attempted to use the above-average profitability of their firms to gain above average wage increases could now be put under moral pressures for violating a core norm of the movement. Even though there was general support within the labor move-ment for more income equality as far as redistribution from employers to wage earners was concerned, the many status differentials within the working class meant that larger income equality between wage earners was by no means a self-evident goal. The centrality the goal of equalization acquired in post-1945 Sweden thus was not a mere correlate of the (political) strength of the labor movement, but rather the result of a historically specific attempt to solve the problem of inflationary wage leap-frogging. However, while the policy of equal pay for equal work initially solved the LO's dilemma, continuous tensions arising from full employment required increasingly ambitious interpretations of equality in order to fulfill its function. Since the late sixties equality came to be interpreted more and more in terms of an overall compression of differentials – "equal pay for all" – rather than equal pay for equal work. Moreover, the demand for equality came to encompass sectors outside the LO constituency. The stricter interpretation of equality, however, caused opposition mainly within the industrial sector with the result that wage drift became an ever more important instrument for restoring wage differentials. Public-sector unions in turn sought to compensate for wage drift in the private sector by including so-called compensation clauses in their contracts. The wage earner funds were the outcome of the LO's increasing difficulties in implementing wage moderation under full employment, rather than the start of a socialist offensive. By making employers pay part of their profits into a fund managed by the LO, it was hoped that wage drift might be contained.

As the LO had to have recourse to ever more radical measures to ensure its internal cohesion, the SAF came to seek the solution in decentralization. The SAF offensive started in 1983 with the breaking away of the engineering employers from national-level bargaining and was completed in 1991 when the organization as a whole abandoned its bargaining role. Although they had been watered down substantially, the wage earner funds did provide a motivation for the SAF's new strategy. More important, however, may have been that centralization in fact had come to promote wage escalation by provoking wage drift. Given the dissatisfaction within the LO about equalization, the SAF's new strategy was not frustrated by a united LO front. Rather the industrial unions generally were sympathetic to such moves.

In response to the inter- and intraunion pressures it had increasingly called forth, the LO started to tone down demands for equalization in the mideighties. Equalization now was to be realized by career development, which would allow individual workers to move into higher-paid jobs. Because the LO seemed to abandon wage equalization and the SAF came to realize that under tight labor markets decentralization of bargaining did not promote wage moderation either,[77] the time of centralized bargaining briefly seemed to have returned in the mideighties. Under pressure from Feldt, the LO and the SAF concluded a two-year agreement again in 1986. Centralized bargaining did not, however, mean the return of wage moderation. Within the LO especially, the lower-paid public-sector workers objected to the policy of increasing wage differentiation. Moreover, as unemployment dropped below 2 percent in 1987, acute labor scarcity precluded the implementation of moderate agreements. As Table 5.6 shows, wage drift exceeded contractual increases from 1988 to 1990, reaching a peak in the last year.

In a last desperate attempt to restore some degree of moderation and centralization to the labor market, Feldt proposed a general ban on wage and price increases as well as a ban on strikes in February 1990. Although the leadership of both the LO and the SAF originally supported the proposal, opposition from their members rapidly made their position untenable. Moreover, the measures failed to secure a majority in the Riksdag.[78] With not only financial markets but also wage bargaining out of control, the regime change had become inevitable. In response to his defeat in parliament, Feldt stepped down and the new finance minister, Alan Larsson, announced that full employment was no longer a policy goal.

In Norway the emphasis on wage equalization increased as the LO found it harder to maintain discipline. But the Norwegian LO has been plagued somewhat less by stifling struggles over relative wages, in large part owing to the different role played by the state. In contrast to Sweden, the Norwegian government maintains the right to force the parties in a labor market conflict to accept arbitration. Although Norwegian labor law does not provide for direct state interference in wage bargaining, the government, contingent upon approval by parliament, can bind unions and employers to arbitration by the tripartite National Wage Board. According to Frøland (1997: 13), compulsory arbitration has been used about ninety times since 1953. Moreover, the state has used additional legal means to interfere directly in wage bargaining. Compulsory arbitration has at times provided a useful scapegoat function for the union

Table 5.6. *Contractual wages and wage drift of Swedish industrial workers, 1971–90*

Period	Total increase in wages (%)	Contractual increase (%)	Wage drift (%)	Wage drift/ contractual increase	Unemployment rate (%)
1971	10.5	6.3	4.2	0.7	2.1
1972	11.8	7.5	4.3	0.6	2.2
1973	8.1	4.1	4.0	1.0	2.0
1974	11.8	5.0	6.8	1.4	1.6
1975	18.0	10.5	7.5	0.7	1.3
1976	13.3	7.9	5.4	0.7	1.3
1977	7.2	3.7	3.5	0.9	1.5
1978	8.0	4.8	3.2	0.7	2.2
1979	8.2	4.4	3.8	0.9	2.1
1980	9.3	6.1	3.2	0.5	2.0
1981	10.1	5.9	4.2	0.7	2.5
1982	7.6	4.1	3.5	0.9	3.2
1983	6.7	3.8	2.9	0.8	3.5
1984	10.3	6.2	4.1	0.7	3.1
1985	7.5	3.8	3.7	1.0	2.9
1986	7.4	3.9	3.5	0.9	2.7
1987	6.4	n.a	n.a	—	2.1
1988	8.4	3.4	5.0	1.5	1.7
1989	10.1	4.5	5.6	1.2	1.5
1990	8.8	2.8	6.7	2.4	1.6

Sources: "The Swedish Economy," several issues. Unemployment figures, OECD Economic Outlook.

leadership as it can transfer the task of getting militant member unions to accept a moderate central agreement to the state.[79] Moreover, it has at times been used to force non-LO unions to accept the agreement reached between the LO and employers.

However, compulsory arbitration is an instrument that has to be applied with care. A general wage freeze that is not combined with measures to contain other incomes can too easily be seen as an attempt to solve economic problems on the backs of the wage earners. To the extent that labor market conditions provoke substantial wage drift, it will disadvantage the public sector where little drift occurs. Finally, the LO finds it much easier to accept compulsory arbitration from a social democratic than from a conservative government.

Accordingly, the conservative governments of the eighties decided to largely refrain from formal income policies, although they issued frequent appeals for wage moderation. Given labor market conditions this approach was not very effective. Wildcat strikes increased substantially in the first part of the decade compared to the seventies. Consequently, central unions themselves felt the need to bargain for higher wage increases. In the 1986 bargaining round, the LO, for the first time in several years, was not satisfied with protection of the existing real wage but demanded an increase plus a reduction of the workweek from 40 to 37.5 hours. Not willing to agree, the employers association called a large-scale lockout. Calling a large lockout in fairly tight labor market conditions soon turned out to be a mistake, and soon the employers had to make a humiliating retreat. As a result, contractual wages in industry virtually exploded in 1986–87, despite the fact that wage drift even increased with respect to the previous year (see Table 5.7).

Given the disintegration of Norwegian wage bargaining, Brundtland's attempt to pursue a Third Way strategy had to be short-lived. To compensate for a reduction in spending by means of devaluation was a rather inappropriate measure to contain a boom that by now was mainly driven by inflationary expectations. Despite the fall in oil prices inflation rates started to edge upward again in 1986, and the growth of credit continued unabated. In early 1987, the social democrats felt that a radical change in expectations was needed to put the economy on an even keel again. Both fiscal and monetary policies were considerably tightened, and the central bank was de facto freed from its commitment to full employment. The government stressed that the May devaluation was to be the last one. The "Turning Operation" of the social democratic government, in short, signaled a decisive change from a policy regime of flexible exchange rates and domestic stimulation to a regime of a fixed external constraint and domestic austerity.

Policy Mistakes or Institutional Breakdown?

Whereas Brundtland may not have had many options at the time she assumed office, the SAP had been in government ever since the boom of the eighties started. Why, then, did Feldt allow the boom to continue for so long instead of temporarily resorting to macroeconomic restriction, as was the common pattern in the fifties and sixties? Did the government carry macroeconomic expansion too far so that in the end it was left with the only option of creating a massive crisis? Were the policy patterns of the fifties still viable in the eighties?

As far as monetary policy is concerned, the reluctance to tighten conditions or even consider a revaluation was partly the result of the bourgeois strategies of the seventies. According to the analysis of Feldt, and Dennis at the Riksbank, the cardinal sin of the strategies of the seventies was to have tried to maintain prosperity by means of public-sector expansion while conditions for the private economy were allowed to deteriorate, partly because of the revaluation resulting

Table 5.7. *Yearly increase in wages in Norwegian manufacturing of adult males, by contractual increase and wage drift*

Period	Total increase in wages (%)	Contractual increase (%)	Wage drift (%)	Wage drift/ contractual increase	Unemployment rate (%)
1971–72	9.3	4.4	4.9	1.1	1.4
1972–73	9.6	3.8	5.8	1.5	1.7
1973–74	12.2	4.9	7.3	1.5	1.5
1974–75	25.2	17.2	8.0	0.5	1.4
1975–76	13.0	8.9	4.1	0.5	2.2
1976–77	15.6	9.4	6.2	0.7	1.8
1977–78	9.7	2.9	6.8	2.3	1.4
1978–79	5.3	1.8	3.5	1.9	1.8
1979–80	2.2	0.0	2.2	—	1.9
1980–81	13.8	5.2	8.6	1.7	1.7
1981–82	7.7	1.9	5.8	3.1	2.0
1982–83	11.6	5.6	6.0	1.1	2.7
1983–84	7.5	1.1	6.4	5.8	3.4
1984–85	9.5	2.9	6.6	2.3	3.2
1985–86	7.6	0.3	7.3	24.3	2.6
1986–87	18.7	10.4	8.3	0.8	2.0
1987–88	7.3	0.2	7.1	35.5	2.1
1988–89	3.0	1.7	1.3	0.8	3.2
1989–90	4.9	4.2	0.7	0.2	4.9
1990–91	7.3	3.8	3.5	0.9	5.2
1991–92	3.8	1.5	2.3	1.5	5.5

Note: Figures are for the period from first quarter of respective year until first quarter of next year. Figures for 1986–1987 include compensation for the reduction in the normal hours of work per week as from 1 January 1987. Unemployment figures refer to the calendar year.
Source: Lønnstatistik 1991. Oslo: Statistisk Sentralbyrå, 1992: 29. Unemployment figures: OECD Economic Outlook.

from higher inflation and partly because of a misguided industrial policy. Quite in keeping with the SAP's view of the fifties and sixties, the ministry of finance and the Riksbank felt that the private sector provided the foundations of prosperity. The task, therefore, was to stimulate private-sector activity and undo some of the excessive public-sector expansion of the seventies. From that perspective, employing restrictive monetary policies to cool down the economy would have been rather perverse because it would hurt private investment activity and exports first but leave the public sector unscathed. Instead, more restrictive monetary policies might even strengthen those in the SAP whose recipe for all economic ills was public-sector expansion.

Accordingly, the ministry and the bank focused almost exclusively on fiscal restriction in order to cool down the economy. Riksbank governor Dennis even argued that restrictive monetary policies simply were not possible. As long as the krona was to be maintained at its parity with the currency basket, no room for increased interest rates was said to exist. A revaluation, it was asserted, would not have been credible on international financial markets. However, even within the theoretical framework used by the Riksbank, Dennis's justification can hardly be considered convincing. If a revaluation had indeed not been credible, higher interest rates would have been required to maintain the new parity. Accordingly the lack of credibility would have allowed the Riksbank to exceed international interest rates levels and hence would have strengthened rather than weakened the dampening effects.[80]

For fiscal austerity, however, no political majority could be found. Given the state of the budget deficit in 1982, Feldt was able to convince the party and parliament of the need for moderation. The strategy of fiscal moderation was opposed from the beginning by what may be called the Keynesian wing of the SAP and LO. During its time in opposition, the SAP had criticized the government for its cuts in public-sector spending. Former finance minister Gunnar Sträng was not thrilled by Feldt's calls for fiscal moderation. As Keynesian policies could supposedly increase employment without the increase in private-sector profits Feldt called for, this view quite naturally held a greater appeal for the LO. On several previous occasions, the emergence of high profits had undermined the member's acceptance of the LO's wage moderation. Irrespective of the question of private-sector profits, the Keynesian strategy was obviously inherently more attractive to the public-sector unions.[81] The ferocity of the international crisis of 1979–82 and the escalating budget deficit helped the SAP leadership to overcome these objections. Yet, as the success of the Third Way materialized, pressures for increased fiscal spending intensified. Moreover, being in a minority position in parliament, the government would have to convince part of the opposition. But like the SAP in opposition and the DNA who had voted against spending cuts proposed by the Willoch government even as late as 1986, the bourgeois parties were not eager to take partial responsibility for unpopular policies.

Fiscal policies can be made responsible for the boom only in a very restrictive sense, however. Swedish budget deficits declined rapidly after 1982, and during the late eighties the budget was in surplus. Because a budget surplus implies that demand is drained from the economy, it would hardly be appropriate to label fiscal policies expansionary. If fiscal policies are to be blamed for the overheating, this could only be true in the sense that they were not restrictive enough to prevent overheating, given the buoyant demand in the private sector.

Accordingly, the criticism of fiscal policies cannot be subsumed under the new neoclassical policy orthodoxy in which ill-advised fiscal policies are held to be the cause of disturbances in the real sector. At best, fiscal management can be accused of a failure to appropriately counteract the dynamism of the private sector.

Moreover, it is questionable whether fiscal and/or monetary restrictions would have had the same effects in the second part of the eighties as they did in the fifties and sixties. As shown earlier, the higher interest rates that accompanied the deregulation of credit rationing failed to have any noticeable effects. Similarly, higher budget surpluses might simply have created room for a faster expansion of the private sector. More important, the difficulties in the wage bargaining system were no longer only driven by excessively tight labor markets, as during the fifties and sixties, but by disagreements about relative wage levels. As long as this problem was not solved, a return to the post-1973 policies would not be possible.

In sum, during the eighties the basic dilemma, which had already frustrated the SAP's economic policies in the late teens and early twenties, reemerged. In order to promote growth and full employment investment activity had to be stimulated at all costs, yet without the ability to effectively curb inflationary expectations, investment would gradually acquire the character of a flight out of money and into highly speculative transactions. In order to regain the stability of the monetary economy social democrats had to discourage investment and use unemployment in order to compensate for the disruption of the labor market partners' ability to moderate wages. The SAP of the eighties, not surprisingly, attempted to avoid this choice as long as possible.

DEREGULATION OF EXCHANGE CONTROLS

Deregulation of credit rationing in both countries was soon followed by the abolition of foreign exchange controls. The SAP government lifted exchange controls in steps between 1986 and 1989. In 1988, the forward exchange market was liberalized. By January 1989, all restrictions concerning the purchase and sale of Swedish and foreign shares and direct investment were lifted. In June 1989, most of the remaining restrictions were abolished. Swedish residents were now free to borrow and lend abroad and trade with domestic and foreign assets, irrespective of purpose or maturity. In Norway, most of the remaining exchange controls were abolished on July 1, 1990. The deregulation measures of July 1990 mainly affected the household sector; most restrictions on foreign exchange dealings concerning the corporate sector had already been lifted.

Given that many social democrats in other Western European countries were convinced that the internationalization of financial relations was the major cause for their economic policy failures since the seventies, the deregulatory policies pursued by Scandinavian social democrats would seem rather perverse.

It seemed that the two strongest social democratic parties in Europe were voluntarily demolishing the foundations of their success.

Yet, the success of full-employment policies never depended critically upon exchange controls. Maintaining more extensive exchange controls in large part was a necessary result of both countries' more extensive reliance on credit rationing. If domestic borrowers had had the ability to borrow abroad, credit-rationing measures aimed at *cooling down* the economy might easily be circumvented. Therefore, exchange regulation during the fifties and sixties did not perform the function of defending a more expansionary policy from restrictive foreign influences. Indeed, with a booming world economy and a general commitment to growth policies, there was no serious external threat to the goal of full employment.

In the restrictive international environment of the eighties and nineties, the defense of full employment had to depend on a more flexible exchange rate management. Such policies can also be pursued without tight exchange regulations, though controls may somewhat limit disturbing capital flows, which might occur in connection with excepted exchange rate changes. In the early seventies, both countries altered exchange regulations with the aim of promoting inflows while limiting outflows. In 1974, Sweden abolished the general prohibition of borrowing abroad, although the provision was made that foreign loans should have a maturity of at least five years. The same provision was applied by Norwegian authorities. Swedish rules required, as of 1974, that outgoing direct investment be financed by foreign currency loans. Exchange regulations never were tight enough, however, to prevent large-scale financial flows like the ones that occurred at the time of the Swedish elections of 1982.

As the domestic preconditions for the successful pursuit of a growth regime disintegrated, and adherence to a fixed exchange rate and tight money came to be considered essential for containing inflation, exchange controls lost their rationale. At best, exchange control now was an instrument that served no macroeconomic purposes but caused microeconomic distortions and placed domestic financial firms at a disadvantage in international competition. At worst, exchange controls might weaken the case for the restrictive macroeconomic strategy policy makers now considered necessary for domestic reasons.

Indeed, even before the shift in policy regime, policy makers in both countries adjusted regulation so as to increase external pressures and assist them in the fight against inflation. The most conspicuous of these measures was the imposition of a ban on borrowing abroad by public authorities. In Sweden, public foreign borrowing was introduced by the bourgeois government in 1976. The downward pressures on the krona in that period seemed to call for an increase in domestic interest rates, but the government feared that this would have a negative effect on investment. Public borrowing abroad in this constellation served as a way to improve the balance of payments by increasing capital inflows without an increase in domestic interest rates. During the period 1975–

79, when the trade balance was in deficit, Norwegian governments applied the same technique.

The imposition of a ban on public borrowing in Sweden in 1984 was an attempt to reduce demand pressures in the economy by increasing external constraints on fiscal policies. As Swedish deputy minister of finance Erik Åsbrink (SAP) argued:

> There are many indications that [the policy of public foreign borrowing] has tempted, in a longer perspective, a too expansionary fiscal policy. Due to the state's foreign borrowing it has been possible to have a deficit on the current account year after year without the negative effects becoming sufficiently clear. When the state started to borrow abroad in 1977 to cover the current account deficit, a natural corrective mechanism was abolished.[82]

In 1986, the Norwegian government decided to ban public official borrowing, even though a renewed deficit on the trade balance emerged in that year. There also the argument was that public official borrowing might hinder the necessary fiscal moderation.[83]

In 1985, the Swedish commission on exchange regulations published its report. Now it was the bourgeois parties who argued that deregulation of exchange controls was indeed desirable in order to impose greater discipline on domestic macroeconomic policies.[84] The main source of the disturbances besetting Sweden was argued to be an excessively accommodating economic policy, and removing exchange controls would hence increase domestic stability as it would make such policies more difficult to pursue. This view, by the way, was shared by central bank governor Bengt Dennis, an SAP appointee.[85] The majority of the commission, mainly SAP members, held that exchange controls were still desirable in order to shield Sweden from foreign disturbances and maintain some autonomy in macroeconomic policies. This argument suffered, however, from a strange inconsistency caused by the SAP's traditional rhetoric of exchange controls as a protective device and the needs of the economy, which seemed to dictate tighter policies instead. On the one hand, they claimed that it would be easier to maintain higher interest rates with exchange controls; on the other hand, they argued that abolition of exchange controls would lead to more restrictive policies.[86]

The social democratic finance ministry did not share this inconsistency. Since the mideighties, Feldt and his deputy Erik Åsbrink were openly arguing for an abolition of exchange controls. The official arguments for the abolition of exchange controls, contained in the budget proposal for 1989, did not embrace the view that external constraints on the economy needed to be increased, and it would indeed have been difficult for the minister of finance to agree with the opposition. Instead, it was put forth that exchange controls had become ineffective and that past experience had shown that in times of downward pressure on the currency, confidence could only be restored by means of monetary and fiscal policy measures. Moreover, it was pointed out that exchange controls had a negative effect on the competitiveness of small and medium-size firms in particular, and that Sweden should not remain aloof when EC countries liberalized their financial transactions. Regardless of whether Feldt thought that controls were ineffective or that their abolition would increase pressures for tighter policies, it is clear that by 1989 the SAP did not have any more use for an instrument that would have facilitated more expansionary macroeconomic policies.

In Norway, the government and the central bank stressed the positive microeconomic effects of exchange control deregulation.[87] Moreover, the need to adjust to EC regulations now also was introduced as an argument in favor of deregulation. Again, such considerations could only become important on the basis of a prior conclusion that a macroeconomic policy that deviated strongly from the EC pattern was no longer desirable. The Norwegian Kleppe committee, for example, which published its report on ways to reduce unemployment in 1992, was instructed by the government to assume a fixed exchange rate policy. Accordingly, interest rate policies necessarily had to be tied to the defense of the parity.[88]

Because policy makers believed that the boom of the eighties and the ensuing crisis had to be attributed primarily to domestic factors, continued mass unemployment and speculation on the currency could not induce them to reimpose exchange regulations. For Norwegian and Swedish policy makers, as for most of their counterparts in other countries, the lesson to be learned from the experience of the eighties was that a strategy that attempted to maintain full employment by means of a soft currency policy will lead to escalating nominal wages, a burgeoning public sector, financial speculation, and inflation rather than growth of productive investment and productivity. Because macroeconomic strategies apparently only postponed but did not solve the problems, the solution now was sought in policies of microlevel adjustment. Despite the fact that policy makers in recent years have regularly invoked the argument that external constraints stand in the way of a more relaxed monetary policy, imposition of exchange controls will be ruled out because such measures are feared to signal to both unions and business that the need for microlevel adjustments is less urgent because macroeconomic policies will again bail them out.[89] If, however, policy makers overcome the fear of a repetition of the experience of the eighties in response to more relaxed macroeconomic policies, exchange controls will be unnecessary.

6

SOCIAL DEMOCRACY IN THE
TWENTY-FIRST CENTURY

In recent decades, social democracy has repeatedly been declared dead. In response to the collapse of the growth regime in the seventies, many analysts concluded that the social democratic model had become either economically or electorally unfeasible.[1] According to liberal supply-side economists, the ever-increasing regulation of the economy was strangling entrepreneurial activity. In order for prosperity to be regained, a decisive turn to liberal economic policies was required.

Sociologists and political scientists with more sympathies for the social democratic project instead predicted the inevitable decline of social democracy due to the erosion of its electoral base.[2] Because social democracy appealed to the common interests of the traditional working class, it seemed that it could only thrive politically in a society in which blue-collar workers not only formed the majority but also identified themselves as belonging to one class.

Since the sixties, these alleged preconditions for social democratic success seemed to be waning rapidly. Industrial jobs started disappearing so rapidly that by the midnineties, at best only 20 percent to 30 percent of employment relations could be characterized as blue collar. Moreover, the blue-collar class itself seemed to increasingly abandon its traditional social democratic values. To the extent that the expanding welfare states of Western Europe remedied the disadvantaged position of labor, the conditions of work became less important as a focal point for identity formation. Moreover, the conditions of work themselves were subjected to rapid change as the mass production plants that employed large amounts of low-skilled labor gave way to smaller-scale processes in which skills and motivation acquired greater importance and the concept of an irreconcilable antagonism between capitalists and the proletariat seemed rather anachronistic.

The shrinking of the blue-collar class poses much less of a problem for social democracy than frequently assumed. Although blue-collar labor may have provided a fertile recruiting ground for social democrats, the concept of class-based political governance has never been particularly viable. Blue-collar labor only rarely came to constitute more than 50 percent of the workforce. Moreover, in many cases religious allegiance hindered the emergence of a common political identity. Consequently, social democrats have had to extend their appeal beyond the blue-collar segment if they were to be politically successful, not only since the sixties, but since the introduction of general suffrage. Economically, the class analysis of society pointed to nationalization of the means of production as the appropriate economy remedy. Yet, as argued above, for a party that wished to abide by democratic rules and therefore had to derive its support from policies that actually improved the conditions of its constituents, such a strategy was not feasible. Even in those rare instances in which social democrats enjoyed a parliamentary majority, they came to embrace strategies under which both labor and business could prosper.

Social democracy enjoyed its greatest successes when it managed to convince wide segments of society that recurrent crises of mass unemployment and gaping income disparities were not, as liberals and conservatives claimed, an inevitable price to be paid for the increasing wealth generated by market economies. The political appeal of social democracy accordingly did not rest primarily on its promise to shift the income distribution in favor of blue-collar labor, but on its vision of a politically managed market economic in which prosperity, economic stability, a fair distribution of income, and political democracy were not conflicting goals.

The real threat to the social democratic program in the seventies and eighties did not derive from the changes in composition and identity of the labor force, but from neoliberal supply-side policies. If it were indeed possible to regain prosperity by means of liberal microeconomic policies, then the social democratic program would appear to be a strategy that benefited the segments of low-paid labor and public-sector workers at the expense of the majority of society. Yet, as was the case during the twenties, liberalism was very effective in eliminating inflation but at the price of stagnation and mass unemployment. With almost twenty million Western Europeans out of work by the late nineties, the neoliberal promise of a reinvigoration of the economy by means of deregulation and tight macropolicies seemed increasingly utopian. The failure of its supply-side policies inevitably undermined the support for liberal economic policies. As a result, European social democracy made an astonishing comeback since the midnineties. By early 1999, labor parties governed eleven out of the fifteen states of the European Union, and, for the first time in history, all of the four major economies. The Labour Party scored a landslide victory in 1997 under Tony Blair. Gerhard Schröder and the SPD did so in the general elections of September 1998. After its dismal performance in the 1991 election, the Swedish SAP came close to an absolute majority in 1994. Apparently, the Swedish electorate trusted that the SAP would be better able to design remedies against the economic crisis than the bourgeois parties. In Norway, admittedly, the DNA was replaced by a coalition of Christians, liberals, and farmers in 1997. The defeat of Norwegian labor, however, does not signal increased popularity of neoliberal policies. Instead, the bourgeois coalition promised to spend more of the oil wealth than the social democrats were willing to do.

Whether social democracy will be able to consolidate its present electoral successes will depend first and foremost on the success of its economic policies. Also during the late twenties, the disappointment with the liberal policies swept many social democratic parties into office. The Norwegian labor party formed its first government in 1928. In the same year, the SPD returned to office after five years in opposition. The following year Ramsay MacDonald won the British general election on the basis of a promise to reduce unemployment. Success was short lived, however. DNA's Christian Hornsrud only survived for eighteen days in the prime minister's office. The SPD returned to the opposition benches in 1930 to support Brüning's fiercely deflationary policies, and Mac-Donald deeply embarrassed the British labor movement by his ill-fated defense of the pound in 1931. Similarly in the nineties, government tenure does not seem to have strengthened the popularity of social democracy. The PvdA's electoral fortunes have gradually declined since the late eighties.[3] In Sweden, opinion polls indicate that, mainly because it proved unable to bring about the rapid reduction in unemployment that voters expected, the SAP now for the first time since the early decades of this century is not much more popular than the conservative party.[4] And if they prove equally unable to solve the economic problems that seemed so intractable to neoliberal economic policies, Blair and Schröder may suffer the same fate.

As the historical analysis of its economic policies presented here suggests, in order for social democracy to consolidate its recent success it will have to govern on the basis of a program of macroeconomic expansion and microeconomic liberalism. Macroeconomic expansion (i.e., a regime based on the principle of cheap money) is a necessary precondition for tackling the problems of unemployment and rising social inequalities to which social democrats owe their present popularity. Microeconomic liberalism, in turn, is called for not only to answer the dissatisfaction with the inefficiency and inflexibility of the large public sector social democrats have created after 1945, but more important, to help fight any inflationary tendencies that a successful macroeconomic strategy might give rise to.

"New social democracy," however, sets out to address the problems of the twenty-first century on the basis of a program of macroeconomic restriction and microeconomic liberalism. In their effort to present a policy program in line with the "spirit of the time," social democrats have embraced a strategy that was appropriate to the inflationary problems of the seventies and eighties but that has become outdated in the new millennium. Worse, the present program is not only inappropriate for the current economic conditions in Europe; it may also serve to actively undermine the conditions on which social democracy can govern effectively. The longer social democracy clings to its macroeconomic fatalism, the harder it may become to resist political demands for an end to microeconomic liberalism.

NEW SOCIAL DEMOCRACY

The failure of the neoliberal policies of the eighties to address the problems of unemployment and economic stagnation did not automatically imply electoral success for social democracy. As long as conservative and liberal parties could credibly argue that the return of social democracy to power would be tantamount to the return of inflation, current account and budget deficits, and the industrial strife of the seventies, labor parties might still appear to many to be the worse alternative. For social democracy to reap the electoral benefits of the liberal failure, it had to adjust.

Because they remained in office, or returned quickly after a brief period in opposition, the adoption of a interpretative framework that rested on a combination of external constraints and leftist supply-side policies was fairly rapid in the two Scandinavian countries, and driven primarily by the party elite. As the foundations of the old regime disintegrated, there were not many policy options left for a government to pursue, nor were there many options concerning how social democrats should interpret these new policies. The three other parties instead were evicted from office while still trying to pursue a version of the old policies. Moreover, they faced extended periods in opposition. Without the constraint of government office, the transition to a new policy interpretation took longer.

Initially, the other three labor parties seemed to radicalize in response to the policy failures of the seventies. The loss of government responsibility in many cases strengthened those groups within the parties that had become increasingly frustrated with the spending cuts and wage restraint that social democratic governments also found increasingly necessary to impose. But the apparent electoral unpopularity of such a leftist program prompted a search for policies that would allow labor parties to regain the reputation of being able to manage the economy in a superior way. The adjustment of labor's economic policy program, which in most cases was completed during the eighties, consisted of three main elements.

First, expansionary macroeconomic strategies now were considered not feasible because of the rapid internationalization of economic relations. In a highly open economy, fiscal spending would serve to increase the current account deficit rather than to reduce unemployment. Expansionary monetary policies, in turn, would only promote capital flight as soon as the domestic interest rate threatened to fall below the rate set by international markets. Second, because macroeconomic stimulation was no longer available, the required growth in private investment activity would have to be brought about by means of supply-side policies, which increased competitiveness. The traditional emphasis on statist solutions like public ownership, subsidies, and extensive microeconomic regulations was toned down dramatically. In contrast to neoliberal emphasis on public abstention, social democrats saw a clear need for activist policies to create a favorable framework for private industry to innovate and prosper. Improving the education of the workforce and stimulating research and development in particular, came to occupy a central place. Finally, social democrats came to argue that the welfare state, though not the obstacle to prosperity it was made out to be by neoliberalism, was in need of fundamental reform. The ever-expanding welfare bureaucracy of the post-1945 period now was said to have aggravated rather than solved some problems because it stimulated passivity and dependence on the parts of its recipients. Instead of subsidizing inactivity, the new welfare state should encourage people to take their fate into their own hands again. Rather than providing potentially unlimited benefits, welfare programs should be aimed at assisting recipients to become independent of state transfers as soon as possible.

In Britain, the initial reaction of the Labour Party to its defeat and the emergence of Thatcherism consisted of a sharp turn to the left. Under Callaghan's labor government, the leftist opposition had been greatly strengthened in response to the hated income policies, rising unemployment, and budget austerity. After 1979 the so-called hard left succeeded in controlling the party for several years. Labour's new economic policy was the so-called alternative economic strategy (AES). The AES was driven by a desire to promote growth and full employment without having to resort to income policies, that is, without having to discipline the trade unions. Since such a strategy would most likely involve higher inflation, a loss of competitiveness, and current account deficits, it foresaw strict import controls and the reimposition of tight exchange controls. Because it was feared that private business under such a strategy would not be willing to invest sufficiently, a large degree of economic planning with a prominent role for trade unions was anticipated. The electorate did not put great faith in the ability of the AES to deliver economic results superior to those of Thatcherism, and Labour suffered a momentous electoral defeat in 1983.

In response to the defeat, the Labour Party quietly abandoned the AES and came to emphasize expansionary macromanagement again.[5] According to prominent members, such as Roy Hattersly, the key to higher growth and productiveness lay in stimulating demand by macroeconomic means. In order to prevent the balance-of-payments problems of the seventies, expansionary demand management should be coupled with an initial devaluation and a policy of flexible exchange rates.

Such views only managed to enter official Labour Party documents in a watered-down form. The far-reaching review of Labour's economic policy that chairman Neil Kinnock set in motion after another election defeat in 1987 argued that Thatcher's macroeconomic policies had served the interest of the City, whereas Labour would subordinate them to the interests of industry.[6] The policy review, however, failed to explain what type of macroeconomic policies that entailed. Indeed, in Andrew Gamble's words (1992: 71), "The sections on macroeconomic policy are undoubtedly the weakest and least convincing in the Policy Review." The reasons for this weakness are obvious. Because of the centrality of tight money in the Thatcher strategy, the Labour Party had to distance itself from such policies. It could not embrace the position that tight money would eventually lead to more jobs by bringing down inflation. Yet, for Labour to espouse macroeconomic expansion inevitably prompted the question of how inflation was to be contained if not by tight money. To that question, however, Labour could not respond, because the obvious answer – income policies – was unavailable, not only because trade unions adamantly rejected any such policies, but also because such a position would have reminded the electorate, no doubt prodded along by the Conservatives, of what had happened last time Labour had put its eggs in the basket of income policies.

When also the policy review failed to have the desired electoral effects, the Labour Party's economic strategy now came to emphasize the leftist version of supply-side policies.[7] Improving the international competitiveness of British industry was now identified as the solution to low growth and high unemployment.[8] To do so, a more active industrial policy was required. However, industrial policy for Labour no longer entailed direct intervention. Rather than suppressing market forces, it should be the task of economic policies to equip business and labor to succeed in international competition. An essential element of such a strategy would be increased investment in upgrading the skills of British labor. The emphasis on modernization of the British economy as the prime task was rather reminiscent of Margaret Thatcher's strategy. The Labour Party emphasized, however, that it was not merely copying the Conservatives' recipes. Whereas the conservative strategy was socially unjust, the improved competitiveness that would result from Labour's policies was a precondition for social justice. In particular, higher investment in skills would improve the situation of wage earners.[9]

The weak point in Labour's strategy, income policies, now was eliminated by assigning the responsibility for low inflation mainly to macroeconomic management. In order to dispel the fear of a return to income policies, Labour was more in need of constraints on macroeconomic policies than the Conservatives, whose autonomy from the unions could not be doubted. Since the late eighties the party came to advocate participation in the exchange rate mechanism (ERM) of the EMS, and subsequently EMU membership. The 1992 election manifesto stated explicitly that a fixed exchange rate commitment would have beneficial effects on inflation because it operated as a constraint on fiscal and monetary policies.[10] One of the first acts of the new Labour government that was elected in 1997 was to grant more independence to the Bank of England.

To be sure, macroeconomic stimulation was not completely eliminated. Such policies might have a useful role to play, but as long as Britain's competitive position was so weak they would benefit foreign suppliers instead. Expansionary demand management thus was conditional upon a radical improvement of international competitiveness. Moreover, expansionary policies should be internationally coordinated. However, since the modernization of the economy was no short-term task, and international reflation was not on the agenda, expansionary demand management was relegated to the long run, leaving only its short-run counterinflation role.

In Germany, the fall of the Schmidt government in 1982 exacerbated internal disagreement about the SPD's economic policies. On the one side stood the trade union wing that had become increasingly frustrated with welfare cuts during Schmidt's last years in government and who advocated a Schiller-type Keynesian policy. On the other side of the divide stood those who, also prompted by the rapid growth of the Green Party, predicted that the rise of postmaterialist values was making the SPD's emphasis on material wealth, growth, and industry increasingly outdated. The latter group had the upper hand in the commission that drafted a new SPD program.[11] The disappointing election outcome of 1987, however, seemed to suggest that an electoral success would be possible on the basis of neither strategy. The postmaterial skepticism regarding growth drove more voters to the Christian Democrats than it attracted from the Greens, and the dogged resistance against welfare cutbacks to many voters seemed to threaten German competitiveness. The party leadership analyzed the causes of the election defeat in the following terms: "So long as important sections of the electorate do not trust the SPD for the tasks of economic modernization, but only for ensuring that social safeguards are maintained, it will be very difficult to build a majority."[12]

After 1987, the SPD set out to shed its image of a party that defended the prerogatives of blue-collar labor and at the same time rejected growth and modern industrial society. In a first step to signal its willingness to ask sacrifices from blue-collar labor, Oskar Lafontaine, the ambitious prime minister of the state of Saarland, argued that more flexibility was required in the labor market and, in particular, that a shortening of the workweek was also acceptable if it implied lower wages. The DGB protested fiercely, and Lafontaine's proposals were defeated at the party's annual congress in 1988. Mass unemployment, however, kept undermining the strength of the DGB, and since the early nineties such proposals became generally accepted. At the same time, the party attempted to integrate the concerns of the Greens with a positive attitude toward industry, by means of the concept of the "ecological renewal of industry." In essence, the idea was to create jobs by stimulating environmental technology.

When mass unemployment accelerated in the nineties and started to make serious inroads on the new middle classes, the Green Party, who at times seemed to seriously threaten the SPD, found it increasingly difficult to maintain that economic growth undermined well-being. As a result, the heavy emphasis on "green" technology, which characterized the SPD's early views, was toned down somewhat. The microeconomic analysis of unemployment, which emerged after 1987, was strengthened.

As for the Labour Party, from which Gerhard Schröder in particular takes many cues, modernization of the economy is the prime task for the SPD. According to Schröder, Germany threatens to become an unattractive location in the global economy. Promoting competitiveness by means of innovation is to be the answer. Cost reduction does play a role in improving competitiveness, and the SPD proposes to cut taxes on business and labor in exchange for higher taxes on consumption. But, innovation is to be the main cure for Germany's economic ills. For the SPD, a policy of promoting innovation implies creating a favorable framework for business to do so, rather than direct government intervention. Regulations retarding the rapid adoption of new technologies are to be abolished; research and development are to be promoted; small and medium-size firms are to have easier access to risk capital; and the quality of education is to be raised.

Schröder's emphasis on microeconomic solutions to the unemployment problem, however, did not go uncontested. Not unlike the forces that eventually prompted the WTB plan of the thirties, the rapidly increasing unemployment of the nineties drove the labor wing of the party, headed by Oskar Lafontaine, in the direction of macroeconomic expansion. Given Germany's current-account surplus, Lafontaine argued, a lack of competitiveness could not possibly be Germany's main problem. What was needed instead was internationally coordinated reflation and, in particular, less restrictive monetary policies.

Lafontaine seemed to realize, however, that it would be politically unwise to place such demands at the center of the SPD's election platform. A program of monetary expansion would inevitably bring the SPD into conflict with the Bundesbank and thus jeopardize the party's decade-long effort to convince voters that it had the better answers to Germany's economic problems. As opinion polls consistently showed since 1992, the majority of the German electorate rather seemed to fear monetary expansion as a result of European monetary union. That Germany needed more innovation, instead, was an uncontroversial conclusion with which even the Christian Democrats found it hard to disagree.

As soon as he had become finance minister, however, Lafontaine set out to implement his program. He fiercely criticized the Bundesbank and its successor, the European Central Bank (ECB), for their restrictive policies; called upon the United States and Japan to stabilize exchange rates; and embarked on a tax reform program aimed at stimulating consumption. His tax reform, however, called forth fierce opposition from German business and strong criticism from Chancellor Schröder. Calls for monetary expansion proved unpopular, and Lafontaine was widely held responsible for the weakening of the euro relative to the dollar during the first few months of its existence. Finally, Lafontaine himself found it hard to explain how he could demand a reorientation of monetary policies toward employment creation while simultaneously calling for stable exchange rates with the dollar and the yen. Largely as a result of unbridgeable conflicts between himself and the chancellor, Lafontaine stepped down in the spring of 1999, after barely four months in office. With that, the proposal for macroeconomic expansion disappeared from the German policy agenda.

The Dutch labor party, as discussed earlier, for historical and ideological reasons was traditionally more inclined to analyze the problem of unemployment primarily in microeconomic terms. Accordingly, a theory that claimed that high wages improved competitiveness over the somewhat longer run because they promoted innovation never gained widespread popularity in the party. Instead, the party sought to distinguish itself from the governing Christian Democrats and liberals by making the defense of the welfare state its core issue. In particular the party focused on maintaining the income of the economically inactive. Given its relatively weak hold among blue-collar labor and the high proportion of the economically inactive in the Netherlands, such a strategy might seem electorally appealing. Yet, as other parties had to experience, in the absence of strong growth the attempt to turn social democracy into a party that appealed primarily to those directly dependent on public transfers was a cul-de-sac. The PvdA was hard pressed to answer the question of how the welfare state was to be financed in future. The middle class would not be enthusiastic about tax increases for the benefit of lower-income groups. In addition, the PvdA could not wholeheartedly support the substantial tax increases required for such a policy because it also felt that the Dutch cost level needed to be reduced. In sum, the emphasis on defending the welfare state earned the PvdA the reputation of being fiscally irresponsible.

The threat of being left on the opposition benches indefinitely led to a programmatic review also in the PvdA. The review got under way in earnest after the election defeat of 1986 when the party had made defense of the welfare state its main campaign theme.[13] The main result of the review was that in the 1989 election campaign the party stressed its fiscal responsibility. This strategy was successful to the extent that the PvdA was invited to form a government with the Christian Democrats in 1989. At the same time the welfare state cutbacks of the new PvdA finance minister, Wim Kok, caused major tension within the party and between the party and the FNV. The 1991 cuts in benefits for disabled workers[14] in particular caused a major conflict with the trade unions, similar to the SPD-DGB conflict of 1982.[15] Although unpopular, the strategy paradoxically increased the party's chance to hold government office. As it now also accepted cost reduction and deficit reduction as the prime economic tasks, it became an acceptable partner for the liberals and hence no longer depended on the consent of the Christian Democrats. Despite an election defeat in 1994 the PvdA was called upon to form a government with the liberals and left-liberals under the leadership of Wim Kok in 1994.

Since 1994, the PvdA has continued the economic strategy of reducing costs faster than its main trading partners and reforming the welfare state. Given high unemployment, no extensive intervention in wage bargaining was required to contain wages. Instead, the strategy of cost reduction came to focus on lowering social security contributions and welfare entitlements. Merely cutting welfare entitlements and wages would probably have had intolerable consequences for the party's popularity, however. Instead, Kok's government embarked on a rather successful program of reducing the number of economically inactive by means of a rapid expansion of part-time labor, which allowed the available work to be spread more evenly.

THE MYTH OF EXTERNAL CONSTRAINTS

During the sixties, when European countries adhered to an expansionary regime, capital mobility was generally said to frustrate expansionary policies. Any attempt to combat inflation by means of tight money would provoke capital inflows, thereby defeating the purpose of the policy.[16] In response to experiences like the British IMF crisis of 1975–76 and President Mitterrand's U-turn in 1982–83, however, the argument was inverted. European social democrats now concluded that, due to the internationalization of financial markets, the option of pursuing an expansionary macroeconomic regime in isolation did no longer exist.[17] Keynesianism in one country was dead, and if it ever were to be revived it would have to be on the level of the European Union. A cheap money policy aimed at promoting investment by lowering the interest rate below the expected profit rate will provoke capital outflows. Consequently, countries that want to pursue more expansionary policies than their neighbors will have to allow the currency to depreciate. In a world of globalized finance, so the argument went, depreciating the currency is no longer an available option because it provokes an uncontrollable run on the currency. Financial investors will interpret a depreciation of the currency as a commitment to unsound policies and hence will expect further devaluations. The result is a flight out of the domestic currency that can only be stopped by a turn to restrictive policies. But confidence is easily lost, and gained only with great difficulty. Countries with a history of devaluations and expansionary policies will be suspect in the eyes of wealth holders, and the latter's distrust will need to be compensated for by higher interest rates in order to convince them to hold the domestic currency. But it is not only a history of actual devaluations that may damage a country's reputation. Even the mere suspicion that a country might be willing to pursue policies that eventually could become incompatible with fixed exchange rates might have the same effect. To the extent that international financial markets interpret budget deficits as an indication of waning adherence to fixed exchange rates, a failure to balance the budget, irrespective of actual devaluations, may prompt capital outflows. Even domestic political opposition to the policies pursued may damage the interests of the country as it undermines the credibility of the government's exchange rate commitment. Since the interest rate is beyond the control of national policy makers, and the option of devaluation no longer exists, policies to stimulate investment will have to focus on improving profits. Or, put in more political terms: as capital gains an exit option it can impose its will on domestic policy makers regardless of the specific balance of political power.

In short, the lesson drawn from the experiences of the seventies and early eighties was that because devaluations and expansionary policies inevitably lead to exchange rate crises and higher interest rates for a long time to come, the best service a government can perform to the economy is to give priority to a fixed exchange rate and institutionalize this priority in such a way that wealth holders will have no reason whatsoever to suspect a rekindling of expansionary policy experiments.

At first glance there would seem to be good historical evidence for such a position. At the end of World War II, Keynes himself had already warned that open financial markets might seriously hamper full employment policies. Keynes strongly advised British policy makers to "retain control of our domestic rate of interest, so that we can keep it as low as suits our own purposes, without interference from the ebb and flow of international capital movements or flights of hot money."[18] The subsequent decades seemed to prove him right. The unprecedented growth period of the fifties and sixties coincided with the widespread use of exchange controls. Soon after the liberalization of financial markets had started in the midsixties, mass unemployment reemerged in the Western economies and growth rates dropped to a substantially lower level.

Yet, that open financial markets inevitably impose a restrictive macroeconomic regime is mainly a myth that may have served the useful purpose of allowing social democrats to combat inflation with less political resistance but which has tragic results when adhered to in a period in which such policies are no longer required. It is an almost irresistible temptation for social democrats to blame the failure of their policies on "capitalists," and foreign ones in particular. The history of social democratic economic policies of the past eighty years, however, rather supports the conclusion that short-term financial flows have benefited social democracy. Because a closed economy does not allow governments to ignore inflation, the exchange rate crises of the seventies and eighties merely speeded up a regime change that had become inevitable anyway. In the thirties, and for some countries in 1992, speculation against the currency greatly helped governments to muster the courage to abandon excessively restrictive policies.

INFLATION AND FINANCIAL OPENNESS

The argument that open financial markets frustrate expansionary macroeconomic policies is essentially Keynesian in nature. Since neoclassical theory maintains that macroeconomic management is not effective in the long run anyway (see Chapter 2), the emergence of international financial mobility cannot be considered problematic. Surprisingly, the standard Keynesian approach to economic policy making in open economies – the so-called Flemming-Mundell model – does not at all support the contention that open financial markets reduce or even annihilate domestic policy autonomy.[19]

The Flemming-Mundell results are straightforward. If international capital mobility is perfect, domestic interest rates cannot deviate from foreign rates, and if exchange rates are assumed fixed, fiscal expansion is a very powerful instrument. The higher domestic demand resulting from expansionary fiscal policies drives up domestic interest rates, which immediately provokes capital inflows. In other words, under financial openness, fiscal expansion automatically brings about the monetary expansion required to accommodate it, irrespective of whether the central bank is willing to do so or not. In the case of flexible exchange rates, monetary policy becomes a powerful tool. Monetary expansion will provoke a depreciation of the currency, which will provide an additional stimulus to domestic demand. When pursued in isolation fiscal expansion under flexible exchange rates will have no effects because higher interest rates will provoke appreciation of the currency. Fiscal expansion accompanied by monetary accommodation, however, is perfectly possible because it will leave the domestic exchange rate unchanged and because the current account deficit resulting from a higher level of gross domestic product at an unchanged exchange rate is by definition unproblematic in a situation of perfect capital mobility.

To arrive at the conclusion that policy autonomy has evaporated due to the internationalization of finance, Keynesians have had to resort to ad hoc assumptions, in particular concerning the behavior of international financial investors. However, to equate closed financial markets with monetary policy autonomy implies committing the analytical error of restricting the possibility of disruptive financial flows and speculation to a constellation in which domestic wealth holders have an international exit option. Acquiring assets denominated in a foreign currency or investing in domestic productive enterprises are by no means the only options open to wealth holders. In the hypothetical case of completely closed financial markets the possibility of a flight out of money exists by means of the option of acquiring (speculative) real assets and/or debt. Accordingly, the closure of financial markets does not free governments from the need to address inflationary problems through restrictive macroeconomic policies if price and income policies are no longer available.

If expectations of continued inflation have sufficiently undermined the confidence in the solidity of the domestic currency, then closing the loophole of capital outflows will not increase the number of macroeconomic options the government faces. Exchange controls can and have been used successfully to contain short-term flows of funds and hence may allow for a smoother and more orderly adjustment of exchange rates. Even in the eighties, for example, exchange controls have been used in the EMS framework to limit short-term speculative flows related to exchange rate realignments.[20] If, however, capital outflows are a reflection of a long-term distrust in the solidity of the domestic currency, rather than just the manifestation of expectations of a change in exchange rates, closing off the avenue of capital exports will not restore confidence but will rather rechannel the flight out of the domestic money into speculative real assets rather than foreign currency. The Reichsbank, for example, used exchange controls during hyperinflation to prevent additional price impulses through devaluation, but as long as the domestic causes of inflation were not removed, such controls did nothing to solve the basic problem. The Scandinavian boom of the eighties might not have developed as far is it did, had financial markets been more open. Hence, effective exchange controls may very well be counterproductive as they contribute to a domestic financial "greenhouse" climate.

To allow the exchange rate to depreciate in order to avoid more restrictive monetary policies in response to capital outflows obviously cannot provide solace in a situation in which the domestic inflation rate is getting out of hand. To relax the exchange rate constraint in such a constellation can only be interpreted as a political refusal to combat inflation and hence must aggravate the flight out of the domestic money. The result is a cumulative interaction between domestic inflation and depreciation.

It is not at all surprising that the mounting inflationary pressures since the sixties would give rise to a resurgence of international capital mobility, deregulation of exchange controls, and the proliferation of fixed exchange rate commitments culminating in the project of economic and monetary union. High inflation stimulated the demand for financial openness by wealth holders seeking protection of their assets by shifting into another currency. The welcome assistance that a stronger external constraint might provide in the macroeconomic fight against inflation, in turn, meant that governments were increasingly willing to supply financial openness.

In the absence of serious inflationary problems, a more expansionary monetary regime is possible, even if financial markets are open. The present disinflationary regime works its restrictive effects on economic growth, not primarily through high interest rates, but through the expectations it engenders. To be sure, high interest rates stood at the cradle of the regime. As can be seen from Figure 6.1 short-term rates peaked markedly in each country at the start of the new regime. Yet as it becomes clear that high rates are not the reflection of a temporary policy to cool down the economy, but rather the beginning of a fundamentally different policy orientation, both the supply of and demand for private investment are durably reduced. Supply decreases because long-term investment becomes riskier. With the reduced prospect of future growth, the demand for credit likewise diminishes. Or, in terms of Figure 2.4, both the Gs and the Gd curves shift to the left. The result may very well be lower interest rates. Conversely, a turn to an expansionary monetary regime in the long run does not necessarily imply lower interest rates as both the demand for and supply of credit increase. Such a regime change accordingly would also be possible if it were indeed true that international financial mobility equalizes interest rates across countries.

Admittedly, in the short run the turn to an expansionary regime will be accompanied by lower interest rates. Without pressing inflationary problems, the answer to capital outflows is to let the currency depreciate. Depreciation in such a constellation simply is an adjustment that brings the exchange rate in line with the government's policy priorities. Analytically, the position that a devaluation will create expectations of further devaluations is quite peculiar as it maintains that by seeking a cure for economic problems governments will create expectations of more economic problems.[21] Financial markets do continuously monitor economic policies and may frequently arrive at the conclusion that a country's policies are incompatible with its exchange rate level. But this in no way implies that financial markets enjoy primacy over politics. Instead, politics might exert its primacy by adjusting the exchange rate level to current policies rather then adjusting policies to the current exchange rate. Governments do have the option of adjusting the exchange rate to policy preference, and may even strengthen the confidence in the currency by correcting an obviously unrealistic exchange rate level.

It would be preferable to coordinate expansionary monetary policies in Western Europe. Because the EU is a rather closed economy in terms of external trade, inflationary effects due to higher import prices would be minimal. Moreover, international coordination would prevent any potentially disturbing change in real exchange rates between countries. But open financial markets pose no hindrance to countries that wish to pursue expansionary monetary polices in isolation. Due to their combined size the inflationary effects of a depreciating euro will be rather small for the eleven countries participating in EMU. Even small countries do have the option of pursuing a more expansionary regime in isolation as long as agreement can be reached that reducing unemployment should enjoy priority and depreciation hence should not be allowed to lead to higher inflation.

A SECULAR INCREASE IN FINANCIAL INTEGRATION?

Given its theoretical deficiencies, it is not surprising that the historical evidence in favor of the hypothesis of overwhelming external constraints is not very strong. Rather than showing a linear increase, as the external constraints hypothesis would predict, the intensity of international financial transactions has described a cyclical pattern. Although the extent of cross-border financial flows has increased rapidly since the sixties, the present situation is not without historical precedent. With the establishment of international telegraph and telephone services in the final decades of the nineteenth century, the technology for rapid international transfers of funds was in place. Because the classical gold standard, in theory at least, relied on international financial flows in order to correct domestic imbalances, governments were not inclined to create hurdles for the use of that technology. Accordingly, capital mobility was at a very high level. German economist Ludwig von Mises (1980: 413) could already argue in 1912 that

> the mobility of capital goods, which nowadays is but little restricted by legislative provisions such as customs duties, or by other obstacles, has led to the formation of a homogeneous world capital market. In the loan markets of the countries that take part in international trade, the net rate of interest is no longer determined according to national, but according to international, considerations. Its level is settled, not by the natural rate of interest in the country, but by the natural rate of interest *anywhere*.[22]

According to Robert Zevin (1992: 51–52), the empirical evidence even suggests that national financial markets were more tightly integrated in the late nineteenth and early twentieth centuries than they are at present.

World War I put an abrupt but temporary end to open financial markets. Many of the regulations fell victim to the bonfire of controls at the end of the war. Some, like the ban on the export of gold, had to be maintained as long as the gold parity of the currency was not yet reestablished. By 1925, however, international capital flows in the developed world found few obstacles in their way. With the exception of Germany, the Great Depression brought few restrictions on financial transactions. In most cases, it was the immediate threat of war that prompted the use of extensive exchange controls. Accordingly, the interwar period was characterized by a high level of international capital mobility.[23]

After 1945, international financial flows remained at a historically low level for almost two decades. At the end of the war, exchange regulations were kept in force and even tightened. As the problems of postwar reconstruction were gradually overcome, a general phase of liberalization set in that culminated in the convertibility of European currencies in 1959.

The sixties saw a divergent trend between countries like Germany and the Netherlands with a liberal regime, and the Scandinavian countries, which made more extensive use of exchange controls. As divergent economic policies increasingly made the exchange rates of the Bretton Woods system seem misaligned, capital flows increased rapidly, prompting increased regulation in all countries. The trend turned again in the midseventies, culminating in the Single Economic Act of 1988 in which all European Union countries agreed to completely abolish exchange controls.

Given that the extent of international financial flows displays a cyclical pattern, the renewed increase since the sixties cannot be interpreted as the inevitable result of new communications technologies. Accordingly, one might conclude that governments could regain much of their policy autonomy by reinstalling controls. More important, it might be asked why governments voluntarily gave up their policy autonomy in the first place. The answer – that, unlike the liberalization of foreign trade, the costs of financial deregulation are dispersed, which allowed neoliberal finance ministers and central bankers to pursue their policies unopposed by powerful interest groups (Helleiner 1996: 194, 196) – would seem rather unconvincing. If the liberalization of financial markets indeed spelled the demise of a highly successful Keynesian growth regime, then such policies should have been opposed by virtually everyone, except perhaps internationally oriented financial firms. Social democratic policy entrepreneurs, in particular, should have made deregulation a political issue if only because their fate, perhaps more so than for other political parties, depends on their ability to effectively control the economy. But nothing of the sort happened. Neither in the countries examined here, nor in most other Western countries, was the abolition of exchange controls a hotly contested political issue.[24] Rather, the political ease with which deregulation proceeded suggests that its effects on domestic policy autonomy were not nearly as decisive as commonly assumed.

INTEREST RATE CONVERGENCE?

If the internationalization hypothesis is correct, nominal interest rates should have converged since the sixties. Convergence of real interest rates should obtain only if goods markets are also perfectly integrated and differential inflation rates thus become impossible. In the markets for (very) short-term funds, convergence seems indeed to have increased. The ability of domestic authorities to stimulate private investment is primarily related to longer-term rates, but longer-term rates have not converged markedly since the sixties. Figure 6.1 plots the development of three-month money market rates since 1966. For these relatively short-term rates it is hard to detect convergence. Instead, interest rates have diverged more since 1980, when a clear separation emerged between low rates in Germany and the Netherlands and higher rates in the other three countries. Since 1992, rates have converged again, but this can hardly count as evidence of the dominance of market forces because that year brought a political decision to tightly coordinate economic policies in preparation for economic and monetary union.

Figure 6.2 plots the development of government bond yields since 1966, as an indicator for long-term rates. With the exception of Britain, rates converged more in the eighties than during the previous period. Since 1992, a marked convergence toward the level of Germany and the Netherlands can be observed.

Several in-depth studies of international interest rate formation have produced similar findings. In a study of monetary regimes from 1881 to 1990, Michael Bordo and Lars Jonung (1994), for example, found that short-term rates indeed converged more strongly from 1974 to 1990 than during any previous time, although no linear historical trend toward greater convergence could be detected. Real long-term interest rates instead did not converge more during

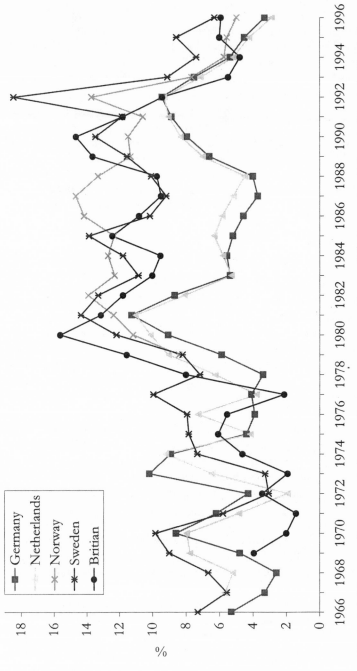

Figure 6.1. Money market rates: period averages in percent per annum. (Source: IMF International Financial Statistics Yearbook, 1997.)

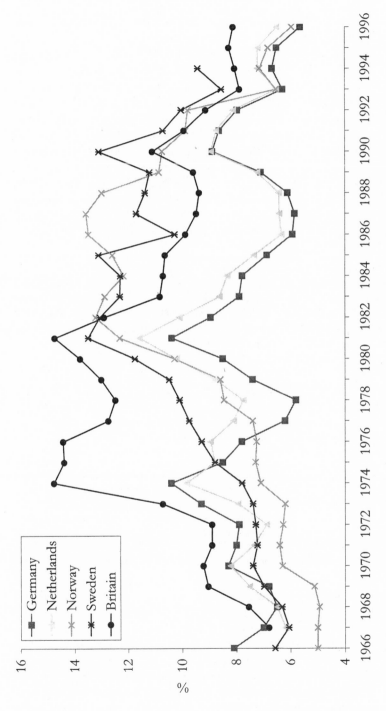

Figure 6.2. Government bond yields: average yields to maturity in percent per annum. (Source: IMF International Financial Statistics Yearbook, 1997.)

1974–90 than during 1946–70. Long-term real rates did converge more strongly after European currencies became convertible in 1959, but during 1974–90 convergence decreased again compared to 1959–70, albeit minimally.

In a detailed study of Swedish financial markets, Lars Oxelheim (1990) failed to find evidence of a dramatically increased integration during the preceding two decades. On the contrary, in surveying the differentials of real long-term interest rates between Sweden and a host of other countries, it seemed that total financial integration decreased in the early eighties. "Whatever perspective we adopt in relation to real interest rate developments, the conclusion is that during the first half of the 1980s total financial integration decreased compared with the immediately preceding period" (Oxelheim 1990: 344).[25] For Norway, Axel Damman (1991: 54–56) has shown that both the real and the nominal interest rates for Norwegian and U.S. state bonds moved very close up to roughly 1980. After 1980, however, large interest rate differentials appeared.[26]

LESSONS FROM THE THIRTIES

That an expansionary monetary regime is not precluded, and is sometimes even promoted, by open financial markets is perhaps most spectacularly illustrated by the regime changes during the Great Depression, when it proved possible to embark on more expansionary policies without having to impose any serious restraints on international financial flows.

Quite reminiscent of much of the present policy discourse in social democratic parties, Philip Snowden, Chancellor of the Exchequer in the second Labour government, argued on January 14, 1931, that one of the reasons why budgets needed to be balanced was to appease international holders of sterling and thereby avoid economic mayhem:

> There are disquieting indications that the national finances, and especially the continuously increasing load of debt upon the Unemployment Insurance Fund, are being watched and criticized abroad. . . . It is believed that there is a steady trickle of money being transferred from this country abroad. We cannot afford to let this movement increase. . . . Any flight from the pound would be fraught with the most disastrous consequences – not merely to the money market but to the whole economic organization of the country.[27]

The speculation against the British pound that set in during the late twenties was inspired not by the fear of expansionary policies but by a belief that the pound had been reestablished at too high a parity and that British society was less and less likely to be willing to bear the costs of such a commitment. To be sure, rather than question the wisdom of its commitment to gold, the Labour Party claimed that the wave of speculation that had brought down the second Labour government was a "bankers' ramp," meaning that financial circles had engineered the crisis of the pound in order to topple the government and achieve a cut in spending, in particular on unemployment benefits.[28] Apart from Norman's continuous demands for budget cuts, this view could derive support from New York's J. P. Morgan & Co.'s insistence that budget cuts were a precondition for a loan to defend the pound. The trauma of Snowden's defense of the pound prompted the Labour Party's decision to make exchange controls an integral part of monetary policy.

Exchange controls proved unnecessary. No run on sterling developed once the link to gold had been cut. Especially during November and December 1931, there was considerable downward pressure on the pound, and on December 3, it reached a low point of $3.24.[29] Although the Bank of England, partly because of lack of funds, stayed aloof, downward pressure on sterling abated. From March 1932 onward, sterling came under upward pressure. Nor did the national government's policy of cheap money require exchange controls. Fearful of an uncontrollable downward slide, the Bank of England did introduce some exchange controls in September 1931 but relaxed these restrictions the same year and abolished them altogether in March 1932.[30] Foreign issues in the London capital market, however, were maintained under informal control after 1932 as the BoE tried to discourage foreign lending.[31]

In Sweden and Norway, speculation against both currencies largely abated after the gold standard was abandoned. No flight out of the Swedish krona occurred after the SAP came to power in 1932 on the basis of an explicitly reflationary program. The Riksbank introduced some foreign exchange restrictions in the autumn of 1931, but they proved superfluous. The Swedish ministry of finance drafted a law on exchange controls during 1932.[32] But because the feared erratic hot money flows and the flight of investors from the country failed to materialize after the SAP came to power, the draft proposal for a foreign exchange law was never presented to parliament.[33] Far-reaching exchange controls were only introduced by the Foreign Exchange Law of 1939 and the Foreign Exchange Decree of 1940. Nor did Norway experience an exchange rate crisis when the social democratic Nygaardsvold government took office in 1935. Tight foreign exchange controls, as in Germany after 1931,[34] were only necessary to protect a more expansionary policy orientation, as long as the commitment to a fixed gold parity was maintained.

Erratic financial flows, instead, made the life of those governments, like the Dutch, who at all costs wanted to defend a restrictive regime after 1931, more difficult. After the fall of 1931, the Netherlands actually experienced an inflow of capital. Gold and foreign currency reserves of the DNB increased from NLG 931 million in September 1931 to NLG 1,106 million in January 1933.[35] The initial credibility of the exchange rate target waned, however, as more and more countries devalued and the depressing effects of deflationary policies to neutralize the overvaluation of exchange rate became more pronounced. Especially from 1933 to 1936, the DNB continuously had to ward off speculation against the guilder. Large outflows occurred in response to the devaluation of the yen (December 31, 1931), the devaluation of the dollar (March 1933), Germany's announcement of a transfer payments moratorium (June 1933), the devaluation of the belga, and in May 1936, after the victory of the Popular Front in France. Whenever a change in the domestic political situation seemed to imply a weakening of the support for the gold parity, capital flowed out. When it seemed in September 1935, for example, that the government did not have a majority for the proposed budget cuts, speculation against the guilder was massive and calmed down only after the proposal was approved.[36]

As was the case in Britain and Scandinavia, the depreciation of the guilder in 1936 restored rather than destroyed confidence in the currency. Quite contrary to the expectations of the government and the DNB, who feared that a serious crisis of confidence in the guilder would follow on the heels of depreciation, the Dutch EEA soon was confronted with the task of preventing excessive appreciation instead of depreciation. The DNB lowered its discount rate in December 1936 and ended the ban on long-term foreign lending and the export of private gold (mid-1937). Equally in contrast to the government's expectations, government bonds rallied strongly in response to the depreciation of September 26, 1936.[37]

EMU: THE RETURN OF THE GOLD STANDARD?

Whether exchange rates are fixed or flexible is not crucial to the success of the social democratic program. Social democratic policies experienced their greatest success under the Bretton Woods regime of fixed exchange rates. They witnessed their most dismal period under another fixed exchange rate regime, namely, the interwar gold standard. Decisive for the fate of social democratic policies, then, is the general policy philosophy in which a fixed exchange rate regime is embedded. The Bretton Woods system linked the currencies of countries that were all committed to a macroeconomic growth regime, and for that reason maintaining the exchange rate did not fundamentally conflict with the goal of full employment. Indeed, the Bretton Woods system was created in 1944 as an attempt to maintain an open trading system without jeopardizing each participating government's ability to pursue expansionary macroeconomic policies. The commitment to fixed exchange rates was to prevent competitive devaluations. Nevertheless, in order not to subordinate macromanagement to the exigencies of external balance, the system provided short-term lending facilities and provided for exchange rate adjustment in the event of a "fundamental disequilibrium," a fundamental disequilibrium comprising problems resulting from a more expansionary policy stance. Moreover, the use of exchange controls was permissible. The interwar gold standard instead was motivated by the desire to reduce domestic policy autonomy by means of institutionalizing a restrictive macroeconomic regime.

There is nothing in a project of economic and monetary union in Western Europe that would intrinsically discriminate against a social democratic policy program. Whether European social democracy will thrive or stagnate under monetary union depends on the policy orientation of the ECB and the national macroeconomic authorities. Although undoubtedly having had favorable effects on productivity, supply-side policies have disappointed the hopes placed in them in the eighties and nineties, as indeed they did during the twenties. After two decades of mass unemployment and stagnation, Western Europe first of all needs a decisive and highly visible break with the current philosophy of monetary policy. In the interwar period, the decision to resurrect and then abandon the gold standard marked the regime change. In the seventies and eighties, the official acceptance of the neutrality-of-money doctrine and/or a fixed exchange rate commitment to Germany performed the same function. At present, a visible rejection of neutral money, possibly combined with agreements on income policies, would be required.

Many social democrats tend to herald monetary integration as the only possible road to recovering at least some of the national policy autonomy that was lost as a result of internationalization. As the party leaders of the Confederation of the Socialist Parties of the European Community declared: "The ever increasing internationalization of the economy and interdependence of our societies at every level mean that it is increasingly difficult to respond on a national level to the new challenges which arise. Democratic control of the future remains possible, provided that those elements of sovereignty which can no longer be exercised in a purely national framework are pooled."[38] However, the EMU project owes its success primarily to the desire of European countries to employ the tight policies of the German Bundesbank as an external constraint for their own policies, instead of to the wish to overcome external constraints. If other European countries had wished to pursue a monetary policy independent of the Bundesbank, there would have been a much less circuitous way than to sign a treaty designed to institutionalize German-style monetary policies at the EU level. The much more obvious solution would have been to form an EMS without Germany during the exchange rate crises of 1992–93, when the Bundesbank's tight monetary policies unleashed speculation against almost all other currencies. Given the appreciation of the mark this would have entailed, and the importance German policy makers attach to current-account surpluses, such a strategy would likely have exerted more pressures on Germany than the present EMU.[39]

As the European Monetary Union, which came into force on January 1, 1999, was primarily designed as a means to institutionalize a disinflationary regime, it is rather more reminiscent of the interwar gold standard than of the Bretton Woods system. The treaty on monetary union was signed at a time when European governments had come to share the view that fighting inflation should be the sole responsibility of monetary authorities. As in the case of the gold standard, inflation was perceived to have been the result of misguided policies. As in the case of the gold standard, politicians deemed an institutionalization of tight monetary policies by means of an independent central bank necessary in order to prevent a repetition of the inflationary sins of the past. Accordingly, the independent Bundesbank became the template for the ECB. In fact, the ECB enjoys an even greater independence: a change in its statutes requires the unanimous consent of all the EU member states, whereas the statutes of the Bundesbank can be changed by a parliamentary majority.

By institutionalizing the disinflationary monetary regime on a European level, the EMU sends a signal that makes a rapid recovery from Western Europe's low-growth and high-unemployment trap rather unlikely. Indeed, the project of monetary union carries a substantial part of the responsibility for the rapid increase in unemployment rates since the early nineties (see Figure 5.2). When the Bundesbank, in the early nineties, decided to punish the unions and the government for their alleged mishandling of German unification, the determination of other EU members to maintain the fixed exchange rate with the Deutsche mark ensured a rapid spread of restrictive policies throughout Europe. Moreover, in order to meet the Maastricht criterion of a budget deficit not in excess of 3 percent of GDP, countries were forced to pursue even tighter fiscal policies in the midst of a recession.

To be sure, the institutional structure of the ECB is no guarantee that its policies will closely resemble those of the Bundesbank. As with the Bundesbank, the ECB statutes do not mention a specific inflation target, and so there is room for discretion on the part of the ECB. Neither the European governments nor the European Commission will have the right to issue directives to the ECB, but this does not prevent board members who come from another tradition of monetary policy making from closely coordinating their actions with their own government. And even though independent central banks have an institutional incentive to embrace a theory that holds monetary policies to have no lasting effects on unemployment, independence does not necessarily imply a preference for the tight monetary policies pursued by the Bundesbank. Rather, the trade-off the ECB will make between price stability and stimulating employment will depend on the specific outlook of the majority of its members. However, even if they cannot be recalled by their governments or the Commission, they are not immune from being influenced by the political and economic developments around them.

Inflation does not stand in the way of such an expansionary regime. With almost twenty million Western Europeans out of work and virtual price stability, the threat of inflation is negligible, at least in the short run. In Sweden, the fact that the post-1992 depreciation of the krona did not call forth compensating wage claims indicated that unions were again willing and able to show moderation. Eighteen years of conservative rule in Britain have weakened the unions to such an extent that a return of the problems of the seventies seems rather unlikely. Under the pressure of almost five million unemployed, German unions find it increasingly difficult to prevent nominal wage cuts.

Admittedly, it is harder to predict whether labor market relations in the Europe of the late nineties are such that a return to the unemployment rates of the fifties and sixties will not set off serious inflationary pressures again in the longer run. The experience of Norway seems to indicate that the breakdown of bargaining during the mideighties was primarily a conjunctural phenomenon. Due to an explicit tripartite social contract, it has been possible to reduce unemployment again to below 5 percent in 1996 without causing serious inflationary pressures.[40] But the Norwegian system in which the state has the fiscal means to award moderation and the legal means to seriously curtail the bargaining autonomy of non-LO unions and wage earners in general may not be readily exported to other countries.

Nevertheless, the need to satisfy the strict convergence criteria of the Maastricht treaty in terms of low inflation and budget deficits has sparked widespread attempts at social concentration. So-called social pacts have recently been concluded in Norway, Italy, Ireland, Portugal, Spain, and Finland. In the Netherlands, the agreement of Wassenaar has survived unscathed since 1982. In Germany, Chancellor Schröder is attempting to construct an "alliance for jobs." And even in Sweden, unions and employers have made attempts to arrive at a greater degree of coordination despite the traumatic breakdown of wage moderation in the late eighties, albeit the LO has had only very limited success in recentralizing bargaining.

With the exception of Norway, none of these social pacts has been tested under conditions of low unemployment, and it seems unlikely that they will be able to revive the successful income policies of the fifties and sixties. With the decline of blue-collar labor and the increasing diversification of the workforce, the demand for local autonomy on the part of workers has increased noticeably, making a return to the centralization of older days unlikely. Likewise, support for the high degree of income equalization that accompanied the policies of nominal wage moderation, in Scandinavia in particular, seems to have disappeared for good. Finally, due to the rapid growth of the public sector since the fifties there is now a large segment of the workforce that is relatively impervious to market pressures. Indeed, the breakdown of wage moderation in the seventies and eighties was frequently spearheaded by the public-sector unions.

Negotiated policies of nominal wage moderation will therefore most likely have to be supplemented by larger market pressures than was the case in the fifties and sixties. In such a context, the recent abandonment of interventionist supply-side policies in favor of deregulation and privatization, and in particular the ongoing process of market liberalization in the European Union, will even have beneficial *macroeconomic* effects. As tariff and nontariff barriers disappear between the countries of the EU, a substantial part of the previously sheltered sectors are opened to more competition, leading market pressures on wage to increase in each national context. Moreover, the fiscal constraint of the stability pact that generally limits acceptable deficits to 3 percent of gross domestic product might play a positive role in stabilizing a regime of low employment, as it puts governments under pressure to cut public employment in response to excessive wage growth.

NEW HOPES?

Political strategists generally advise candidates not to campaign on issues for which they cannot provide a solution. For social democrats not to make Europe's mass unemployment the major campaign issue would have been impossible. If there was any hope of convincing a substantial part of the electorate that social democracy had not become an anachronism in the postindustrial societies of the late twentieth century, then it had to be argued that the stagnation and mass unemployment that came to characterize the reign of neoliberal policies were not inevitable.

Although after the recent election victories of a host of social democratic parties mass unemployment in the European Union shows no sign of disappearing, there would seem to be rays of hope. In Norway and the Netherlands, social democratic governments have been able to reduce unemployment below the 5 percent mark. The Norwegian success rests mainly on public-sector job creation funded by oil wealth and hence holds few lessons for other countries. The Dutch strategy, in contrast, is increasingly presented by its social democratic sister parties as an example to emulate.

In the Netherlands, the social democratic–liberal coalition has continuously reduced the unemployment rate since 1994 while at the same time significantly improving the budget balance. Yet, it is doubtful whether the Dutch strategy holds the key to Europe's problems. Despite substantial reductions in disposable real wages, the Dutch success rests largely on distributing the available work more evenly than on creating more work. Measured in hours worked, employment increased by roughly 14 percent from 1983 to 1996 while the unemployment rate fell from 11.0 percent to 6.7 percent. During the same period, however, the Dutch labor force increased by roughly 19 percent.[41] Despite rapidly falling unemployment, the amount of labor available per member of the labor force hence has declined. Correcting for the large share of part-time employment and the low participation rate, Dutch unemployment ranges somewhere in the area of 20 percent rather than the 6.7 percent recorded in 1996 (see Figure 5.2). Moreover, the strong emphasis on improving competitiveness by means of cost reduction has led to the reemergence of poverty to such an extent that even the Dutch bishops have seen fit to caution the social democrats not to ignore the problem. More important perhaps, the jobs gained from improved competitiveness have come largely at the expense of other European countries. Prime Minister Kok has repeatedly prided himself on having succeeded in lowering the Dutch cost level substantially below the German level.

By distributing the available work more evenly, the Dutch social democrats have employed a solidaristic labor market policy, which contrasts positively with the high level of open unemployment in most other European nations. Yet, overall a strategy that relies on cutting costs below the level of European competitors holds few lessons for Europe. Moreover, it is doubtful whether the combination of substantial cuts in disposable income and welfare entitlements, combined with an only very limited growth in the demand for labor, will be politically acceptable in many countries outside the Netherlands.

As was the case during the thirties, for Europe to solve the problems of mass unemployment and stagnation, first of all a decisive change in the monetary regime is required. Yet, at present only very few European social democrats are willing to change course. German and Dutch social democrats are mainly preoccupied with the fear that the ECB will become less fixated on price stability than their central banks were. Despite Lafontaine's brief intermezzo as minister of finance, the dogma of tight money nowhere else remains as uncontested as in Germany. Notwithstanding the continuously high export volumes and current account surpluses, the SPD remains convinced that Germany's problem is one of competitiveness. A strategy that insists on tight money while trying to reduce unemployment by means of ever greater trade surpluses with its EU partners will prove counterproductive in the long run for both Germany and the EU.

Southern European social democrats seem to value the EMU, especially for the constraints it puts on domestic policy making. Indeed, at the Maastricht negotiations the Spanish social democratic government was one of those that pushed most strongly for tight criteria. And even the French socialists, who have frequently claimed that the EMU is the only way to break the dominance of the Bundesbank, are ambiguous as they also see the EMU as a vehicle for realizing General de Gaulle's long-standing dream of dislodging the dollar from its position as the world's foremost reserve currency. To accomplish the latter, however, the ECB would have to build a reputation by means of a prolonged period of very tight policies.

For social democrats to disappoint the hopes again placed in them might have dire consequences, not only for the parties themselves, but for society in general. The most benign of the consequences would be the reemergence of the budget deficit problems of the seventies and eighties. Continuous mass unemployment will put increasingly strong pressures on governments to implement measures that can be effective in the short run. Fiscal policies can do so, especially if they are used to expand the public sector. Moreover, without any exchange rate consequences to fear from fiscal expansion, such policies may again seem increasingly attractive to many governments. Admittedly, EMU members have committed themselves to maintaining budget deficits below the 3 percent mark, except in serious recessions; but if a majority of members favor fiscal expansion it would seem hard for the minority to insist on sanctions. However, without support from the ECB fiscal expansion will again end up in the familiar cul-de-sac of the seventies.

More seriously, a stubborn commitment to a tight money regime may serve to reverse the liberal microeconomic policies on which social democrats embarked during the eighties and usher in a period of growing protectionism and interventionism. Indeed, there is a rapidly growing movement in Europe that interprets the current economic malaise as the result of the allegedly unbridled capitalism that the neoliberal policies of the preceding decades bestowed on European workers. Social democrats might find it hard to resist the argument that if the level of employment is determined by international competitiveness, and if socially unacceptable cost reduction of a draconian size is required to regain competitiveness, then protectionist measures should be employed to provide relief.[42] During the thirties, protectionism, although microeconomically inefficient, had a macroeconomic justification in that it helped counteract the deflationary effects of a misplaced monetary policy. In the highly trade dependent European economies of the 1990s, which do not suffer from deflation, increased protectionism can only spell disaster as it implies that microeconomic policies have joined the monetary authorities in their effort to keep people out of work.

Politically, a failure of social democrats to provide an alternative to the economic policies of their predecessors definitely opens up the space for movements of an extremist nature. That the virulently xenophobic French Front National has managed to become the most popular political party among blue-collar workers on the basis of slogans like "Globalization threatens your job, the Front National fights globalization" may be a sign of things to come. Alternatively, a failure of social democracy may spark a withdrawal into political apathy, thereby undermining one of the core foundations on which any democratic polity must rest.

Fortunately, the political situation at the end of the nineties does not warrant unbridled pessimism. Even though no government is willing to openly advocate a change in regime, the increasingly sharp contrast between U.S. prosperity and European stagnation is rapidly swelling the ranks of those who advocate that the ECB shed its Bundesbank legacy and adopt the strategy of the Federal Reserve, which recognizes that, apart from holding inflation down, stimulating growth and employment is an important responsibility for monetary policies. The series of interest rate cuts during the first months of 1999 may be a sign that the ECB finds it increasingly difficult to resist such calls.

In addition, non-EMU members Britain and Sweden seem to be taking the first steps toward abandoning the dogma of tight money. In both cases, international financial markets provided the impetus. In a wave of financial speculation, sterling and the krona were forced to abandon their fixed exchange rate in September and November 1992, respectively. As in September 1931, the Bank of England refused to go to great lengths in terms of higher interest rates to defend the pound. Subsequently, the bank has made use of its larger room for maneuvering to pursue a more relaxed policy. As a result, Britain has ranked among the countries with the highest growth rates in Western Europe since 1992.

In Sweden, the social democrats initially supported the conservative government's desperate attempts to calm speculation on the currency by means of drastic spending cuts. By mid-November, however, the SAP had concluded that a floating currency might be preferred to an extremely restrictive fiscal and monetary policy. On November 19, 1992, four days after the SAP announced it was no longer willing to support the government's policies, the krona was floated. As in September 1931, the Riksbank followed the depreciation by a declaration that it would not relax its fight against inflation. But although the krona depreciated by more than 20 percent, the inflation rate did not turn upward. Instead, the immediate effects of the depreciation were that some of the major banks were saved from failing and the export industry managed to recover. The longer-term effect of the absence of inflationary pressures under a floating currency has been to convince the SAP that it has more policy options than it originally thought. In 1997 the government decided that it did not wish to join EMU for the time being, mainly because, given the high unemployment rate, it did not wish to give up its monetary policy autonomy – the same policy autonomy that was said not to exist only a few years before.

Admittedly, the ECB, and Swedish and British social democrats are treading very carefully in the monetary policy area. But as the view that no alternatives to tight money exist is admitted to be increasingly untenable, the first necessary step toward a new era of social democratic prosperity has been taken. As during the twenties and the Great Depression, it is the monetary policy decisions that will determine whether the social democratic program succeeds.

NOTES

CHAPTER 1. SOCIAL DEMOCRACY IN THE MACROECONOMY

1. For a recent version see Matzner & Streeck 1991, and Streeck 1991. For Sweden see Erixon 1989. As early as 1923, the SAP's economic policy expert, Ernst Wigforss, could point out that the argument that high wages would stimulate employers to "rationalize" production was an old one within the labor movement. See Unga 1976: 60.
2. For example, see Streeck 1991: 23, 31.
3. On the concept of the feasible real wage see Layard 1986, chap. 3.
4. See Korpi 1978 and Stephens 1986.
5. See Goldthorpe 1984.
6. See Gourevitch 1986 and Cerny 1990, chap. 8.
7. See Riese 1987.
8. For this view see Korpi 1978 and Stephens 1986.
9. See Przeworski 1985, Przeworski 1991, and Przeworski & Sprague 1986. Given the history of economic policies it would seem a rather odd argument that policy programs that cause a short-term economic crisis with the promise of superior economic performance in the long run are electorally unfeasible. Most disinflationary policies rest on this type of argument.

CHAPTER 2. POLITICS, ECONOMICS, AND POLITICAL ECONOMY

1. British Conservative Chancellor of the Exchequer Nigel Lawson (1993: 414–5) explained the policy change under the Thatcher government in rather similar terms: "The conclusion on which the present Government's economic policy is based is that there is indeed a proper distinction between the objectives of macroeconomic and microeconomic policy, and a need to be concerned with both of them. But the proper role of each is precisely the opposite of that assigned to it by the conventional post-War wisdom. It is the conquest of

inflation, and not the pursuit of growth and employment, which is or should be the objective of macroeconomic policy. And it is the creation of conditions conducive to growth and employment, and not the suppression of price rises which is or should be the objective of microeconomic policy."

2. According to Susan Strange (1986: 79): "there is also ample evidence that economic theories are like detergents on a supermarket shelf. Politicians decide on other grounds what ends they wish to achieve and will pick on the appropriate legitimating economic theory as a shopper picks off the shelf the detergent that suits the kind of washing or cleaning he or she wants to do." For related views see Alan Budd in Solow et al. 1987: 187 and Lowi 1992: 3.

3. See Cross 1982.

4. To avoid misunderstandings, the argument is not that economics has achieved no progress. The development from Adam Smith's vague notion of the "invisible hand" to the Arrow-Debreu-Hahn general equilibrium theory does indeed constitute major progress. The same holds true for Friedman's version of the quantity theory as compared to Hume's early formulation. Sraffa's (1960) modeling of the classical theory of value is a significant step ahead from Marx's inconsistent solution of the transformation problem. Similarly, the step from mercantilist notions of the stimulating effects of cheap money to Keynes's views on monetary policy is a major advance.

5. Net taxes, in the case of transfers.

6. An equivalent formulation of the question whether money is neutral in the long run is whether saving determines investment or investment determines saving. Is it possible for the central bank to induce a rise in investment and thereby an increase in income which in turn will lead to higher savings? Or does increased investment require a prior decision of households to save more?

7. In Milton Friedman's version of the quantity theory, the velocity of money is seen to increase somewhat in response to higher inflation. For our purposes, this point is not crucial.

8. See Hahn 1984: 125.

9. Robinson (1972: 4) points out that in order to arrive at the conclusion that markets tend toward equilibrium, "either the whole of future time is collapsed into today or else every individual has correct foresight about what all others will do, while they have correct foresight about what he will do, so that the argument runs into the problem of free will and predestination."

10. See also Riese 1987B: 26.

11. See Hahn (1984: 308): "Now one of the mysteries which future historians of thought will surely wish to unravel is how it came about that the Arrow-Debreu model came to be taken descriptively; that is, as sufficient in itself for the study and perhaps control of actual economies. Having spent most of my life as an economist on this theory I confess that such an interpretation never occurred to me. Indeed it was clear from the beginning that we only had half a theory anyway since there was (and is) no rigourous account, derived from first principles, of how the Arrow-Debreu equilibrium comes to be established."

12. See also Hahn (1984: 332): "The proposition that a k-fold change in the stock of money appropriately defined will lead to a k-fold change in money prices and money wages and no changes in any real magnitude is not a proposition deducible from serious theory."

13. High-powered money denotes notes and coins in circulation plus the amount of commercial bank borrowing at the central bank.

14. Moreover, uncertainty does not necessarily imply instability to the extent that actors prefer not to change behavior when confronted with alternatives of which the consequences are uncertain. See Coddington 1982.

15. See Keynes 1973, chap. 23.

16. As Leijonhufvud 1968 and Meltzer 1988 have brought to our attention again, there is much more in Keynes's work than the IS-LM model.

17. Cf. Keynes 1973: 168.

18. Put differently, the credit market is not an auction market but instead is naturally rationed. Banks cannot afford to indiscriminately lend to those who are willing to pay the highest interest rates. Because credit contracts, in contrast to the sale of a good, are commitments for the future, banks and lenders in general will have to determine the creditworthiness of the borrower, i.e., they will have to form an opinion whether it is likely that the borrower will be able to fulfill his commitment.

19. This figure was taken from Spahn 1986: 159.

20. Note that the real interest rate always is an expected value as it consists of the nominal interest rate discounted for the expected inflation for the duration of the credit contract.

21. For example, Keynes 1973: 12.

22. See also Layard 1986, chap. 3, and Staderman 1987: 312–17.

23. Historically the view that, in the short run, a fall in money wages was likely to lower the price level instead of real wages was not confined to Keynes and his followers. As Blaug (1985: 674) notes: "Now as Keynes himself made clear in chapter 19 of the General Theory on 'Changes in Money Wages', it was orthodox doctrine that money wage cuts cannot directly affect employment in the short run because the demand for labor depends on real wages; since in the short run all variable costs are labor costs, prices must fall in the same proportion as wages, leaving real wages the same."

24. See Keynes 1963: 189–90.

25. See Keynes 1963: 172–3.

26. "The very effort of individuals to lessen their burden of debts increases it, because of the mass effect of the stampede to liquidate in swelling each dollar owed. Then we have the great paradox, which, I submit, is the chief secret of most, if not all, great depressions: *The more the debtors pay, the more they owe.* The more the economic boat tips, the more it tends to tip. It is not tending to right itself, but is capsizing." Irving Fisher 1934, quoted in Herr 1986: 188. Emphasis in the original.

27. See Keynes 1963: 168–78.

28. See Tobin 1980: 4.

29. See, for example, Hibbs 1997, Garrett & Lange 1991, and, for the interwar period, Simmons 1994.

30. See Riese 1986, 1987B.

31. See "The End of Laissez Faire" in Keynes 1963.

32. See Polanyi 1957: 251.

33. For the SPD, see Könke 1987: 206.

34. For a fuller definition of a laissez-faire monetary regime see Selgin & White 1994: 1718–19.
35. On demand management policies in general see also Bispham & Boltho (1982: 290): "experience up to the late 1970s suggests that there was little real change in the way governments used their instruments. What gradually changed were the goals of policy-makers. The decade was marked not so much by a retreat from demand management as by a retreat from the short-term full employment goal toward policies aimed at controlling inflation."
36. See Bowden & Collins 1992.
37. See, e.g., Blyth 1997.
38. See also Garrett & Lange 1991 and Cerny 1990, chap. 8.

CHAPTER 3. WHY WAS THERE NO SOCIAL DEMOCRATIC BREAKTHROUGH IN THE TWENTIES?

1. For a summary of the commission's findings, see Maurseth 1987: 101–7.
2. For a discussion of the Swedish socialization commission, see Tilton 1991: 86–102.
3. See Winkler 1979: 40–41 and Schönhoven 1987: 123, 127.
4. In the November 1918 elections, the Labour Party polled 2,374,385 votes and the coalition 5,091,128. Due to the peculiarities of the electoral system it gained only 59 seats in the House of Commons compared to the coalition's 484. Source: Mowat 1964: 6. In the Norwegian general election of October 1918, the liberals and DNA roughly polled the same number of votes, yet the former held 54 seats and the DNA only 18. In the 1921 elections, which were held under a reformed electoral system, labor increased its seats from 18 to 29 while the liberals declined from 54 to 39. The Dutch social democrats gained 22 seats in the elections to the Lower House in 1918 compared to 15 in 1913.
5. See Cronin 1984, Maier 1988, and Middlemas 1979, chap. 5.
6. Lloyd George election campaign speech, November 24, 1918. Quoted in Boyle 1967: 467.
7. See Tilton 1991: 90–91 on the SAP leadership.
8. Östlind 1945: 390, 456.
9. See Maier 1988 and Cronin 1984.
10. Moreover, to argue that demands for a certain type of policy can only be formulated on the basis of a consistent economic theory is most certainly to strongly overestimate the role of economic ideas in policy making. History provides many examples of governments pursuing policies that lack thorough theoretical justification.
11. Cf. Axelsson, Löfgren, & Nilsson 1987: 33–34.
12. See Winch 1969: 53–55.
13. See Skidelsky 1967: 40 and Thompson 1996: 69.
14. See Danielsen 1984: 118–19.
15. Quoted in Ousland 1949, vol. 2:17. My translation.
16. See *Det Norske Arbeiderpartis Kriseprogram 1922*. Reproduced in Maurseth 1987: 258.

17. See *Stortings Forhandlinger* 1920, 7a, Finansdebatten April 26, 1920, 1286–87.
18. See Wigforss 1967: 527–28, Öhman 1969: 42, Öhman 1970: 35–52, Steiger 1971: 99–110, Erlander 1972: 173–74, Axelsson et al. 1987: 35–36.
19. According to Unga 1976: 25, the SAP had already in 1905 advocated communal works creation at market wages.
20. Sveriges Riksdag, Motioner I Andra Kammaren 1912:250 and Sveriges Riksdag, Motioner I Första Kammaren 1912:98. For a detailed discussion see Öhman 1970: 43–49 and Steiger 1971: 108–10.
21. Sveriges Riksdag, Motioner I Första Kammaren 1919:181 and Sveriges Riksdag, Motioner I Första Kammaren 1921:108. See Steiger 1971: 121.
22. See Öhman 1970: 39
23. See also Steiger 1971: 110–11.
24. See Held 1982: 98–99.
25. See Held 1982: 98.
26. See Held 1982: 98–99 and Könke 1987: 214–15.
27. Keynes 1973, chap. 23.
28. The competing political faction, "the Caps," held that an increase in the money supply only creates inflation and that restrictive monetary policies have no effect on unemployment. See Kindleberger 1987: 132.
29. See Kindleberger 1987: 61.
30. Sejersted 1973: 21.
31. See Öhman 1970: 39 and Unga 1976: 34.
32. See also Clarke 1988: 145–46.
33. See also Eichengreen 1992: 107.
34. See Maier 1987, esp. 168–76.
35. See Eichengreen 1992: 106.
36. See Moggridge 1992: 358 and Howson 1975: 11.
37. Howson 1975: 10.
38. See Kindleberger 1987: 332.
39. See Hume 1970: 124.
40. See Jahn, Eriksen, & Munthe 1966: 221.
41. A. Sandberg, "Saken som nu beskjaeftiger vor Handelsstand sterkest," *Verdens Gang*, no. 304, Saturday December 6, 1919, page 9. My translation.
42. Norges Bank's Arkiv, Folder Hovedsetet 485, Letter from "Direktionen for Norges Bank" to "Norges Banks Repræsentantskap," Kristiania, February 28, 1919. The letter was signed by Governor Bomhoff and Director Sandberg.
43. The new rules governing the volume of money in circulation were proposed in Odelstings Proposisjon 1919 (50). See Bergh & Hanisch 1984: 134.
44. Quoted in Östlind 1945: 342.
45. Östlind 1945: 342.
46. See Thunholm 1991: 112–15.
47. See Keesing 1978: 11–14.
48. See Keesing 1978: 16.
49. See Feldman 1993: 156–57, 214–15 and Webb 1989: 23–25, 120, 122.
50. See Webb 1985.
51. Britain imposed a ban on the export of gold in March 1919.
52. Since June 1919 the dollar was the only currency on a fixed parity with gold again.

53. Östlind 1945: 311.
54. Fuglum 1989: 390.
55. See van Seenus 1945: 115.
56. Holtfrerich 1980: 15.
57. For Germany see Winkler 1979: 27; for Britain, Tawney 1943.
58. Railways, mines, electric power generation, industrial insurance companies, canals, harbors, and steamship lines as well as the retailing of alcoholic drinks. See Milliband 1960: 61.
59. See Milliband 1960: 63 and Tawney 1943: 13, 19–20.
60. See Schönhoven 1987: 122.
61. See Keesing 1978: 64.
62. See Jahn 1966: 212 and Rygg 1954: 445.
63. Pollard 1962: 66.
64. Current accounts plus the budget for crisis measures.
65. Keesing 1978: 55.
66. Östlind 1945: 423–24.
67. Fuglum 1989: 390.
68. Quoted in Webb 1989: 36.
69. Quoted in Howson 1975: 10.
70. See Thomas 1936: section 1.7, Mowat 1963: 25–26, Howson 1974: 89.
71. LO Archives, Sekretariatet Representantskapsprotokoll, Box A2A:2.
72. On unions' views on speculation see Olstad 1990, vol. 1: 267.
73. See Stortings Forhandlinger 1920, 7A, Trontalen: 62.
74. See, for example, the argument of Norges Bank director A. Sandberg in "Saken som nu Beskjaeftiger vor Handelsstand Sterkest," *Verdens Gang*, No. 304, Saturday December 6, 1919: 9. Social democrats also agreed that it would be counterproductive to fight inflation by means of tight money. DNA's financial spokesman Hornsrud argued during the finance debate in parliament on April 26, 1920, that the only way to get rid of inflation (*dyrtiden*) was to increase production (See Stortings Forhandlinger 1920, 7A Finansdebatten April 26, 1920: 1290).
75. See also Eichengreen 1991: 111–12.
76. Quoted in Östlind 1945: 353. For similar attempts of the DNB to persuade commercial banks to reduce lending see van Seenus 1945: 119.
77. See "Betaenkninger over pengevaerdien og valutaspörmaalene" av Arbeidsutvalget i det Norske Finansraad, Kristiania 1918: 16 and Tidskrift for Bank- og finansvaesen (1918: 181).
78. See Rygg 1950: 6.
79. Norges Bank's Arkiv Folder Hoveds. Akt U32, 7/8/1920, "Til den Norske Almenhet."
80. Norges Bank's Arkiv Folder Hoveds. Akt. U32. My translation.
81. See Keesing 1978: 16 and van Seenus 1945: 119.
82. Östlind 1945: 452.
83. Keesing 1978: 39.
84. Middlemas 1979: 124.
85. Laursen & Pedersen 1964: 134.
86. Hodne 1983: 27.
87. See Östlind 1945: 341, 355, and Bergh & Hanisch 1984: 133.

88. It should be noted that before the calamity of the early thirties the term "Great Depression" referred to the crisis of 1873–96.
89. This does not apply to Sweden, where matters of exchange rate policy are the prerogative of the central bank. However, the central bank, since its foundation, has been subjected to parliamentary control, and in practice to government control during this century.
90. Odelstings Proposisjon 50, 1919; see above.
91. See Bergh & Hanisch 1984: 134.
92. Stortings Forhandlinger 1920, d. 8, O. No. 112: 890.
93. Tawney (1942: 15) described the effects of higher interest rates as follows: "Then the incredible happened. The government betrayed uneasiness. Bankrate was raised – too late – to 6 percent in November, 1919 and to 7 percent in April 1920. It was evident that an attempt was about to be made to recover control of the monetary situation. The change of policy was a pinprick, not an earthquake; but coming when it did, it let the gas out of the balloon."
94. As in Norway and Sweden, British economists, including Keynes, were strongly in favor of more restrictive policies. Keynes, in fact, was willing to go further in raising the interest rate than the Treasury (see Howson 1975: 20). After he had written the *General Theory*, Keynes still held that because all controls had been abandoned, restrictive monetary policies had been inevitable at that point (see Howson 1973: 461–62).
95. Riksdagens Protokoll, Första Kammaren 1920, No. 23: 80–97. Söndagen den 14. Mars 1920: 80, 83.
96. See also Östlind 1945: 353.
97. "Bankoutskottet anger riktlinjen för valutapolitiken." *Social Demokraten*, April 20, 1921, page 1. My translation.
98. In 1931, however, Wigforss recognized the dangers of deflation Nylander and Kreuger already pointed out in 1921. See Wigforss 1980B: 388–89.
99. See also Wigforss 1951: 155, where he argues that the gold standard was to be preferred to "a managed monetary system" because of the inevitable human weakness.
100. LO Arkiv, Representantstkapsprotokoll, Box A2A:3; 1920–22, April 27–28, 1921. Dagordningens punkt X, Det Allmäna Krisläget.
101. LO Arkiv, Representantstkapsprotokoll, Box A2A:3; 1920–22, October 10–11, 1921. Dagordningens punkt VIII, Behandling av det nuvarande krisläget och därmed sammanhörande frågor.
102. For Norway see Hanisch 1979: 239.
103. Stortings Forhandlinger 1920, 7a, Finansdebatten April 26, 1920: 1288.
104. Stortings Forhandlinger 7a, January 27, 1920, Trontalen: 62.
105. See also Sejersted 1973.
106. See Perry 1994: 301.
107. See Nekkers 1985: 107.
108. Norges Bank governor Nicolai Rygg also saw this as one of the arguments in favor of deflation. See Derry 1973: 308.
109. See Ousland 1949, vol. 2: 13.
110. See "Dokumenter offentliggjort av Arbeidsutvalget i det Norske finansraad: Pengevaerdien – valutaspörsmaalene, Kreditgivning til utlandet." Kristiania 1918: 34.

111. See Hveding 1974.
112. See van Seenus 1945: 115.
113. See Unga 1976: 58, Thunholm 1991: 113–14, and Östlind 1945: 356–57.
114. See Östlind 1945: 361.
115. See Boyce 1987: 36–38.
116. Quoted in Nysæter 1972: 27. My translation.
117. Quoted in Nysæter 1972: 27. My translation.
118. See Odelstings Melding no. 5 (1928) and Rygg 1949: 499.
119. See Keilhau 1950.
120. See Holtfrerich 1980: 329.
121. See Ehrenberg 1991: 79–80 and Goodman 1991: 32. The government, by the way, never used its right.
122. Cf. Feldman 1993: 404. See also Webb 1989: 123.
123. See Holtfrerich 1988: 118–21.
124. Riese 1986: 226
125. Östlind 1945: 312.
126. See Eichengreen 1992: 110–11.
127. See Laursen & Pedersen 1964, chap. 7, and Hanisch 1979: 254–67.
128. See Riese 1986: 215.
129. In 1913 prices. Webb 1989: 76.
130. Sweden, Britain, and the UK.
131. See Laursen & Pedersen 1964: 123.
132. For an overview, see Hardach 1973.
133. See Mathews 1986.
134. See Laursen & Pedersen 1964: 57.
135. See Webb 1989: 42.
136. See also Feldman 1993: 211.
137. See Riese 1986: 214–31.
138. Riese 1986: 217–18.
139. See Maier 1987: 169.
140. See Mowat 1963: 298–304.
141. Dutch labor was organized in three main trade unions: a Catholic, a social democratic, and a Protestant one.
142. See Harmsen 1975: 144–45.
143. See chap. 4 and Windmuller et al. 1985: 64–66.
144. See Middlemas 1979: 139–41.
145. For a somewhat different interpretation, see Dahl 1981. See also Knutsen 1984 and Galenson 1949.
146. I.e., the encyclicals *Rerum novarum* and *Quadragesimo anno*.
147. General male suffrage was introduced in 1917, limited female suffrage in 1919.
148. See van Kersbergen 1995.
149. See Zimmerman 1986: 58.
150. The two exceptions were the fall of the first Labour government in October 1924 and the withdrawal of the SPD from the Grand Coalition under Stresemann in October 1923.
151. For the UK see Boyce 1987: 150.
152. See de Hen 1980: 162, 353.

153. See also Unga 1976: 58.
154. See also Erlander 1972: 171–72.
155. Arbettarrörelsens Arkiv SAP Rulle 4 A:I:A 11–16. Partistyrelsens och VU protokoll 1915–30. My translation.
156. Arbetarrörelsens Arkiv SAP Rulle 4 A:I:A 11–16. Partistyrelsens och VU protokoll 1915–30. My translation.
157. My translation.
158. Indeed, its demand in 1930 for productive public works at market wages is generally seen to signal its acceptance of Keynesianism, because more demand rather than lower wages now was considered the best solution to unemployment. See Axelsson et al. 1987: 36, Öhman 1970: 81–83, and Steiger 1971.
159. See Öhman 1970: 134–35 and Unga 1976: 83, 184.
160. See Jörberg & Krantz 1986: 316 and Hamilton 1989, chap. 3.
161. See Perry 1994: 306.
162. See Mowat 1963: 128.
163. See Hanisch 1978.
164. Ousland 1949, vol. 2: 205.
165. Unga 1976: 80.
166. On the contracyclical policies of 1926 see Hertz-Eichenrode 1982, Blaich 1977, and Leuschen-Seppel 1981, Section 2.5.
167. See Schönhoven 1987: 157.
168. Keynes 1963: 77. Kindleberger 1987: 332, however, notes that "it is impossible to find a statement to that effect in Lenin's writings."
169. See Held 1982: 104, 114.
170. See Könke 1987: 204.
171. See Moses 1986: 158.
172. See Unga 1976: 35. In a slightly different form, the argument that high wages promote structural adjustment of industry would return after World War II in the so-called Rehn-Meidner model.
173. See Unga 1976: 59.
174. See Thompson 1996: 71.
175. *Socialism in Our Time* and *The Living Wage*.
176. See also Unga (1976: 62) on the SAP in the twenties: "Because for *moral* reasons they considered the road to wage reduction closed but nevertheless thought it necessary to reduce production costs, cost reductions were to be accomplished in a completely new way, i.e., by means of rationalizations." My translation, emphasis in the original. See also Könke 1987: 100, who argued that the ADGB's concept of economic democracy initially reflected the increased cooperation between labor and capital made necessary by economic developments.
177. See Unga 1976, chap. 6, on the SAP and Könke 1987, chap. 6, on the discussion within the SPD and ADGB.
178. Within the ADGB the discussion about the more microlevel concept of industrial democracy set in after the breakdown of the macrocorporatism of the ZAG.
179. For Germany see Könke 1987: 204–5. The ADGB itself realized that its demand of a forty-hour workweek might lead to reduced competitiveness. See Schneider 1973: 227.
180. See de Hen 1980: 162.

181. See Thompson 1996: 71–73.
182. See Schönhoven 1989: 102–3.

CHAPTER 4. THE CREATION OF THE SOCIAL DEMOCRATIC
CONSENSUS

1. See Gourevitch 1986 and Luebbert 1991.
2. Temin 1989: 90.
3. See Gourevitch 1986: 166–68.
4. See also Neumann 1972: 260–61.
5. My translation.
6. See also James 1986: 418.
7. Kalecki 1977.
8. "The fear of inflation prevented the various German governments under the Weimar republic from adopting after 1929 effective measures designed to put an end to the depression, and this failure led in the end to the breakdown of the political and social system in Germany. . . . The same train of thoughts was behind the herostratic efforts of the Labour government in Britain to balance the budget and to prevent the central bank from maintaining liquidity during the financial crisis in the summer of 1931: Had not the experience of the German inflation taught a sufficiently clear lesson as to what financial leniency and irresponsibility would lead to?" Laursen & Pedersen 1964: 11. See also Temin 1989.
9. See Temin 1989 and Eichengreen 1992.
10. See Rüstow 1981: 451 and Houwink ten Cate 1987: 192 f.
11. The Dawes Plan provided for reparations to be handed over to the reparations agent in German currency. Actual payments to the Allies would take place only if the reparations agent judged that the Reichsbank had sufficient reserves so as not to jeopardize the exchange rate. If the Reichsbank's reserves were not deemed sufficient the first RM 2 billion were to be invested in short-term German paper while amounts in excess of 2 billion (with a maximum of RM 5 billion) would be invested in long-term paper. Capital inflows, of course, would improve the Reichsbank's currency reserve and hence make transfer more likely.
12. See McNeil 1986: 175–76.
13. Eichengreen 1992: 226.
14. See also Eichengreen 1992: 242 and McNeil 1986: 103–9.
15. McNeil 1986: 241.
16. On the Labour Party see Skidelsky 1967: 44.
17. See also Gerschenkron 1970: 3.
18. As Held 1982: 10, 125, points out, Woytinski's aversion to Hilferding may have tempted him to give a not entirely accurate account.
19. See also Gourevitch 1986: 143–44.
20. Emphasis added. See also Lewin 1967: 59–64, who argues that Ernst Wigforss anticipated Keynes.
21. The Australian social democratic party was the only one to openly propose abandoning gold in order to stimulate the economy. See McKibbin 1975: 97 on the Theodore Plan of early 1931.
22. See Keynes 1963, part II, chap. 4.

23. On the DNA's policy proposals during the Great Depression see Maurseth 1987: 557–65, Nordvik 1977, and Sejersted 1985: 108–10.
24. Colbjørnsen & Sømme 1933.
25. On the *Plan van de Arbeid* see Abma 1981: 170–75, Griffiths 1989: 157, Goudriaan 1986: 47–149, Hansen 1981, and Nekkers 1985: 12–13.
26. See Klein 1975: 127.
27. See Tingsten 1941, vol. I: 323–24.
28. Quoted in Tingsten 1941, vol. I: 340.
29. On the discussion within the party leadership see Meijer 1977.
30. Quoted in Moses 1986: 159. See also Zollitsch 1982.
31. The plan was published on January 26, 1932. The national council (Bundesvorstand) accepted the WTB Plan on February 16, 1932; the ADGB "crisis congress" did so on April 13, 1932.
32. See Unga 1976, chap. 9, and Steiger 1971: 135–42.
33. See Maurseth 1987: 559.
34. "Valutakrisen og Arbeidslønnen," *Arbeiderbladet*, October 12, 1931.
35. "Voldsom Prisstigning i Anmarsj?" *Arbeiderbladet*, September 28, 1931.
36. See the interviews with MPs Alfred Madsen and Oscar Torp, "Den Nuværende Diskonto er Unødig Høi," *Arbeiderbladet*, September 30, 1931, and "Diskontoen og Prisene," *Arbeiderbladet*, October 7, 1931.
37. *Arbeiderbladet*, September 29, 1931: 1. Oscar Torp makes a similar argument on October 7, 1931. See "Diskontoen og Prisene," *Arbeiderbladet*.
38. "Prisstigning-Samfundskontrol," *Arbeiderbladet*, September 29, 1931: 4.
39. "Valutakrisen og Arbeidslønnen," *Arbeiderbladet*, October 12, 1931.
40. "Vår Linje," *Arbeiderbladet*, October 1, 1931: 4.
41. "Den Nuværende Diskonto er Unødig Høi," *Arbeiderbladet*, September 30, 1931.
42. Riksdagens Protokoll 1932, Första Kammaren, vol. 3, no. 33: 29. See also Riksdagens Protokoll 1932, Andra Kammaren, vol. 4, no. 42: 17.
43. Arbetarrörelsens Arkiv, SAP Rulle 20, A:II:B: 13–15, V.U. Bilagor 1931–33, Bilaga 170, 1931.
44. On the NVV see Fritschy & Werkman 1987: 71.
45. The first Dutch MP to publicly suggest devaluation of the currency, in fact, was the liberal S. E. B. Bierema in the fall of 1933. See Vlak 1967: 36.
46. See Abma 1981: 175.
47. Handelingen Tweede Kamer, November 12, 1935: 281.
48. Nekkers 1985: 57.
49. See Macmillan 1966: 246.
50. See Clarke 1988: 74–75, and chap. 4.
51. See also Tomlinson 1981: 79.
52. See Howson 1975: 69–71.
53. See also Clarke 1988: 159–60.
54. See Clarke 1988: 153.
55. Especially during the latter months of the gold standard, the Treasury and the BoE feared that an increase in interest rates would only be interpreted as a sign of weakness.
56. See Boyce 1987: 303–4.
57. McKibbin 1965: 110–11, 114. See also Skidelsky 1992: 393.

58. Quoted in Howson & Winch 1977: 89. Emphasis in the original.
59. Quoted in Kunz 1987: 96.
60. Quoted in Howson & Winch 1977: 93.
61. On Mosley's proposals see Skidelsky 1967: 47–50, and chap. 8.
62. See Kunz 1987: 101–2, and Boyce 1987: 351.
63. See Schneider 1974 and Zollitsch 1982. The fear of inflation and weakening of the currency had already led Hilferding, in line with the majority of participants, to reject the Lautenbach Plan – an early proposal for fiscal expansion – at a secret conference held by the Reichsbank on September 15, 1931. See Salin 1964: 23.
64. Cf. Könke 1987: 211–12.
65. See Landmann 1981: 386–89.
66. Quoted in Landmann 1981: 83.
67. See also Gates 1973: 214, 220.
68. See McNeil 1986, chap. 4, and Hertz-Eichenrode 1982.
69. See Erlander 1972.
70. See Bergström 1969: 49, 1988: 23, Gustafsson 1973: 128, Jonung 1989: 46, Jörberg & Krantz, 1986: 318, Lindbeck 1974: 23, and Myhrman & Söderström 1987: 82.
71. Gustafsson 1973: 128.
72. See also Beckman 1974: 40.
73. See Nordvik 1979, Beckman 1974: 39, and Hodne 1983: 94.
74. See also Klein 1975: 129.
75. See Howson 1975: 92. This, of course, was a view that Hawtrey, the main exponent of the Treasury view, had already expressed in 1925. See Clarke 1988: 52.
76. Stadermann 1987: 230.
77. See Maier 1987: 97.
78. Jaeger 1988: 185.
79. See also James 1989: 243.
80. On the failure of voluntary agriculture associations under the deflationary policies of the early twenties in Britain, see Pollard 1962.
81. See Hveding 1982: 196–97.
82. See Bank & Vos 1988: 88–89.
83. Cartel prices already had been the target for a deflation decree on July 26, 1930.
84. On this inconsistency in Brüning's policies see Jaeger 1988: 171 and Koops 1973.
85. For figures on German agricultural prices see Rolfes 1976: 748.
86. See Holt 1975, chap. 17.
87. The Corn Production and Agriculture Acts were repealed in 1921. See Pollard 1962: 134–35.
88. Pollard 1962: 139.
89. See Cooper 1989: 131.
90. Cf. Peden 1985: 102. Some of the more important schemes that were organized in the wake of this act were the Milk Marketing Board (1933), the Bacon and Pig Marketing Board (1933), and the Potato Marketing Board (1934).
91. For useful overviews of Swedish agricultural policies, see Hellström 1976, chap.

4–8, and Seyler 1983, chap. 4. On the regulation of the milk market see also Rothstein 1992.
92. On the SPD, see Leuschen-Seppel 1981: 257, 263. For Norway, Hveding 1982. On Sweden, see Thullberg 1974.
93. For Sweden, see Thullberg 1974. On the SPD, see Leuschen-Seppel 1981, part 2, chap. 4, especially 208–9, and Holt 1975: 111. As late as 1930 the second Labour government in Britain still hoped to mitigate the crisis in agriculture by setting up model farms to help increase productivity.
94. For Sweden, see Andersson 1990: 19.
95. See Nordvik 1977.
96. Quoted in Ousland 1949, vol. 3: 126.
97. See Unga 1976: 167–68.
98. Wigforss 1951: 292. By late 1931 Wigforss argued that the SAP's policy of rejecting help to agriculture that placed any significant burdens on the budget would have to be abandoned. See Partistyrelsens sammanträden den 9–14 November 1931. Arbetarrörelsens Arkiv, SAP rulle 5 A:I:A 17–19, Partistyrelsens protokoll 1931–39.
99. Wigforss 1951: 293.
100. Quoted in Thullberg 1974: 162.
101. See also Rothstein 1992.
102. Rothstein 1992.
103. Quoted in Neumann 1972: 266.
104. See Peden 1985: 103–6 and Mowat 1963: 439–40.
105. See Stocking & Watkins 1946: 192–98.
106. DNB president Trip opposed this law because it would hamper reduction of prices. See de Hen 1980: 200.
107. This was a popular expression among Dutch businessmen at the time. See *De Nederlandsche Werkgever*, January 25, 1934: 39. Quoted in de Hen 1980: 203.
108. See Windmuller et al. 1985: 71–75.
109. See also Pollard 1974: 242–43, for figures indicating falling nominal and rising real wages from 1929 to 1932.
110. During 1933 also the fascist "unions" were trying to prevent wage cuts. See Mai 1983: 608.
111. Quoted in Siegel 1982: 70. For a shortened English version of this article see Siegel 1985.
112. See Schweitzer 1964: 401.
113. Kjellstrom 1934: 27.
114. See Nordvik 1990: 17.
115. Klein 1975: 135.
116. See Bank & Vos 1987: 68.
117. Quoted in Vlak 1967: 38.
118. Irmler 1976: 292.
119. See Sayers 1976: 413.
120. Quoted in Kock 1961: 101.
121. See Wigforss 1980B: 387–88.
122. See Wigforss 1980A.
123. See Riksdagens Protokoll, Första Kammaren, vol. 3, no. 33: 19.
124. See Riksdagens Protokoll, Första Kammaren, vol. 3, no. 33: 29–30, and Riksdagens Protokoll, Andra Kammaren, vol. 4, no. 42: 16–18.

125. See Howson 1975: 86.
126. See also Luther 1964: 250–68.
127. See Landmann 1981 and Schneider 1986.
128. Compare this with his statement from 1932: "We don't lack monetary means of circulation in Germany but we lack capital. Capital, however, can not be printed by a paper press. Capital has to be created by savings and work." Quoted in Korsch 1976: 75. My translation.
129. See also Goodhart 1994: 1427.
130. See Durbin 1988: 34.
131. Quoted in Howson 1989: 404.
132. See Rooth 1988: 68.
133. Vikbladh 1973: 386.
134. See Rooth 1988: 67–70, and appendix.
135. Lieftinck 1987: 184, 1989: 116–18.
136. See Lieftinck 1987: 168.
137. In Britain, the manifesto of the Liberal Party argued: "This war has forced us to accept controls which cannot be suddenly relaxed without incurring the dangers of soaring prices and inflation." The Conservative Manifesto maintained that "as long as shortage of food remains, rationing must obviously be accepted: the dangers of inflation also must be guarded against." Quoted in Cairncross 1985: 300. For Norway, see Bergh 1989: 33–44.
138. See Howson 1987: 433–34. Keynes (1977: 185–86) wrote on January 7, 1942, evaluating the lessons of 1921: "The main one [lesson] seems to be that all controls – rationing control, raw material control, new issue control, bank credit control and high taxation control – must be retained in principle for a period of at least two years and only gradually relaxed as and when consumer goods become available in greater quantities. If the vast bulk of purchasing power which must necessarily exist at the end of the war, is released in psychological conditions necessarily surrounding the end of the war, the result cannot be different from what it was in 1919 to 1921."
139. See Lie 1994.
140. See Jones 1987: 37.
141. See Leiserson 1959: 45–52.
142. See Lewin 1989: 208 for a similar discussion.
143. On the SAP see Lewin 1967: 219.
144. See Nekkers 1985: 39. In 1934, SDAP board member Oudegeest was forced to conclude that the policy proposals of the annual congress, which mainly consisted of a plea for more planning, actually had already been taken up by the Christian democratic government. See Meijer 1977: 73.
145. See Meijer 1977 and Abma 1981: esp. 176–77.
146. See Colbjørnsen & Sømme 1933, Ousland 1949, vol. 3: 104, and Førsund 1978: 27.
147. See Førsund 1978: 29.
148. In contrast to the Dutch proposals, the national level council was not to have an explicitly tripartite composition but was to be nominated by parliament along lines of party proportionality. See Bergh 1978.
149. My translation. Quoted in Könke 1987: 207. See also 210.
150. See Miller & Potthoff 1986.
151. See also Miller & Potthoff 1986: 155.

152. See Klotzbach 1982: 61–62.
153. Quoted in Mowat 1955: 548.
154. Those were civil aviation, cable and wireless, coal, railways, long-distance road haulage, electricity, gas, iron and steel, and the Bank of England.
155. See Morgan 1985: 130.
156. See also Morgan 1985: 130.
157. See Morgan 1985: 137.
158. In unanimous advice from the Stichting van de Arbeid in March 1946.
159. See Klotzbach 1982: 287, 292.
160. Derry 1973: 413.
161. See Bergh 1989: 65–67, Lange & Pharo 1991, and Slagstad 1993.
162. Those were cotton, clothing, furniture, and jewelry.
163. See also Shonfield 1969: 97.
164. Tomlinson 1989: 17.
165. See Beer 1965: 200–208.

CHAPTER 5. THE BREAKDOWN OF THE SOCIAL DEMOCRATIC CONSENSUS

1. See Frøland 1992.
2. See Beer 1965: 195–96, Cairncross 1985: 410, and Hatton & Chrystal 1991: 68 on the UK, and Bergh 1989 on Norway.
3. See Knoester 1989: 95–98.
4. See Dow 1964: 235–42.
5. For a description of the short-term policy cycles, see Martin 1985 and Swenson 1989: 144–47.
6. See also Shonfield 1969: 64.
7. See also Hatton & Chrystal 1991: 74–77, and Cairncross 1981: 374.
8. See Jonung 1994: 236.
9. See Bjerve 1989, and Jahn, Eriksen, & Munthe 1966: 347–48.
10. See Allen 1989.
11. See Altvater et al. 1980, vol. 2: 303–4.
12. Especially in Britain there has been extensive debate on whether there was a "Keynesian revolution" in economic policy after 1945. See Booth 1983, 1984, 1985, Rollings 1985, 1988, and Tomlinson 1981, 1984.
13. See Meltzer 1988: 4.
14. The 1973 Labour Party program spoke of a "fundamental and irreversible shift of the balance of power and wealth to working people and their families." Quoted in Smith 1992: 22.
15. In the original proposal, the funds would have come to own more than half of the stock of Swedish shares after about 20 years.
16. See Korpi 1978 and Stephens 1986.
17. This, in fact, is an example of beggar-your-neighbor policies by means of a fixed nominal exchange rate.
18. See Szász 1974.
19. See Goldthorpe 1984.
20. The literature on corporatism is vast. See, for example, Blaas & Guger 1985,

Cameron 1984, Cawson 1986, Keman 1984, Pekkarinen, Pohjola, & Rowthorn 1992, Schmidt 1982, and Schmitter 1979.

21. Subsequently the concept of corporatism changed meaning so as to adjust to the new economic orthodoxy. In a mixed form, Garrett & Lange 1986 would attribute employment success both to Keynesian policies in the corporatist countries, and to neoclassical real wage flexibility in noncorporatist countries. Theoretically more consistent, Calmfors & Driffil 1988 came to interpret policy success in corporatist countries also in a neoclassical manner as centralized trade unions were assumed to pursue a wage policy that simulated the outcomes of a neoclassical labor market because they, unlike decentralized unions, could not externalize the negative employment consequences of a rigid real wage policy. Katzenstein 1985 finally provided the supply-side interpretation as corporatism now came to signify a superior ability for microeconomic adjustment.

22. See Scharpf 1987: 180.

23. I.e., transfer system plus state expenditure.

24. Scharpf 1987: 189.

25. See also Scholten 1987: 121.

26. See Scholten 1987: 146.

27. Indeed, the formulation of article 3 was left vague on purpose because a concrete definition of what "safeguarding the currency" meant might have entailed the risk of legal action against the bank in case it failed to reach its goal. See Hentschel 1988B: 104.

28. Section 73, article 4 of the Basic Law states that monetary affairs are the exclusive prerogative of the federal authorities while sec. 88 simply states that the federal authorities create a central bank. *Tarifautonomie*, in contrast, is guaranteed by the Basic Law (sec. 9).

29. See Brugmans 1983, de Jong 1960, and Schotsman 1987.

30. See Hentschel 1988B: 107.

31. See Hentschel 1988B: 92.

32. Schlesinger 1976: 556, 559.

33. See also the Bundesbank's annual report for 1960 (which was published after the revaluation of March 7, 1961), in which it strongly warns against further revaluations because of the damage to exports.

34. See Balkhausen 1992: 103.

35. See Goodman 1992: 74 and Scharpf 1987: 170.

36. Helmut Schmidt, interview with the *Economist*, September and October 1979, reprinted in Hanrieder 1982: 211.

37. See Goodman 1992: 90.

38. In an interview given years after he left office, the Christian democratic minister of social affairs in the Den Uyl government of 1973–77 complained that it was frustrating to urge workers to moderate wages in order to increase employment while the bank was revaluing at the same time. See Visser & Wijnhoven 1989: 91.

39. See Schotsman 1987: 324–27.

40. Quoted in Visser & Wijnhoven 1989: 96. My translation.

41. Sometimes this principle is also seen to imply that unions should try to frustrate non–social democratic governments.

42. The scientific advisory council of the economics ministry (Wissenschaftlicher

Beirat beim Bundeswirtschaftsministerium) pleaded for the introduction of income policies in 1956. See Cassel 1972.

43. See Hildebrand 1984: 160–70.
44. See Altvater, Hoffmann, & Semmler 1980: 306.
45. Cassel 1972: 253.
46. For an excellent analysis of the decline of Dutch corporatism see Hemerijck 1992.
47. Zimmerman 1986.
48. See Visser & Wijnhoven 1989: 50.
49. Max van de Berg, former PvdA chairman and one of the few who seemed to be willing to take some inflationary risks, pointed out in 1989: "It went terribly wrong once. No one dares to risk that inflation anymore, and hence I believe that growth will always be relatively low." Quoted in Visser & Wijnhoven 1989: 65. My translation.
50. See Matthews 1968.
51. See Healey 1989: 393.
52. Jones 1987: 79.
53. On Heath's U-turn see Beer 1982: 84–87.
54. My translation.
55. My translation.
56. Finansplan 1991, quoted in Magnus Henrekson & Lars Hultkranz 1991. My translation.
57. See also Merkel 1993: 222.
58. Per Kleppe, October 6, 1975, Stortings Forhandlinger 1975–76, 7a: 22.
59. See also Armingeon 1985: 36–39.
60. Inflation also had an indirect negative effect on real wages as it moved wage earners into higher tax brackets. See Per Kleppe, Stortings Forhandlinger 1973–74, 7B: 2724.
61. See, for example, SV MP Berge Furre, Stortings Forhandlinger 1973–74, 7C: 2931. For the academic version of this argument see Panitch 1979.
62. See Per Kleppe, Stortings Forhandlinger 1973–74, 7B: 2722–27.
63. See Stortings Forhandlinger 1973–74, 7B: 2723.
64. Per Kleppe, 6 October 1975, Stortings Forhandlinger 1975–76, 7A: 22.
65. See Dahl 1989: 10.
66. Figures from Lybeck 1982: 92.
67. See Dobloug 1993: 53–54.
68. Feldt 1991: 57–58, 60.
69. Damman 1991: 77.
70. See Martin 1985, Sabel 1981, and Swenson 1989.
71. See Dow 1988.
72. Stenius 1987: 109.
73. See Biljer 1985: 23–33.
74. See Feldt 1991: 282.
75. See Martin 1991.
76. See, for example, *LO Tidning*, no. 33, October 28, 1994: 10.
77. Having realized that, Per Gyllenhamar of Volvo in 1984 actually took an initiative for national-level negotiations with government involvement. See Feldt 1991: 173.

78. See Feldt 1991: 453–69.
79. See also Dølvik et al. 1997: 90.
80. See also Wohlin 1991: 382.
81. See Bergström 1987, 1991 on the SAP's 1981 congress.
82. Åsbrink & Heikensten 1986: 27. My translation. See also Hansson & Lindberg (1989: 20): "The foreign exchange norm was introduced in the knowledge that the rate of price increases in the seventies and early eighties had proved incompatible with a fixed exchange rate. There had been a number of devaluations and an appreciable risk existed that future wage settlements would be based on expectations of recurrent devaluations if competitiveness weakened once more. There was thus a need for further commitments to ensure that the direction of economic policy would be consistent with a given exchange rate."
83. See NOU 1989:1: 164.
84. See SOU 1985: 52. Among those supporting the minority position was Anne Wibble, future finance minister in the Bildt government.
85. See Wihlborg 1993: 274.
86. See also Calmfors 1985.
87. See Olsen 1990: 166–67 and NOU 1989:1: 24–25.
88. See NOU 1992:26: 42.
89. That governments are more concerned with preventing domestic inflation than overcoming external constraints is also indicated by some tax reforms implemented after the regime change. Even on the assumption that international capital mobility equalizes interest rates, domestic real interest rates can still be made to deviate by tax measures as, for example, the deductibility of interest payments. Yet both governments have argued that the tax deductibility contributed to the credit explosion and have moved to reduce this tax deductibility.

CHAPTER 6. SOCIAL DEMOCRACY IN THE TWENTY-FIRST CENTURY

1. For an overview of theories predicting the inevitable decline of social democracy see Merkel 1993, chap. 2.
2. Prezworksi and Sprague (1986), for example, have argued that as the size of the blue-collar class shrank, social democrats were forced to water down their class appeal in an effort to gain support from the middle class. In so doing, however, they lost support from blue-collar voters. Social democracy thus faced an inescapable electoral dilemma.
3. See Wolinetz 1993: 109.
4. By early November 1996, support for the SAP had declined to 29.5 percent. *Dagens Nyheter*, November 1, 1996: A13.
5. See Thompson 1996, chap. 17.
6. On the policy review see Shaw 1993, 1994, chap. 4.
7. See Thompson 1996, chap. 18.
8. See Gamble 1992 and Kinnock 1986.
9. See Thompson 1996: 277–78.
10. See Thompson 1996: 269.
11. See Lösche & Walter 1992: 125–27.
12. Quoted in Padgett 1993: 29.

13. See Wolinetz 1993.
14. The disability program in the Netherlands is extensively used as a reservoir for unemployed workers.
15. See van Praag 1994.
16. See Block 1977: 206 and Gilpin 1987: 144.
17. Arguing that the internationalization of economic relations terminated the successful Keynesian regime of the post-1945 decades has become a veritable growth industry since the eighties. For some of the more sophisticated arguments see Scharpf 1987, chap. 11, Stewart 1983, and Webb 1991. Cornwall 1989, 1990 attributes restrictive policies in the larger economies to the lack of adequate labor market institutions that could have contained inflation. Given the internationalization of economic relations, the policies of the larger economies left the smaller countries no option but to follow suit.
18. Keynes 1980: 16. See also Keynes 1973: 339.
19. See Argy 1981, chap. 22, and Dornbusch 1980, chaps. 10–11.
20. See Giavazzi & Giovannini 1989 and Artis 1987.
21. Peter Temin 1989: 71–72 has made the same argument with respect to the German policies during the Great Depression: "The argument that devaluation would increase capital flight confuses the cure with the disease. Capital was fleeing because people holding Reichsmarks were afraid the currency would lose its value. Once devaluation had taken place, only the expectation of further devaluation would have led to flight. In any case further flight would only lower the price of the mark, leading other people to want to buy it. Devaluation, therefore, would have reduced capital flight and its effects, not increased it."
22. Emphasis in the original.
23. See also Brown 1987, chap. 1.
24. See also Helleiner 1996: 194.
25. See also Zevin 1992: 53–54.
26. For Sweden, see Gottfries, Nilsson, & Ohlson 1992: 25.
27. Quoted in Howson 1975: 70.
28. The DNA also interpreted the British crisis in such terms. See, for example, *Arbeiderbladet* (September 21, 1931: 6): "It is haute finance that governs England. After the details of the English government crisis became known, it turned out that all of it had been a maneuver of haute finance to get rid of the Labour government." My translation.
29. Sayers 1976: 422.
30. See Oye 1992: 113–14 and Helleiner 1994: 32.
31. See Cairncross & Eichengreen 1983: 94.
32. See Thomas 1936: 195.
33. Cf. Kock 1961: 203.
34. For a description of German exchange controls since the summer of 1931, see Luther 1964, chap. 11.
35. Griffiths 1987: 169.
36. See Brugmans 1983: 534 and Keesing 1978: 133–36.
37. See Vlak 1967, chap. 3.
38. Declaration of the party leaders of the Confederation of the Socialist Parties of the European Community, Madrid, December 1990. Quoted in Ladrech 1993:

139. The European Trade Unions Congress adopts a similar position: "The economic and monetary integration of the European economies is happening anyway . . . what is required is the empowering of democratically-accountable institutions so as to regain at the European level those powers to manage our economies which have increasingly been lost at the national level." *Declaration on the Treaty on European Union* adopted by the ETUC Executive Committee, March 5–6, 1992, 3. See also Wilde 1994: 181

39. Indeed, in early August 1993 German finance minister Theo Waigel proposed that the Deutsche mark leave the EMS, but no majority could be found. Instead, the solution was to expand the exchange rate bandwidth of the EMS to 15 percent.

40. The Norwegian unemployment rate for the last quarter of 1996 was 4.2 percent. SSB 1997.

41. Employment figures: CBS, "Tijdreeksen Arbeidsrekeningen 1950-heden, Werkgelegenheid," http://statline.cbs.nl/witch/etc/scratch/43027407/6383ART00.html. Labor force figures: *OECD Economic Outlook*, various issues.

42. For some cautiously formulated steps in that direction, see Scharpf 1996.

REFERENCES

Abma, R. (1981), "The Labour Plan and the Social Democratic Workers Party." *Acta Historiae Neerlandicae, The Low Countries History Yearbook*, vol. 14:154–81.

Allen, Christopher S. (1989), "The Underdevelopment of Keynesianism in the Federal Republic of Germany." In: Peter A. Hall, ed., *The Political Power of Economic Ideas*." Princeton: Princeton University Press.

Altvater, Elmar, Jürgen Hoffmann, & Willi Semmler (1980), *Vom Wirtschaftswunder zur Wirtschaftskrise*. 2 volumes. Berlin: Olle & Wolter.

Andersen, Tore (1978), "Ødegaardismen: Klassesamarbeid i den Lokalpolitiske Hverdag." *Tidsskrift for Arbeiderbevegelsens Historie*, 1:81–93.

Andersson, Sten (1990), "Mellan Åkarp och Saltsjöbaden." Ph.D. dissertation, Department of History, University of Stockholm.

Argy, Victor (1981), *The Postwar International Money Crisis*. London: George Allen & Unwin.

Argy, Victor, Anthony Brennan, & Glenn Stevens (1990), "Monetary Targeting: The International Experience." *Economic Record*, vol. 66, no. 192:37–62.

Armingeon, Klaus (1985), "Neo-Korporatistische Inkomenspolitiek." In: Hans Keman, Jaap Woldendorp, & Dietmar Braun, eds., *Het Neo-Korporatisme als Nieuwe Politieke Strategie*. Amsterdam: CT Press.

Artis, Michael J. (1987), "Devisenkontrollen und EWS." *Europäische Wirtschaft*, no. 36.

Asard, Erik (1986), "Industrial and Economic Democracy in Sweden: From Consensus to Confrontation." *European Journal of Political Research*, 14:207–19.

Åsbrink, Erik, & Lars Heikenstein (1986), "Valutaflödena 1985 och den Ekonomiska Politiken." *Skandinaviska Enskilda Banken Kvartalskrift*, no. 1:21–27.

Aufricht, Hans, ed. (1967), *Central Bank Legislation*. Volume II: *Europe*. Washington, D.C.: International Monetary Fund.

Axelsson, Roger, Karl-Gustaf Löfgren, & Lars Gunnar Nilsson (1987)[1979], *Den Svenska Arbetsmarknadspolitiken under 1900 Talet*. Stockholm: Prisma.

Axilrod, Stephen H. (1985), "U.S. Monetary Policy in Recent Years: An Overview," *Federal Reserve Bulletin*, January: 14–24.

Bakke, Egil (1984), "Hvilken Rolle Norges Bank?" *Farmand*, no. 20:28–30.

Balkhausen, Dieter (1992), *Gutes Geld & schlechte Politik*. Düsseldorf: ECON Verlag.

Bank, J. (1987), "Het Socialisme." In: P. Luykx & N. Bootsma, eds., *De Laatste Tijd*. Utrecht: Aula.

Bank, J., & C. Vos (1987), *Hendrikus Colijn, Antirevolutionair*. Houten: De Haan.

Bank of England (1979), "Speech by the Governor Given at the Lord Mayor's Dinner to the Bankers and Merchants of the City of London on 18 October 1979." *Bank of England Quarterly Bulletin*, vol. 19, no. 4:407–9.

Beckman, Svante, et al. (1974), "Ekonomisk Politik och Teori i Norden under Mellankrigstiden." In: *Kriser och Krispolitik i Norden under Mellankrigstiden*. Mötesrapport. Uppsala: Nordiska historikermötet.

Beer, Samuel H. (1965), *Modern British Politics*. London: Faber and Faber.

——— (1982), *Britain against Itself: The Political Contradictions of Collectivism*. New York: W. W. Norton.

Bergh, Trond (1978), "Ideal and Reality in Norwegian Macroeconomic Planning 1945–1965." *Scandinavian Journal of History*, 1:75–104.

——— (1987), *Storhetstid (1945–1965). Arbeiderbevegelsens historie I Norge-5*. Oslo: Tiden Norsk Forlag.

——— (1989), "Norsk Økonomisk Politikk." In: Trond Bergh, ed., *Vekst og Velstand*. Oslo: Universitetsforlaget.

Bergh, Trond, & Tore J. Hanisch (1984), *Vitenskap og Politikk*. Oslo: Aschehoug.

Bergström, Hans (1987), *Rivstart?* Stockholm: Tidens Förlag.

——— (1991), "Devalveringens Politiska Tillkomst och Logik." In: Lars Jonung, ed., *Devalveringen 1982. Rivstart eller Snedtändning?* Stockholm: SNS Förlag.

Bergström, Villy (1969), *Den Ekonomiska Politiken i Sverige och dess Verkningar*. Stockholm: Almqvist & Wicksell.

——— (1984), "Arvet från Tjugotalet Präglar Dagens Politik." *Tiden*, vol. 75 no. 8: 471–83.

——— (1988), *Socialdemokratin i Regeringsställning*. Stockholm: Fackföreningsrörelsens Institut för Ekonomisk Forskning.

——— (1989), "Vårt Ekonomiska Läge." In: *Vårt Ekonomiska Läge 1989*. N.p: Sparfrämjandet AB.

Biljer, Marianne (1985), "Finance Houses in Sweden." *Sveriges Riksbank Quarterly Review*, 1:23–33.

Bispham, John, & Andrea Boltho (1982), "Demand Management." In: Andrea Boltho, ed., *The European Economy. Growth and Crisis*. Oxford: Oxford University Press.

Bjerve, Petter Jakob (1981), "Kva Hendte i Norge i 1970-åra Konjunkturpolitisk?" *Sosialøkonomen*, no. 5:10–21.

——— (1989), "Strategiar for den Økonomiske Politikken i Etterkrigstida." In: Guttorm Hansen et al., eds., *Mennesket I Sentrum. Festskrift til Helge Seips 70-årsdag*. Oslo: Tanno.

——— (1993), "Feilslegen Politikk? Analyse og Vurdering av den Makroøkonomiske Politikken i 1986–1992." *Sosialøkonomen*, no.11:22–27.

Bjørgum, Jorunn (1970), *Venstre og Kriseforliket*. Oslo: Universitetsforlaget.

Björlin, Lars (1974), "Jordfrågan i Svensk Arbetarrörelse 1890–1920." *Arbetarrörelsens Årsbok*: 55–126.

Bjørnson, Øyvind (1990), *På Klassekampens Grunn. Arbeiderbevegelsens Historie I Norge-2*. Oslo: Tiden Norsk Forlag.

Blaas, Wolfgang, & Alois Guger (1985), "Arbeitsbeziehungen und makroökonomische Stabilität im internationalen Vergleich." In: Peter Gerlich, Edgar Grande, & Wolfgang C. Müller, eds., *Sozialpartnerschaft in der Krise*. Vienna: Böhlau.

Blackburn, Keith, & Michael Christensen (1989), "Monetary Policy and Policy Credibility: Theories and Evidence." *Journal of Economic Literature*, vol. 27: 1–45.

Blaich, Fritz (1977), *Die Wirtschaftskrise 1925–26 und die Reichsregierung*. Kallmünz: Verlag Lassleben.

Blaug, Mark (1976), "Kuhn versus Lakatos; or, Paradigms versus Research Programs in the History of Economics." In: S. Latsis, ed., *Method and Appraisal in Economics*. Cambridge: Cambridge University Press.

(1985), *Economic Theory in Retrospect*. Cambridge: Cambridge University Press.

Blessing, Karl (1957), "Einführung." In: Joachim von Spindler, Willy Becker, & O.-Ernst Starke (1969), *Die Deutsche Bundesbank*. 3d ed. Stuttgart: W. Kohlhammer Verlag.

Block, Fred (1977), *The Origins of International Economic Disorder*. Berkeley: University of California Press.

(1987), *Revising State Theory. Essays in Politics and Postindustrialism*. Philadelphia: Temple University Press.

Bloemen, E. S. A. (1987), "The Employers' Associations." In: Richard T. Griffiths, ed., *The Netherlands and the Gold Standard, 1931–1936*. Amsterdam: NEHA.

Blom, J. C. H. (1977), "De Politieke Machtspositie van H. Colijn in de Jaren '30." In: P. W. Klein & G. J. Borger, eds., *De Jaren Dertig. Aspecten van Crisis en Werkloosheid*. Amsterdam: Meulenhoff Educatief.

Blyth, Mark (1997), "Moving the Middle: Redefining the Boundaries of State Action." *Political Quarterly*, July/August:231–40.

Boltho, Andrea (1982), "Growth." In: Andrea Boltho, ed., *The European Economy: Growth and Crisis*. Oxford: Oxford University Press.

Booth, Alan (1983), "The 'Keynesian Revolution' in Economic Policymaking." *Economic History Review*, 2d ser., 36:103–23.

(1984), "Defining a 'Keynesian Revolution.'" *Economic History Review*, 2d ser., 37:2:263–67.

(1985), "The 'Keynesian Revolution' and Economic Policy Making: A Reply." *Economic History Review*, 2d ser., 38:101–6.

(1987), "Britain in the 1930s: A Managed Economy?" *Economic History Review*, 2d ser., 40, 4:499–522.

(1989), "Britain in the 1930s: A Managed Economy? A Reply to Peden and Middleton." *Economic History Review*, 2d ser., 42, 4:548–56.

Borchardt, Knut (1982), *Wachstum, Krisen, Handlungsspielräume der Wirtschaftspolitik*. Göttingen: Vandenhoeck & Ruprecht.

(1984), "Could and Should Germany Have Followed Great Britain in Leaving the Gold Standard?" *Journal of European Economic History*, vol. 13, no. 3: 471–97.

Bordo, Michael D., & Lars Jonung (1994), "Monetary Regimes, Inflation and Monetary Reform: An Essay in Honor of Axel Leijonhufvud." *Stockholm School of Economics*, Working Paper No. 16.

Born, Karl Erich (1972), "Government Action against the Great Depression." In: Herman van der Wee, ed., *The Great Depression Revisited*. The Hague: Martinus Nijhoff.

Bosman, H. W. J. (1974), "Enkele Gedachten over de Positie van De Nederlandsche Bank N.V." In: *Economie in Overleg*. Leiden: H. E. Stenfert Kroese.

Bosworth, Barry P., & Alice M. Rivlin (1987), eds., *The Swedish Economy*. Washington, D.C.: The Brookings Institution.

Bots, A. C. A. M. (1987), "De Volkshuishouding." In: P. Luykx & N. Bootsma, eds., *De Laatste Tijd*. Utrecht: Aula.

Bowden, Sue, & Michael Collins (1992), "The Bank of England, Industrial Regeneration, and Hire Purchase between the Wars." *Economic History Review*, 2d ser., vol. 45, I:120–36.

Boyce, Robert (1987), *British Capitalism at the Crossroads*. Cambridge: Cambridge University Press.

Boyle, Andrew (1967), *Montagu Norman*. London: Cassell.

Brand, Carl F. (1974), *The British Labour Party. A Short History*. Revised Edition. Stanford, Calif.: Hoover Institution Press.

Braun, Dietmar (1988), "Der Niederländische Weg in die Masssenarbeitslosigkeit (1973–1981)." Ph.D. Dissertation, Department of Political Science, University of Amsterdam.

Brittan, Samuel (1978), "Inflation and Democracy." In: Fred Hirsch & John H. Goldthorpe, eds., *The Political Economy of Inflation*. Oxford: Martin Robertson.

Brown, Alice, & Desmond S. King (1988), "Economic Change and Labour Market Policy: Corporatist and Dualist Tendencies in Britain and Sweden." *West European Politics*, vol. 11, no. 3:75–91.

Brown, Brendan (1987), *The Flight of International Capital: A Contemporary History*. London: Routledge.

Brugmans, I. J. (1983)[1940], *Paardenkracht en Mensenmacht: Sociaal-economische Geschiedenis van Nederland 1795–1940*. Leiden: Martinus Nijhoff.

Brulin, Göran (1989), *Från den 'Svenska Modellen' til Företagskorporatism?"* Lund: Arkiv.

Brüning, Heinrich (1970), *Memoiren 1918–1934*. Stuttgart: DVA.

Caesar, Rolf (1983), "Central Banks in the Political Arena." *Intereconomics*, vol. 18, no. 1:3–10.

Cairncross, Alec (1981), "The Postwar Years 1945–77." In: Roderick Floud & Donald McCloskey, eds., *The Economic History of Britain since 1700*. Volume 2: *1860 to the 1970s*. Cambridge: Cambridge University Press.

(1985), *The Years of Recovery*. London: Methuen.

(1988), "The Bank of England: Relationships with the Government, the Civil Service and Parliament." In: Gianni Toniolo, ed., *Central Banks' Independence in Historical Perspective*. Berlin: W. de Gruyter.

Cairncross, Alec, & Barry Eichengreen (1983), *Sterling in Decline*. Oxford: Basil Blackwell.

Callaghan, James (1987), *Time and Chance*. London: Collins.

Calmfors, Lars, & John Driffil (1988), "Centralization of Wage Bargaining." *Economic Policy*, 6:13–61.

Calmfors, Lars (1985), "Valutaregleringen Kan Avvecklas!" *Skandinaviska Enskilda Banken Kvartalsskrift*, no. 4:88–93.

(1993), "Lessons from the Macroeconomic Experience of Sweden." *European Journal of Political Economy*, vol. 9, no. 1: 25–72.

Cameron, David R. (1984), "Social Democracy, Corporatism, Labor Quiescence, and the Representation of Economic Interests in Advanced Capitalist Society." In: John H. Goldthorpe, ed., *Order and Conflict in Contemporary Capitalism*. Oxford: Clarendon Press.

Campbell, Robert (1977), "The Keynesian Revolution 1920–1970: Economics in the Twentieth Century." In: Carlo M. Cipolla, ed., *The Fontana Economic History of Europe. The Twentieth Century I*. Hassocks, Sussex: Harvester Press.

Carlsson, Stig, ed. (1991), *Arbetarrörelsen och den Ekonomiska Politiken*. Stockholm: Tiden.

Casparsson, Ragnar (1947), *LO Under Fem Årtionden. Första Delen*. Stockholm: LO.

(1948), *LO Under Fem Årtionden. Andra Delen*. Stockholm: LO.

Cassel, Gustav (1933), "Sveriges Valutapolitik." *Skandinaviska Kreditaktiebolaget Kvartalsskrift*, July:41–44.

Cassel, Dieter (1972), "Die Konzertierte Aktion: Instrument einer rationalen Stabilisierungspolitik?" In: D. Cassel, G. Gutmann, & H. J. Thieme, eds., *25 Jahre Marktwirtschaft in der Bundesrepublik Deutschland*. Stuttgart: Gustav Fischer Verlag.

Castles, Francis G. (1978), *The Social Democratic Image of Society*. London: Routledge & Kegan Paul.

Cavanagh Hodge, Carl (1993), "The Long Fifties: The Politics of Socialist Programmatic Revision in Britain, France and Germany." *Contemporary European History*, no. 1:17–34.

Cawson, Alan (1986), *Corporatism and Political Theory*. Oxford: Basil Blackwell.

Cerny, Philip G. (1990), *The Changing Architecture of Politics*. London: Sage.

Christiansen, Anne Berit (1990), "The New Exchange Rate System." *Norges Bank Economic Bulletin*, vol. 61, no. 4:262–65.

Clark, Simon (1989), *Keynesianism, Monetarism, and the Crisis of the State*. Brookfield, Vt.: Gower.

Clarke, Peter (1988), *The Keynesian Revolution in the Making 1924–1936*. Oxford: Clarendon Press.

Coddington, Alan (1982), "Deficient Foresight: A Troublesome Theme in Keynesian Economics." *American Economic Review*, vol. 72, no. 3:480–87.

Cohen, H. F. (1977), "Democratisch Socialisme in de Jaren '30." In: P. W. Klein & G. J. Borger, eds., *De Jaren Dertig. Aspecten van Crisis en Werkloosheid*. Amsterdam: Meulenhoff Educatief.

Colbjørnsen, Ole, & Axel Sømme (1933), *En Norsk 3-Årsplan: Veien Frem Til en Socialistisk Planøkonomi i Norge*. Oslo: Det Norske Arbeiderpartis Forlag.

Cooper, Andrew Fenton (1989), *British Agricultural Policy 1912–36*. Manchester: Manchester University Press.

Cornwall, John (1989), "Inflation as a Cause of Economic Stagnation: A Dual

Model." In: Jan A. Kregel, ed., *Inflation and Income Distribution in Capitalist Crisis*. New York: New York University Press.

(1990), *The Theory of Economic Breakdown: An Institutional-Analytical Approach*. Oxford: Basil Blackwell.

Cronin, James E. (1982), "Coping with Labour, 1918–1926." In: James E. Cronin & Jonathan Schneer, eds., *Social Conflict and the Political Order in Modern Britain*. New Brunswick, N.J.: Rutgers University Press.

(1984), *Labour and Society in Britain 1918–1979*. London: Batsford Academic and Educational.

Cross, Rod (1982), "The Duhem-Quine Thesis, Lakatos and the Appraisal of Theories in Macroeconomics." *Economic Journal*, vol. 92:320–40.

Crotty, James (1983), "On Keynes and Capital Flight." *Journal of Economic Literature*, vol. 21:59–65.

Dahl, Hans Frederik (1971), *Norge Mellom Krigene*. Oslo: Pax Forlag.

Dahl, Svein (1979), "Høyres Syn på Statens Rolle i det Økonomiske Liv i Mellomkrigstiden." *(Norsk) Historisk Tidsskrift*, vol. 58:239–68.

(1981), "Norsk Arbeidgiverforening 1927/28. Tilbaketog og revurdering." *(Norsk) Historisk Tidsskrift*, vol. 60:1–25.

(1989), *Kleppepakkene – Feilgrep eller Sunn Fornuft?* Oslo: Solum Forlag A/S.

Dammann, Axel (1991), *Fra Penger og Kreditt til Gjeld og Fallitt*. Oslo: Self-published.

Danielsen, Rolf (1981), "F. L. Konow og Paritragediens Siste Akt." *(Norsk) Historisk Tidsskrift*, vol. 60: 266–81.

(1984), *Borgerlig Oppdemmingspolitikk. Høyres Historie 2*. Oslo: J. W. Cappelens Forlag.

Davidson, David (1920), "Valutaproblemets Teoretiska Innebörd." *Ekonomisk Tidsskrift*, no. 3–4:71–123.

Davidson, Paul (1989), "Keynes and Money." In: Roger Hill, ed., *Keynes, Money and Monetarism: The Eighth Keynes Seminar Held at the University of Kent at Canterbury, 1987*. London: Macmillan.

Davies, Gavyn (1985), "The Macroeconomic Record of the Conservatives." *Harvard University Center for Europan Studies Working Paper Series*, no. 2.

De Boissieu, Christian (1987), "Lessons from the French Experience as Compared with Some Other OECD Countries." In: Marcello De Cecco, ed., *Changing Money*. London: Basil Blackwell.

De Geer, Hans (1989), *I Vänstervind och Högervåg*. Stockholm: Almänna Förlaget.

(1991), "Arbetsfred och Partitaktik." *(Svensk) Historisk Tidsskrift*, vol. 3:132–38.

de Hen, P. E. (1980), *Actieve en Re-Actieve Industrialisatiepolitiek in Nederland*. Amsterdam: De Arbeiderspers.

de Jong, A. M. (1960), *De Wetgeving nopens De Nederlandsche Bank, 1814–1958*. The Hague: Martinus Nijhoff.

De Kock, M. H. (1974)[1939], *Central Banking*. 3d ed. London: Crosby, Lockwood, Staples.

De Long, J. Bradford, & Lawrence H. Summers (1986), "Is Increased Price Flexibility Stabilizing?" *American Economic Review*, vol. 76, no. 5:1031–44.

De Vries, Joh. (1977), *De Nederlandse Economie Tijdens de 20ste Eeuw*. Bussum: Unieboek.

den Bakker, G. P., C. A. van Bochove, & Th. A. Huitker (1987), *Macro-economische Ontwikkelingen, 1921–1939 en 1969–1985: Een Vergelijking op Basis van Herziene Gegevens voor het Interbellum*. The Hague: CBS/Staatsuitgeverij.

den Dunnen, Emile (1987), *Instrumenten van het Geld- en Valutamarktbeleid in Nederland*. Amsterdam: NIBE.

Den Norske Creditbank (1990), *The Swedish Money and Bond Markets*. Stockholm: Den Norske Creditbank.

den Uyl, J. M. (1988), *Inzicht en Uitzicht*. Amsterdam: Bert Bakker.

Derry, T. K. (1973), *A History of Modern Norway 1814–1972*. Oxford: Clarendon Press.

Dimsdale, N. H. (1991), "British Monetary Policy since 1945." In: N. F. R. Crafts & N. W. C. Woodward, eds., *The British Economy since 1945*. Oxford: Clarendon Press.

Dobloug, Tore Anstein (1992), "Norsk Valutakurspolitikk 1971–90." Master's Thesis, Department of Political Science, University of Oslo.

Dølvik, Jon Erik, Mona Bråten, Frode Longva, & Arild H. Steen (1997), "Norwegian Labour Market Institutions and Regulations." In: Jon Erik Dølvik & Arild Steen, eds., *Making Solidarity Work?* Oslo: Universitetsforlaget.

Dornbusch, Rudiger (1980), *Open Economy Macroeconomics*. New York: Basic Books.

Dow, Alexander C., & Sheila C. Dow (1989), "Endogenous Money Creation and Idle Balances." In: John Pheby, ed., *New Directions in Post Keynesian Economics*. Aldershot: Edward Elgar.

Dow, J. C. R. (1964), *The Management of the British Economy 1945–60*. Cambridge: Cambridge University Press.

——— (1988), "Uncertainty and the Financial Process and Its Consequences for the Power of the Central Bank." *Banca Nazionale Del Lavoro Quarterly Review*, no. 166:311–25.

Drukker, J. W. (1990), *Waarom de Crisis Hier Langer Duurde*. Amsterdam: NEHA.

Durbin, Elizabeth (1988), "Keynes, the British Labour Party and the Economics of Democratic Socialism." In: Omar F. Hamouda & John N. Smithin, eds., *Keynes and Public Policy after Fifty Years*. Volume I: *Economics and Policy*. Aldershot: Edward Elgar.

Ehrenberg, Herbert (1991), *Abstieg vom Währungsolymp*. Frankfurt am Main: Fischer Taschenbuch Verlag.

Eichengreen, Barry (1990), "One Money for Europe? Lessons from the US Currency Union." *Economic Policy*, no. 10:117–87.

——— (1992), *Golden Fetters*. New York: Oxford University Press.

Eichengreen, Barry, & T. J. Hatton (1988), "Interwar Unemployment in International Perspective: An Overview." In: Barry Eichengreen & T. J. Hatton, eds., *Interwar Unemployment in International Perspective*. Dordrecht: Kluwer Academic Publishers.

Eichengreen, Barry, & Jeffrey D. Sachs (1990), "Exchange Rates and Economic Recovery in the 1930s." In: Barry Eichengreen, *Elusive Stability*. Cambridge: Cambridge University Press.

Eklöf, Kurt (1990), "Penningpolitikens Mål och Medel 1955–1967." *Sveriges Riksbank Occasional Paper*, no. 7. Stockholm: Sveriges Riksbank.

——— (1990), "Tre Valutakriser 1967–1977." *Sveriges Riksbank Occasional Paper*, no. 8. Stockholm: Sveriges Riksbank.

(1993), " 'Originella och Värdefulla' Källor." Unpublished paper.

Elster, Jon (1989), "Wage Bargaining and Social Norms." *Acta Sociologica*, 2:113–136.

(1989), *The Cement of Society*. Cambridge: Cambridge University Press.

Emminger, Otmar (1987), *D-Mark, Dollar, Währungskrisen*. Stuttgart: DVA.

Englund, Peter (1990), "Financial Deregulation in Sweden." *European Economic Review*, 34:385–93.

Epstein, Gerald (1996), "International Capital Mobility and the Scope for National Economic Management." In: Robert Boyer & Daniel Drache, eds., *States against Markets*. London: Routledge.

Eriksen, Erik Oddvar (1993), "Norwegian Social Democracy and Political Governance." In: Anne Cohen Kiel, ed., *Continuity and Change*. Oslo: Scandinavian University Press.

Erixon, Lennart (1989), "Den Tredje Vägen-Inlåsning Eller Förnyelse?" *Ekonomisk Debatt*, 3:181–95.

Erlander, Tage (1972), *Tage Erlander, 1901–1939*. Stockholm: Tidens Förlag.

(1973), *Tage Erlander, 1940–1949*. Stockholm: Tidens Förlag.

Erlander, Tage, & Björn von Sydow (1976), "Efterskrift." In: Nils Karleby, *Socialismen Inför Verkligheten*. Stockholm: Tidens Förlag.

Esping-Andersen, Gösta (1985), *Politics against Markets: The Social Democratic Road to Power*. Princeton, N.J.: Princeton University Press.

(1990), *The Three Worlds of Welfare Capitalism*. Princeton, N.J.: Princeton University Press.

Evans, Peter, Dietrich Rueschemeyer, & Theda Skocpol (1985), eds., *Bringing the State Back In*. Cambridge: Cambridge University Press.

Fagerberg, Jan (1988), "Willoch-Periodens Politiske Økonomi." *Samtiden*, 2:20–26.

Fagerberg, Jan, Ådne Capellen, Lars Mjøset, & Rune Skarstein (1990), "The Decline of State Capitalism in Norway." *New Left Review*, 181:60–91.

Fase, W. J. P. M. (1980), *Vijfendertig Jaar Loonbeleid in Nederland*. Alphen aan den Rijn: Samson.

Feldman, Gerald (1993), *The Great Disorder*. New York: Oxford University Press.

Feldt, Kjell-Olof (1991), *Alla Dessa Dagar . . . I Regeringen 1982–1990*. Stockholm: Norstedts Förlag.

Finansdepartementet (1991), *Pressmeddelande*. March 3.

Fischer, Benno (1987), *Theoriediskussion der SPD in der Weimarer Republik*. Frankfurt am Main: Peter Lang.

Fischer, Wolfram (1968), *Deutsche Wirtschaftspolitik*. Opladen: Leske.

Flanagan, Robert J., David W. Soskice, & Lloyd Ulman (1983), *Unionism, Economic Stabilization and Income Policies*. Washington, D.C.: Brookings Institution.

Flora, Peter, et al. (1983), *State, Economy, and Society in Western Europe 1815–1975. Volume I: The Growth of Mass Democracies and Welfare States*. Frankfurt am Main: Campus Verlag.

(1987), *State, Economy, and Society in Western Europe 1815–1975. Volume II: The Growth of Industrial Societies and Capitalist Economies*. Frankfurt am Main: Campus Verlag.

Førsund, Finn B. (1975), "Det Norske Arbeiderparti 1930–33. Krisepolitikken og Vegen til Sosialismen." Master's Thesis, Department of History, University of Bergen.

(1978), "Krisepolitikken og Vegen till Sosialismen." *Tidsskrift For Arbeiderbevegelsens Historie*, 1:27–55.

Franzén, Thomas (1986), "The Forward Exchange Market in Sweden." *Sveriges Riksbank Quarterly Review*, 2:16–25.

Fraser, Steve (1989), "The 'Labor Question.' " In: Steve Fraser & Gary Gerstle, eds., *The Rise and Fall of the New Deal Order*. Princeton, N.J.: Princeton University Press.

Freeman, Richard B. (1988), "Labour Market Institutions and Economic Performance." *Economic Policy*, April:63–80.

Frey, Bruno S., & Friedrich Schneider (1981), "Central Bank Behaviour." *Journal of Monetary Economics*, 7:291–315.

Frieden, Jeffrey A. (1991), "National Economic Policies in a World of Global Finance." *International Organization*, vol. 45, no. 4: 425–51.

Fritschy, W., & P. E. Werkman (1987), "The Trade Unions." In: Richard T. Griffiths, ed., *The Netherlands and the Gold Standard 1931–1936*. Amsterdam: NEHA.

Frøland, Hans Otto (1992), "Fem Påstander om Korporatisme som Inntektspolitisk Styringsmiddel i LO–N. A. F. Området etter 1945." *Søkelys på Arbeidsmarkedet*, vol. 9:57–64.

(1997), "Utvidet Inntektspolitisk Samarbeid som Svar på Ytre Utfordringer." *ARENA Working Paper*, No. 7.

Fuglum, Per (1989), *En Skute–En Skipper*. Oslo: Tapir.

Furre, Berge (1971), *Mjølk, Bønder og Tingmenn*. Oslo: Det Norske Samlaget.

(1992), *Norsk Historie 1905–1990*. Oslo: Det Norske Samlaget.

Galbraith, John Kenneth (1988)[1954], *The Great Crash 1929*. Boston: Houghton Mifflin.

Galenson, Walter (1949), *Labor in Norway*. Cambridge, Mass.: Harvard University Press.

Gamble, Andrew (1992), "The Labour Party and Economic Management." In: Martin J. Smith & Joanna Spear, eds., *The Changing Labour Party*. London: Routledge.

Gardner, Richard N. (1980), *Sterling-Dollar Diplomacy*. New York: Columbia University Press.

Garrett, Geoffrey, & Peter Lange (1986), "Performance in a Hostile World: Domestic and International Determinants of Economic Growth in the Advanced Capitalist Democracies." *World Politics*, 39:517–45.

(1991), "Political Responses to Interdependence: What Is 'Left' for the Left?" *International Organization*, vol. 45, no. 4: 539–64.

Garvy, George (1976), "Keynesianer vor Keynes." In: G. Bombach, H.-J. Ramser, M. Timmermann, & W. Wittmann, eds., *Der Keynesianismus*. Volume 2. Berlin: Springer-Verlag.

Gates, Robert A. (1973), "Von der Sozialpolitik zur Wirtschaftspolitik? Das Dilemma der deutschen Sozialdemokratie in der Krise 1929–1933." In: Hans Mommsen, Dietmar Petzina, & Bernd Weisbrod, eds., *Industrielles System und politische Entwicklung in der Weimarer Republik*. Düsseldorf: Droste Verlag.

Gerhardsen, Einar (1972), *Samarbete och Strid. Minnen 1945–1955*. Stockholm: Tidens Förlag.

Gerschenkron, Alexander (1970), "Reflections on European Socialism." In: Gregory Grossman, ed., *Essays in Socialism and Planning in Honor of Carl Landauer*. Englewood Cliffs, N.J.: Prentice Hall.

Giavazzi, Francesco, & Alberto Giovannini (1989), *Limiting Exchange Rate Flexibility*. Cambridge, Mass.: MIT Press.

Gilpin, Robert (1987), *The Political Economy of International Relations*. Princeton, N.J.: Princeton University Press.

Glynn, Andrew (1992), "Exhange Controls and Policy Autonomy: The Case of Australia 1983–88." In: Tariq Banuri & Juliet B. Schor, eds., *Financial Openness and National Autonomy*. Oxford: Clarendon Press.

Glynn, Sean, & John Oxborrow (1976), *Interwar Britain*. New York: Harper & Row.

Goldthopre, John H. (1984), "The End of Convergence: Corporatist and Dualist Tendencies in Modern Western Societies." In: John H. Goldthorpe, ed., *Order and Conflict in Contemporary Capitalism*. Oxford: Clarendon Press.

(1978), "The Current Inflation: Toward A Sociological Account." In: Fred Hirsch & John H. Goldthorpe, eds., *The Political Economy of Inflation*. Oxford: Martin Robertson.

Gonn, Audun (1985), "Toward Market Oriented Monetary and Credit Policy." *Norges Bank Economic Bulletin*, vol. 56, no. 3:220–29.

Goodhart, Charles A. E. (1989), *Money, Information and Uncertainty*. London: Macmillan.

(1994), "What Should Central Banks Do? What Should Be Their Macroeconomic Objectives and Operations?" *Economic Journal*, vol. 104:1424–36.

Goodman, John B. (1991), "The Politics of Central Bank Independence." *Comparative Politics*, April :329–49.

(1992), *Monetary Sovereignty. The Politics of Central Banking in Western Europe*. Ithaca, N.Y.: Cornell University Press.

Gottfries, Nils, Christian B. Nilsson, & Kerstin Ohlson (1992), "Has Swedish Monetary Policy Been Countercyclical?" *Sveriges Riksbank Arbetsraport*, no. 7. Stockholm: Sveriges Riksbank.

Goudriaan, F. G. W. (1986), *Geeft ons Nederlanders Toch Werk*. 's-Gravenhage: Staatsuitgeverij.

Gourevitch, Peter (1986), *Politics in Hard Times: Comparative Responses to International Economic Crises*. Ithaca, N.Y.: Cornell University Press.

(1989), "Keynesian Politics: The Political Sources of Economic Policy." In: Peter A. Hall, ed., *The Political Power of Economic Ideas*." Princeton, N.J.: Princeton University Press.

Griffiths, Richard T. (1987), "The Policy Makers." In: Richard T. Griffiths, ed., *The Netherlands and the Gold Standard 1931–1936*. Amsterdam: NEHA.

(1989), "De Grote Depressie, 1929–1939." In: J. L. van Zanden & R. T. Griffiths, eds., *Economische Geschiedenis van Nederland in de 20e Eeuw*. Utrecht: Het Spectrum.

Grotkopp, Wilhelm (1954), *Die grosse Krise*. Düsseldorf: Econ Verlag.

Gustafsson, Bo (1973), "A Perennial of Doctrinal History: Keynes and 'the Stockholm School.' " *Economy and History*, 16:114–28.

(1974), "Perspektiv på den Offentliga Sektorn under 1930-talet." In: *Kriser och krispolitik i Norden under Mellankrigstiden*. Mötesrapport. Uppsala: Nordiska historikermötet.

Habermas, Jürgen (1973), *Legitimationsprobleme im Spätkapitalismus*. Frankfurt am Main: Campus Verlag.

Hahn, Frank (1984), *Equilibrium and Macroeconomics*. Oxford: Basil Blackwell.

Hall, Peter (1986), *Governing the Economy: The Politics of State Intervention in Britain and France*. Cambridge: Polity Press.

(1989), "Conclusion: The Politics of Keynesian Ideas." In: Peter A. Hall, ed., *The Political Power of Economic Ideas*. Princeton, N.J.: Princeton University Press.

(1992), "The Movement from Keynesianism to Monetarism: Institutional Analysis and British Economic Policy in the 1970s." In: Sven Steinmo, Kathleen Thelen, & Frank Longstreth, eds., *Structuring Politics*. Cambridge: Cambridge University Press.

Hamilton, Malcolm B. (1989), *Democratic Socialism in Britain and Sweden*. Basingstoke: Macmillan.

Hanisch, Ted (1977), *Hele Folket i Arbeid*. Oslo: Pax Forlag.

Hanisch, Tore Jørgen (1978), "The Economic Crisis in Norway in the 1930s: A Tentative Analysis of Its Causes." *Scandinavian Economic History Review*, vol. 26, no. 2:145–55.

(1979), "Om Virkninger av Paripolitikken." (*Norsk*) *Historisk Tidsskrift*, vol. 58:239–68.

Hanrieder, Wolfgang, ed., (1982), *Helmut Schmidt: Perspectives on Politics*. Boulder, Colo.: Westview Press.

Hansen, Erik (1981), "Depression Decade Crisis: Social Democracy and Planisme in Belgium and the Netherlands." *Journal of Contemporary History*, vol. 16: 293–322.

Hansson, Lars, & Hans Lindberg (1989), "The Foreign Exchange Norm and the Dismantling of Exchange Controls." *Sveriges Riksbank Quarterly Review*, 2: 18–22.

Hardach, Karl (1973), "Zur zeitgenössischen Debatte der Nationalökonomen über die Ursachen der deutschen Nachkriegsinflation." In: Hans Mommsen, Dietmar Petzina, & Bernd Weisbrod, eds., *Industrielles System und politische Entwicklung in der Weimarer Republik*. Düsseldorf: Droste Verlag.

(1980), *The Political Economy of Germany in the Twentieth Century*. Berkeley: University of California Press.

Harmsen, Ger (1975), *Voor de Bevrijding van de Arbeid*. Nijmegen: SUN.

Harrod, R. F. (1969), *The Life of John Maynard Keynes*. New York: Augustus M. Kelley Publishers.

Hatton, T. J. & K. Alec Chrystal (1991), "The Budget and Fiscal Policy." In: N. F. R. Crafts & N. W. C. Woodward, eds., *The British Economy since 1945*. Oxford: Clarendon Press.

Hayek, Friedrich (1960), *The Constitution of Liberty*. Chicago: University of Chicago Press.

Healey, Denis (1989), *The Time of My Life*. New York: W. W. Norton.

Heckscher, Eli F. (1931), *Sveriges Penningpolitik*. Stockholm: P. A. Norstedt & Söner.

Held, Michael (1982), *Sozialdemokratie und Keynesianismus*. Frankfurt am Main: Campus Verlag.

Helleiner, Eric (1994), *States and the Reemergence of Global Finance.* Ithaca, N.Y.: Cornell University Press.

(1996). "Post-Globalization: Is the Financial Liberalization Trend Likely to Be Reversed?" In: Robert Boyer & Daniel Drache, eds., *States against Markets.* London: Routledge.

Hellström, Gunnar (1976), *Jordbrukspolitik i Industrisamhället.* Stockholm: LTs Förlag.

Hemerijck, Anton (1992), "The Historical Contingencies of Dutch Corporatism." Ph.D. Dissertation, Balliol College, Oxford.

Henrekson, Magnus (1991), *Sweden: Monetary and Financial System.* Stockholm: Fackföreningsrörelsens Institut för Ekonomisk Forskning.

Henrekson, Magnus, & Lars Hultkranz (1991), "Hur Hög Skall Arbetslösheten Fa Bli?" *Ekonomisk Debatt* 4:301–3.

Hentschel, Volker (1988A), "Die Entstehung des Bundesbankgesetzes. (Teil I)." *Bankhistorisches Archiv,* vol. 14, no.1:3–31.

(1988B), "Die Entstehung des Bundesbankgesetzes. (Teil II)." *Bankhistorisches Archiv,* vol. 14, no. 2:79–115.

Herr, Hansjörg (1986), *Geld, Kredit und ökonomische Dynamik in marktvermittelten Ökonomien: Die Vision einer Geldwirtschaft.* Munich: Verlag V. Florentz.

(1989), "On Post-Keynesian Crisis Theory: The Meaning of Financial Instability." In: Werner Vaeth, ed., *Political Regulation in the "Great Crisis."* Berlin: Edition Sigma.

Hersoug, Tor (1987), "Norge." In: Marianne Stenius, ed., *Penningpolitik i Norden.* N.p.: Nordisk Ekonomiska Forskningsradet, Dialogos.

Hertz-Eichenrode, Dieter (1982), *Wirtschaftskrise und Arbeitsbeschaffung.* Frankfurt am Main: Campus Verlag.

Hetzel, Robert L. (1990), "Central Bank's Independence in Historical Perspective: A Review Essay." *Journal of Monetary Economics,* 25:165–76.

Hibbs, Douglass A. (1977), "Political Parties and Macroeconomic Policy." *American Political Science Review,* December: 1467–87.

Hildebrand, Karl-Gustaf (1971), *I Omwandlingens Tjänst.* Stockholm: Svenska Handelsbanken.

Hildebrand, Klaus (1984), "Von Erhard zur grossen Koalition 1963–1969." In: Karl Dietrich Bracher et al., eds., *Geschichte der Bundesrepublik Deutschland.* Volume 4. Stuttgart: DVA.

Hirsch, Fred (1978), "The Ideological Underlay of Inflation." In: Fred Hirsch & John H. Goldthorpe, eds., *The Political Economy of Inflation.* Oxford: Martin Robertson.

Hirsch, Fred, & Peter Oppenheimer (1977), "The Trial of Managed Money: Currency, Credit and Prices 1920–1970." In: Carlo M. Cipolla, ed., *The Fontana Economic History of Europe. The Twentieth Century – 2.* Brighton: Harvester Press.

Hodne, Fritz (1983), *The Norwegian Economy 1920–1980.* London: Croon Helm.

Holli, Knut (1978), "New Rules for Norges Bank's Liquidity Loans to Banks." *Norges Bank Economic Bulletin,* 4:266–71.

Holt, John Bradshaw (1975)[1936], *German Agricultural Policy.* New York: Russel & Russel.

Holtfrerich, Carl-Ludwig (1980), *Die deutsche Inflation 1914–1923*. Berlin: Walter de Gruyter.

(1988), "Relations between Monetary Authorities and Governmental Institutions: The Case of Germany from the 19th Century to the Present." In: Gianni Toniolo, ed., *Central Banks' Independence in Historical Perspective*. Berlin: Walter de Gruyter.

Horvei, Tore, Lars Jagrén, Lars Mitek, & Sinikka Salo (1987), "Financial Markets in the Nordic Countries." In: Pentti Vartia et al., eds., *Growth Policies in a Nordic Perspective*. Helsinki: ETLA.

Houwink ten Cate, Johannes (1987), "Hjalmar Schacht als Reparationspolitiker." *Vierteljahresschrift für Sozial- und Wirtschaftsgeschichte*, vol. 74, no. 2:186–228.

Howson, Susan (1973), " 'A Dear Money Man?' Keynes on Monetary Policy, 1920." *Economic Journal*, vol. 83:456–64.

(1974), "The Origins of Dear Money, 1919–20." *Economic History Review, 2d ser.*, vol. 17, no. 1:88–107.

(1975), *Domestic Monetary Management in Britain 1919–38*. Cambridge: Cambridge University Press.

(1987), "The Origins of Cheaper Money, 1945–47." *Economic History Review, 2d ser.*, vol. 40, no. 3:433–52.

(1989), "Cheap Money versus Cheaper Money: A Reply to Professor Wood." *Economic History Review, 2d. ser.*, vol. 42, no. 3:401–5.

Howson, Susan, & Donald Winch (1977), *The Economic Advisory Council 1930–1939*. Cambridge: Cambridge University Press.

Huber, Evelyne, & John Stephens (1992), "Economic Internationalization, the European Community, and the Social Democratic Welfare State." Paper for the Annual Meeting of the American Political Science Association, Chicago, September.

Hume, L. J. (1970), "The Gold Standard and Deflation: Issues and Attitudes in the 1920s." In: Sidney Pollard, ed., *The Gold Standard and Employment Policies between the Wars*. London: Methuen.

Humphrey, Thomas M. (1990), "Cumulative Process Models from Thornton to Wicksell." In: Donald E. Moggridge, ed., *Perspectives on the History of Economic Thought*. Volume 4: *Keynes, Macroeconomics and Methods*. London: Edward Elgar.

Hveding, Øistein (1982), *Landbrukets Gjeldskrise i Mellomkrigstiden*. Oslo: Statens Lånekasse for Jordbrukere.

Irmler, Heinrich (1976), "Bankenkrise und Vollbeschäftigungspolitik." In: Deutsche Bundesbank, ed., *Währung und Wirtschaft in Deutschland 1876–1975*. Frankfurt am Main: Verlag Fritz Knapp.

Jaeger, Hans (1988), *Geschichte der Wirtschaftsordnung in Deutschland*. Frankfurt am Main: Suhrkamp.

Jahn, Gunnar, Alf Eriksen, & Preben Munthe (1966), *Norges Bank Gjennom 150 År*. Oslo: Norges Bank.

James, Harold (1986), *The German Slump*. Oxford: Clarendon Press.

(1989), "What Is Keynesian about Deficit Financing? The Case of Interwar Germany." In: Peter Hall, ed., *The Political Power of Economic Ideas*. Princeton, N.J.: Princeton University Press.

(1992), "Financial Flows across Frontiers during the Interwar Depression." *Economic History Review 2d ser.*, vol. 45, no. 3:594–613.

Jones, Russel (1987), *Wages and Employment Policy 1936–1985.* London: Allen & Unwin.

Jonung, Lars (1989), "En Stabil Stabiliseringspolitik." In: Lars Jonung, ed., *Stabiliseringspolitik.* Stockholm: SNS Förlag.

(1992), "Den Svenska Prisstabiliseringspolitiken 1931–39: Riksbanken och Knut Wicksells Norm." In: Sveriges Riksbank, *Penningpolitik under Rörlig Växelkurs.* Stockholm: Sveriges Riksbank.

(1993), "Riksbankens Politik 1945–1990." In: Lars Werin, ed., *Från Räntereglering till Inflationsnorm.* Stockholm: SNS Förlag.

(1994), "Etterskrift. 1990-talets Ekonomiska Kris i Historisk Belysning." In: Erik Lundberg, *Ekonomiska Kriser Förr och Nu.* 2d ed. Stockholm: SNS Förlag.

Jörberg, Lennart, & Olle Krantz (1986)[1977], "Skandinavien." In: Carlo M. Cipolla & K. Borchardt, eds., *Europäische Wirtschaftsgeschichte.* Volume 5. *Die Europäischen Volkswirtschaften im 20. Jahrhundert.* Stuttgart: Gustav Fischer Verlag.

Kaldor, Nicholas (1983), *The Economic Consequences of Mrs Thatcher.* London: Duckworth.

Kalecki, Michael (1977)[1943], "Political Aspects of Full-Employment." In: Michael Kalecki, *Selected Essays on the Dynamics of the Capitalist Economy 1933–1970.* Cambridge: Cambridge University Press.

Karleby, Nils (1921), "En Prisfallsperiod och dess Följder." *Tiden*, vol. 12:289–308.

(1926), *Socialismen inför Verkeligheten.* Stockholm: Tidens Förlag.

Katzenstein, Peter (1985), *Small States in World Markets.* Ithaca, N.Y.: Cornell University Press.

Keesing, F. A. G. (1978)[1947], *De Conjuncturele Ontwikkeling van Nederland en de Evolutie van de Economische Politiek, 1918–1939.* Nijmegen: SUN.

Keilhau, Wilhelm (1950), "Deflasjonstragedien og Ministeriet Hornsrud." *Samtiden*, vol. 19:167–75.

(1952), *Den Norske Pengehistorie.* Oslo: Aschehoug.

Keman, Hans (1984), "Politics, Policies and Consequences: A Cross National Analysis of Public Policy Formation in Advanced Capitalist Democracies (1967–1981)." *European Journal of Political Research*, 12:142–69.

Kennedy, Ellen (1991), *The Bundesbank.* London: Royal Insitute of International Affairs/Pinter Publishers.

Keohane, Robert (1984), *After Hegemony.* Princeton, N.J.: Princeton University Press.

Keynes, John Maynard (1937), "The General Theory of Employment." In: Donald Moggridge, ed., *The Collected Writings of John Maynard Keynes.* Vol. 14. London: Macmillan.

(1963), *Essays in Persuasion.* New York: W. W. Norton.

(1973)[1936], *The General Theory of Employment, Interest and Money.* London: Macmillan.

(1977), *The Collected Writings of John Maynard Keynes.* Vol. 17. Edited by Elizabeth Johnson. London: Macmillan.

(1980), Speech to the House of Lords, May 23, 1944. Reproduced in: Donald

Moggridge, ed., *The Collected Writings of John Maynard Keynes*. Vol. 26. London: Macmillan.

Kindleberger, Charles P. (1973), *Die Weltwirtschaftskrise*. Munich: DTV.

(1985A), "A Structural View of the German Inflation." In: Charles P. Kindleberger, *Keynesianism versus Monetarism and Other Essays in Financial History*. London: George Allen & Unwin.

(1985B), "Keynesianism versus Monetarism in Eighteenth Century France." In: Charles P. Kindleberger, *Keynesianism versus Monetarism and Other Essays in Financial History*. London: George Allen & Unwin.

(1986)[1973], *The World in Depression, 1929–1939*. 2d ed. Berkeley: University of California Press.

(1987), *A Financial History of Western Europe*. London: George Allen & Unwin.

Kinnock, Neil (1986), *Making Our Way*. Oxford: Basil Blackwell.

Kjellstrom, Erik T. H. (1934), *Managed Money: The Experience of Sweden*. New York: Columbia University Press.

Klein, P. W. (1975), "Depression and Policy in the Thirties." *Acta Historiae Neerlandicae, Studies in the History of the Netherlands*, vol. 8:123–58.

Klemann, Hein (1990), *Tussen Reich en Empire*. Amsterdam: NEHA.

Kloten, Norbert, Karl-Heinz Ketterer, & Rainer Vollmer (1985), "West Germany's Stabilization Performance." In: Leon N. Lindberg & Charles Maier, eds., *The Politics of Inflation and Economic Stagnation*. Washington, D.C.: Brookings Institution.

Klotzbach, Kurt (1982), *Der Weg zur Staatspartei*. Berlin: Verlag J. H. W. Dietz Nachf.

Knoester, A. (1989), *Economische Politiek in Nederland*. Leiden: Stenfert Kroese.

Knutsen, Paul (1984), "Norsk Arbeidsgiverforening i 1920 Åra: Problemer og Perspektiver." *(Norsk) Historisk Tidsskrift*, vol. 63:52–67.

Kock, Karin (1961), *Kreditmarknad och Räntepolitik 1924–1958. Första Delen*. Stockholm: Sveriges Allmänna Hypoteksbank.

(1962), *Kreditmarknad och Räntepolitik 1924–1958. Andra Delen*. Stockholm: Sveriges Allmänna Hypoteksbank.

Koerfer, Daniel (1987), *Kampf ums Kanzleramt*. Stuttgart: DVA.

Könke, Günter (1987), *Organisierter Kapitalismus, Sozialdemokratie und Staat*. Wiesbaden: Franz Steiner Verlag.

(1990), "Planwirtschaft oder Marktwirtschaft? Ordnungspolitische Vorstellungen sozialdemokratischer Nationalökonomen in der Weimarer Republik." *Vierteljahresschrift für Sozial- und Wirtschaftsgeschichte*, vol. 77, no. 4:457–87.

Koops, Tilman P. (1973), "Zielkonflikte der Agrar- und Wirtschaftspolitik in der Ära Brüning." In: Hans Mommsen, Dietmar Petzina, & Bernd Weisbrod, eds., *Industrielles System und politische Entwicklung in der Weimarer Republik*. Düsseldorf: Droste Verlag.

Korkman, Sixten (1988), "The Relevance of the Monetary Regime for Macroeconomic Developments in Small Open Economies." Mimeo. Helsinki: WIDER.

Korpi, Walter (1978), *The Working Class in Welfare Capitalism*. London: Routledge & Kegan Paul.

Korsch, A. (1976), "Der Stand der beschäftigungspolitischen Diskussion zur Zeit der Weltwirtschaftskrise in Deutschland." In: G. Bombach, H.-J. Ramser,

M. Timmermann, & W. Wittmann, eds., *Der Keynesianismus*. Volume 1. Berlin: Springer-Verlag.

Kragh, Börje (1944), "Den Penningpolitiska Diskussionen i Sverige under och Efter Första Världskriget." *Ekonomisk Tidskrift*, no. 1:74–85.

Kregel, Jan (1987), "Rational Spirits and the Post-Keynesian Macrotheory of Microeconomics." *Economist*, vol. 135, no. 4:520–32.

Krugman, Paul (1992), *The Age of Diminished Expectations*. Cambridge: MIT Press.

Kunz, Diane B. (1987), *The Battle for Britain's Gold Standard in 1931*. London: Croon Helm.

Ladrech, Robert (1993), "The European Left and Political Integration: A New Stage in Social Democracy?" In: Carl F. Lankowksi, ed., *Germany and the European Community*. New York: St. Martin's Press.

Lakatos, I. (1970), "Falsification and the Methodology of Scientific Research Programs." In: I. Lakatos & A. Musgrave, eds., *Criticism and the Growth of Knowledge*. Cambridge: Cambridge University Press.

Landgren, Karl-Gustav (1960), *Den 'Nya Ekonomin' i Sverige. J. M. Keynes, E. Wigforss, B. Ohlin och Utvecklingen 1927–39*. Stockholm: Almqvist & Wiksell.

Landsorganisasjon i Sverige (1984), *Den Produktiva Rättvisan*. Stockholm: Tidens Förlag.

(1992), *I Vår Makt*. Stockholm: LO.

Lange, Even, & Helge Pharo (1991), "Planning and Economic Policy in Norway, 1945–1960." *Scandinavian Journal of History*, vol. 16, no. 3:215–28.

Larsson, Mats (1991), "State, Banks and Industry in Sweden, with Some Reference to the Scandinavian Countries." In: H. James, H. Lindgren, & A. Teichova, eds., *The Role of the Banks in the Interwar Period*. Cambridge: Cambridge University Press.

Lash, Scott (1985), "The End of Neo-Corporatism? The Breakdown of Centralised Bargaining in Sweden." *British Journal of Industrial Relations*, 23, 2:215–39.

Laursen, Karsten, & Jørgen Pedersen (1964), *The German Inflation 1918–1923*. Amsterdam: North-Holland.

Lawson, Nigel (1988), "An Independent Central Bank." Minute from the Chancellor of the Exchequer to the Prime Minister. Reprinted in: Nigel Lawson (1993), *The View from No. 11*. New York: Doubleday.

(1993), *The View from No. 11*. New York: Doubleday.

Layard, Richard (1986), *How to Beat Unemployment*. Oxford: Oxford University Press.

Lee, Bradford A. (1989), "The Miscarriage of Necessity and Invention: Proto-Keynesianism and Democratic States in the 1930s." In: Peter A. Hall, ed., *The Political Power of Economic Ideas*. Princeton, N.J.: Princeton University Press.

Lehnert, Detlef (1983), *Sozialdemokratie zwischen Protestbewegung und Regierungspartei 1848–1983*. Frankfurt am Main: Suhrkamp.

Leijonhufvud, Axel (1968), *On Keynesian Economics and the Economics of Keynes*. New York: Oxford University Press.

Leiserson, Mark W. (1959), *Wages and Economic Control in Norway 1945–1957*. Cambridge, Mass.: Harvard University Press.

Leuschen-Seppel, Rosemarie (1981), *Zwischen Staatsverantwortung und Klasseninteresse*. Bonn: Verlag Neue Gesellschaft.

Lewin, Leif (1967), *Planhushållningsdebatten*. Uppsala: Almqvist & Wiksell.

(1989), *Ideologi och Strategi: Svensk Politik Under 100 År*. 3d ed. Stockholm: Norstedts Förlag.

Lie, Arne (1987), "Det Europeiske Monetære System (EMS) og Norsk Valutapolitikk." *Internasjonal Politikk*, no. 1–2: 67–89.

Lie, Einar (1994), "Pengesanering og Reguleringsøkonomi." *(Norsk) Historisk Tidsskrift*, vol. 73:54–71.

Lieftinck, Pieter (1987), "Het Nederlandsche Financiële Herstel 1945–1952: Een Terugblik." In: A. Knoester, ed., *Lessen Uit het Verleden*. Leiden: Stenfert Kroese.

(1989), *Pieter Lieftinck 1902–1989: Een Leven in Vogelvlucht. Herrinneringen Opgetekend Door A. Bakker. & M. M. P. van Lent*. Utrecht: Van Veen.

Limmer, Hans (1986), *Die deutsche Gewerkschaftsbewegung*. München: Günter Olzog Verlag.

Lindahl, Erik (1943), "Sveriges Penning- och Prispolitik Efter Kriget." *Ekonomisk Tidsskrift*, no. 2: 91–105.

Lindbeck, Assar (1974), *Swedish Economic Policy*. Berkeley: University of California Press.

Lindenius, Christina (1990), "Exchange Deregulation: Short- and Long-Run Effects." *Sveriges Riksbank Quarterly Review*, 3:15–22.

Linder, Erik (1920), "Kapitalknappheten och Vårt Fallande Penningvärde." *Tiden* vol. 11:11–16.

Lindgren, Håkan (1987), *Bank, Investmentbolag, Bankfirma. Stockholms Enskilda Bank 1924–1945*. Uppsala: Self-published.

Lindkvist, Lars (1982), "Karleby och den Socialdemokratiska Ekonomiläran." *Tiden* vol. 73:306–315.

Lösche, Peter, & Franz Walter (1992), *Die SPD*. Darmstadt: Wissenschaftliche Buchgesellschaft.

Lotsberg, Kari (1985), "Monetary and Credit Policy in the Nordic Countries." *Sveriges Riksbank Quarterly Review*, 4:17–32.

Lowi, Theodore J. (1992), "The State in Political Science: How We Became What We Study." *American Political Science Review*, vol. 86, no. 1:1–7.

Luebbert, Gregory M. (1991), *Liberalism, Fascism or Social Democracy*. New York: Oxford University Press.

Luihn, Hans (1986), *Arbeid og Samfunn: Arbeidsmarkedspolitikk i Norge Gjennom 100 År*. Oslo: NKS Forlaget.

Lundberg, Erik (1983), *Ekonomiska Kriser Förr och Nu*. Stockholm: SNS Förlag.

(1985), "The Rise and Fall of the Swedish Model." *Journal of Economic Literature*, 23:1–36.

Luther, Hans (1964), *Vor dem Abgrund*. Berlin: Propyläen Verlag.

Lybeck, Johan A. (1982), "Varning for Variabla Växelkurser!" *Ekonomisk Debatt*, 2: 92–106.

(1992), *Finansiella Kriser Förr Och Nu*. Stockholm: SNS Förlag.

Macmillan, Harold (1966), *Winds of Change 1914–1939*. London: Macmillan.

Maddison, Angus (1982), *Ontwikkelingsphasen van het Kapitalisme*. Utrecht: Aula.

Mai, Günther (1983), "Die Nationalsozialistische Betriebszellenorganisation." *Vierteljahrshefte für Zeitgeschichte*, vol. 31:573–613.

Maier, Charles S. (1987), *In Search of Stability*. Cambridge: Cambridge University Press.

(1988) [1975], *Recasting Bourgeois Europe*. Princeton, N.J.: Princeton University Press.

Maier, Charles S., & Leon N. Lindberg (1985), "Alternatives for Future Crises." In: Leon N. Lindberg & Charles Maier, eds., *The Politics of Inflation and Economic Stagnation*. Washington, D.C.: Brookings Institution.

Marsh, David (1993), *The Bundesbank: The Bank That Rules Europe*. London: Mandarin.

Martin, Andrew (1985), "Wages, Profits, and Investment in Sweden." In: Leon N. Lindberg & Charles Maier, eds., *The Politics of Inflation and Economic Stagnation*. Washington, D.C.: Brookings Institution.

(1991), "Wage Bargaining and Swedish Politics: The Political Implications of the End of Central Negotiations." Mimeo, Harvard University.

Mason, Tim W. (1974), "Zur Entstehung des Gesetzes zur Ordnung der nationalen Arbeit vom 20. Januar 1934: Ein Versuch über das Verhältnis von 'archaischer' und 'moderner' Momente in der neuesten deutschen Geschichte." In: Hans Mommsen, Dietmar Petzina, & Bernd Weisbrod, eds., *Industrielles System und politische Entwicklung in der Weimarer Republik*. Düsseldorf: Droste Verlag.

Mason, Timothy (1982), "Die Bändigung der Arbeiterklasse im nationalsozialistischen Deutschland. Eine Einleitung." In: Carola Sachse, Tilla Siegel, Hasso Spode, & Wolfgang Spohn, eds., *Angst, Belohnung, Zucht und Ordnung. Herrschaftsmechanismen im Nationalsozialismus*. Opladen: Westdeutscher Verlag.

Mathews, William Carl (1986), "The Continuity of Social Democratic Economic Policy 1919 to 1920: The Bauer Schmidt Policy." In: Gerald D. Feldman, Carl Ludwig Holtfrerich, Gerhard A. Ritter, & Peter Christian Witt, eds., *Die Anpassung an die Inflation*. Berlin: Walter de Gruyter.

Matthews, R. G. O. (1968), "Why Has Britain Had Full Employment Since the War?" *Economic Journal*, vol. 78, no. 311:555–69.

Maurseth, Per (1987), *Gjennom Kriser til Makt (1920–1935). Arbeiderbevegelsens Historie I Norge – 3*. Oslo: Tiden Norsk Forlag.

McKibbin, Ross (1975), "The Economic Policy of the Second Labour Government 1929–1931," *Past and Present*, no. 68:95–123.

McNeil, William C. (1986), *American Money and the Weimar Republic*. New York: Columbia University Press.

Meidner, Rudolf (1984) [1948], "Lönepolitikens Dilemma vid Full Sysselsättning." In: Rudolf Meidner, *I Arbetets Tjänst*. Stockholm: Tidens Förlag.

Meijer, G. J. (1977), "Naar het Plan van de Arbeid. Het Partijbestuur van de SDAP en de Crisisbestrijding." In: P. W. Klein & G. J. Borger, eds., *De Jaren Dertig: Aspecten van Crisis en Werkloosheid*. Amsterdam: Meulenhoff Educatief.

Meltzer, Allan H. (1988), *Keynes's Monetary Theory: A Different Interpretation*. Cambridge: Cambridge University Press.

Merkel, Wolfgang (1993), *Ende der Sozialdemokratie?* Frankfurt am Main: Campus.

Meyer, Håkon (1934), ed., *Det Norske Arbeiderparti. Samtlige Landsmøtebeslutninger, Resolusjoner, Valg Etc. 1912–1933*. Oslo: Det Norske Arbeiderpartis Forlag.

Middlemas, Keith (1979), *Politics in Industrial Society*. London: Andre Deutsch.

Midgaard, John (1989) [1963], *Eine kurze Geschichte Norwegens*. Oslo: Aschehoug.

Miller, Susanne, & Heinrich Potthoff (1986), *A History of German Social Democracy.* New York: St. Martin's Press.

Milliband, Ralph (1960), *Parliamentary Socialism.* London: Merlin Press.

Milward, Alan S. (1984), *The Reconstruction of Western Europe 1945–51.* Berkeley: University of California Press.

Mitchell, B. R. (1981), *European Historical Statistics 1750–1975.* 2d rev. ed. London: Macmillan.

  (1992), *International Historical Statistics. Europe 1750–1988.* 3d ed. New York: Stockton Press.

Moggridge, D. E. (1972), *British Monetary Policy 1924–1931: The Norman Conquest of $4.86.* Cambridge: Cambridge University Press.

  (1990), "Foreword." In: Patrick Deutscher, *R. G. Hawtrey and the Development of Macroeconomics.* London: Macmillan.

  (1992), *Maynard Keynes: An Economist's Biography.* London: Routledge.

Moland, Torstein (1994), "Economic Perspectives. Address by Governor Torstein Moland at the Meeting of the Supervisory Council of Norges Bank on 10 February 1994." *Norges Bank Economic Bulletin,* vol. 65, no. 1:1–14.

Moore, Basil J. (1988), *Horizontalists and Verticalists: The Macroeconomics of Credit Money.* Cambridge: Cambridge University Press.

Moravcsik, Andrew (1991), "Negotiating the Single European Act." In: Robert O. Keohane & Stanley Hoffmann, eds., *The New European Community.* Boulder, Colo.: Westview Press.

Morgan, Kenneth O. (1979), *Consensus and Disunity. The Lloyd George Coalition Government 1918–1922.* Oxford: Clarendon Press.

  (1985), *Labour in Power 1945–51.* Oxford: Oxford University Press.

Moses, John A. (1986), "The German Free Trade Unions and the Problem of Mass Unemployment in the Weimar Republic." In: Peter D. Stachura, ed., *Unemployment and the Great Depression in Weimar Germany.* London: Macmillan.

Mowat, Charles Loch (1963) [1955], *Britain between the Wars.* Chicago: University of Chicago Press.

Munthe, Preben (1991), "Streiftog i Norges Bank Historie." In: Norges Bank 175 År. *Norges Bank Skriftserie,* no. 19. Oslo: Norges Bank.

Myhrman, Johan, & Hans Tson Söderström (1982), "Svensk Stabiliseringspolitik: Erfahrenheter och Nya Villkor." In: Bo Södersten, ed., *Svensk Ekonomi.* 3d ed. Stockholm: Rabén & Sjögren.

Nekkers, Jan (1985), "Sentiment en Program." In: J. Jansen van Galen, J. Nekkers, D. Pels, & J. P. Pronk, *Het Moet, Het Kan, Op Voor Het Plan! Vijftig Jaar Plan van de Arbeid.* Amsterdam: Bert Bakker.

Neumann, Franz (1972)[1942], *Behemoth. The Structure and Practice of National Socialism 1933–1944.* New York: Octagon Books.

Nilson, Alexander (1988), "Household Liabilities and Wealth in the Eighties." *Sveriges Riksbank Quarterly Review,* 1:21–29.

Nissen, Bernt A. (1933), "Venstre efter 1905." In: Jacob S. Worm-Müller, Arne Bergsgård, & Bernt A. Nissen, *Venstre I Norge.* Oslo: Olaf Norlis Forlag.

Nordvik, Helge W. (1977), "Krisepolitikken og den Teoretiske Nyoreintering av den Økonomiske Politikken i Norge i 1930-Årene." *(Norsk) Historisk Tidsskrift,* vol. 56:289–317.

(1979), "Finanspolitikken og den Offentlige Sektors Rolle i Norsk Økonomi i Mellomkrigstiden." *(Norsk) Historisk Tidsskrift*, vol. 58:223–38.

(1990), "Penge- og Valutapolitikk, Bank- og Kredittvesen og Krisen i Norsk Økonomi pa 1930-tallet." In: O. Abrahamsen, M. Larsson, and H. W. Nordvik, *Norsk og Svensk Bankvesen Under Mellomkrigstidens Krise.* Oslo: NORAS.

(1992), "Den Norske Bankkrisen i Mellomkrigstiden – En Sammenligning med Dagens Bankkrise." In: *Kreditliberalisering og Bankkrise.* Oslo: NORAS.

Norges Bank (1989), "Norwegian Credit Markets: Norwegian Monetary and Credit Policy." *Norges Bank Skriftserie*, no. 17. Oslo: Norges Bank.

(1991), "Economic Perspectives." *Norges Bank Economic Bulletin*, vol. 62, No. 1: 3–6.

Norges Offentlige Utredninger 1989:1, *Penger og Kredit i en Omstillingstid.* Oslo: Statens Trykningskontor.

Norges Offentlige Utredninger 1992:26, *En Nasjonal Strategi for Økt Sysselsetting i 1990-Årene.* Oslo: Statens Trykningskontor.

Notermans, Ton (1997), "Social Democracy and External Constraints." In: Kevin R. Cox, ed., *Spaces of Globalization.* New York: Guilford Press.

Nyhamar, Jostein (1990), *Nye Utfordringer (1965–1990). Arbeiderbevegelsens Historie I Norge-6.* Oslo: Tiden Norsk Forlag.

Nysæter, Egil (1972), "Sosialistane og Pengepolitikken." Master's Thesis, Department of History, University of Bergen.

Odhner, Clas-Erik (1988), "Arbetare och Bönder Formar den Svenska Modellen. Socialdemokratin och Jordbrukspolitiken." In: Klaus Misgeld, Karl Molin, & Klas Åmark, eds., *Socialdemokratins Samhälle.* Stockholm: Tiden.

(1992), *Ekonomi och Pengar i Europa.* Stockholm: Tiden.

Öhman, Berndt (1969), "Krispolitikens Förhistoria." *Tiden*, vol. 61:39–44.

(1970), *Svensk Arbetsmarknadspolitik 1900–1947.* Stockholm: Prisma.

Olsen, Kari (1990), "The Dismantling of Norwegian Foreign Exchange Regulations." *Norges Bank Economic Bulletin*, vol. 61, no. 3:164–170.

Olstad, Finn (1990), *Jern og Metall 100 År. Bind 1, 1891–1940.* Oslo: Tiden Norsk Forlag.

Organization for Economic Cooperation and Development (1988), *Why Economic Policies Change Course. Eleven Case Studies.* Paris: OECD.

Östlind, Anders (1945), *Svensk Samhällsekonomi, 1914–1922.* Stockholm: Svenska Bankföreningen.

Ousland, Gunnar (1949), *Fagorganisasjonen i Norge. Vol. 2.* Oslo: Arbeidernes Faglige Landsorganisasjon i Norge.

Oxelheim, Lars (1990), *International Financial Integration.* Berlin: Springer-Verlag.

Oye, Kenneth A. (1992), *Economic Discrimination and Political Exchange.* Princeton, N.J.: Princeton University Press.

Padgett, Stephen (1993), "The German Social Democrats: A Redefinition of Social Democracy or Bad Godesberg Mark II?" *West European Politics*, vol. 16, no. 1:20–38.

Panitch, Leo (1979), "The Development of Corporatism in Liberal Democracies." In: Philippe Schmitter & Gerhard Lehmbruch, eds., *Trends toward Corporatist Intermediation.* London: Sage.

Paterson, William E., & Alistair H. Thomas (1986), "Introduction." In: William

E. Paterson & Alistair H. Thomas, eds., *The Future of Social Democracy*. Oxford: Clarendon Press.

Patinkin, Don (1982), *Anticipations of the General Theory?* Chicago: University of Chicago Press.

Peden, G. C. (1985), *British Economic and Social Policy: Lloyd George to Margaret Thatcher*. Deddington: Philip Allan.

Pekkarinen, Jukka, Matti Pohjola, and Bob Rowthorn, eds. (1992), *Social Corporatism: A Superior Economic System?* Oxford: Clarendon Press.

Perry, Jos (1994), *De Voorman. Een Biografie van Willem Hubert Vliegen*. Amsterdam: Uitgeverij De Arbeiderspers.

Pettersson, Karl-Henrik (1993), *Bankkrisen Inifrån*. Stockholm: SNS Förlag.

Petzina, Dietmar (1977), *Die deutsche Wirtschaft in der Zwisschenkriegszeit*. Wiesbaden: Franz Steiner Verlag.

Pimlott, Ben (1977), *Labour and the Left in the 1930s*. London: Allen & Unwin.

Piore, Michael J., & Charles F. Sabel (1984), *The Second Industrial Divide*. New York: Basic Books.

Polanyi, Karl (1957)[1944], *The Great Transformation*. Boston: Beacon Press.

Pollard, Sidney (1962), *The Development of the British Economy 1914–1950*. London: Edward Arnold.

    (1970), "Editor's Introduction." In: Sidney Pollard, ed., *The Gold Standard and Employment Policies between the Wars*. London: Methuen.

    (1973), "The Trade Unions and the Depression of 1929–1933." In: Hans Mommsen, Dietmar Petzina, & Bernd Weisbrod, eds., *Industrielles System und politische Entwicklung in der Weimarer Republik*. Düsseldorf: Droste Verlag.

Pronk, J. P. (1985), "Bestaanszekerheid bij een Behoorlijk Levenspeil voor Iedereen." In: J. Jansen van Galen, J. Nekkers, D. Pels, & J. P. Pronk, *Het Moet, Het Kan, Op Voor Het Plan! Vijftig Jaar Plan van de Arbeid*. Amsterdam: Bert Bakker.

Przeworski, Adam (1985), "Social Democracy as a Historical Phenomenon." In: Adam Przeworski, *Capitalism and Social Democracy*. Cambridge: Cambridge University Press.

    (1991), "Could We Feed Everyone? The Irrationality of Capitalism and the Infeasibility of Socialism." *Politics and Society*, vol. 19, no. 1:1–38.

Przeworski, Adam, & John Sprague (1986), *Paper Stones: A History of Electoral Socialism*. Chicago: University of Chicago Press.

Przeworski, Adam, & Michael Wallerstein (1985), "Democratic Capitalism at the Crossroads." In: Adam Przeworski, *Capitalism and Social Democracy*. Cambridge: Cambridge University Press.

Putnam, Robert D., & C. Randall Henning (1986), "The Bonn Summit of 1978: How Does International Economic Policy Coordination Actually Work?" *Brookings Discussion Papers in International Economics*, no. 53. Washington, D.C.: Brookings Institution.

Qvigstad, Jan F., & Arent Skjæveland (1994), "Valutakursregimes–Historiske Erfaringer og Fremtidige Utfordringer." In: *Stabilitet og Langsiktighet. Festskrift til Hermod Skånland*. Oslo: Aschehoug/Norges Bank.

Riese, Hajo (1986), *Theorie der Inflation*. Tübingen: J. C. B. Mohr.

    (1987A), "Aspekte eines monetären Keynesianismus – Kritik und Gegenentwurf." In K. Dietrich et al., *Postkeynesianismus.* Marburg: Metropolis Verlag.

(1987B), "Wider den Dezisionismus der Theorie der Wirtschaftspolitik." Unpublished manuscript, Fachbereich Wirstchaftswissenschaft, Freie Universität Berlin.

(1988), "Keynesianische Kapitaltheorie." In: Harald Hagemann & Otto Steiger, eds., *Keynes' General Theory nach fünfzig Jahren.* Berlin: Duncker & Humblot.

Ritschl, Albrecht (1990), "Zu hohe Löhne in der Weimarer Republik?" *Geschichte und Gesellschaft*, 16–3:375–402.

Robinson, Joan (1972), "The Second Crisis of Economic Theory." *American Economic Review*, vol. 62, no. 2: 1–10.

Rødseth, Asbjørn (1994), "Om Konjunkturane i Norge etter 1980: Vegen til Høg Arbeidsløyse." In: Agnar Sandmo, ed., *Perspektiv på Arbeidsledigheten.* Bergen: Fagbokforlaget.

Rolfes, Max (1976), "Landwirtschaft 1914–1970." In: Wolfgang Zorn, ed., *Handbuch der Deutschen Wirtschafts- und Sozialgeschichte. vol. 2, Das 19. und 20. Jahrhundert.* Stuttgart: Ernst Klett Verlag.

Rollings, Neil (1985), "The 'Keynesian Revolution' and Economic Policy-Making: A Comment." *Economic History Review, 2d ser.*, 38:95–100.

(1988), "British Budgetary Policy 1945–1954: A 'Keynesian Revolution'? *Economic History Review, 2d ser.*, 41:238–98.

Rooth, Gösta (1988), *Ivar Rooth, Riksbankchef 1929–1948.* Uppsala: Self-published.

Rosenberg, Irma (1986), "Norms for Foreign Exchange Flows and External Borrowing by the Government." *Sveriges Riksbank Quarterly Review*, 4:17–26.

Rothstein, Bo (1992), "Explaining Swedish Corporatism: The Formative Moment." *Scandinavian Political Studies*, vol. 15, no. 3:173–91.

(1992), *Den Korporativa Staten.* Stockholm: Norstedts.

Rowland, Peter (1975), *David Lloyd George: A Biography.* New York: Macmillan.

Ruggie, John Gerard (1982), "International Regimes, Transactions, and Change: Embedded Liberalism in the Postwar Economic Order." *International Organization*, vol. 36, no. 2:379–415.

Rüstow, Hanns-Joachim (1981), "Die Wende zur aktiven Krisenbekämpfung: Der Papen Plan." In: G. Bombach et al., eds., *Der Keynesianismus.* Volume 3. Berlin: Springer-Verlag.

Rygg, Nicolai (1949), "Vitenskap, Politikk og Legende." *Samtiden*, vol. 58:486–510.

(1950), *Norges Bank i Mellomkrigstiden.* Oslo: Gyldendal Norsk Forlag.

(1954), *Norges Bank Historie.* Volume 2. Oslo: n.p.

Sabel, Charles F. (1993), "Can the End of the Social Democratic Trade Unions Be the Beginning of a New Kind of Social Democratic Politics?" In: Steven R. Sleigh, ed., *Economic Restructuring and Emerging Patterns of Industrial Relations.* Kalamazoo, Mich.: Upjohn Institute for Employment Research.

Sachs, Jeffrey, & Charles Wyplosz (1986), "The Economic Consequences of President Mitterrand." *Economic Policy*, 2:262–306.

Salin, Edgar (1964), "Zur Einführung." In: Hans Luther, *Vor dem Abgrund.* Berlin: Propyläen Verlag.

Samuelson, Kurt (1972), *From Great Power to Welfare State.* 2nd printing. London: George Allen & Unwin.

Sargent, Thomas J. (1983), "The Ends of Four Big Inflations." In: Robert E. Hall, ed., *Inflation: Causes and Effects.* Chicago: University of Chicago Press.

Sayers, R. S. (1976), *The Bank of England, 1891–1944.* 3 volumes. Cambridge: Cambridge University Press.

Schacht, Hjalmar (1950), *Gold for Europe.* London: Gerald Duckworth.

Schager, Nils Henrik (1991), "Kommentar." In: Lars Jonung, ed., *Devalveringen 1982: Rivstart eller Snedtändning?* Stockholm: SNS Förlag.

Scharpf, Fritz W. (1987), *Sozialdemokratische Krisenpolitik in Europa.* Frankfurt am Main: Campus.

⎯⎯ (1996), "Politische Optionen im vollendeten Binnenmarkt." In: Markus Jachtenfuchs & Beate Kohler-Koch, eds., *Europäische Integration.* Opladen: Leske & Budrich.

Schlesinger, Helmut (1976), "Geldpolitik in der Phase des Wiederaufbaus (1950–1958)." In: Deutsche Bundesbank, ed., *Währung und Wirtschaft in Deutschland 1876–1975.* Frankfurt am Main: Verlag Fritz Knapp.

Schmidt, Manfred G. (1982), *Wohlfahrtstaatliche Politik unter bürgerlichen und sozialdemokratischen Regierungen.* Frankfurt am Main: Campus.

Schmitter, Philippe C. (1979), "Still the Century of Corporatism?" In: Philippe C. Schmitter & Gerhard Lehmbruch, eds., *Trends toward Corporatist Intermediation.* Beverly Hills: Sage Publications.

Schneider, Michael (1973), "Konjunkturpolitische Vorstellungen der Gewerkschaften in den letzten Jahren der Weimarer Republik. Zur Entwicklung des Arbeitsbeschaffungsplans des ADGB." In: Hans Mommsen, Dietmar Petzina, & Bernd Weisbrod, eds., *Industrielles System und politische Entwicklung in der Weimarer Republik.* Düsseldorf: Droste Verlag.

Scholten, Ilja (1987), "Corporatism and the Neo-Liberal backlash in the Netherlands." In: Ilja Scholten, ed., *Political Stability and Neo-Corporatism.* London: Sage.

Schönhoven, Klaus (1987), *Die Deutschen Gewerkschaften.* Frankfurt am Main: Suhrkamp.

⎯⎯ (1989), *Reformismus und Radikalismus: Gespaltene Arbeiterbewegung im Weimarer Sozialstaat.* Munich: DTV.

Schotsman, R. J. (1987), *De Parlementaire Behandeling van het Monetaire Beleid in Nederland sinds 1863.* Amsterdam: NIBE/Staatsuitgeverij.

Schweitzer, Arthur (1964), *Big Business in the Third Reich.* Bloomington: Indiana University Press.

Sejersted, Francis (1973), *Ideal, Teori, og Verkelighet. Nycolai Rygg og Pengepolitikken i 1920-Årene.* Oslo: J. W. Cappelens Forlag.

⎯⎯ (1985), *Historisk Introduksjon til Økonomien.* Oslo: J. W. Cappelens Forlag.

Selgin, George A., & Lawrence H. White (1994), "How Would the Invisible Hand Handle Money?" *Journal of Economic Literature,* vol. 32:1718–49.

Seyler, Hans (1983), *Hur Bonden Blev Lönarbetare.* Lund: Arkiv.

Shackle, G. L. S. (1983)[1967]. *The Years of High Theory.* Cambridge: Cambridge University Press.

Shaw, Eric (1993), "Toward Renewal? The British Labour Party's Policy Review." *West European Politics,* vol. 16, no. 1:112–32.

(1994), *The Labour Party since 1979: Crisis and Transformation*. London: Routledge.

Sheffrin, Steven M. (1989), *The Making of Economic Policy*. Cambridge: Basil Blackwell.

Shonfield, Andrew (1969), *Modern Capitalism*. New York: Oxford University Press.

Siegel, Tilla (1982), "Lohnpolitik im nationalsozialistischen Deutschland." In: Carola Sachse, Tilla Siegel, Hasso Spode, & Wolfgang Spohn, eds., *Angst, Belohnung, Zucht und Ordnung: Herrschaftsmechanismen im Nationalsozialismus*. Opladen: Westdeutscher Verlag.

(1985), "Wage Policy in Nazi Germany." *Politics and Society*, vol. 14, no. 1:1–51.

Sijben, Jac. J. (1977), *Money and Economic Growth*. Leiden: Martinus Nijhoff.

Silenstam, Per (1970), *Arbetskraftsutbudets Utveckling i Sverige 1870–1965*. Stockholm: Almqvist & Wiksell.

Simmons, Beth (1994), *Who Adjusts?* Princeton, N.J.: Princeton University Press.

Skånland, Hermod (1992), "Oppgavefordelingen mellom Norges Bank og Finansdepartmentet – Hvordan den var og hvordan den bør være." In: *Kredittliberalisering og Bankkrise*. NORAS Rapport no. 35. Oslo: NORAS.

Skånland, Hermod, & Arent Skjæveland (1992), "Det Økonomiske Opplegget for 1993." *Penger og Kreditt*, 4:246–51.

Skarstein, Rune (1989), "Economic Model-Time and Historical Time." In: Jan Bohlin et al., eds., *Samhällsvetenskap, Ekonomi och Historia*. Göteborg: Daidalos.

Skidelsky, Robert (1967), *Politicians and the Slump*. London: Macmillan.

(1992), *John Maynard Keynes. Volume Two: The Economist as Saviour 1920–1937*. London: Macmillan.

Slagstad, Rune (1993), "Da Arbeiderpartiet Fant Seg Selv." In: Trond Nordby, ed., *Arbeiderpartiet og Planstyre 1945–1965*. Oslo: Universitetsforlaget.

Smith, Adam (1981)[1776], *An Inquiry into the Nature and Causes of the Wealth of Nations*. 2 vols. Indianapolis: Liberty Classics.

Smith, Martin J. (1992), "A Return to Revisionism? The Labour Party's Policy Review." In: Martin J. Smith & Joanna Spear, eds., *The Changing Labour Party*. London: Routledge.

Söderpalm, Sven Anders (1980), *Arbetsgivarna och Saltsjöbadspolitiken*. Stockholm: SAF.

Söderström, Hans Tson (1991), "Den Ekonomiska Politikens Möjligheter. Svar till Agell och Vredin." *Ekonomisk Debatt* 6:525–30.

Solow, Robert, Alan Budd, & Christian von Weiszacker (1987), "The Conservative Revolution: A Roundtable Discussion." *Economic Policy*, October:181–200.

Spahn, Heinz-Peter (1986), *Stagnation in der Geldwirtschaft*. Frankfurt am Main: Campus Verlag.

(1988A), *Bundesbank und Wirtschaftskrise*. Regensburg: Transfer Verlag.

(1988B), "Bundesbankpolitik 1970–1987." *WZB Mitteilungen*, no. 42:18–20.

Sraffa, Piero (1960), *Production of Commodities by Means of Commodities*. Cambridge: Cambridge University Press.

SSB (1997), "Sterk Sysselsettningsvekst gjennom Hele 1996." *Ukens Statistikk*, no. 7.

Stadermann, Hans-Joachim (1987), *Ökonomische Vernunft*. Tübingen: J. C. B. Mohr.

Statens Offentliga Utredningar 1985:52 Översyn av Valutaregleringen. Stockholm.

Steiger, Otto (1971), Studien zur Entstehung der neuen Wirtschaftslehre in Schweden. Berlin: Duncker & Humblot.

Steigum, Erling, Jr. (1994), "Nordisk Økonomisk Krise: Hvilken Rolle Kan Finans- og Pengepolitikken Spille?" In: Agnar Sandmo, ed., Perspektiv på Arbeidsledigheten. Bergen: Fagbokforlaget.

Stenius, Marianne (1987), ed., Penningpolitik i Norden. Nordisk Ekonomiska Forskningsradet, Dialogos.

Stephens, John (1986)[1979], The Transition from Capitalism to Socialism. Urbana: University of Illinois Press.

Stevenson, Frances (1971), Lloyd George. Edited by A. J. P. Taylor. New York: Harper & Row.

Stewart, Michael (1983), The Age of Interdependence, Cambridge, Mass.: MIT Press.

Stocking, George W., & Myron W. Watkins (1946), Cartels in Action: Case Studies in International Business Diplomacy. New York: Twentieth Century Fund.

Strange, Susan (1986), Casino Capitalism. Oxford: Basil Blackwell.

Streeck, Wolfgang (1991), "On the Institutional Conditions of Diversified Quality Production." In: Egon Matzner & Wolfgang Streeck, eds., Beyond Keynesianism. Aldershot: Edward Elgar.

Sveriges Riksbank (1985), "Deregulation Continues." Sveriges Riksbank Quarterly Review 1:14–16.

Swenson, Peter (1989), Fair Shares. Ithaca, N.Y.: Cornell University Press.

Szász, A. (1974), "De Rol van Deviezenrestricties bij de Regulering van het Internationale Kapitaalverkeer." In: Economie in Overleg. Leiden: H. E. Stenfert Kroese.

Tawney, R. H. (1943), "The Abolition of Economic Controls, 1918–1921." Economic History Review, vol. 13:1–30.

Temin, Peter (1989), Lessons from the Great Depression. Cambridge, Mass.: MIT Press.

Thatcher, Margaret (1993), The Downing Street Years. New York: HarperCollins.

Thomas, Brinley (1936), Monetary Policy and Crises: A Study of Swedish Experience. London: George Routledge and Sons.

Thompson, Noel (1996), Political Economy and the Labour Party. London: UCL Press.

Thullberg, Per (1974), "SAP och Jordbruksnäringen 1920–1940" Arbetarrörelsens Årsbok 1974:127–68.

Thunholm, Lars Erik (1987), "Sverige." In: Marianne Stenius, ed., Penningpolitik i Norden. Nordisk Ekonomiska Forskningsradet, Dialogos.

(1991), Oscar Rydbeck och Hans Tid. Stockholm: T. Fischer.

Tietmeyer, Hans (1990), "Voraussetzungen eines Europäischen Zentralbankensystems," Aussenwirtschaft, vol. 45, no.3:301–11.

Tilton, Tim (1988), "Ideologins Roll i Socialdemokratisk Politik." In: Klaus Misgeld, Karl Molin, & Klas Åmark, eds., Socialdemokratins Samhälle. Stockholm: Tiden.

(1991), The Political Theory of Swedish Social Democracy. Oxford: Clarendon Press.

Tingsten, Herbert (1941), Den Svenska Socialdemokratins Idéutveckling. Vol. 1. Stockholm: Tidens Förlag.

Tjelmeland, Hallvard (1986), "Politikk og Historie. Om Ulike Syn på dei Sosiale Drivkreftene Bak Danninga av Regjeringa Nygaardsvold." Tidsskrift for Arbeidersbevegelsens Historie, no. 2:131–62.

Tobin, James (1978), "A Proposal for International Monetary Reform." *Eastern Economic Journal*, 4:153–59.

(1980), *Asset Accumulation and Economic Activity*. Chicago: University of Chicago Press.

Tomlinson, Jim (1981), "Why Was There Never a 'Keynesian Revolution' in Economic Policy?" *Economy and Society*, vol. 10, no.1:72–87.

(1984), "A 'Keynesian Revolution' in Economic Policy-Making?" *Economic History Review, 2d. ser.*, 37:258–62.

(1989), "Labour's Management of the National Economy 1945–51: Survey and Speculations." *Economy and Society*, vol. 18, no. 1:1–23.

Unga, Nils (1976), *Socialdemokratin och Arbetslöshetsfrågan 1912–34*. Kristianstad: Arkiv.

van Kersbergen, Kees (1995), *Social Capitalism*. London: Routledge.

van Praag, Philip Jr. (1994), "Conflict and Cohesion in the Dutch Labour Party." In: David S. Bell & Eric Shaw, eds., *Conflict and Cohesion in Western European Social Democratic Parties*. London: Pinter.

van Seenus, Richard (1945), *Bankpolitiek en Conjunctuur: Het Nederlandsche Bankwezen in het Conjunctuurverloop na den Wereldoorlog 1914–1918*. Amsterdam: H. J. Paris.

van Straaten, A. J. (1989), *Veertig Jaar Monetaire en Financiële Analyse door de Nederlandsche Bank, 1947–1986*. Amsterdam: NIBE.

Vikbladh, Inge (1973), "Monetary Policy in Sweden." In: Karel Holbik, ed., *Monetary Policy in Twelve Industrial Countries*. Boston: Federal Reserve Bank of Boston.

Visser, Wessel, & Rien Wijnhoven (1989), *Baan Brekende Politiek*. Kampen: Kok Agora.

Vissering, G. (1917), *Het Vraagstuk van de Geldruimte in Nederland en de Goudpolitiek van De Nederlandsche Bank*. Rotterdam: Nijgh & van Ditmar.

Vlak, Gerard Johan Maria (1967), "Het Nederlandse Valuta-Egalisatiefonds 1936–1940." Ph.D. Dissertation, Department of Economics, Katholieke Hogeschool Tilburg.

Vogt, Martin (1973), "Die Stellung der Koalitionsparteien zur Finanzpolitik 1928–30." In: Hans Mommsen, Dietmar Petzina, & Bernd Weisbrod, eds., *Industrielles System und politische Entwicklung in der Weimarer Republik*. Düsseldorf: Droste Verlag.

von Mises, Ludwig (1980)[1934], *The Theory of Money and Credit*. Indianapolis: Liberty Classics.

Wallerstein, Immanuel (1974), *The Modern World-System*. New York: Academic Press.

Webb, Michael C. (1991), "International Economic Structures, Government Interests, and International Coordination of Macroeconomic Adjustment Policies." *International Organization*, vol. 45, no. 3:309–42.

Webb, Steven B. (1985), "Government Debt and Inflationary Expectations as Determinants of the Money Supply in Germany 1919–1923." *Journal of Money, Credit and Banking*, vol. 17, no. 4:479–92.

(1989), *Hyperinflation and Stabilization in Weimar Germany*. New York: Oxford University Press.

Wigforss, Ernst (1941), *Från Klasskamp til Samverkan*. Stockholm: Tidens Förlag.

(1950), *Minnen.* Volume 1. Stockholm: Tidens Förlag.

(1951), *Minnen.* Volume 2. Stockholm: Tidens Förlag.

(1967), "Ideologiska Linjer i Praktisk Politik." *Tiden*, vol. 59:525–33.

(1980A)[1932], "Varken Inflation eller Deflation." In: Ernst Wigforss, *Skriften i Urval. II, Agitatorn.* Stockholm: Tidens Förlag.

(1980B)[1931], "Kronan och Guldet." In: Ernst Wigforss, *Skriften i Urval. II, Agitatorn.* Stockholm: Tidens Förlag.

Wihlborg, Clas (1993), "Valutapolitiken." In: Lars Werin, ed., *Från Räntereglering till Inflationsnorm.* Stockholm: SNS Förlag.

Wilde, Lawrence (1994), *Modern European Socialism.* Aldershot: Dartmouth.

Winch, Donald (1969), *Economics and Policy.* New York: Walker.

Windmuller, J. P., C. de Galan, & A. F. van Zweeden (1985), *Arbeidsverhoudingen in Nederland.* Utrecht: Het Spectrum.

Winkler, Heinrich August (1979), *Die Sozialdemokratie und die Revolution von 1918/19.* Berlin: Verlag J. H. W. Dietz Nachf.

(1982), "Klassenbewegung oder Volkspartei? Zur Programmdiskussion in der Weimarer Sozialdemokratie 1920–1925." *Geschichte und Gesellschaft*, 8:9–54.

Wohlin, Lars (1991), "Svensk Valutapolitik – Tillbakablick och Framtid i ett Integrerat Europa." In: Lars Jonung, ed., *Devalveringen 1982. Rivstart eller Snedtändning?* Stockholm: SNS Förlag.

Wolfbrandt, Marianne (1989), "Impact of Financial Integration on Central Bank Policy." *Sveriges Riksbank Quarterly Review*, 3:11–20.

Wolinetz, Steven B. (1993), "Reconstructing Dutch Social Democracy." *West European Politics*, vol. 16, no. 1:97–111.

Zevin, Robert (1992), "Are World Financial Markets More Open? If So Why and with What Effects?" In: Tariq Banuri & Juliet B. Schor, eds., *Financial Openness and National Autonomy.* Oxford: Clarendon Press.

Zimmermann, Erwin (1986), *Neokorporative Politikformen in den Niederlanden.* Frankfurt am Main: Campus Verlag.

Zollitsch, Wolfgang (1982), "Einzelgewerkschaften und Arbeitsbeschaffung: Zum Handlungsspielraum der Arbeiterbewegung in der Spätphase der Weimarer Republik." *Geschichte und Gesellschaft* 8:87–115.

INDEX